AGRARIANISM

in American Literature

PERSPECTIVES ON AMERICAN LITERATURE
Robert H. Woodward and James J. Clark
General Editors

AGRARIANISM
in American Literature

———•———

EDITED BY

M. THOMAS INGE
Michigan State University

THE ODYSSEY PRESS
NEW YORK

ACKNOWLEDGMENTS

Acknowledgment is gratefully made for permission to reprint the following material:

Astor-Honor, Inc. For "Jericho, Jericho, Jericho" from *A Novel, A Novella and Four Short Stories* by Andrew Lytle, © 1958 by Andrew Lytle. Reprinted by permission of Astor-Honor, Inc., New York.

Donald Davidson. For "I'll Take My Stand: A History" from *American Review*, summer, 1935, published by Bookman Publishing Company. Reprinted by permission of Donald Davidson.

Delta Council. For *"The Rights of Man"* by William Faulkner, address to the Delta Council, May 15, 1952. Reprinted by permission of the Delta Council.

Harcourt, Brace & World, Inc. For "The Patented Gate and the Mean Hamburger," by Robert Penn Warren. Copyright, 1947, by Robert Penn Warren. Reprinted from his volume *The Circus in the Attic and Other Stories* by permission of Harcourt, Brace & World, Inc.

Harper and Row, Publishers. For passage from "Out of the Sea" and from "Epilogue: A Philosophical Excursion" from *Out of the Earth* by Louis Bromfield. Copyright 1948, 1949, 1950 by Louis Bromfield. For "The Community and Rural Life" from *The Human Community* by Baker Brownell. Copyright 1950 by Harper & Row, Publishers, Incorporated. For "Introduction: A Statement of Principles" and excerpt from "The Hind Tit" by Andrew Nelson Lytle, from *I'll Take My Stand* by Twelve Southerners. Copyright 1930 by Harper & Brothers; renewed 1958 by Donald Davidson. All reprinted by permission of Harper & Row, Publishers.

Holt, Rinehart and Winston, Inc. For "Mowing" and "A Lone Striker" from *Complete Poems of Robert Frost*. Copyright 1934 by Holt, Rinehart and Winston, Inc. Copyright 1936, © 1962 by Robert Frost. Copyright © 1964 by Lesley Frost Ballantine. Reprinted by permission of Holt, Rinehart and Winston, Inc.

Houghton Mifflin Company. For "At the Forks" from *Let Us Now Praise Famous Men* by James Agee and Walker Evans. Published by Houghton Mifflin, 1941, 1960. Reprinted by permission of Houghton Mifflin Company.

Alfred A. Knopf, Inc. For "Captain Carpenter" by John Crowe Ransom. Copyright 1924 by Alfred A. Knopf, Inc., and renewed 1952 by John Crowe Ransom. For "Antique Harvesters" by John Crowe Ransom. Copyright 1927 by Alfred A. Knopf, Inc. and renewed in 1955 by John Crowe Ransom. Both reprinted from *Selected Poems* by John Crowe Ransom by permission of the publisher. For "The Husbandman" by H. L. Mencken. Copyright 1924 by Alfred A. Knopf, Inc. and renewed 1952 by H. L. Mencken. Reprinted from A *Mencken Chrestomathy* by permission of the publisher. For excerpt from *Lanterns on the Levee* by William Alexander Percy. Copyright 1941 by Alfred A. Knopf, Inc. Reprinted by permission.

Harold Ober Associates, Inc. For "Blue Smoke" by Sherwood Anderson, from *Puzzled America*. Copyright 1935 by Charles Scribner's Sons. Renewed 1963 by Eleanor Anderson. Reprinted by permission of Harold Ober Associates Inc.

Quadrangle Books, Inc. For extract from *Every Man A King* by Huey P. Long, published 1964 by Quadrangle Books, Inc. Reprinted by permission of the publishers.

Time, The Weekly Newsmagazine. For "The Pushbutton Cornucopia," *Time,* March 9, 1959. Reprinted by permission from *Time,* The Weekly Newsmagazine; Copyright Time Inc. 1959.

University of Minnesota Press. For "Prologue: The Long Street" and "On a Replica of the Parthenon" from *Poems 1922-1961,* by Donald Davidson. University of Minnesota Press, Minneapolis. Copyright © 1924, 1927, 1934, 1935, 1938, 1952, 1961, 1966 by Donald Davidson. Reprinted by permission of University of Minnesota Press.

University of North Carolina Press. For extract from *Agrarianism: A Program for Farmers* by Troy J. Cauley. University of North Carolina Press, 1935. Reprinted by permission of the publishers.

The Viking Press, Inc. For "On the Mountainside" by Elizabeth Madox Roberts from *The Haunted Mirror* by Elizabeth Madox Roberts. Copyright 1932 by Elizabeth Madox Roberts, © 1960 by Ivor S. Roberts. For "The Independent Farmer" by Thorstein Veblen from *The Portable Veblen,* edited by Max Lerner. Copyright 1923 by B. W. Huebsch, Inc., 1951 by Ann B. Sims. Reprinted by permission of The Viking Press, Inc.

For my parents
RICHARD *and* LUCILLE HARVELL
and my wife's parents
BERNARD *and* LENA MEREDITH
who appreciate
good country people

CONTENTS

INTRODUCTION

*The heaven, even the heavens are the
Lord's: but the earth hath he given to
the children of men.*

PSALMS 115: 16

THE IMPORTANCE of agrarian thought in the development of American culture cannot be overestimated. In fact, one distinguished contemporary historian, Henry Bamford Parkes, maintains that no genuine appreciation of the distinctive qualities of American civilization is possible without taking full account of the force and influence of the agrarian tradition, and his perceptive study *The American Experience* (1947) focuses upon the drive toward an agrarian democracy, toward an ideal society of independent property owners and husbandmen, in the political and economic history of our nation. Not all historians will entirely agree with Parkes' generalization, but to examine the full development of American thought from the cultural perspective, from an analysis of literary and historical documents, is to come away convinced that agrarianism forms one of the most persistent and pervasive strains of symbolic and political ideas in the native mind.

The word "agrarianism" is being used here purposely with a good deal of looseness and imprecision. Originally, the word "agrarian" was probably derived from the Roman *lex agraria,* the agrarian law that called for an equal division of public lands, and during the past three centuries the term has had wide currency with application to any social or political movement requiring a forced equalization or redistribution of ownership in cultivated land. Thus during the eighteenth century the word became in aristocratic circles an epithet of insult and abuse, and was used with an ambiguity and emotional coloration of the same sort that today accompanies the use of "communist." As late as 1859, we find an anonymous writer in the April issue of the *Atlantic Monthly* for that year attempting to extricate the word from its undeserved degeneration, as "one of the most reproachful terms that violent politicians have ever used when seeking to bespatter their foes," by going back to its Roman origins to prove that "strictly speaking, an Agrarian is a conservative, a man who asks for justice—not a destructive, who, in his desire to advance his own selfish ends or those of his class, would trample on law and order alike." It is correct that today, technically speaking, an agrarian is one who places his political faith in achieving a predominantly agricultural economy. But in other countries and at other times, "agrarian" has been no more than a synonym for "agricultural." In any case, the selection of materials for this book has been guided by a very general use of the word as suggestive of a set of ideas or attitudes toward the farmer and his craft of husbandry in American writing from a philosophical, imaginative, mythical, political, or economic perspective.

Some of the basic ideas voiced by the agrarians represented in this volume, thoughts which are generally to be understood as "agrarian," include the following:

1. The cultivation of the soil, the mother of all arts, has within it a positive spiritual good and instills in the cultivator such virtues as honor, manliness, self-reliance, courage, moral integrity, and hospitality. These follow from his direct contact with physical nature, the medium through which God is directly revealed and which serves to remind man of his finite nature and dependence on God. It is an occupation singularly blessed by God, since He was the first husbandman, having wrought order and creation out of confusion and chaos, and it was the first employment ordained by Him of Adam, the first man.

2. Only farming offers complete independence and self-sufficiency, because regardless of the state of the national economy (provided the farmer and not the bank owns his land), his basic needs of food and shelter are provided through his cooperative relationship with nature. The standard by which an economic system is judged is not how much prosperity or wealth it produces, but how effectively it encourages freedom, individuality, and morality.

3. The farmer has a sense of identity, a sense of historical and religious tradition, a feeling of belonging to a concrete family, place, and region, which are psychologically and culturally beneficial. His life is harmonious, orderly, and whole, and counteracts tendencies in modern society toward abstraction, fragmentation, and alienation.

4. Industry, capitalism, and technology, and the thriving metropolises they have created, are often destructive of independence and dignity, and encourage corruption, vice, and weakness.

5. Agricultural communities, where the brotherhoods of labor and cooperation bring about increased understanding, provide a potential model for an ideal social order.

Not all those who write in this tradition would subscribe to all
of these basic ideas, of course, but this summary does reflect the
more commonly expressed beliefs about the agricultural life and
provides convenient touchstones for understanding the term "agrarian" as it has been used in compiling this book.

It should be recognized that these ideas are not peculiarly American, but come as the culmination of an extensive philosophical
development throughout the history of Western civilization. Great
minds of nearly every age and time have repeatedly reiterated the
superior advantages of husbandry and country life over other occupations and modes of existence.

In the eighth century B.C., Hesiod, a Greek poet, farmer, and contemporary of Homer, compiled his *Works and Days,* largely a collection of maxims on farming, in which his preference for husbandry
over the life of commerce and even soldiering is indicated. In *The
Economist,* over 300 years later, the Athenian soldier-author Xeno-
phon noted that the "earth of her own good will gives lessons in
justice and uprightness to all who can understand her meaning,"
and he also quoted the wise teacher Socrates as having said "Husbandry is the mother and nurse of the other arts. For when
husbandry flourishes, all the other arts thrive, but whenever the
land is compelled to lie waste, the other arts . . . nearly perish."
Writing around the middle of the fourth century B.C., Aristotle suggested in his *Politics* a relationship between agriculture and good
citizenship:

> The best common people are the agricultural population, so that it is
> possible to introduce democracy as well as other forms of constitution
> where the multitude lives by agriculture or by pasturing cattle. For
> owing to their not having much property they are busy, so that they
> cannot often meet in assembly, while owing to their having the neces-
> saries of life they pass their time attending to their framework and do
> not covet their neighbor's goods.

Rome, whose government spent over a century trying to persuade
the city dwellers to move back on the land, in an attempt to revive
the declining Republic, also had its agrarian exponents. One of the
oldest surviving prose works in Latin is an agricultural manual
De Agri Cultura (or *De Re Rustica*) by Cato the Elder, in which he
notes that among his ancestors, to call a man a good farmer and a
good tiller of the soil was to pay him the highest possible compli-
ment, and the great orator and statesman Cicero declared in *On
Ethics,* "of all the occupations by which gain is received, none is
better than agriculture, none more delightful, none more becoming
to a freeman." Numerous other writers turned their hands to practical handbooks on farming, each with its inevitable paean to the

humble countryman and his noble employment, such as the learned
satirist Varro's *Rerum Rusticarum* and Columella's exhaustive summary of all such previous works *De Re Rustica,* while Vergil attempted the same thing but entirely in verse in his masterpiece the
Georgics. Pliny the Elder devoted several sections of his encyclopedic
Natural History to agriculture, and celebrations of country life are
frequently found in the poetry and satires of Horace, whose second
epode on the subject begins (as Dryden translated it):

> How happy in his low degree,
> How rich in humble poverty, is he,
> Who leads a quiet country life;
> Discharg'd of business, void of strife,
> And from the griping scrivener free!
> Thus, ere the seeds of vice are sown,
> Liv'd men in better ages born,
> When plow'd with oxen of their own
> Their small paternal field of corn.

In addition to the prolific classical literature, there existed also a
body of legends and folklore on the subject, such as those surrounding Arcadia, a district of the Greek Peloponnesus, about which
Vergil wrote. Although in fact the Arcadians were a primitive, savage people, their simple, pastoral existence suggested to the poetic
mind certain virtues lost in the more civilized urban areas, and thus
the name *Arcadia* came to be applied to any idealistic attempt to
reconstruct a pastoral form of society.

The influence of these ideas, by now standardized and stereotyped,
extended through the Middle Ages into the Renaissance, such that
we find Chaucer waxing eloquent on the simple, rustic life as incorporated in the myth of the Golden Age, and even cursing the
decadence brought about by the new spirits of commercial zeal
and progress:

> But cursed was the time, I dare well say,
> That man first did their sweaty business
> To grub up metal, lurking in darkness,
> And in the rivers first gems sought.
> Alas! then sprung up all the cursedness
> Of covetousness, that first our sorrow brought!

The contrast between the corrupt, disorderly life of the city and the
virtuous, simple life in the country became during the Elizabethan
period and afterward one of the most common thematic motifs in

English literature. Perhaps Sidney put it more succinctly than anyone else when he wrote:

> Greater was that shepherds treasure
> Than their false, fine, courtly pleasure.

The theme is found in many of Shakespeare's plays, and *The Temp-
est* seems to have been inspired in part by contemporary travel
accounts of America by European explorers, who idealized the New
World as a potential Arcadia where a simple Edenic existence for
civilized man was yet possible. Much of the pastoral subject matter
was also inspired by renewed interests in classical literature, which
prompted in Italy, France, Germany, and England the composition
of agricultural handbooks patterned after those of the ancients.

A new emphasis came during the eighteenth century when the
place of agriculture in the wealth of nations became an issue, with
the radical French physiocrats insisting that agriculture was the
only productive occupation and the sole source of wealth, with
others such as Adam Smith agreeing, up to a point, that it was at
least an indispensable and necessary part of any prosperous national
economy. Agriculture became a fad in England among certain members of the aristocratic class during the early eighteenth century, and
while the government was engaged in agricultural reform, the
populace eagerly read the writings of the zealous innovator Arthur
Young (whom George Washington consulted for advice on how to
manage his farm) and dabbled half-seriously in farming. These
concerns are reflected in the writings of the eminent worthies of
the Restoration and Augustan Ages—Dryden, Steele, Swift, Pope,
and Johnson—and subsequently prompted the growth of a quantity
of romantic and sentimental poetry on the subject of the decaying
peasant life and the qualities of his past existence, by such poets
as Goldsmith, Crabbe, Burns, Gray, Wordsworth, and Thomson.
Oliver Goldsmith's idyllic "The Deserted Village," with its sentimental praise of the rural life and somber prophecy of what vices
urban existence, commerce, and the British Enclosure Acts were in-
flicting on man, stands as a prime example of their art. After carefully developing in impassioned detail his basic theme, "Ill fares the
land, to hastening ills a prey,/ Where wealth accumulates and men
decay," the poet notes:

> Even now, methinks, as pondering here I stand,
> I see the rural virtues leave the land;
> Down where yon anchoring vessel spreads the sail,
> That idly waiting flaps with every gale,

Downward they move, a melancholy band,
Pass from the shore, and darken all the strand.
Contented Toil, and hospitable Care,
The kind connubial Tenderness are there;
And Piety with wishes placed above,
And steady Loyalty, and faithful Love
And thou, sweet Poetry, thou loveliest maid,
Still first to fly where sensual joys invade,
Unfit, in these degenerate times of shame,
To catch the heart, or strike for honest fame.

The vessel carrying all the agrarian virtues is bound for the New World, where perhaps the climate and environment will better suit their health. Appropriately enough, only ten years after Goldsmith published his poem in 1770, we find a young American named Thomas Jefferson, recent author of the Declaration of Independence, governor of the state of Virginia, beginning work on a statistical survey in answer to a questionnaire from the secretary of the French legation at Philadelphia about the resources of American states. The final product was a book, *Notes on the State of Virginia,* wherein Jefferson warmly greeted the recently arrived agrarian virtues by formulating for them what was to become the classic statement and source of inspiration for America's chapter in the history of agrarian thought: "Those who labour in the earth are the chosen people of God, if ever he had a chosen people, whose breasts he has made his peculiar deposit for substantial and genuine virtue." At that moment, Jefferson touched hands with Hesiod, Socrates, Aristotle, and the other ancients, and breathed new life for another century or two into one of the great traditions of Western civilization.

The present volume is designed primarily as a controlled-research textbook in order to enable the student to trace and evaluate for himself the impact of agrarianism on American life and thought. Except for the editor's indicated formulation of what seems to constitute agrarianism, the intent of the book is not to argue any thesis about the subject but to provide sufficient primary source material for the student to formulate his own reactions and conclusions. Because agrarian thought is so closely related to other significant historical and mythical concepts (such as the frontier thesis, the concept of the noble savage, the myth of the West as a new Eden, the pastoral theme in literature, and pantheism in religion and philosophy), occasionally the selections may lapse over into these areas, but an effort has been made for the most part to keep the subject sharply in focus.

So as to give the material some sense of order, a strict chronological arrangement is avoided in favor of one that follows a logical division. The first section provides a sampling of theoretical statements about the farmer and the virtues of his way of life within a wide time span, from colonial days into the twentieth century, while Section 2 illustrates agrarianism by bringing together a lively set of autobiographical and fictional depictions of the good life. Section 3 focuses upon the impact of agrarian thought on American democracy, Section 4 upon disillusionment over the discrepancy between the ideal and the real in American agriculture, and Section 5 upon the struggle between industrialism and agrarianism, between progress and tradition, or between urbanism and ruralism, for the control of the American destiny. In an epilogue, William Faulkner, speaking as a novelist and occasional husbandman, reiterates an important agrarian theme for the consideration of twentieth-century man. The editor has not hestitated to place literary selections alongside historical documents, in the belief that both offer rich primary source material for understanding American life and culture without warping the essential integrity of either. Whenever possible, the editor has favored the use of full selections rather than abridgements, complete works of short fiction and poetry rather than excerpts from novels and larger works. It is recommended that a few select whole books, fictional or historical, be used along with this casebook.

The introductions are intended to be suggestive overviews of the material that follows, and the study questions at the end of the book hope to suggest fruitful paths for understanding, discussing, and writing about the issues and ideas expressed in the selections. A brief list of suggestions for further reading and notes on the authors conclude the volume. To facilitate use of the material for controlled research, standard texts have been quoted and full bibliographical data included for each selection. Original pagination is indicated in brackets, the number before the virgule (/) indicating the end of the page and the number after it signaling the beginning of a new page.

I am pleased to express my gratitude to Professor C. Merton Babcock, Michigan State University, through whose recommendation the opportunity to do this book was extended; to my wife Betty, who has provided both material and moral encouragement; and to Mrs. Gay Post, whose secretarial assistance has been invaluable. I am also indebted for suggestions and other favors to Professors James J.

Clark and Robert H. Woodward of San Jose State College, Virginia
Rock of York University in Toronto, M. E. Bradford of the University of Dallas, the late Donald Davidson of Vanderbilt University
(retired), Russel B. Nye of Michigan State University, Kenneth Cra-
ven of the University of Wyoming, and John D. Wilson of Michigan
State University.

M. THOMAS INGE
Salamanca, Spain

AGRARIANISM

in American Literature

I

An American Arcadia: Theoretical Perspectives

To THE MIND of the European during the age of discovery, America suggested a virgin land, an unspoiled and undefiled garden of Eden, a new Arcadia. Sir Thomas More used the Americas as a setting for his Utopia for this reason. The extent to which preconception overrode reality is indicated by the English explorers' description of the Indian girls of Roanoke Island as nymphs, or the insistence of Christopher Columbus that he heard nightingales singing throughout the night in this country where they never existed. Captain Arthur Barlow in 1584 described Virginia as a lush garden of "incredible abundance," overladen with fragrant flowers, fruits, and succulent grapes, and blessed with soil—"the most plentifull, sweete, fruitfull, and wholesome of all the worlde." Little wonder that the highest John Donne could reach metaphorically in describing the voluptuousness of his mistress' body was to exclaim, "My America! My new-found-land."

A myth was also generated that the European could regain in the New World his lost innocence by a primal relationship with nature. The source of regenerative power is the soil, a repository of moral, civic, and economic values. The immigrant, therefore, who settled in this "paradise regained" and tilled the soil brought with him an inherited baggage of pastoral and classical myth surrounding his vocation. Whatever the realities of existence in the labor of settling a new continent, these notions were never entirely to leave the mind of the new American and were to be tested for their truth and potency in the founding of a new political state.

Even the sober, logical minds of the New England Puritan colonists, all of whom farmed of necessity, shared in this agrarian heritage. They saw America as the place where Christ's army was to realize an advance Calvinistic millennium, "a specimen of what shall be over all the earth in the glorious times which are expected," said In-

1

crease Mather. But they were more inclined to view their struggle with the wilderness and their labor in the soil as a part of the universal conflict with evil, as satanical devices employed against them in defense of what once was "the devil's territories," according to Cotton Mather.

Less pietistic, and more straightforward in style, are the *Essays Upon Field-Husbandry in New England* by Jared Eliot, colonial Connecticut's leading clergyman-physician. His book, the first important American handbook on agriculture, is mostly taken up with practical advice on manuring, crop rotation, stock breeding, and such, but in the two excerpts reprinted here, he reiterates in his simple style (so the farmer can understand it) the virtues of husbandry and its importance in the national economy.

The New Englanders for the most part farmed of necessity for subsistence, since their hard, stony soil yielded insufficient crops for commercial farming. While they turned to commerce to make a living, food raising as a business was left to the Middle Colonies and especially the South, where fertile soil and an amenable climate made agriculture the economic basis for the entire society. No one better represents that society than Thomas Jefferson, often called both the father of American agriculture and the father of American democracy because of his abiding passions for the cultivation of the soil and the rights of the common man.

Among his contemporaries, Jefferson did more to advance agricultural experiment and technique than anyone else, by adapting European methods to American crops and livestock, by introducing new inventions (such as the threshing machine) and improved breeds, by founding agricultural societies and recommending the inclusion of agricultural science in the curriculum of the University of Virginia, and by surrendering all patent rights to his improvements and innovations to the public domain. Of greater importance to the development of American thought is his early formulation of his version of the agrarian ideal in Query XIX of his *Notes on the State of Virginia*. In a concise statement of fewer than four hundred words, couched in the rich metaphoric language of the poet, Jefferson made perhaps the most vivid, appealing statement of the theory of agrarianism in American literature. From this paragraph have sprung almost two centuries of literary, social, economic, and political thought.

The quality of Jefferson's succinctness and verbal grace is especially apparent when his statement is compared with a similar one written by a fellow planter from Caroline County, Virginia, John Taylor. Taylor was a man with whom, Jefferson said, he "rarely, if ever, differed in any political principle of importance." Because of

his highly systematic and detailed development of agrarian principles in his writings and his uncompromising support of them in his
political actions, the historian Charles A. Beard recognized him as
"the philosopher and statesman of agrarianism." But Taylor is
known less to literature than to history because of his unfortunate
tendency to write a rambling, repetitious, and poorly organized
prose. Yet his works are distinguished by their reflection of a truly
original mind. Both characteristics are illustrated in the excerpt included here from *Arator,* Taylor's knowledgeable analysis of the
problems of American agriculture and their remedies.

Both the nineteenth and twentieth centuries have had their expos-
itors of agrarian ideals, all specifically colored by the changing philosophical and historical currents in America. The literature of both
the North and the South gave voice to them, with distinctive flavors.
In New England, speaking from the Transcendental point of view,
Ralph Waldo Emerson wrote respectfully of farming as the most sacred of all callings. This naturally follows as a result of his philosophy of Transcendentalism, which recognizes nature as the source of
the all-pervading spiritual power, the Oversoul, through which man
has a share in the Godhead. Since the farmer stands closest to nature
and participates in the creation of bodily sustenance, he deserves the
most respect in the division of human labors. Like Jefferson, Emerson recognized that the soil remained a potent political and economic force, and believed that city life fatally attracted the youth of
husbandry and turned them into corrupted, artificial people. In
Georgia, speaking from a more traditional Christian ethical point of
view, Sidney Lanier celebrated in lilting but often diffuse iambics
the independent Southern yeoman who wisely rotates his crops and
grows "the universal food"—corn—instead of the commercially valuable King Cotton. Following the Jeffersonian dualism, Lanier also
rebukes those who choose to occupy the flimsy city, "built on the
shifting sands of trade" and "capricious commerce." Both Emerson
and Lanier offer essentially romanticized versions of the agrarian
ideals, but perhaps Emerson's essay has more of the cerebral and less
of the emotional than Lanier's poem.

It is surprising to find that Horace Greeley, the great reformer
and advocate of American opportunism, not only supported agrarian political policies but also felt that he knew enough about agriculture himself to write a book on the subject—*What I Know of
Farming.* He makes it clear, however, that he does not fall for the
romantic concept of the farmer as "more virtuous, upright, unselfish,
or deserving, than other people." The good farmer is a useful and
valuable citizen, but "so is a good merchant, doctor or lawyer." His
admiration for farming, he says, is a very practical matter, in that

"There is no other business in which success is so nearly certain as in this." Yet, in spite of his disclaimer, he too partakes of the agrarian mystique when he recommends agriculture as a vocation conducive to honesty, truth, and manliness of character. Greeley's essay is an interesting application of the opportunistic ethics of the Gilded Age to agriculture.

The final three authors represented in this section are all of the present century, and their writings represent respectively the application of the modern tools of economics, sociology, and science to the agrarian ideal. All three, Troy J. Cauley, Baker Brownell, and Louis Bromfield, attempt to justify agrarianism by marshaling factual evidence, the result being three stimulating, realistic, pragmatic statements and defenses of Jefferson's basic philosophy. The most distinguished writer of the three is Louis Bromfield, who early in his career wrote a series of impressive novels and later turned to agriculture to become a famous and successful practical farmer. In 1939 he bought a thousand-acre farm in Richland, Ohio, which he called "Malabar," and through the application of his scientific theories of the balance of nature to soil depletion, he created what remains one of the nation's agricultural show places. He wrote *Out of the Earth* as an agricultural textbook to answer the great volume of queries he received about his practices at Malabar Farm. In the two excerpts reprinted here he explains how biology and chemistry affect the soil and how this in turn relates to the life and welfare of the farmer. Bromfield wished to bring all the modern resources of science and technology to husbandry so as to enable it to survive as a way of life.

The selections included here are intended to suggest the perseverance of agrarianism as a viable strain in American thought, from colonial days to the present, and to establish a set of philosophical perspectives from which to view the latter sections.

JARED ELIOT

Essays upon Field-Husbandry

THE PREFACE

THERE ARE sundry books on *husbandry* wrote in *England:* Having read all on that subject I could obtain; yet such is the difference of climate and method of management between them and us, arising from causes that must make them always differ, so that those books are not very userful to us. Besides this, the terms of art made use of are so unknown to us, that a great deal they write is quite unintelligible to the generality of *New-England* readers.

Altho' *Great-Britain* in its situation be above six hundred miles more northerly than this country, yet the winters there are ordinarily so mild, that their books direct to ploughing in lays all the winter months; whereas at that season we are commonly bound fast in frost and snow.

For these reasons books of *husbandry* calculated to the state and circumstances of the country may be of great service; not an *history* of our practice, not an *account* of what we do in our present husbandry, but rather what we might do, to our advantage.

Having spent more than thirty years in a business that required a great deal of travel, altho' it did not much [iii/iv] hinder reading and study, gave me an opportunity to see much of the country, of making many observations, and of being acquainted with very many persons of worth and ingenuity, both farmers and others.

Yet all this while I was in a great measure prevented hereby, from making trials and experiments of those things which occured to my mind. Having had but one years leasure, am not so well furnished as the readers may expect. If it doth no more, it may serve to excite those who are more sufficient and more equal to the business, and set on foot what is so much wanted.

From Jared Eliot, *Essays Upon Field-Husbandry in New England, As it is or may be Ordered* (Boston: Edes and Gill, 1760), pp. iii–vi, 96–98.

It may be thought that a subject of this nature is not very suitable
for one of my calling.

Certainly the cultivation of the earth affords the most useful philosophy, opens to us a glorious scene and discovery of the wisdom
and power of the Creator and Governor of the world. It is what has
imployed men of all rank and orders, from the prince to the peasant.

Besides, useful knowledge has come from a quarter from whence it
was not so natural to expect it: A monk first discovered gun powder,
and the useful art of printing was the invention of a soldier.

It is acknowledged by our best writers, that while other parts of
learning less useful, have been cultivated, agriculture or husbandry,
has been strangely neglected. Some suppose the reason of this neglect
is, that the subject is too low [iv/v] for polite writers. It was not so
accounted by King Solomon; he did not think it below his dignity as
a king, nor inconsistent with his character as a preacher. The text
saith, *For he spake of the trees, from the cedar tree that is in Leba-
non, to the hyssop that springeth out of the wall.* This must include
all useful plants, grain and grass, even the whole vegetable kingdom.

This useful branch of learning is revived in Ireland, where some
hundreds of very considerable persons in the kingdom are associated
together to promote husbandry and other manufactures, and are
made a chartered corporation by the government: pens and hands
are set to work; it hath set a new face upon the country, and the
whole kingdom feel the advantage of this fine institution.

I rather think husbandry has been neglected as being too high;
that is, writers do not care to be at the trouble of projecting, nor at
the charge of trials and experiments upon what hath been projected:
it being a great deal easier to write a book upon the known arts and
sciences that shall be accepted and applauded, than to write upon
husbandry so as not to be despised; for some think we do not need
it, and that we know all that can be known already.

If any think that I am mistaken, I would desire them to try; the
subject needs all the help that can be afforded, especially at a time
when there is such a heavy load of debt upon the country. [v/vi]

If in this essay, or any other way I may be so happy as in the least
degree to promote the temporal or spiritual interest of my dear
friends and country-men, it is what will afford me a sensible pleasure.

The plain stile in which the following pages are written, is what
will render the whole the more intelligible and useful to farmers.

Killingworth, December 31, 1747   J. ELIOT. [vi]

From THE FIFTH ESSAY

For your sakes no doubt this is written; that he that plougheth should plough in hope, and that he that thresheth in hope, should be partaker of this hope.

I Cor. ix. 10.

The sluggard will not plough by reason of the cold, therefore shall he beg in harvest, and have nothing.

Prov. xx. 4.

WEALTH OR RICHES may be considered as nominal or real, natural or artificial: Nominal or artificial are those things which derive all, or the greatest part of their value, from opinion, custom, common consent, or a stamp of authority, by which a value is set; such as silver, gold, pearls, precious stones, pictures, bills of credit. Some of these things have a degree of intrinsick value in them, but not in any proportion to the value to which they are raised by custom or consent: For instance, silver and gold have a certain degree of intrinsick worth, but nothing equal to iron in the necessary service of life, either for instrument or medicine. A diamond hath an intrinsick [96/97] worth from its hardness; but as to many other precious stones, a load-stone, a mill-stone, or a grind-stone, is of much more real worth and use to mankind. Pearls are prescribed in medicine for great people: But is not of use but as a testacous powder; and for that use an oyster shell will do as well: But many things in high esteem have no intrinsick worth at all.

Natural or real wealth are such things as supply the necessities or conveniences of life: These are obtained from the earth, or the sea; such as corn, flesh, or fish, fruits, food and raiment.

Husbandry and navigation are the true source of natural or real wealth, without husbandry, even navigation cannot be carried on; without it we should want many of the comforts and conveniences of life. Husbandry then is a subject of great importance, without which all commerce and communication must come to an end, all social advantages, cease, comfort and earthly pleasure be no more. Nay, this is the very basis and foundation of all nominal or artificial wealth and riches. This rises and falls, lives or dies, just in proportion to the plenty or scarcity of real riches or natural wealth, we have a pregnant proof of this, *2 Kings* vi. 25. *And there was a great famine in Samaria; and behold they besieged it until an asses head was sold for four score pieces of silver, and the fourth part of a kab of doves dung for five pieces of silver.* With submission, I rather think it should be rendered, the contents of the dove's crop. The dove's returning home from the field with crops full of pease and other grain, would, when extracted, be a welcome entertainment to the hungry inhabitants, and sell for a good price; whereas the proper excrements or dung, especially of such animals who void no urine, is so loathsome, and [97/98] so destitute of nourishment, as to be unfit for food, even in times of greatest extremity.

If second hand food has been so high in the market, how valuable are the clean productions of the earth? Husbandry is the true mine from whence are drawn true riches and real wealth. [98]

THOMAS JEFFERSON

Notes on the State of Virginia

QUERY XIX.

The present state of manufactures, commerce, interior and exterior trade?

WE NEVER had an interior trade of any importance. Our exterior commerce has suffered very much from the beginning of the present contest. During this time we have manufactured within our families the most necessary articles of cloathing. Those of cotton will bear some comparison with the same kinds of manufacture in Europe; but those of wool, flax and hemp are very coarse, unsightly, and unpleasant: and such is our attachment to agriculture, and such our preference for foreign manufactures, that be it wise or unwise, our people will certainly return as soon as they can, to the raising [of] raw materials, and exchanging them for finer manufactures than they are able to execute themselves.

The political economists of Europe have established it as a principle that every State should endeavour to manufacture for itself; and this principle, like many others, we transfer to America, without calculating the difference of circumstance which should often produce a difference of result. In Europe the lands are either cultivated, or locked up against the cultivator. Manufacture must therefore be resorted to of necessity [239/240] not of choice, to support the surplus of their people. But we have an immensity of land courting the industry of the husbandman. Is it best then that all our citizens should be employed in its improvement, or that one half should be called off from that to exercise manufactures and handicraft arts for the other? Those who labour in the earth are the chosen people of God, if ever he had a chosen people, whose breasts he has made his peculiar deposit for substantial and genuine virtue. It is the focus in

From Thomas Jefferson, *Notes on the State of Virginia*, Second American Edition (Philadelphia: Mathew Carey, 1794), pp. 239–241. First published in 1787.

9

which he keeps alive that sacred fire, which otherwise might escape from the face of the earth. Corruption of morals in the mass of cultivators is a phaenomenon of which no age nor nation has furnished an example. It is the mark set on those, who not looking up to heaven, to their own soil and industry, as does the husbandman, for their subsistence, depend for it on casualties and caprice of customers. Dependance begets subservience and venality, suffocates the germ of virtue, and prepares fit tools for the designs of ambition. This, the natural progress and consequence of the arts, has sometimes perhaps been retarded by accidental circumstances: but, generally speaking, the proportion which the aggregate of the other classes of citizens bears in any state to that of its husbandmen, is the proportion of its unsound to its healthy parts, and is a good enough barometer whereby to measure its degree of corruption. While we have land to labour then, let us never wish to see our citizens occupied [240/241] at a workbench, or twirling a distaff. Carpenters, masons, smiths, are wanting in husbandry: but, for the general operations of manufacture, let our workshops remain in Europe. It is better to carry provisions and materials to workmen there, than bring them to the provisions and materials, and with them their manners and principles. The loss by the transportation of commodities across the Atlantic will be made up in happiness and permanence of government. The mobs of great cities add just so much to the support of pure government, as sores do to the strenth of the human body. It is the manners, and spirit of a people which preserve a republic in vigour. A degeneracy in these is a canker which soon eats to the heart of its laws and constitution. [241]

JOHN TAYLOR

The Pleasures of Agriculture

THE PLEASURES of agriculture, in free countries, are more, and in enslaved, fewer, than the pleasures of most other employments. The reason of it is, that agriculture both from its nature, and also as being generally the employment of a great portion of a nation, cannot be united with power, considered as an exclusive interest. It must of course be enslaved, wherever despotism exists, and its masters will enjoy more pleasures in that case, than it can ever reach. On the contrary, where power is not an exclusive, but a general interest, agriculture can employ its own energies for the attainment of its own happiness.

Under a free government it has before it, the inexhaustible sources of human pleasure, of fitting ideas to substances, and substances to ideas; and of a constant rotation of hope and fruition.

The novelty, frequency and exactness of accommodations between our ideas and operations, constitutes the most exquisite source of mental pleasures. Agriculture feeds it with endless supplies in the natures of soils, plants, climates manures, instruments of culture and domestic animals. Their combinations are inexhaustible, the novelty of results is endles, discrimination and adaption are never idle, and an unsatiated interest receives gratifications in quick succession.

Benevolence is so closely associated with this interest, that its exertion in numberless instances, is necessary to foster it. Liberality in supplying its labourers with the comforts of life, is the best sponsor for the prosperity of agriculture, and the practice of almost every moral virtue is amply remunerated in this world, whilst it is also the best surety for attaining the blessings of the next. [138/139] Poetry, in allowing more virtue to agriculture, than to any other profession, has abandoned her privilege of fiction, and yielded to the natural moral effect of the absence of temptation. The same fact is commem-

From John Taylor, *Arator, Being a Series of Agricultural Essays, Practical and Political*, Fifth Edition, Revised and Enlarged (Petersburg, Va.: Whitworth & Yancey, 1818), pp. 138–141. First published in 1813.

orated by religion, upon an occasion the most solemn, within the
scope of the human imagination. At the awful day of judgment, the
discrimination of the good from the wicked, is not made by the criterion of sects or of dogmas, but by one which constitutes the daily
employment and the great end of agriculture. The judge upon this
occasion has by anticipation pronounced, that to feed the hungry,
clothe the naked, and give drink to the thirsty, are the passports to
future happiness; and the divine intelligence which selected an agricultural state as a paradise for its first favourites, has here again prescribed the agricultural virtues as the means for the admission of
their posterity into heaven.

With the pleasures of religion, agriculture unites those of patriotism, and among the worthy competitors for pre-eminence in the
practice of this cardinal virtue, a profound author assigns a high station to him who has made two blades of grass grow instead of one;
an idea capable of a signal amplification, by a comparison between a
system of agriculture which doubles the fertility of a country, and a
successful war which doubles its territory. By the first the territory
itself is also substantially doubled, without wasting the lives, the
wealth, or the liberty of the nation which has thus subdued sterility,
and drawn prosperity from a willing source. By the second, the
blood pretended to be enriched, is spilt; the wealth pretended to be
increased, is wasted; the liberty said to be secured, is immolated to
the patriotism of a victorious army; and desolation in every form is
made to stalk in the glittering garb of false glory, throughout some
neighboring country. Moral law decides the preference with unde-
viating consistency, in assigning to the nation, which elects true patriotism, the recompense of truth, and to the electors of the false, the
expiation of error. To the respective agents, the same law assigns the
remorses of a conqueror, and the quiet conscience of the agriculturist. [139/140]

The capacity of agriculture for affording luxuries to the body, is
not less conspicuous than its capacity for affording luxuries to the
mind; it being a science singularly possessing the double qualities of
feeding with unbounded liberality, both the moral appetites of the
one, and the physical wants of the other. It can even feed a morbid
love for money, whilst it is habituating us to the practice of virtue;
and whilst it provides for the wants of the philosopher, it affords
him ample room for the most curious and yet useful researches. In
short, by the exercise it gives both to the body and to the mind, it
secures health and vigour to both; and by combining a thorough
knowledge of the real affairs of life, with a necessity for investigating
the arcana of nature, and the strongest invitations to the practice of
morality, it becomes the best architect of a complete man.

If this eulogy should succeed in awakening the attention of men of science to a skilful practice of agriculture they will become models for individuals, and guardians for national happiness. The discoveries of the learned will be practised by the ignorant; and a system which sheds happiness, plenty and virtue all around, will be gradually substituted for one, which fosters vice, breeds want, and begets misery.

Politicians (who ought to know the most, and generally know the least, of a science in which the United States are more deeply interested than in any other) will appear, of more practical knowledge, or at least of better theoretical instruction: and the hopeless habit of confiding our greatest interest to people most ignorant of it, will be abandoned.

The errors of politicians ignorant of agriculture, or their projects designed to oppress it, can only rob it of its pleasures, and consign it to contempt and misery. This revolution of its natural state, is invariably effected by war, armies, heavy taxes, or exclusive privileges. In two cases alone, have nations ever gained any thing by war. Those of repelling invasion and emigrating into a more fruitful territory. In every other case, the industrious of all professions suffer by war, the effects of which in its modern form, are precisely the same to the [140/141] victorious and the vanquished nation. The least evil to be apprehended from victorious armies, is a permanent system of heavy taxation, than which, nothing can more vitally wound or kill the pleasures of agriculture. Of the same stamp, are exclusive privileges in every form; and to pillage or steal under the sanction of the statute books, is no less fatal to the happiness of agriculture than the hierarchical tyranny over the soul, under the pretended sanction of God, or the feudal tyranny over the body, under the equally fraudulent pretence of defending the nation. In a climate and soil, where good culture never fails to beget plenty, where bad cannot produce famine, begirt by nature against the risque of invasion, and favoured by accident with the power of self government, agriculture can only lose its happiness by the folly or fraud of statesmen, or by its own ignorance. [141]

RALPH WALDO EMERSON

Farming

THE GLORY of the farmer is that, in the division of labors, it is his part to create. All trade rests at last on his primitive activity. He stands close to nature; he obtains from the earth the bread and the meat. The food which was not, he causes to be. The first farmer was the first man, and all historic nobility rests on possession and use of land. Men do not like hard work, but every man has an exceptional respect for tillage, and a feeling that this is the original calling of his race, that he himself is only excused from it by some circumstance which made him delegate it for a time to other hands. If he have not some skill which recommends him to the farmer, some product for which the farmer will give him corn, he must himself return into his due place among the planters. And the profession has in all eyes its ancient charm, as standing nearest to God, the first cause.

Then the beauty of nature, the tranquillity and innocence of the countryman, his independence, and his pleasing arts,—the care of bees, of poultry, of sheep, of cows, the dairy, the care of hay, of fruits, [123/124] of orchards and forests, and the reaction of these on the workmen, in giving him a strength and plain dignity, like the face and manners of nature, all men acknowledge. All men keep the farm in reserve as an asylum where, in case of mischance, to hide their poverty,—or a solitude, if they do not succeed in society. And who knows how many glances of remorse are turned this way from the bankrupts of trade, from mortified pleaders in courts and senates, or from the victims of idleness and pleasure? Poisoned by town life and town vices, the sufferer resolves: 'Well, my children, whom I have injured, shall go back to the land, to be recruited and cured by that which should have been my nursery, and now shall be their hospital.'

The farmer's office is precise and important, but you must not try

From Ralph Waldo Emerson, *Society and Solitude* (Boston: Fields, Osgood & Company, 1870), pp. 123–128, 135–138.

to paint him in rose-color; you cannot make pretty compliments to fate and gravitation, whose minister he is. He represents the necessities. It is the beauty of the great economy of the world that makes his comeliness. He bends to the order of the seasons, the weather, the soils and crops, as the sails of a ship bend to the wind. He represents continuous hard labor, year in, year out, and small gains. He is a slow person, timed to nature, and not to city watches. He takes the pace of seasons, plants, and chemistry. Nature never hurries: atom by atom, little by little, she achieves her work. The lesson one learns in fishing, yachting, [124/125] hunting, or planting, is the manners of Nature; patience with the delays of wind and sun, delays of the seasons, bad weather, excess or lack of water,—patience with the slowness of our feet, with the parsimony of our strength, with the largeness of sea and land we must traverse, etc. The farmer times himself to Nature, and acquires that livelong patience which belongs to her. Slow, narrow man, his rule is, that the earth shall feed and clothe him; and he must wait for his crop to grow. His entertainments, his liberties, and his spending must be on a farmer's scale, and not on a merchant's. It were as false for farmers to use a wholesale and massy expense, as for states to use a minute economy. But if thus pinched on one side, he has compensatory advantages. He is permanent, clings to his land as the rocks do. In the town where I live, farms remain in the same families for seven and eight generations; and most of the first settlers (in 1635), should they reappear on the farms to-day, would find their own blood and names still in possession. And the like fact holds in the surrounding towns.

This hard work will always be done by one kind of man; not by scheming speculators, nor by soldiers, nor professors, nor readers of Tennyson; but by men of endurance,—deep-chested, long-winded, tough, slow and sure, and timely. The farmer has a great health, and the appetite of health, and means to his end: he has broad lands for his home, wood to [125/126] burn great fires, plenty of plain food; his milk, at least, is unwatered; and for sleep he has cheaper and better and more of it than citizens.

He has grave trusts confided to him. In the great household of Nature, the farmer stands at the door of the bread-room, and weighs to each his loaf. It is for him to say whether men shall marry or not. Early marriages and the number of births are indissolubly connected with abundance of food; or, as Bruke said, "Man breeds at the mouth." Then he is the Board of Quarantine. The farmer is a hoarded capital of health, as the farm is the capital of wealth; and it is from him that the health and power, moral and intellectual, of the cities came. The city is always recruited from the country. The men in cities who are the centres of energy, the driving-wheels of trade, politics, or practical arts, and the women of beauty and genius are the children or grandchildren of farmers, and are spending the energies which their fathers' hardy, silent life accumulated in frosty furrows, in poverty, necessity, and darkness.

He is the continuous benefactor. He who digs a well, constructs a stone fountain, plants a grove of trees by the roadside, plants an orchard, builds a durable house, reclaims a swamp, or so much as puts a stone seat by the wayside, makes the land so far lovely and desirable, makes a fortune which he cannot carry away with him, but which is useful to his [126/127] country long afterwards. The man that works at home helps society at large with somewhat more of certainty than he who devotes himself to charities. If it be true that, not by votes of political parties, but by the eternal laws of political economy, slaves are driven out of a slave State as fast as it is surrounded by free States, then the true abolitionist is the farmer, who, heedless of laws and constitutions, stands all day in the field, investing his labor in the land, and making a product with which no forced labor can compete.

We commonly say that the rich man can speak the truth, can afford honesty, can afford independence of opinion and action;—and that is the theory of nobility. But it is the rich man in a true sense, that is to say, not the man of large income and large expenditure, but solely the man whose outlay is less than his income and is steadily kept so.

In English factories, the boy that watches the loom, to tie the thread when the wheel stops to indicate that a thread is broken, is called a *minder*. And in this great factory of our Copernican globe, shifting its slides; rotating its constellations, times, and tides; bringing now the day of planting, then of watering, then of weeding, then of reaping, then of curing and storing,—the farmer is the *minder*. His machine is of colossal proportions,—the diameter of the water-wheel, the arms of the levers, the power of the battery, are out of all mechanic measure;[127/128]—and it takes him long to understand its parts and its working. This pump never "sucks"; these screws are never loose; this machine is never out of gear; the vat and piston, wheels and tires, never wear out, but are self-repairing. . . . [128/135]

There has been a nightmare bred in England of indigestion and spleen among landlords and loomlords, namely, the dogma that men breed too fast for the powers of the soil; that men multiply in a geometrical ratio, whilst corn only in an arithmetical; and hence that, the more prosperous we are, the faster we approach these frightful limits: nay, the plight of every new generation is worse than of the foregoing, because the first comers take up the best lands; the next, the second best; and each succeeding wave of population is driven to poorer, so that the land is ever yielding less returns to enlarging hosts of eaters. Henry Carey of Philadelphia replied: 'Not so, Mr. Malthus, but just the opposite of so is the fact.'

The first planter, the savage, without helpers, without tools, looking chiefly to safety from his enemy,—man or beast,—takes poor land. The better lands are loaded with timber, which he cannot clear; they need drainage, which he cannot attempt. He cannot plough, or fell trees, or drain the rich swamp. He is a poor creature; he scratches with a sharp [135/136] stick, lives in a cave or a hutch, has no road but the trail of the moose or bear; he lives on their flesh when he can kill one, on roots and fruits when he cannot. He falls, and is lame; he coughes, he has a stitch in his side, he has a fever and chills: when he is hungry, he cannot always kill and eat a bear; —chances of war,—sometimes the bear eats him. 'T is long before he digs or plants at all, and then only a patch. Later he learns that his planting is better than hunting; that the earth works faster for him than he can work for himself,—works for him when he is asleep, when it rains, when heat overcomes him. The sunstroke which knocks him down brings his corn up. As his family thrive, and other planters come up around him, he begins to fell trees, and clear good land; and when, by and by, there is more skill, and tools and roads, the new generations are strong enough to open the lowlands, where the wash of mountains has accumulated the best soil, which yield a hundred-fold the former crops. The last lands are the best lands. It needs science and great numbers to cultivate the best lands, and in the best manner. Thus true political economy is not mean, but liberal, and on the pattern of the sun and sky. Population increases in the ratio of morality: credit exists in the ratio of morality.

Meantime we cannot enumerate the incidents and agents of the farm without reverting to their influence on the farmers. He carries out this cumulative [136/137] preparation of means to their last effect. This crust of soil which ages have refined he refines again for the feeding of a civil and instructed people. The great elements with which he deals cannot leave him unaffected, or unconscious of his ministry; but their influence somewhat resembles that which the same Nature has on the child,—of subduing and silencing him. We see the farmer with pleasure and respect, when we think what powers and utilities are so meekly worn. He knows every secret of labor: he changes the face of the landscape. Put him on a new planet, and he would know where to begin; yet there is no arrogance in his bearing, but a perfect gentleness. The farmer stands well on the world. Plain in manners as in dress, he would not shine in palaces; he is absolutely unknown and inadmissible therein; living or dying, he never shall be heard of in them; yet the drawing-room heroes put down beside him would shrivel in his presence,—he solid and unexpressive, they expressed to gold-leaf. But he stands well on the world, —as Adam did, as an Indian does, as Homer's heroes, Agamemnon or Achilles, do. He is a person whom a poet of any clime—Milton, Firdusi, or Cervantes—would appreciate as being really a piece of the old Nature, comparable to sun and moon, rainbow and flood; because he is, as all natural persons are, representative of Nature as much as these. [137/138]

That uncorrupted behavior which we admire in animals and in young children belongs to him, to the hunter, the sailor,—the man who lives in the presence of Nature. Cities force growth, and make men talkative and entertaining, but they make them artificial. What possesses interest for us is the *naturel* of each, his constitutional excellence. This is forever a surprise, engaging and lovely; we cannot be satiated with knowing it, and about it; and it is this which the conversation with Nature cherishes and guards. [138]

HORACE GREELEY

The Farmer's Calling

IF ANY ONE fancies that he ever heard *me* flattering farmers as a class, or saying anything which implied that they were more virtuous, upright, unselfish, or deserving, than other people, I am sure he must have misunderstood or that he now misrecollects me. I do not even join in the cant, which speaks of farmers as supporting everybody else—of farming as the only indispensable vocation. You may say if you will that mankind could not subsist if there were no tillers of the soil; but the same is true of house-builders, and of some other classes. A thoroughly good farmer is a useful, valuable citizen: so is a good merchant, doctor, or lawyer. It is not essential to the true nobility and genuine worth of the farmer's calling that any other should be assailed or disparaged.

Still, if one of my three sons had been spared to attain manhood, I should have advised him to try to make himself a good farmer; and this without any romantic or poetic notions of Agriculture as a pursuit. I know well, from personal though youthful experience, that the farmer's life is one of labor, [183/184] anxiety, and care; that hail, and flood, and hurricane, and untimely frosts, over which he can exert no control, will often destroy in an hour the net results of months of his persistent, well-directed toil; that disease will sometimes sweep away his animals, in spite of the most judicious treatment, the most thoughtful providence, on his part; and that insects blight, and rust, will often blast his well-grounded hopes of a generous harvest, when they seem on the very point of realization. I know that he is necessarily exposed, more than most other men, to the caprices and inclemencies of weather and climate; and that, if he begins responsible life without other means than those he finds in his own clear head and strong arms, with those of his helpmeet, he must expect to struggle through years of poverty, frugality, and resolute,

From Horace Greeley, *What I Know of Farming: A Series of Brief and Plain Expositions of Practical Agriculture as an Art Based Upon Science* (New York: G. W. Carleton & Co., 1871), pp. 183–188.

persistent, industry, before he can reasonably hope to attain a position of independence, comfort, and comparative leisure. I know that much of his work is rugged, and some of it absolutely repulsive; I know that he will seem, even with unbroken good fortune, to be making money much more slowly than his neighbor, the merchant, the broker, or eloquent lawyer, who fills the general eye while he prospers and, when he fails, sinks out of sight and is soon forgotten; and yet, I should have advised my sons to choose farming as their vocation, for these among other reasons:

I. There is no other business in which success is so nearly certain as in this. Of one hundred men who [184/185] embark in trade, a careful observer reports that ninety-five fail; and, while I think this proportion too large, I am sure that a large majority do, and must fail, because competition is so eager and traffic so enormously overdone. If ten men endeavor to support their families by merchandise in a township which affords adequate business for but three, it is certain that a majority must fail, no matter how judicious their management or how frugal their living. But you may double the number of farmers in any agricultural county I ever traversed, without necessarily dooming one to failure, or even abridging his gains. If half the traders and professional men in this country were to betake themselves to farming tomorrow, they would not render that pursuit one whit less profitable, while they would largely increase the comfort and wealth of the entire community; and, while a good merchant, lawyer, or doctor, may be starved out of any township, simply because the work he could do well is already confided to others, I never yet heard of a temperate, industrious, intelligent, frugal, and energetic farmer who failed to make a living, or who, unless prostrated by disease or disabled by casualty, was precluded from securing a modest independence before age and decrepitude divested him of the ability to labor.

II. I regard farming as that vocation which conduces most directly and palpably to a reverence for Honesty and Truth. The young lawyer is often constrained, or at least tempted, by his necessities, to do [185/186] the dirty professional work of a rascal intent on cheating his neighbor out of his righteous dues. The young doctor may be likewise incited to resort to a quackery he despises in order to secure instant bread; the unknown author is often impelled to write what will sell rather than what the public ought to buy; but the young farmer, acting *as* a farmer, must realize that his success depends upon his absolute verity and integrity. He deals directly with Nature, which never was and never will be cheated. He has no temptation to sow beach sand for plaster, dock-seed for clover, or stoop to any trick or juggle whatever. "Whatsoever a man soweth that shall he also reap," while true, in the long run, of all men, is instantly and palpably true as to him. When he, having grown his crop, shall attempt to sell it—in other words, when he ceases to be a farmer and becomes a trader—he may possibly be tempted into one of the many devious ways of rascality; but, so long as he is acting simply as a farmer, he can hardly be lured from the broad, straight highway of integrity and righteousness.

III. The farmer's calling seems to me that most conducive to thorough manliness of character. Nobody expects him to cringe, or smirk, or curry favor, in order to sell his produce. No merchant refuses to buy it because his politics are detested or his religious opinions heterodox. He may be a Mormon, a Rebel, a Millerite, or a Communist, yet his Grain or his Pork will sell for exactly what it is worth—not a [186/187] fraction less or more than the price commanded by the kindred product of like quality and intrinsic value of his neighbor, whose opinions on all points are faultlessly orthodox and popular. On the other hand, the merchant, the lawyer, the doctor, especially if young and still struggling dubiously for a position, are continually tempted to sacrifice or suppress their profoundest convictions in deference to the vehement and often irrational prepossessions of the community, whose favor is to them the breath of life. "She will find that *that* won't go down here," was the comment of an old woman on a Mississippi steamboat, when told that the plain, deaf stranger, who seemed the focus of general interest, was Miss Martineau, the celebrated Unitarian; and in so saying she gave expression to a feeling which pervades and governs many if not most communities. I doubt whether the social intolerance of adverse opinions is more vehement anywhere else than throughout the larger portion of our own country. I have repeatedly been stung by the receipt of letters gravely informing me that my course and views on a current topic were adverse to public opinion: the writers evidently assuming, as a matter of course, that I was a mere jumping-jack, who only needed to know what other people thought to insure my instant and abject conformity to their prejudices. Very often, in other days, I was favored with letters from indignant subscribers, who, dissenting from my views on some question, took this method of informing me that they [187/188] should no longer take my journal —a superfluous trouble, which could only have meant dictation or insult, since they had only to refrain from renewing their subscriptions, and their *Tribune* would stop coming, whenever they should have received what we owed them; and it would in no case stop till then. That a journalist was in any sense a public teacher—that he necessarily had convictions, and was not likely to suppress them because they were not shared by others—in short, that his calling was other and higher than that of a waiter at a restaurant, expected to furnish whatever was called for, so long as the pay was forthcoming —these ex-subscribees had evidently not for one moment suspected. That such persons have little or no capacity to insult, is very true; and yet, a man is somewhat degraded in his own regard by learning that his vocation is held in such low esteem by others. The true farmer is proudly aware that it is quite otherwise with *his* pursuit— that no one expects him to swallow any creed, support any party, or defer to any prejudice, as a condition precedent to the sale of his products. Hence, I feel that it is easier and more natural in his pursuit than in any other for a man to work for a living, and aspire to success and consideration, without sacrificing self-respect, compromising integrity, or ceasing to be essentially and thoroughly a gentleman. [188]

SIDNEY LANIER

Corn

TODAY the woods are trembling through and through
With shimmering forms, that flash before my view,
Then melt in green as dawn-stars melt in blue.
   The leaves that wave against my cheek caress
   Like women's hands; the embracing boughs express
      A subtlety of mighty tenderness;
   The copse-depths into little noises start,
   That sound anon like beatings of a heart,
   Anon like talk 'twixt lips not far apart.
   The beech dreams balm, as a dreamer hums a song;
   Through that vague wafture, expirations strong
   Throb from young hickories breathing deep and long
With stress and urgence bold of prisoned spring
      And ecstasy of burgeoning.
   Now, since the dew-plashed road of morn is dry,
   Forth venture odors of more quality
   And heavenlier giving. Like Jove's locks awry,
      Long muscadines
Rich-wreathe the spacious foreheads of great pines,
And breathe ambrosial passion from their vines.
   I pray with mosses, ferns and flowers shy
   That hide like gentle nuns from human eye
   To lift adoring perfumes to the sky.
I hear faint bridal-sighs of brown and green
Dying to silent hints of kisses keen
As far lights fringe into a pleasant sheen.
   I start at fragmentary whispers, blown
   From undertalks of leafy souls unknown,
   Vague purports sweet, of inarticulate tone. [53/54]

From *Poems of Sidney Lanier*, edited by His Wife, New Edition (New York: Charles Scribner's Sons, 1906), pp. 53–59. First published in *Lippincott's Magazine*, February, 1875.

Dreaming of gods, men, nuns and brides, between
Old companies of oaks that inward lean
To join their radiant amplitudes of green
  I slowly move, with ranging looks that pass
  Up from the matted miracles of grass
Into yon veined complex of space
Where sky and leafage interlace
  So close, the heaven of blue is seen
  Inwoven with a heaven of green.

I wander to the zigzag-cornered fence
Where sassafras, intrenched in brambles dense,
Contests with stolid vehemence
  The march of culture, setting limb and thorn
  As pikes against the army of the corn.

There, while I pause, my fieldward-faring eyes
Take harvests, where the stately corn-ranks rise,
     Of inward dignities
And large benignities and insights wise,
    Graces and modest majesties.
Thus, without theft, I reap another's field;
Thus, without tilth, I house a wondrous yield,
And heap my heart with quintuple crops concealed.

Look, out of line one tall corn-captain stands
Advanced beyond the foremost of his bands,
  And waves his blades upon the very edge
  And hottest thicket of the battling hedge.
Thou lustrous stalk, that ne'er mayst walk nor talk,
  Still shalt thou type the poet-soul sublime
  That leads the vanward of his timid time
  And sings up cowards with commanding rhyme—[54/55]
Soul calm, like thee, yet fain, like thee, to grow
By double increment, above, below;
  Soul homely, as thou art, yet rich in grace like thee,
  Teaching the yeomen selfless chivalry
  That moves in gentle curves of courtesy;
Soul filled like thy long veins with sweetness tense,
    By every godlike sense
Transmuted from the four wild elements.
      Drawn to high plans,
  Thou lift'st more stature than a mortal man's,
Yet ever piercest downward in the mould
    And keepest hold

Upon the reverend and steadfast earth
    That gave thee birth;
Yea, standest smiling in thy future grave,
    Serene and brave,
With unremitting breath
Inhaling life from death,
Thine epitaph writ fair in fruitage eloquent,
    Thyself thy monument.

    As poets should,
Thou hast built up thy hardihood
With universal food,
  Drawn in select proportions fair
  From honest mould and vagabond air;
From darkness of the dreadful night,
    And joyful light;
  From antique ashes, whose departed flame
  In thee has finer life and longer fame;
From wounds and balms,
From storms and dry calms,
From potsherds and dry bones
    And ruin-stones. [55/56]
Into they vigorous substance thou hast wrought
Whate'er the hand of Circumstance hath brought;
  Yea, into cool solacing green hast spun
  White radiance hot from out the sun.
So thou dost mutually leaven
Strength of earth with grace of heaven;
  So thou dost marry new and old
  Into a one of higher mould;
  So thou dost reconcile the hot and cold,
    The dark and bright,
And many a heart-perplexing opposite,
    And so,
  Akin by blood to high and low,
Fitly thou playest out thy poet's part,
Richly expending thy much-bruiséd heart
  In equal care to nourish lord in hall
    Or beast in stall:
  Thou took'st from all that thou mightst give to all.

O steadfast dweller on the selfsame spot
Where thou wast born, that still repinest not—
Type of the home-fond heart, the happy lot!—
  Deeply thy mild content rebukes the land

Whose flimsy homes, built on the shifting sand
Of trade, for ever rise and fall
With alternation whimsical,
      Enduring scarce a day,
      Then swept away
By swift engulfments of incalculable tides
Whereon capricious Commerce rides.
Look, thou substantial spirit of content!
Across this little vale, thy continent,
      To where, beyond the mouldering mill,
      Yon old deserted Georgian hill [56/57]
Bares to the sun his piteous aged crest
            And seamy breast,
      By restless-hearted children left to lie
      Untended there beneath the heedless sky,
      As barbarous folk expose their old to die.
Upon that generous-rounding side,
            With gullies scarified
      Where keen Neglect his lash hath plied,
Dwelt one I knew of old, who played at toil,
And gave to coquette Cotton soul and soil.
      Scorning the slow reward of patient grain,
      He sowed his heart with hopes of swifter gain,
      Then sat him down and waited for the rain.
He sailed in borrowed ships of usury—
A foolish Jason on a treacherous sea,
Seeking the Fleece and finding misery.
      Lulled by smooth-rippled loans, in idle trance
      He lay, content that unthrift Circumstance
      Should plough for him the stony field of Chance.
Yea, gathering crops whose worth no man might tell,
He staked his life on games of Buy-and-Sell,
And turned each field into a gambler's hell.
      Aye, as each year began,
      My farmer to the neighboring city ran;
Passed with a mournful anxious face
Into the banker's inner place;
Parleyed, excused, pleaded for longer grace;
      Railed at the drought, the worm, the rust, the grass;
      Protested ne'er again 'twould come to pass;
      With many an *oh* and *if* and *but alas*
Parried or swallowed searching questions rude,
And kissed the dust to soften Dives's mood.
At last, small loans by pledges great renewed,
      He issues smiling from the fatal door,

And buys with lavish hand his yearly store [57/58]
Till his small borrowings will yield no more.
Aye, as each year declined,
With bitter heart and ever-brooding mind
He mourned his fate unkind.
　In dust, in rain, with might and main,
　He nursed his cotton, cursed his grain,
　Fretted for news that made him fret again,
Snatched at each telegram of Future Sale,
And thrilled with Bulls' or Bears' alternate wail—
In hope or fear alike for ever pale.
　And thus from year to year, through hope and fear,
　With many a curse and many a secret tear,
　Striving in vain his cloud of debt to clear,
　　　At last
He woke to find his foolish dreaming past,
　And all his best-of-life the easy prey
　Of squandering scamps and quacks that lined his way
　　　With vile array,
From rascal statesman down to petty knave;
Himself, at best, for all his bragging brave,
A gamester's catspaw and a banker's slave.
　Then, worn and gray, and sick with deep unrest,
　He fled away into the oblivious West,
　　　Unmourned, unblest.

Old hill! old hill! thou gashed and hairy Lear
Whom the divine Cordelia of the year,
E'en pitying Spring, will vainly strive to cheer—
　King, that no subject man nor beast may own,
　Discrowned, undaughtered and alone—
Yet shall the great God turn thy fate,
And bring thee back into thy monarch state
　　　And majesty immaculate.
　Lo, through hot waverings of the August morn, [58/59]
　Thou givest from thy vasty sides forlorn
　Visions of golden treasuries of corn—
Ripe largesse lingering for some bolder heart
That manfully shall take thy part,
　　　And tend thee,
　　　And defend thee,
With antique sinew and with modern art.

　　SUNNYSIDE, GEORGIA, August, 1874 [59]

TROY J. CAULEY

The Merits of Agrarianism

IN THE BEGINNING, we tentatively defined Agrarianism as an economic and social system under which the chief method of making a living is that of tilling the soil, with a consequent rather wide dispersion of population and a relative meagerness of commercial intercourse. From this beginning we may proceed to an elaboration of its nature.... [104/109]

A farmer engaging in relatively self-sufficing farming on a farm which he owns outright can be about the most independent specimen to be discovered in this country. He can be independent in politics, in ethics, in his general behavior. He can *afford* to be independent. He has no customers and no creditors to offend; he has no business competitors to fear. There is no Dean or Board of Trustees to review his moral convictions and pass judgment thereupon. He can be an Individual and not a Babbitt. Certainly he is not removed from all social pressure to conform to the mores of the herd, but such pressure is at a minimum in his case. It is infinitely to be regretted that there are not more of his sort in our country.

To defend private property as a desirable social and economic arrangement is not, by any means, to defend the present arrangement in this country. Although our present Industrial Capitalism is usually spoken of as a system of private property, this is fundamentally false. The great bulk of the property in this country has come to be owned by large corporations; and these corporations, in turn, are controlled by a relative handful of men, mostly financiers. Ownership of farm lands is not concentrated to the same degree as is that of urban property, but the mortgage companies are operating rapidly in that direction. To the great mass of people in this [109/110] country, the ownership of property beyond a few personal items, utterly incapable of yielding the owner a living, is an absolutely non-

From Troy J. Cauley, *Agrarianism: A Program for Farmers* (Chapel Hill, N.C.: University of North Carolina Press, 1935), pp. 104, 109–114, 117–121, 124–127. Reprinted with the kind permission of the University of North Carolina Press.

existent state of affairs. Thus private property in the true sense of the term has disappeared from among us. Its restoration is an essential to the restoration of an agrarian economy of a satisfactory sort.

Widespread ownership of property will not give to people complete and absolute economic security. Such security, along with perfection, is not of this earth. But the insecurity which results from such uncontrollable natural factors as wind and rain and frost and drought is an insecurity much less cruel in its effects than that of the wage-earner who is totally dependent upon the employer for the opportunity to earn a living. There is something invigorating and inspiring in the struggle with the untoward forces of nature; there is nothing of the sort in the process of standing in line in front of an employment agency.

The fundamental purpose of an economic system is to satisfy our material wants and to contribute as much as possible toward the creation of an environment in which we may satisfy our non-material wants as well. Let us outline the ultimate methods of attacking the problem of satisfying material wants. They appear to be the following:

I. By increasing the quantity of goods and services available.

    A. By increasing the total quantity. [110/111]
    B. By increasing the quantity available to the average person by a more equitable distribution.

II. By reducing the number and variety of our wants.

    A. By reducing the number of wanters, i.e., control of population growth.
    B. By reducing the number of wants per wanter, i.e., lower material standards of living.

"Scarcity" may be defined as a low ratio between the amount of goods and services available and the amount wanted. From the standpoint of human welfare as against that of business expediency, scarcity is certainly not desirable, inasmuch as it simply means the inability of great numbers of people to satisfy their wants.

On the whole, urban industrial economy proposes to eliminate scarcity by increasing the quantity of goods and services available. In this project it generally fails for two reasons: (1) ths insistence of a capitalistic exchange economy that goods of any particular sort be kept relatively scarce in order to bolster up exchange-values, as previously explained; and (2) the development on the part of the peo-

ple of high material, or more nearly, pecuniary, standards which are
an inevitable accompaniment of highly organized urban communities, and which call always for more goods and services regardless of
the quantity already available.

Resolved into its essentials, our present pecuniary urban culture
means simply "more and faster." Contentment has [111/112] no
place in its philosophy or practice. With its standards of conspicuous
consumption and ostentation, there is never any stopping place. A
six-cylinder automobile is good until an eight-cylinder machine appears, which in turn is eclipsed by a twelve-cylinder projectile, and
so on *ad infinitum* and no where. "Progress" is the great slogan of
such a culture, and translated into concrete terms "Progress" has
meant quantity and speed. And quantity and speed have meant, in
turn, surfeit and jangled nerves.

We dig a tunnel under a river to save ten minutes' time. We fabri-
cate thousands of "time-saving and labor-saving" devices. And what
do we do with the time and energy thus saved? We devise still other
machines to consume them. The workman has two extra hours of
"leisure" as the result of "time-saving" machinery, and he spends
them looking at mechanical jumping-jacks and listening to mechanical music at a "talkie." Or he drives an automobile at forty miles an
hour a block at a time, stopping at regular intervals at the red lights
to let other emancipated workmen drive forty miles an hour a block
at a time between the red lights in the other direction.

More and faster, more and faster!

An agrarian economy has a different method of dealing with the
problem of scarcity. It devotes some effort to the matter of increasing
the amount of goods available, but comparatively little. Chiefly it
meets the problem *by reducing the* [112/113] *number and variety
of material wants.* How is it enabled to do this? Why is an agrarian
community any more successful than an urban community in limiting material wants to a relatively low level? There are several factors
which are responsible for this.

In the first place you don't want what other people have unless you
see them or otherwise learn of their having it. Country people do not
see each other in nearly so great numbers or nearly so often as do
city people.This follows simply from the fact that rural people are
widely dispersed geographically as compared with urban groups. In
sparsely settled rural areas, a family may go for days without seeing
anyone outside the pecuniary class in which it itself is situated. On
the other hand, a city man, and more particularly his wife and
daughters, never pass a day without seeing at close range the members of greatly superior pecuniary groups. To put all of this into
very simple terms, it isn't so bad to be poor if all your neighbors are
poor too.

In the second place, truly rural communities are not afflicted by that most efficient creator of scarcity of all time, modern advertising. The great bulk of modern advertising has as its essential purpose that of making people dissatisfied with what they already have or of making them want something which they have never wanted before. In both cases the result is the creation of scarcity to an extent almost beyond comprehension. It has been estimated—no telling how accurately—that [113/114] advertising ranks as the fourth largest industry in this country from the standpoint of the "dollar volume" of business done and the number of people employed.

The typical urban community is the happy hunting ground for the advertiser. Present-day rural communities are not entirely free of the nuisance, but then present-day rural communities are not in the great majority of cases typical agrarian communities. In a true agrarian community advertising of the scarcity-creating variety has no place, and in actual historical cases did not exist to any appreciable degree.

High-pressure salesmanship in all of its various manifestations and ramifications is, of course, of the same general nature. It has the same objects as advertising, those of making people dissatisfied with what they have and desirous of things the lack of which they have never felt. Such salesmanship is of the essence of a highly organized exchange economy, and by the same sign utterly alien to a self-sufficing agrarian economy.... [114/117],

The desire for prestige or recognition, among one's fellow beings is an almost universal human characteristic, common alike to rural people and city people. But there are vastly different ways in which prestige may be attained or manifested. Each culture, to a large extent, has its own ways. It is needless to repeat that our present-day industrial culture has money-making as its chief route to prestige. In the typical case money-making alone is not quite sufficient; it is necessary that other people be made aware of the fact. Thus we have conspicuous consumption and ostentation generally as a supplementary technique. These are, of course, based directly upon and dependent upon money-making itself.

Since money-making is not a feature of agrarian life, the struggle for prestige takes other forms. One of the commonest of these is that of physical prowess or skill in the performance of some useful task. In an agrarian community men pit strength against strength at log-rollings, house-raisings, and husking-bees; skill against skill in shooting-matches, horse-races, and horshoe-pitching. None of these requires any particular cash outlay, but the results are certainly as satisfactory from the standpoint of the psychological need involved.

The agrarian method of removing scarcity by reducing the amount of goods wanted has the further great merit that it

[117/118] offers leisure which is capable of being engaged—true leisure as distinct from mere enforced idleness. The essence of the beneficial use of leisure is complete relaxation from any nervous tension and the doing of things purely for the fun of doing them. Although in some cases the industrial worker may in terms of hours and minutes have as much or more leisure time than the farmer, there is the great difference in the majority of cases that the industrial worker is so keyed up by the speed at which he has worked—a pace set by the machine and not by the worker—that he finds it impossible to relax to the point of actually enjoying his non-working hours. Further, the chances are that he will take whatever recreation he does in the form of manipulating or watching the manipulation of other machines, a process which is scarcely refreshing for the person who has spent his day being worked by machines.[1]

Probably the greatest single source of human satisfaction is to be found in human companionship. The truth of this follows simply from the fact that man is essentially a social [118/119] animal. Gregariousness is a fundamental characteristic of human existence on a satisfactory basis. Casual interpretation of this human characteristic might lead one to the conclusion that city life would from this point of view offer great advantages over country life, in that the congregation of large numbers of people in urban communities would make possible much greater opportunities for human companionship. There is, however, only a very small measure of truth in such conclusion. It is true that agricultural communities can be so sparsely settled as to make the opportunities for human companionship very meager, but this is not typically the case. We are more prone to think of rural communities as being of such a nature in this country than do the people of European countries. This is because of the recentness of the pioneering period in our country. The conquest of the frontier did involve a great dispersion of population with consequent isolation and loneliness for many families, but this was essen-

[1] One author puts the problem in this way:

"The question is whether man can live by jumping-jacks alone. The statesmen of imperial Rome had a formula for the diversion of the people. It was bread and circuses. Our machines may be taught to manufacture bread from sawdust but it is also possible that they may find circuses easier. Such appears to have been our recent experience. It would be interesting to attempt to measure how much of the lives of how many of the people are at present given to diverting themselves with cinema circuses and automotive jumping-jacks. This is not said in irony. Perhaps man can achieve his ultimate happiness in playing with machinery. Yet it seems a strange fate for an animal species designed by nature for sunshine and love-making."—W. E. Atkins and others, *Economic Behavior* (Houghton Mifflin Co., Boston, 1931, 2 vols.), II, 502.

tially a passing phase. Taking the country as a whole, it has now passed; and east of the Mississippi River it had largely passed by the time of the Civil War.

Isolation is, of course, a relative term. It is argued by some people that farm families are still isolated, and that the only escape from such isolation is through the ownership of an automobile. There is much evidence to the contrary. In farm communities where the homes are not more than half a mile or so apart, there are ample opportunities for an adequate amount of visiting back and forth without any such [119/120] expensive means of transportation as an automobile. So far as that is concerned, people can walk such distances without any severe strain on heart and nerve and sinew; and walking is possessed of considerable merit from many points of view.

The virtue of hospitality has always flowered best under the conditions of a relatively widely dispersed population, and there is no good reason to suppose that it will not continue.

On the other hand, the aggregation of huge numbers of people in our great cities has quite definitely defeated its own ends so far as providing the opportunity for human companionship of a satisfying nature is concerned. A constant and enforced mingling with too many people can be utterly destructive of true companionship with one's fellow beings. The sight and sound of people can under such circumstances become utterly repulsive. People live within cat-throwing distance of each other in cities for years and never know each other's name. Partly this is from choice, but largely it is from necessity. To form intimate, face-to-face acquaintanceships with as many people as one comes into contact with in a large city would be to lay oneself open to grave dangers of imposition, not to say fraud and criminal violence.

It is possible to experience loneliness on the boundless plains of west Texas, eighty or ninety miles from another human being; and it is possible to experience loneliness at the corner of Broadway and Forty-second Street with people stepping [120/121] all over your toes. It is bad in both cases, but in some respects the latter is the worse. Loneliness in a crowd is somewhat ironic; loneliness in solitude is natural.

The point is that an agrarian community together with the adjacent villages which are an integral part of agrarian economy, offers opportunities for contact with just a sufficient number of persons with the proper degree of leisure for the most satisfying human companionship.

Agrarian life creates the opportunity further, for an intimate, satisfying relationship with nature. The work of the farmer takes him

into the outdoors—into close contact with the earth and its plant
and animal inhabitants. He sees the sunrise and the sunset, feels the
wind and the rain and the cold, hears the myriad sounds of animate
nature. Undoubtedly to many city dwellers, these matters are of no
concern. They are so remote from their experience and so alien to
their ideas of comfort and pleasure as to offer no attraction. There is
in them balm for the human soul just the same. There is food for
the satisfaction of spiritual hunger. . . . [121/124]

A rural community has certain characteristics which are conducive
to physical as well as to mental health. Medical examination of recruits in this country during the World War revealed numerous
physical defects in both the men from urban communities and those
from the farm. There was, however, a significant differential between the two groups. City men had a rejection rate of 21.6 per cent
as against a rate of 16.8 per cent for the country men. Of 19 disquali-
fying defects, the men from the farms had a higher percentage in
only 9. The Surgeon General reported that the total defects per one
hundred recruits was 38.3 for urban men and 33.3 for rural men.[2]

In view of the distinctly inferior medical facilities available to
country people as compared with those to which city people regularly have access, it is obvious that the country communities have
some very important inherent advantages over city areas from the
standpoint of healthfulness. Briefly these advantages are: a lack of
congestion and crowding, making epidemics less likely; an abundance of fresh air and sunshine; frequent occasion for physical exercise; availability of fresh, [124/125] wholesome foods in the typical
case; and a general absence of vicious living habits.

In spite of the fact, however, that farm communities contribute
better raw material for the making of soldiers than do the cities, an
agrarian nation is infinitely less likely to become engaged in war
than is a highly developed capitalistic industrial nation. It might be
argued in this connection that the agrarian interests in the Old
South were largely responsible for the annexation of Texas and the
filibustering raids into Cuba, which matters were to some extent in
the nature of military aggression; but it is to be stressed that the
leadership of this element in the Old South was not truly agrarian
in its interests and objectives but instead was attempting to further
the interests of an industrial or commercial type of agriculture based
upon slave labor and cotton as a cash crop.

Fundamentally, practically all modern wars are caused by economic factors. Briefly, the capitalistic industrial nations push out in

---

[2] F. R. Yoder, *Introduction to Agricultural Economics* (Thomas Y. Crowell
Co., New York, 1929), p. 44.

a struggle for sources of raw materials and markets for finished products. They come to grips with each other in this process, and the outcome, sooner or later, is very likely to be war. Once a war has been generated by these fundamental causes, there are various psychological factors which influence individual men and women to participate in it and to lend their moral support to it; but the underlying causes are economic.

The question of why we have wars is divisible into two parts: (1) how do wars get started? and (2) why do people [125/126] participate in them after they are started? No effort will be made here to go into either one of these questions in an exhaustive manner, but certain facts stand out immediately. The people of an agrarian state may very well participate in a war after it is started by someone else, but they will not start one. By the very nature of an agrarian society, its people are interested in those things which are close to home and in very little else. Certainly they have no sufficiently pressing interests abroad to induce them to go halfway round the world and start a war, as any number of industrial and commercial nations have done. And it follows that if the nations of the earth generally were agrarian in character they would spend their time leaving each other alone. And in view of the fact that modern warfare constitutes the greatest calamity to which the human race is subject, such a state of affairs would have a great deal in its favor.

It follows from the various characteristics of the agrarian community which have been discussed in the preceding pages that such a community possesses a much greater degree of economic and social stability than does an urban industrial and commercial community. Whether this be virtue or fault is, no doubt, largely a matter of personal philosophy. It is urged here as a virtue. American life during the past century and a half has suffered from many things, but very near the top of the list should be placed the lack of stability of community life. That we have developed so few civic virtues, that our local government is the mess that it is, that our towns and [126/127] cities are as hideously ugly as they frequently are—all may be ascribed in very large part to the fact that none of these units has had a sufficient degree of stability to make any considerable number of people deeply interested in their moral or aesthetic welfare. The typical American lives in at least half a dozen relatively widely-scattered communities in the course of his hurried life-time. A novel setting forth the life story of an American who was born, lived, and died in the same community would be a rarity indeed.

Under these conditions it may be stoutly maintained that an increased stability of community life would be largely beneficial in this country, and Agrarianism offers much in that direction.

Finally, what are the rural virtues so far as the people themselves are concerned? Although the following list is not exclusively rural, the fact remains that an agrarian community is peculiarly conducive to the development and perpetuation of these qualities on the part of the rank and file of its members: Self-reliance, physical courage, moral integrity, loyalty, and hospitality. Can definite proof of this claim be presented? Probably not, but then there are so many truths that cannot be finally proved. [127]

BAKER BROWNELL

The Community and Rural Life

THOUGH RURAL LIFE usually is assumed to be the normal context in which the human community emerges and survives, it really is different things to different people. Its central meaning no doubt is the functional cooperation of human beings with vegetable and animal life. It is thus the context of human ecology. Rural life is not the lonely conquest of a hostile wilderness. It is not the life of the hunter or trapper or old-time lumberman killing or capturing his prey. It is a cooperative alliance with Nature in which the survival and abundance of life of many species, including man, are mutually dependent. Rural life, on the other hand, is not a life in cities removed from growing things, nor is it residence in a park or suburb, or visiting a country estate. It is a functional relationship with Nature and is found for the most part in agriculture and husbandry. It may include many members of that increasing group called "rural, non-farm," but only if they are productively close to the life of the country. A country grocer or banker, a small manufacturer, an artificer, a country doctor, or a village housewife may well be as much a part of the rural context of life as a farmer. If they partake of the rhythmic processes associated with the growth of plants and animals and participate in the variegated pattern of rural living, they belong.

This symbiotic relationship of man and growing things called rural life is normally the seat of the small community and, as I shall try to show, of the true community. All human life, of course, is eventually dependent on this relationship, though some men and women live remotely from it. They learn to remove themselves from the close, compelling influences of natural things. They abstract their thoughts and interests and even their activities from the green context and spiritual milieu of life in Nature, and reside in massive

From Baker Brownell, *The Human Community: Its Philosophy and Practice for a Time of Crisis* (New York: Harper & Row, Publishers, Incorporated, 1950), pp. 6–9.

aggregations or in other ways remote from rural interests. But they
have not taken with them into those aggregations the stable human
community or the naturally integrated life. They have renounced
Nature at a price. That price would seem to be something close to
spiritual impoverishment and phyletic discontinuity and decadence.
[6/7]

In this age of wonders and defeat it is conceivable at least that
men might dissolve entirely their alliance with living Nature, reject
their symbiotic ecology, and live entirely by artifice and material
technology. Scientists may find ways to substitute completely an artificial process for the green chemistries, the native photosynthesis, the
animal assimilative processes, of the natural world on which we now
live. They thus would release men wholly from the rhythms and
compulsions of the fields. It would be a senseless procedure, no
doubt; it would be economically and socially inefficient, I am told,
but that might not greatly limit its large-scale development. It has in
fact already been accomplished in part.

The limiting principle in such a substitutive procedure is less the
physical and technological restrictions, or those of common sense,
than the psychological, social, and deeply cultural cast of a man's nature. The pattern of his living, as it were, has been laid out through
millions of years in association with living animals and plants and
the vast music and movement of the natural world. The form of
human life and the structure of its activities are involved in these
natural forms and structures. The values that men have, the accents,
the appreciations, the criteria of morals, even the insistance on living survival itself, were derived initially in this milieu, given form
there, and now evolve—if they evolve at all—as part of that great
order. To abstract human beings by some technological procedure
from this functional relationship with the life and creative persis-
tence of the natural world around them would be literally to abstract them from life itself. They would be no longer men in a complete or formal sense. Their communities would disintegrate; their
values disappear. That indeed is already happening in part, as their
relations with Nature become more indirect. The decline of the
human community as we see it today corresponds to the decline of
rural culture and economy.

The beasts and the plants participate primevally in our communities. They enter our philosophies; mold our natures; help make us
fully human. They are among our greatest teachers. Through the
mutuality and interlocking functions of men and plants and animals
we and they domesticate each other, and create severally characters,
modes of life, and human communities unattainable alone. We still
hold to our totems—or the phyletic identification with animals—

though not in the totemistic faith. When men are deprived of these associations something secure and primitively creative in their lives is lost. When they rebel, like some rural Lucifer, against the order of things within which they were created, they lose somehow the wisdom and the pace of Nature, and invent, as he did, [7/8] disunity and conflict. They invent disorder. For animals and plants bind us functionally to the sun and seasons. Our life and work among them indenture us to wordless patterns of the four winds and the summer solstice. We are more fully unified through them with the sources and sustenance of our lives. We are continuous with Nature and the world. This sense of functional unity with the natural world is a basic condition, we may assume, of what is called a meaningful and stable life.

On the child this revolt against nature, or, to say it more quietly, this removal of our life from the rural community of animals, plants, and human beings, is particularly harmful. John Dewey has pointed it out: when life in the main was rural, the child came into contact with natural things. He knew the care of domestic animals, the cultivation of the soil, the raising of crops. The home was the center of industry and in it all the child took a functional part. His mental and moral training was here. The development here of hand and eye, of skill and deftness, and, above all, his "initiation into self-reliance, independence of judgment and action" were the stimulus to habits of regular and continuous work. In the city these educative influences usually are absent. "Just at the time," Dewey says, "when a child is subjected to a great increase in stimulus and pressure from his environment, he loses the practical and motor training necessary to balance his intellectual development. Facility in acquiring information is gained: the power of using it is lost."[1]

What is this value in the relationship with Nature? It is the working continuity of men with other living things and natural processes. Though an Otis elevator or a subway train is also a natural thing subject to natural processes and in its way as wonderful as a wild rose in June, there is still a difference. The elevator lacks the evaluative continuity and spiritual response in the minds of men that native things possess. It is an artifice without organic continuity and without versatility of value. It forces its design of action on our lives but has no meaning otherwise. Our use of it involves little responsibility and no traditional concern, still it imposes its authority upon us. The elevator has no joy nor thrust of life like that of the maple sapling, the redwing, or the child. It is an instrument to go up and

---

[1] John Dewey, "The Primary Education Fetish," *Education Today* (New York, G. P. Putnam's Sons, 1940), Chap. 2, p. 23.

down. The difference from natural things is indefinable perhaps, but in the life of man critically important.

Beyond all that is the fact that rural life is the normal milieu of the human community. Thousands of years of human culture confirm it. I do not know whether the community must be rural to exist, but the evidence [8/9] of centuries seems to indicate it. Cities have come and gone. Their cultures and philosophies have been epiphenomenal, as it were, upon the deep permanence of their rural background. But the human community as a sustaining, many-functioned, organic pattern of life has rarely, if ever, been in them. The community is rural. It belongs to rural culture, philosophy, and life. [9]

LOUIS BROMFIELD

Out of the Earth

From *OUT OF THE SEA*

THE GOOD FARMER is the man who learns as much as he can about the vast range of things which the good farmer must know concerning veterinary science, economics, chemistry, botany, animal husbandry, nutrition and countless other fields, all of which are tied into the ancient, complex and varied profession of agriculture, and then knows how to apply this knowledge to his own problems.

Perhaps no stupider human saying has ever been formulated than the one that "anybody can farm." Anyone can go through the motions, but not 10 per cent of our agricultural population today could be seriously called "good farmers." Thirty per cent are pretty good, and the remaining 60 per cent do not, through ignorance or laziness or sometimes through the misfortune of living on wretched land fit only for forests, deserve the dignified title of "farmer." Most of them still remain within the range of a completely primitive [5/6] agriculture confined to plowing, scattering seed and harvesting whatever crops with luck turn up at the end of the season. That they perform these operations with the aid of modern machinery does not make them either good or modern farmers. Tragically, a great many of them actually hate the soil which they work, the very soil which, if tended properly, could make them prosperous and proud and dignified and happy men.

You might ask, how is all this concerned with that infinitely tiny spark of life ignited millions, perhaps billions, of years ago in the still steaming waters of this planet. The connection, as we are discovering more and more thoroughly each day, is a closer one than appears on the surface. Out of that tiny spark and the first cell or substance which contained it, all of us were eventually descended, through the myriads of strange monsters which embodied and car-

From Louis Bromfield, *Out of the Earth* (New York: Harper & Brothers, 1950), pp. 5-9, 297-300.

41

ried on that tiny spark as cellular structure multiplied and life
began to take strange shapes, each with its special adaptations for
life and survival and reproduction in a given environment.

As cells multiplied, they became fish, and fish crept ashore and developed lungs and became lizards, and finally birds and horses and
camels and elephants and man in his way followed a similar trans-
mogrification, the long record of which appears in the embryo all
the way from the gills of the fish to the lungs and the formation of
mouth and throat which give him the power of speech and the brain
which has raised him gradually above the level of the other animals.
The whole record is there—a record which none of us can escape,
however much we may try to deceive ourselves and avoid our past.

In the beginning we all came from the sea, and the elements of
the sea—its oxygen, its nitrogen, its infinite range and variety of mineral wealth—are still as necessary to us as the proteins and carbohydrates which they make possible and by which we sustain life. Some
of them we are able to live without as we are able to live without
gills. Some of the organs and glands once necessary to existence and
procreation have become atrophied and useless and will doubtless
disappear one day as our gills have disappeared, but we are, like the
plants themselves, still dependent upon a remarkable range of minerals for the structure of our bodies, for the vigor and health and the
maintenance of that metabolic system which permits us to utilize the
complex proteins and carbohydrates which give us energy and
brains, and for the fertility which permits us to reproduce ourselves
and so [6/7] continue the future of a species which is still in the
process of change and adaptivity.

Once not very long ago it was believed that only phosphorus and
calcium and one or two other major elements were necessary to the
development, birth and growth of a living human organism. Today
we are becoming aware that in the functioning of a normal and
healthy metabolism producing a healthy, vigorous human, or even
an animal or a plant of the same category, an infinitely greater
range of elements and minerals is necessary; and constantly, almost
day by day as new discoveries are being made, the range is growing
larger to include more and more of the minerals from the sea out of
which that first spark of life was born.

The relation of iodine to goiter and cretinism is perhaps the oldest and longest-established case. A child born in a wholly iodine-defi-
cient area stands one chance in ten of being an idiot, one in five of
dying of goiter and virtually one in one of suffering from all the mal-
adies and handicaps that come of the disorder of the thyroid gland,
all because he and his mother before him did not have daily as
much iodine as could be smeared on the head of a pin. The function

of fluorine in the most minute quantities in the creation and maintenance of good teeth and bone has long been established, or that of cobalt, copper and manganese in relation to acute anemia and the capacity to breed. Cobalt in exquisitely minute quantities plays its part in the creation of one of the most recently discovered and important of all vitamins, B–12, a vitamin by which it indeed could be said that we live.

But as the physiologists and men of medicine are beginning to discover, the story of life, complicated as it is, contains still greater complexities, many of them still undiscovered. One may suffer from thyroid derangement through the lack of infinitisimal amounts of iodine, but the thyroid derangement may make it impossible for the human metabolism to absorb sufficient amounts of calcium or phosphorus, no matter the amount taken into the body, or impossible to absorb the infinitesimal amounts of zinc which may be the safeguard against leukemia. The pattern is intricate and extremely difficult to unravel—this pattern of nutrition and the relation of minerals to our health, growth, intelligence and vitality, and to the intricate workings and interdependence of all our glands. We have only begun to unravel the fringes of the whole pattern of metabolism, of minerals and vitamins and enzymes and hormones and the nutrition which, it appears, runs back and back into the steam and fogs of the [7/8] primeval world in which the first tiny spark, born of the minerals and elements themselves, came into existence.

Why, you might well ask again, should this concern the farmer? It concerns the farmer because the chief concern of the farmer is his soil. Out of it comes the health, intelligence and vitality of his animals and his family and, in a broader sense, of his fellow citizens. Out of it also comes his economic prosperity, his independence of banks and of government subsidies and regimentation. If his soil is good and minerally balanced and well managed and productive up to the optimum (which means simply that he is getting maximum potential production in quantity and quality without loss of fertility) he is the most independent man in the world, a world which has never been able to do without him and which becomes daily and hourly and by the minute less and less able to do without him. Slaves do not produce great quantities of food (as Soviet Russia has discovered) nor do they produce, except by accident of Nature, good and highly nutritious foods. The good independent successful farmer produces both. Better than any man he knows, through his plants and animals and his daily contact and struggles with the weather, that out of the earth we come and to the earth we return. Out of the sea, one might almost say.

The men and women of no other profession are as content to die when their time comes as the good farmer and his wife, for, better than the people of any other profession, they know by living with earth and sky and in companionship with their fellow animals that we are all only infinitesimal fragments of a vast universe in which the cycle of birth, growth, death, decay and rebirth is the law which has permitted us to live.

What we have done with out individual lives is another question for which we ourselves must accept the responsiblity. If it has been a good life, full and rich, and especially if it has been lived close to the earth from which we come, there are no terrors and no yearnings for a silly heaven of pink clouds filled with angels twanging harps. Rarely does the good farmer long for any immortality better than the rich fields he has left behind him and the healthy, intelligent children who will carry on his work and his name. If there is an after-life that is pleasant and comfortable, so much the better, but he hopes that it will not be an after-life in which there is no work, for it is by work of hand and brain that he has lived a full, rich life, which leaves him at the end ready to lie down and fall asleep in the quiet knowledge and satisfaction that what he has done will live on and [8/9] on after him into eternity. The good farmer is one of the ultimate peaks of evolution away from that first silly one-celled creature wriggling about in the sea water of a billion years ago. He is the one citizen without whom mankind and civilization cannot exist. As that very great and vigorous old gentleman, Liberty Hyde Bailey, has put it so well, "The first man was a farmer and the last man will be a farmer." [9]

EPILOGUE: A PHILOSOPHICAL EXCURSION

AT MALABAR when the shadows grow longer across the Valley and each day the Big House falls earlier beneath the deep shadow of the low sandstone cliffs, we know that winter is closing in. On a still day when we hear the whistles of the big Diesels on the Pennsylvania Railroad six miles away we know that we shall have fine clear weather, and when the sound comes from the opposite direction from the Baltimore and Ohio, we know that there will be clouds and rain. We know the time by the flight overhead of the big planes going north and south, and some of the pilots know us so well that on summer nights they blink their lights in greeting as they pass through the clear, still sky overhead.

In the barns and the fields, Al and Simon know their cows—a hundred and twenty of them—by name, and they know their dispositions and what they like or do not like, from Jean, the bossy old Guernsey who must be started homeward first on her way from pasture before the others will go properly, to Inez, the Holstein, smart and temperamental, who once struck up a feud with Mummy, the feed-room cat, and was observed on two occasions shaking Mummy as a dog might shake her, when the unfortunate cat came within reach.

As Philip, who lived with us until he grew up and went away on his own, once said, "The trouble with Malabar is that it's always characters—characters never people . . . even down to the ducks." That's true of most farm people and especially true of farm people in hill country where over each rise in the land, just beyond each patch of woods, there lies a new world. In the old days before automobiles and telephones, "character" developed in old age into eccentricity. Today the change is not so great, but the independence, the strength of opinion and willingness to fight for an opinion still remain. These are not regimented people herding at night into subways to return to a cave somewhere high up in a skyscraper, living as man was never meant to live.

For the young people a farm is a kind of Paradise. One never hears the whine of the city child, "Mama, what shall I do now?" On [297/298] a farm no day is ever long enough for the young person to crowd into its meager twenty-four hours all there is to be done. That, too, is true of the good farmer himself. No day is long enough. There is fishing and swimming, explorations of the woods and the caves, trapping, messing about the big tractors, playing in the great mows, a hundred exciting things to do which each day are new and each day adventurous.

But most of all there is the earth and the animals through which one comes very close to eternity and to the secrets of the universe. Out of Gus, the Mallard duck, who comes up from the pond every evening to eat with the dogs, out of Stinker, the bull, with his wise eyes and placid disposition, out of all the dogs which run ahead leaping and barking and luring the small boys farther and farther into the fields, a child learns much, and most of all that warmth and love of Nature which is perhaps the greatest of all resources, not only because its variety and beauty is inexhaustible but because slowly it creates a sense of balance and of values, of philosophy and even of wise resignation to man's own significance which bring the great rewards of wisdom and understanding and tolerance. It is not by senseless accident that the vast majority of the great men and women of the nation and those who have built it have come from farms or hamlets.

There is in all the world no finer figure than a sturdy farmer standing, his feet well planted in the earth, looking over his rich fields and his beautiful shiny cattle. He has a security and an independence unknown to any other member of society, yet, unlike the trapper or the hunter, he is very much a part of society, perhaps its most important member. The sharp eyes with the crow's feet circling them like small halos, the sunburned neck, the big strong hands, all tell their story of values and of living not only overlooked but un-known to far too many of those who live wholly in an industrial civilization where time clocks and machines rule man instead of man ruling them.

Nothing is more beautiful than the big farm kitchen. It has changed with the times. The refrigerator, the electric stove, the quick-freeze and the cold room have supplanted the cellar, the root storage and the great black old range with its tank of boiling water on the side. The woodpile is gone from outside the door and the horses no longer steam as they stand patiently while the farmer comes in for a cup of coffee and a cinnamon bun. We tell the time nowadays not by the whistle of the old steam locomotives but by the [298/299] passage overhead of the big flying flagship. But the good smell is still there in the kitchen and the farmer's wife is the same at heart, although in these times she is not bent with rheumatism at forty from carrying water and wood and bending over a washboard. At forty she is likely to be spry and young and busy with her clubs and neighborhood activities—as young-looking as her eighteen-year-old daughter who is a leader in the 4-H Club. And her husband does not rise at daylight and come in weary and bent long after dark. He keeps city hours, but during the day his work is half fun, because the drudgery has gone out of it. He is out of doors with the smell of fresh-turned earth rising to him from the furrow, the sight of a darting cock pheasant rising before his eyes in a kind of brilliant hymn to the morning. He, too, is young and sturdy at middle age and able to go places with his boys, to fish and hunt with them and attend their meetings.

A lot of things have changed on the farms of today, but the essence of the farm and the open country remains the same. The freedom is unchanged and the sense of security and independence and the good rich food and the beauty that lies for the seeing eye on every side and, above all, that satisfaction, as great as that of Leonardo or Shakespeare or any other creative artist, in having made something great and beautiful out of nothing. The farmer may leave his stamp upon the whole of the landscape seen from his window, and it can be as great and beautiful a creation as Michelangelo's David, for the farmer who takes over a desolate farm, ruined by some evil and ignorant predecessor, and turns it into a Paradise of beauty and abundance is one of the greatest of artists.

Of course, I am talking about the good farmer, the real farmer, and not that category of men who remain on the land because circumstance dropped them there and who go on, hating their land, hating their work and their animals because they have never discovered that they do not belong there, that they have no right to carry in trust the greatest of all gifts Nature can bring to man—a piece of good land, with the independence, the security, the excitement and even the splendor that go with it. The good farmer, working with Nature rather than fighting or trying to outwit her, may have what he wants of those treasures which are the only real ones and the ones by which man lives—his family, his power to create and construct the understanding of his relationship to the universe, and the deep, religious, humble sense of his own insignificance in God's creation. [299/300]

The good farmer of today can have all the good things that his father knew and many that his father never knew, for in the modern world he lives with all the comforts of a luxurious city house plus countless beauties and rewards forever unknown to the city dweller. More than any other member of our society—indeed, perhaps alone in our society—the farmer has learned how to use machinery to serve him rather than his serving machinery. That is a very great secret indeed and one which the other members of our society need desperately to learn. [300]

2

The Good Life:
As It Is Lived

BECAUSE of the numerous great minds in Western thought who have written favorably of agrarianism, the American farmer could take his place at the plow with a feeling that his work was prestigious, that—more than simply a way of making a living—farming was a way of life. In the popular mind in this country, the family farm has remained a potent symbol of the good life. City-dwellers dream of it, and artists find inspiration in it. The politician whose life began on the farm has always had a distinct advantage, and the biographers of great men are pleased to celebrate their subjects' rustic origins. For many, the independent yeoman has been at the root of a democratic state; and his world, perhaps a past but not entirely lost world, they believe, still holds promise for individual and national salvation.

Just as the pastoral tradition centered around the simple, sensitive, and unrestrained shepherd, so does the agrarian tradition center on the rational, hardy, and independent husbandman. It has been suggested that the figure of the farmer is really no more than the pastoral shepherd stripped and reclothed in American homespun. But the one important difference is that while the shepherd was often no more than a literary device used as a subterfuge for criticizing social and political institutions, or at the minimum was a mouthpiece for the poet's peculiar views or emotions, the symbolic figure of the noble, unmaterialistic, democratic son of the soil was based upon a reality, a form of experience in which at one point in our history, around 1850, as much as 90 percent of the entire population was directly or indirectly engaged. As the literature in this unit demonstrates, the farmer as a literary figure, to be effective, has always demanded that the artist and reader share in his experience and accept his attitudes and point of view, rather than remain sub-

missively useful for the expression of any individual ethical or philosophical sentiment.

American literature is impressively rich with essayists, poets, and
fiction writers who have written extensively and well of the good
life, most of them from personal experience. It is usually easy to tell
when the writer is simply waxing eloquent over something he has
read about and when he is drawing from concrete acquaintance with
the soil and life on the farm. For some it proved a limited subject
matter, but for others it proved sourceful enough to engage them in
their lifework. The problem in selecting material for this unit was
not a scarcity of works worthy of reprinting but the achievement of
a sufficient geographic or regional spread. Crèvecoeur, Cooper, and
Whitman represent or reflect the East; Frost, New England; Garland,
the Midwest; Lanier, Lytle, and Roberts, the South; and Norris, the
Far West. What is included is barely an indication of untouched resources.

The three essayists in the unit, from the eighteenth, nineteeth,
and twentieth centuries respectively, Crèvecoeur, William Cooper,
and Andrew Lytle, are all attempting to record in frank prose the
details of rustic existence. Although Crèvecoeur is writing within a
contrived fictional framework, pretending to be a member of long-es-
tablished American native stock, and is highly influenced by his European disposition and attitudes, he did purchase a farm in Orange
County, New York, in 1767, marry an American woman, and relinquish his birth, breeding, and nationality to devote his time to farming. Thus his *Letters from an American Farmer* are based upon experience and convey a sincerity or conviction that would be difficult
to contrive. He was, however, forced to abandon farming when the
Revolution caused a conflict of sympathies. His greatest contribution
to American letters is the earliest definition of "Americanism" in his
series of letters.

Judge William Cooper, the father of James Fenimore Cooper, had
little of his son's literary disposition, but the excerpt included here
from a letter describing the conditions under which he founded
Cooperstown, near Lake Otsego in New York, in 1788, does have a
straightforward and uncomplicated style that clearly communicates.
While Cooper's pride in his frontier effort and love for the cultivated soil are clear, they are tempered by a healthy respect for the
role hard labor, natural disaster, and providence play in the affairs
of pioneering agriculture.

Andrew Lytle was in the 1930's a member of a group of Southern
writers, teachers, and historians who joined in a group effort to save
the South and America from the debasements of industrialism in the
name of a new agrarian ideology. This group will be discussed in

the next unit, where their statement of principles is reprinted, but in writing his defense of the agrarian life for their joint symposium *I'll Take My Stand*, Lytle devoted a large portion of his essay to a full and explicit description of Southern rural life. Lytle knew whereof he spoke, being the son of a cotton farmer in Murfreesboror, Tennessee, having grown up in a rural environment, and later combining his career as a writer with that of a farmer as manager of Cornsilk, his father's farm, during the Depression. While he may overstate his case in "The Hind Tit," by raising reality to a symbolic or ritualistic level, it is hard to find a more convincing or appealing sketch of the good life.

The poet who undertakes to write on the subject must resist the tendency to apply to husbandry the great store of themes, techniques, and figures of speech that have accumulated in the creation of pastoral and nature poetry. In "The Waving of the Corn," this is exactly the trap Sidney Lanier falls into. The commonplace bees, clover, cricket, and dove are there, surrounding the gnarly-handed ploughman and his whistling son, but missing is the real world of the distinctively American soil. What is missing from Lanier's poem is exactly what Whitman's poetry is full of—purely American sights, sounds, smells, people, language, trees, and grass. The brief prose piece reprinted in this unit, "The Common Earth, the Soil," was written while Whitman was visiting with a friendly farm family near Camden, on Timber Creek, in the late 1870's to regain his health following a stroke. Many of the notes written during the stay, published in 1882 in *Specimen Days and Collect*, appear to be potential poems, as this one does, and perhaps Whitman intended to revise it as such later. It illustrates, in any case, the vitality and inspiration he found in this continent's dark, rich soil. Robert Frost, who spent most of his career drawing subject matter for his inimitable poems from the life and activities of the New England farmers, demonstrates in his poem "Mowing" how a very common task, treated with a conservative control of language, metaphor, and emotion, can be brought to the level of a universal symbol of communication between man and nature. This is characteristic of all his poetry—the discovery of a moral in the natural fact—and, like Faulkner, Frost was able to use his regional and parochial experience as the means for making universal statements about man.

The celebrations and examinations of country life in fiction by far are the more numerous than in the essay and poem in American literature. Two nineteenth-century movements gave impetus to the treatment of the good life in novels and stories: realism, with its emphasis on middle and lower class economic and social problems and its use of the common vernacular; and local color, with its conscious use of highly peculiar and distinctive regional characters and customs. Hamlin Garland did not believe in depicting the picturesque and eccentric for its own value, but believed in what he called "veritism," a combination of intense realism (both the ugly and the beautiful, the vulgar and the noble) in content and ethical idealism (a concern for social reform without overt preachment) in theme. His stories in *Main-Traveled Roads,* such as "The Return of a Private," drawn from his own experiences as a member of a pioneer family in Wisconsin, Iowa, and South Dakota, are all clearly written with this attitude. "On the Mountainside," by Elizabeth Madox Roberts, is a twentieth-century example of the continuing interest in the agrarian life. Her stories and novels set in her home Kentucky locale had less in common with the early local colorists than with the modern symbolic realists and novelists of sensibility.

Whatever else may be said about the importance of agrarianism in American thought, few would debate the statement that it has inspired some of the finest imaginative literature produced in this country.

MICHEL-GUILLAUME JEAN DE CRÈVECOEUR

On the Situation, Feelings, and
Pleasures of an American Farmer

As YOU ARE the first enlightened European I have ever had the pleasure of being acquainted with, you will not be surprised that I should, according to your earnest desire and my promise, appear anxious of preserving your friendship and correspondence. By your accounts, I observe a material difference subsists between your husbandry, modes, and customs, and ours; every thing is local; could we enjoy the advantages of the English farmer, we should be much happier, indeed, but this wish, like many others, implies a contradiction; and could the English farmer have some of those privileges we possess, they would be the first of their class in the world. Good and evil I see is to be found in all societies, and it is in vain to seek for any spot where those ingredients are not mixed. I therefore rest satisfied, and thank God that my lot is to be an American farmer, instead of a Russian boor, or an Hungarian peasant. I thank you kindly for the idea, however dreadful, which [22/23] you have given me of their lot and condition; your observations have confirmed me in the justness of my ideas, and I am happier now than I thought myself before. It is strange that misery, when viewed in others, should become to us a sort of real good, though I am far from rejoicing to hear that there are in the world men so thoroughly wretched; they are no doubt as harmless, industrious, and willing to work as we are. Hard is their fate to be thus condemned to a slavery worse than that of our negroes. Yet when young I entertained some thoughts of selling my farm. I thought it afforded but a dull repetition of the same labours and pleasures. I thought the former tedious

From J. Hector St. John Crèvecoeur, *Letters from an American Farmer*, Reprinted from the Original Edition (New York: Fox, Duffield & Company, 1904), pp. 22–29, 45–47. First published in 1782.

and heavy, the latter few and insipid; but when I came to consider myself as divested of my farm, I then found the world so wide, and every place so full, that I began to fear lest there would be no room for me. My farm, my house, my barn, presented to my imagination, objects from which I adduced quite new ideas; they were more forcible than before. Why should not I find myself happy, said I, where my father was before? He left me no good books it is true, he gave me no other education than the art of reading and writing; but he left me a good farm, and his experience; he left me free from debts, and no kind of difficulties to struggle [23/24] with.—I married, and this perfectly reconciled me to my situation; my wife rendered my house all at once chearful and pleasing; it no longer appeared gloomy and solitary as before; when I went to work in my fields I worked with more alacrity and sprightliness; I felt that I did not work for myself alone, and this encouraged me much. My wife would often come with her knitting in her hand, and sit under the shady trees, praising the straightness of my furrows, and the docility of my horses; this swelled my heart and made every thing light and pleasant, and I regretted that I had not married before. I felt myself happy in my new situation, and where is that station which can confer a more substantial system of felicity than that of an American farmer, possessing freedom of action, freedom of thoughts, ruled by a mode of government which requires but little from us? I owe nothing, but a pepper corn to my country, a small tribute to my king, with loyalty and due respect; I know no other landlord than the lord of all land, to whom I owe the most sincere gratitude. My father left me three hundred and seventy-one acres of land, forty-seven of which are good timothy meadow, an excellent orchard, a good house, and a substantial barn. It is my duty to think how happy I am that he lived to build and to pay for all these improvements; [24/25] what are the labours which I have to undergo, what are my fatigues when compared to his, who had every thing to do, from the first tree he felled to the finishing of his house? Every year I kill from 1,500 to 2,000 weight of pork, 1,200 of beef, half a dozen of good wethers in harvest: of fowls my wife has always a great stock: what can I wish more? My negroes are tolerably faithful and healthy; by a long series of industry and honest dealings, my father left behind him the name of a good man; I have but to tread his paths to be happy and a good man like him. I know enough of the law to regulate my little concerns with propriety, nor do I dread its power; these are the grand outlines of my situation, but as I can feel much more than I am able to express, I hardly know how to proceed. When my first son was born, the whole train of my ideas were suddenly altered; never was there a charm that acted so quickly

and powerfully; I ceased to ramble in imagination through the wide
world; my excursions since have not exceeded the bounds of my
farm, and all my principal pleasures are now centered within its
scanty limits: but at the same time there is not an operation belonging to it in which I do not find some food for useful reflections. This
is the reason, I suppose, that when you was here, you used, in
[25/26] your refined stile, to denominate me the farmer of feelings;
how rude must those feelings be in him who daily holds the axe or
the plough, how much more refined on the contrary those of the European, whose mind is improved by education, example, books, and
by every acquired advantage! Those feelings, however, I will delineate as well as I can, agreeably to your earnest request. When I contemplate my wife, by my fire-side, while she either spins, knits,
darns, or suckles our child, I cannot describe the various emotions of
love, of gratitude, of conscious pride which thrill in my heart, and
often overflow in involuntary tears. I feel the necessity, the sweet
pleasure of acting my part, the part of an husband and father, with
an attention and propriety which may entitle me to my good fortune.
It is true these pleasing images vanish with the smoke of my pipe,
but though they disappear from my mind, the impression they have
made on my heart is indelible. When I play with the infant, my
warm imagination runs forward, and eagerly anticipates his future
temper and constitution. I would willingly open the book of fate,
and know in which page his destiny is delineated; alas! where is
the father who in those moments of paternal extacy can delineate
one half of the thoughts which dilate his heart? I am sure I cannot;
then again [26/27] I fear for the health of those who are become so
dear to me, and in their sicknesses I severely pay for the joys I experienced while they were well. Whenever I go abroad it is always involuntary. I never return home without feeling some pleasing emotion, which I often suppress as useless and foolish. The instant I
enter on my own land, the bright idea of property, of exclusive
right, of independence exalt my mind. Precious soil, I say to myself
by what singular custom of law is it that thou wast made to constitute the riches of the freeholder? What should we American farmers be without the distinct possession of that soil? It feeds, it clothes
us, from it we draw even a great exuberancy, our best meat, our richest drink, the very honey of our bees comes from this privileged spot.
No wonder we should thus cherish its possession, no wonder that so
many Europeans who have never been able to say that such portion
of land was theirs, cross the Atlantic to realize that happiness. This
formerly rude soil has been converted by my father into a pleasant
farm, and in return it has established all our rights; on it is founded
our rank, our freedom, our power as citizens, our importance as in-

habitants of such a district. These images I must confess I always behold with pleasure, and extend them as far as my imagination can [27/28] reach: for this is what may be called the true and the only philosophy of an American farmer. Pray do not laugh in thus seeing an artless countryman tracing himself through the simple modifications of his life; remember that you have required it, therefore with candor, though with diffidence, I endeavour to follow the thread of my feelings, but I cannot tell you all. Often when I plough my low ground, I place my little boy on a chair which screws to the beam of the plough—its motion and that of the horses please him, he is perfectly happy and begins to chat. As I lean over the handle, various are the thoughts which croud into my mind. I am now doing for him, I say, what my father formerly did for me, may God enable him to live that he may perform the same operations for the same purposes when I am worn out and old! I relieve his mother of some trouble while I have him with me, the odoriferous furrow exhilarates his spirits, and seems to do the child a great deal of good, for he looks more blooming since I have adopted that practice; can more pleasure, more dignity be added to that primary occupation? The father thus ploughing with his child, and to feed his family, is inferior only to the emperor of China ploughing as an example to his kingdom. In the evening when I return home through my [28/29] low grounds, I am astonished at the myriads of insects which I perceive dancing in the beams of the setting sun. I was before scarcely acquainted with their existence, they are so small that it is difficult to distinguish them; they are carefully improving this short evening space, not daring to expose themselves to the blaze of our meridian sun. I never see an egg brought on my table but I feel penetrated with the wonderful change it would have undergone but for my gluttony; it might have been a gentle useful hen leading her chickens with a care and vigilance which speaks shame to many women. A cock perhaps, arrayed with the most majestic plumes, tender to its mate, bold, courageous, endowed with an astonishing instinct, with thoughts, with memory, and every distinguishing characteristic of the reason of man. I never see my trees drop their leaves and their fruit in the autumn, and bud again in the spring, without wonder; the sagacity of those animals which have long been the tenants of my farm astonish me: some of them seem to surpass even men in memory and sagacity. I could tell you singular instances of that kind.... [29/45]

I never should have done were I to recount the many objects which involuntarily strike my imagination in the midst of my work, and spontaneously afford me the most pleasing relief. These appear insignificant trifles to a person who has travelled through Europe and America, and is acquainted with books and with many sciences; but such simple objects [45/46] of contemplation suffice me, who have no time to bestow on more extensive observations. Happily these require no study, they are obvious, they gild the moments I dedicate to them, and enliven the severe labours which I perform. At home my happiness springs from very different objects; the gradual unfolding of my children's reason, the study of their dawning tempers attract all my paternal attention. I have to contrive little punishments for their little faults, small encouragements for their good actions, and a variety of other expedients dictated by various occasions. But these are themes unworthy your perusal, and which ought not to be carried beyond the walls of my house, being domestic mysteries adapted only to the locality of the small sanctuary wherein my family resides. Sometimes I delight in inventing and executing machines, which simplify my wife's labour. I have been tolerably successful that way; and these, Sir, are the narrow circles within which I constantly revolve, and what can I wish for beyond them? I bless God for all the good he has given me; I envy no man's prosperity, and with no other portion of happiness that I may live to teach the same philosophy to my children; and give each of them a farm, shew them how to cultivate it, and be like their father, good substantial [46/47] independent American farmers—an appellation which will be the most fortunate one, a man of my class can possess, so long as our civil government continues to shed blessings on our husbandry. Adieu. [47]

WILLIAM COOPER

———•─•———

Letter to William Sampson, Esq.

"Sir,—I shall cheerfully answer the queries you have put to me. The manly way in which you have challenged me, and the good sense you have shown upon a subject on which you can have no experience, and the object I perceive you to have at heart, that of procuring information in a matter interesting to your countrymen, do you honor, and make it a pleasure for me to satisfy so fair a curiosity. . . . [xviii/xxii]

"You have desired to know something of my own proceedings, and since I am to speak of myself, I can nowhere better introduce the subject than now, in proof of what I have asserted.

"I began with the disadvantage of a small capital, and the encumbrance of a large family, and yet I have already settled more acres than any man in America. There are forty thousand souls now holding, directly or indirectly, under me; and I trust that not one among so many, can justly impute to me any act resembling oppression. I am now descending into the vale of life, and I must acknowledge that I look back with self-complacency upon what I [xxii/xxiii] have done, and am proud of having been an instrument in reclaiming such large and fruitful tracts from the waste of the creation. And I question whether that sensation is not now a recompense more grateful to me than all the other profits I have reaped. Your good sense and knowledge of the world will excuse this seeming boast; if it be vain, we must all have our vanities, but it will at least serve to show that industry has its reward, and age its pleasures, and thus become an encouragement to others to persevere and prosper.

"In 1785, I visited the rough and hilly country of Otsego, where there existed not an inhabitant, nor any trace of a road; I was alone, three hundred miles from home, without bread, meat, or food of any

From Susan Fenimore Cooper's Introduction to James Fenimore Cooper, *The Pioneers* (Boston and New York: Houghton, Mifflin and Company, 1876), pp. xviii, xxii–xxvii, xxxvi. The letter was written by Judge Cooper in 1805.

kind; fire and fishing-tackle were my only means of subsistence. I
caught trout in the brook, and roasted them on the ashes. My horse
fed on the grass that grew on the edge of the waters. I laid me down
to sleep in my watch-coat, nothing but the melancholy wilderness
about me. In this way I explored the country, formed my plans of
future settlements, and meditated upon the spot where a place of
trade, or a future village should afterwards be established.

"In May, 1786, I opened the sales of 40,000 acres, which in sixteen
days were all taken up by the poorer order of men. I soon after established a store, and went to live among them, and continued to do
so until 1790, when I brought on my family. For the ensuing four
years the scarcity of provisions was a serious calamity; the country
was mountainous, there were neither roads nor bridges.

"But the greatest discouragement lay in the extreme poverty of
the people, none of whom had the means of clearing more than a
small spot, in the middle of the thick and lofty woods, so that their
grain grew chiefly in the shade; their maize did not ripen; their
wheat was blasted; and the little they did gather they had no mill to
grind, within twenty miles' distance. Not one in twenty had a horse,
and the way lay through rapid streams, across swamps, or over
[xxiii/xxiv] bogs. They had neither provisions to take with them,
nor money to purchase them; nor if they had were there any to be
found. If the father of a family went abroad to labor for bread, it
cost him three times its value before he could bring it home, and all
the business on his farm stood still until his return.

"I resided among them, and saw too clearly how bad their condition was. I erected a store-house, and during each winter filled it
with large quantities of grain purchased in distant places. I procured
from my friend Henry Drinker a credit for a large quantity of
sugar-kettles, he also lent me some potash kettles, which we transported as best we could sometimes by partial roads on sleighs, and
sometimes over the ice. By these means I established potash works
among the settlers, and made them debtors for their bread, and laboring utensils. I also gave them credit for their maple sugar and po-
tashes at a price that would bear transportation, and the first year
after the adoption of this plan I collected in one mass forty-three
hogsheads of sugar, and three hundred barrels of pearl ashes, worth
about nine thousand dollars. This kept the people together, and the
country soon assumed a new face.

"I had not funds of my own sufficient for the opening of new
roads, but I collected the people at convenient seasons, and by joint
efforts we were able to throw bridges over the deep streams, and to
make in the cheapest manner such roads as suited our then humble
purposes.

"In the winter preceding the summer of 1789, grain rose in Albany to a price before unknown. The demand swept all the granaries of the Mohawk country. The number of beginners who depended upon it for their bread greatly aggravated the evil, and a famine ensued, which will never be forgotten by those who, though now in the enjoyment of ease and comfort, were then afflicted with the cruelest of wants.

"In the month of April 1789, I arrived among them with several loads of provisions, destined for my own use [xxiv/xxv] and that of laborers I had brought with me for certain necessary operations; but in a few days all was gone, and there remained not one pound of salt meat, nor a single biscuit. Many were reduced to such distress, as to live upon the roots of wild leeks; some more fortunate lived upon milk, while others supported nature by drinking a syrup made of maple sugar and water. The quantity of leeks they ate had such an effect upon their breath that they could be smelled at many paces distance, and when they came together it was like cattle that had pastured in a garlic field. A man of the name of Betts, mistaking some poisonous herb for a leek, ate it, and died in consequence. Judge of my feelings at this epoch, with two hundred families about me, and not a morsel of bread.

"A singular event seemed sent by a good Providence to our relief. It was reported to me that unusual shoals of fish were seen moving in the clear waters of the Susquehanna. I went, and was surprised to find they were herrings. We made something like a small net, by the intertwining of twigs, and by this rude and simple contrivance we were able to take them by thousands. In less than ten days each family had an ample supply, with plenty of salt. I also obtained from the Legislature, then in session, seventeen hundred bushels of corn. This we packed on horses' backs, and on our arrival made a distribution among the families, in proportion to the number of individuals of which each was composed.

"This was the first settlement I made, and the first attempted after the Revolution. It was, of course, attended with the greatest difficulties; nevertheless, to its success many others owed their origin. It was besides the roughest land in all the state, and the most difficult of cultivation of all that has been settled; but for many past years it has produced everything necessary to the support and comfort of man. It maintains at present eight thousand souls, with schools, academies, churches, meeting-houses, turnpike roads, and a market-town. It annually yields to commerce large [xxv/xxvi] droves of fine oxen, great quantities of wheat and other grain, abundance of pork, potash in barrels, and other provisions. Merchants with large capitals, and all kinds of useful mechanics, reside upon it; the waters are stocked with fish, the air is salubrious, and the country thriving and happy. When I contemplate all this, and above all, when I see these good old settlers meet together, and hear them talk of past hardships, of which I bore my share, and compare the misery they then endured with the comforts they now enjoy, my emotions border upon weakness which manhood can scarcely avow.

"Some rich theorists let the property they purchase lie unoccupied and unproductive, and speculate upon a full indemnity from the future rise in property. But I can assert from practical experience, that it is better for a poor man to pay forty shillings an acre to a landlord who heads the settlement, and draws people around him by good plans for their advancement and convenience, than to receive an hundred acres gratis from one of these wealthy theorists. If fity thousand acres be settled so that there is but one man upon a thousand acres, there can be no one convenience of life attainable; neither road, school, church, nor any of those advantages without which man's life would resemble that of a wild beast.

"Of this I had full proof in the circumstances of the Burlington Company. They were rich, and purchased a tract of sixty-nine thousand acres, and made a deed of gift of one hundred acres out of each thousand to actual settlers; and this they were bound to do, in compliance with a condition of the King's Patent. They provided those settlers with many articles of husbandry. But the agent very soon returned, and not long afterwards the settlers followed, saying they could not support themselves so far in the woods in that scattered situation.

"I then resided in Burlington, and when I undertook to make the settlement on those very lands, where so rich a company had failed, it was thought a romantic undertaking [xxvi/xxvii] for a man unprovided with funds, to attempt what gratuitous donations had not been able to achieve. Nevertheless I succeeded, and for that very reason that I made no partial gifts, but sold the whole, at a moderate price, with easy payments, having for myself a handsome profit, and people were readily induced to come when they saw a number of coöperators, and the benefits of association.

"But let me be clearly understood in this, that no man who does not possess a steady mind, a sober judgment, fortitude, perseverance, and above all, common sense, can expect to reap the reward which to him who possesses these qualifications is almost certain. . . . [xxvii/xxxvi]

"After having been employed for twenty years in the same pursuit of improving lands, I am now, by habit, so attached to it, that it is the principal source which remains to me of pleasure and recreation." [xxxvi]

SIDNEY LANIER

The Waving of the Corn

PLOUGHMAN, whose gnarly hand yet kindly wheeled
Thy plough to ring this solitary tree
  With clover, whose round plat, reserved a-field,
In cool green radius twice my length may be—
  Scanting the corn thy furrows else might yield,
To pleasure August, bees, fair thoughts, and me,
    That here come oft together—daily I,
    Stretched prone in summer's mortal ecstasy,
Do stir with thanks to thee, as stirs this morn
    With waving of the corn.

Unseen, the farmer's boy from round the hill
Whistles a snatch that seeks his soul unsought,
  And fills some time with tune, howbeit shrill;
The cricket tells straight on his simple thought—
  Nay, 'tis the cricket's way of being still;
The peddler bee drones in, and gossips naught;
    Far down the wood, a one-desiring dove
    Times me the beating of the heart of love:
And these be all the sounds that mix, each morn,
    With waving of the corn.

From here to where the louder passions dwell,
Green leagues of hilly separation roll:
  Trade ends where yon far clover ridges swell.
Ye terrible Towns, ne'er claim the trembling soul
  That, craftless all to buy or hoard or sell,

From *Poems of Sidney Lanier,* edited by His Wife, New Edition (New York: Charles Scribner's Sons, 1906), p. 23. First published in *Harper's Magazine,* 1877.

From out your deadly complex quarrel stole
    To company with large amiable trees,
    Suck honey summer with unjealous bees,
And take Time's strokes as softly as this morn
    Takes waving of the corn.

WEST CHESTER, PA., 1876. [23]

WALT WHITMAN

———•————

The Common Earth, The Soil

THE SOIL, too—let others pen-and-ink the sea, the air, (as I sometimes try)—but now I feel to choose the common soil for theme—naught else. The brown soil here, just between winter-close and opening spring and vegetation)—the rain-shower at night, and the fresh smell next morning—the red worms wriggling out of the ground—the dead leaves, the incipient grass, and the latent life underneath—the effort to start something—already in shelter'd spots some little flowers—the distant emerald show of winter wheat and the rye-fields—the yet naked trees, with clear interstices, giving prospects hidden in summer—the tough fallow and the plow-team, and the stout boy whistling to his horses for encouragement—and there the dark fat earth in long slanting stripes upturn'd. [100]

From Walt Whitman, *Complete Prose Works* (Philadelphia: David McKay, Publisher, 1892), p. 100. First published in *Specimen Days and Collect*, 1882.

HAMLIN GARLAND

The Return of a Private

THE NEARER the train drew toward La Crosse, the soberer the little group of "vets" became. On the long way from New Orleans they had beguiled tedium with jokes and friendly chaff; or with planning with elaborate detail what they were going to do now, after the war. A long journey, slowly, irregularly, yet persistently pushing northward. When they entered on Wisconsin territory they gave a cheer and another when they reached Madison, but after that they sank into a dumb expectancy. Comrades dropped off at one or two points beyond, until there were only four or five left who were bound for La Crosse County.

Three of them were gaunt and brown, the fourth was gaunt and pale, with signs of fever and ague upon him. One had a great scar down his temple, one limped, and they all had unnaturally large, bright eyes, showing emaciation. There were no hands greeting them at the station, no banks of gayly dressed ladies waving handkerchiefs and shouting "Bravo!" as they came in on the caboose of a freight train into the towns that had cheered and blared at them on their way to war. As they looked out or stepped upon the platform for a moment, while the train stood at the station, the loafers looked at them indifferently. Their blue coats, dusty and grimy, were too familiar now to excite notice, much less a friendly word. They were the last of the army to return, and the loafers were surfeited with such sights.

The train jogged forward so slowly that it seemed likely to be midnight before they should reach La Crosse. The little squad grumbled and swore, but it was no use; the train would not hurry, and, as a matter of fact, it was nearly two o'clock when the engine whistled "down brakes."

All of the group were farmers, living in districts several miles out of the town, and all were poor. [112/113]

From Hamlin Garland, *Main-Travelled Roads* (New York and London: Harper & Brothers, n.d.), pp. 112–129. First published in 1891.

"Now, boys," said Private Smith, he of the fever and ague, "we are landed in La Crosse in the night. We've got to stay somewhere till mornin'. Now I ain't got no two dollars to waste on a hotel. I've got a wife and children, so I'm goin' to roost on a bench and take the cost of a bed out of my hide."

"Same here," put in one of the other men. "Hide'll grow on again, dollars'll come hard. It's going to be mighty hot skirmishin' to find a dollar these days."

"Don't think they'll be a deputation of citizens waitin' to 'scort us to a hotel, eh?" said another. His sarcasm was too obvious to require an answer.

Smith went on, "Then at daybreak we'll start for home—at least, I will."

"Well, I'll be dummed if I'll take two dollars out o' *my* hide," one of the younger men said. "I'm goin' to a hotel, ef I don't never lay up a cent."

"That'll do f'r you," said Smith; "but if you had a wife an' three young uns dependin' on yeh—"

"Which I ain't, thank the Lord! and don't intend havin' while the court knows itself."

The station was deserted, chill, and dark, as they came into it at exactly a quarter to two in the morning. Lit by the oil lamps that flared a dull red light over the dingy benches, the waiting room was not an inviting place. The younger man went off to look up a hotel, while the rest remained and prepared to camp down on the floor and benches. Smith was attended to tenderly by the other men, who spread their blankets on the bench for him, and, by robbing themselves, made quite a comfortable bed, though the narrowness of the bench, made his sleeping precarious.

It was chill, though August, and the two men, sitting with bowed heads, grew stiff with cold and weariness, and were forced to rise now and again and walk about to warm their stiffened limbs. It did not occur to them, probably, to contrast their coming home with their going forth, or with the coming home of the general, colonels, or even captains—but to Private Smith, at any rate, there [113/114] came a sickness at heart almost deadly as he lay there on his hard bed and went over his situation.

In the deep of the night, lying on a board in the town where he had enlisted three years ago, all elation and enthusiasm gone out of him, he faced the fact that with the joy of home-coming was already mingled the bitter juice of care. He saw himself sick, worn out, taking up the work on his half-cleared farm, the inevitable mortgage standing ready with open jaw to swallow half his earnings. He had given three years of his life for a mere pittance of pay, and now!—

Morning dawned at last, slowly, with a pale yellow dome of light rising silently above the bluffs, which stand like some huge storm-devastated castle, just east of the city. Out to the left the great river swept on its massive yet silent way to the south. Bluejays called across the water from hillside to hillside through the clear, beautiful air, and hawks began to skim the tops of the hills. The older men were astir early, but Private Smith had fallen at last into a sleep, and they went out without waking him. He lay on his knapsack, his gaunt face turned toward the ceiling, his hands clasped on his breast, with a curious pathetic effect of weakness and appeal.

An engine switching near woke him at last, and he slowly sat up and stared about. He looked out of the window and saw that the sun was lightening the hills across the river. He rose and brushed his hair as well as he could, folded his blankets up, and went out to find his companions. They stood gazing silently at the river and at the hills.

"Looks natcher'l, don't it?" they said, as he came out.

"That's what it does," he replied. "An' it looks good. D' yeh see that peak?" He pointed at a beautiful symmetrical peak, rising like a slightly truncated cone, so high that it seemed the very highest of them all. It was touched by the morning sun and it glowed like a beacon, and a light scarf of gray morning fog was rolling up its shadowed side.

"My farm's just beyond that. Now, if I can only ketch a ride, we'll be home by dinner-time." [114/115]

"I'm talkin' about breakfast," said one of the others.

"I guess it's one more meal o'hardtack f'r me," said Smith.

They foraged around, and finally found a restaurant with a sleepy old German behind the counter, and procured some coffee, which they drank to wash down their hardtack.

"Time'll come," said Smith, holding up a piece by the corner, "when this'll be a curiosity."

"I hope to God it will! I bet I've chawed hardtack enough to shin-gle every house in the coolly. I've chawed it when my lampers was down, and when they wasn't. I've took it dry, soaked, and mashed. I've had it wormy, musty, sour, and blue-mouldy. I've had it in lit-tle bits and big bits; 'fore coffee an' after coffee. I'm ready f'r a change. I'd like t' git holt jest about now o' some of the hot biscuits my wife c'n make when she lays herself out f'r company."

"Well, if you set there gabblin', you'll never *see* yer wife."

"Come on," said Private Smith. "Wait a moment, boys; less take suthin'. It's on me." He led them to the rusty tin dipper which hung on a nail beside the wooden water-pail, and they grinned and drank.

Then shouldering their blankets and muskets, which they were "taken' home to the boys," they struck out on their last march.

"They called that coffee Jayvy," grumbled one of them, "but it never went by the road where government Jayvy resides. I reckon I know coffee from peas."

They kept together on the road along the turnpike, and up the winding road by the river, which they followed for some miles. The river was very lovely, curving down along its sandy beds, pausing now and then under broad basswood trees, or running in dark, swift, silent currents under tangles of wild grapevines, and drooping alders, and haw trees. At one of these lovely spots the three vets sat down on the thick green sward to rest, "on Smith's account." The leaves of the trees were as fresh and green as in June, the jays called cheery greetings to them, and kingfishers darted to and fro with swooping noiseless flight.

"I tell yeh, boys, this knocks the swamps of Loueesiana into kingdom come." [115/116]

"You bet. All they c'n raise down there is snakes, niggers, and p'rticler hell."

"An' fighting men," put in the older man.

"An' fightin' men. If I had a good hook an' line I'd sneak a pick'rel out o' that pond. Say, remember that time I shot that alligator——"

"I guess we'd better be crawlin' along," interrupted Smith, rising and shouldering his knapsack, with considerable effort, which he tried to hide.

"Say, Smith, lemme give you a lift on that."

"I guess I c'n manage," said Smith, grimly.

"Course. But, yo' see, I may not have a change right off to pay yeh back for the times you've carried my gun and hull caboodle. Say, now, gimme that gun, anyway."

"All right, if yeh feel like it, Jim," Smith replied, and they trudged along doggedly in the sun, which was getting higher and hotter each half-mile.

"Ain't it queer there ain't no teams comin' along," said Smith, after a long silence.

"Well, no, seein's it's Sunday."

"By jinks, that's a fact. It *is* Sunday. I'll git home in time f'r dinner, sure!" he exulted. "She don't hev dinner usially till about *one* on Sundays." And he fell into a muse, in which he smiled.

"Well, I'll git home jest about six o'clock, jest about when the boys are milkin' the cows," said old Jim Cranby. "I'll step into the barn, an' then I'll say: '*Heah!* why ain't this milkin' done before this

time o' day?' An' then won't they yell!" he added, slapping his thigh
in great glee.

Smith went on. "I'll jest go up the path. Old Rover'll come down
the road to meet me. He won't bark; he'll know me, an' he'll come
down waggin' his tail an' showin' his teeth. That's his way of
laughin'. An' so I'll walk up to the kitchen door, an' I'll say, '*Dinner
f'r a hungry man!*' An' then she'll jump up, an'——"

He couldn't go on. His voice choked at the thought of it. Saunders, the third man, hardly uttered a word, but walked silently behind the others. He had lost his wife the first year he was in the
[116/117] army. She died of penumonia, caught in the autumn
rains while working in the fields in his place.

They plodded along till at last they came to a parting of the
ways. To the right the road continued up the main valley; to the left
it went over the big ridge.

"Well, boys," began Smith, as they grounded their muskets and
looked away up the valley, "here's where we shake hands. We've
marched together a good many miles, an' now I s'pose we're done."

"Yes, I don't think we'll do any more of it f'r a while. I don't want
to, I know."

"I hope I'll see yeh once in a while, boys, to talk over old times."

"Of course," said Saunders, whose voice trembled a little, too. "It
ain't *exactly* like dyin'." They all found it hard to look at each
other.

"But we'd ought'r go home with you," said Cranby. "You'll never
climb that ridge with all them things on yer back."

"Oh, I'm all right! Don't worry about me. Every step takes me
nearer home, yeh see. Well, good-by, boys."

They shook hands. "Goody-by. Good luck!"

"Same to you. Lemme know how you find things at home."

"Good-by."

"Good-by."

He turned once before they passed out of sight, and waved his
cap, and they did the same, and all yelled. Then all marched away
with their long, steady, loping, veteran step. The solitary climber in
blue walked on for a time, with his mind filled with the kindness of
his comrades, and musing upon the many wonderful days they had
had together in camp and field.

He thought of his chum, Billy Tripp. Poor Billy! A "minie" ball
fell into his breast one day, fell wailing like a cat, and tore a great
ragged hole in his heart. He looked forward to a sad scene with Billy's mother and sweetheart. They would want to know all about it.
He tried to recall all that Billy had said, and the particulars of it,
but there was little to remember, just that wild wailing sound high

in the air, a dull slap, a short, quick, expulsive groan, [117/118] and the boy lay with his face in the dirt in the ploughed field they were marching across.

That was all. But all the scenes he had since been through had not dimmed the horror, the terror of that moment, when his boy comrade fell, with only a breath between a laugh and a death-groan. Poor handsome Billy! Worth millions of dollars was his young life.

These sombre recollections gave way at length to more cheerful feelings as he began to approach his home coolly. The fields and houses grew familiar, and in one or two he was greeted by people seated in the doorways. But he was in no mood to talk, and pushed on steadily, though he stopped and accepted a drink of milk once at the well-side of a neighbor.

The sun was burning hot on that slope, and his step grew slower, in spite of his iron resolution. He sat down several times to rest. Slowly he crawled up the rough, reddish-brown road, which wound along the hillside, under great trees, through dense groves of jack oaks, with tree-tops far below him on his left hand, and the hills far above him on his right. He crawled along like some minute, wingless variety of fly.

He ate some hardtack, sauced with wild berries, when he reached the summit of the ridge, and sat there for some time, looking down into his home coolly.

Sombre, pathetic figure! His wide, round, eyes gazing down into the beautiful valley, seeing and not seeing, the splendid cloud-shadows sweeping over the western hills and across the green and yellow wheat far below. His head drooped forward on his palm, his shoulders took on a tired stoop, his cheek-bones showed painfully. An observer might have said, "He is looking down upon his own grave."

II

Sunday comes in a Western wheat harvest with such sweet and sudden relaxation to man and beast that it would be holy for that reason, if for no other, and Sundays are usually fair in harvest-time. As one goes out into the field in the hot morning sunshine, with no [118/119] sound abroad save the crickets and the indescribably pleasant silken rustling of the ripened grain, the reaper and the very sheaves in the stubble seem to be resting, dreaming.

Around the house, in the shade of the trees, the men sit, smoking, dozing, or reading the papers, while the women, never resting, move about at the housework. The men eat on Sundays about the same as on other days, and breakfast is no sooner over and out of the way than dinner begins.

But at the Smith farm there were no men dozing or reading. Mrs. Smith was alone with her three children, Mary, nine, Tommy, six, and little Ted, just past four. Her farm, rented to a neighbor, lay at the head of a coolly or narrow gully, made at some far-off post-glacial period by the vast and angry floods of water which gullied these tremendous furrows in the level prairie—furrows so deep that undisturbed portions of the original level rose like hills on either side, rose to quite considerable mountains.

The chickens wakened her as usual that Sabbath morning from dreams of her absent husband, from whom she had not heard for weeks. The shadows drifted over the hills, down the slopes, across the wheat, and up the opposite wall in leisurely way, as if, being Sunday, they could take it easy also. The fowls clustered about the housewife as she went out into the yard. Fuzzy little chickens swarmed out from the coops, where their clucking and perpetually disgruntled mothers tramped about, petulantly thrusting their heads through the spaces between the slats.

A cow called in a deep, musical bass, and a calf answered from a little pen near by, and a pig scurried guiltily out of the cabbages. Seeing all this, seeing the pig in the cabbages, the tangle of grass in the garden, the broken fence which she had mended again and again —the little woman, hardly more than a girl, sat down and cried. The bright Sabbath morning was only a mockery without him!

A few years ago they had bought this farm, paying part, mortgaging the rest in the usual way. Edward Smith was a man of terrible energy. He worked "nights and Sundays," as the saying goes, to clear the farm of its brush and of its insatiate mortgage! In the midst of his Herculean struggle came the call for volunteers, and [119/120] with the grim and unselfish devotion to his country which made the Eagle Brigade able to "whip its weight in wild-cats," he threw down his scythe and grub-axe, turned his cattle loose, and became a blue-coated cog in a vast machine for killing men, and not thistles. While the millionaire sent his money to England for safe-keeping, this man, with his girl-wife and three babies, left them on a mortgaged farm, and went away to fight for an idea. It was foolish, but it was sublime for all that.

That was three years before, and the young wife, sitting on the well-curb on this bright Sabbath harvest morning, was righteously rebellious. It seemed to her that she had borne her share of the country's sorrow. Two brothers had been killed, the renter in whose hands her husband had left the farm had proved a villain; one year the farm had been without crops, and now the overripe grain was waiting the tardy hand of the neighbor who had rented it, and who was cutting his own grain first.

About six weeks before, she had received a letter saying, "We'll be discharged in a little while." But no other word had come from him. She had seen by the papers that his army was being discharged, and from day to day other soldiers percolated in blue streams back into the State and county, but still *her* hero did not return.

Each week she had told the children that he was coming, and she had watched the road so long that it had become unconscious; and as she stood at the well, or by the kitchen door, her eyes were fixed unthinkingly on the road that wound down the coolly.

Nothing wears on the human soul like waiting. If the stranded mariner, searching the sun-bright seas, could once give up hope of a ship, that horrible grinding on his brain would cease. It was this waiting, hoping, on the edge of despair, that gave Emma Smith no rest.

Neighbors said, with kind intentions: "He's sick, maybe, an' can't start north just yet. He'll come along one o' these days."

"Why don't he write?" was her question, which silenced them all. This Sunday morning it seemed to her as if she could not stand it longer. The house seemed intolerably lonely. So she dressed the [120/121] little ones in their best calico dresses and home-made jackets, and, closing-up the house, set off down the coolly to old Mother Gray's.

"Old Widder Gray" lived at the "mouth of the coolly." She was a widow woman with a large family of stalwart boys and laughing girls. She was the visible incarnation of hospitality and optimistic poverty. With Western open-heartedness she fed every mouth that asked food of her, and worked herself to death as cheerfully as her girls danced in the neighborhood harvest dances.

She waddled down the path to meet Mrs. Smith with a broad smile on her face.

"Oh, you little dears! Come right to your granny. Gimme a kiss! Come right in, Mis' Smith. How are yeh, anyway? Nice mornin', ain't it? Come in an' set down. Everything's in a clutter, but that won't scare you any."

She led the way into the best room, a sunny, square room, carpeted with a faded and patched rag carpet, and papered with white-and-green wall-paper, where a few faded effigies of dead members of the family hung in variously sized oval walnut frames. The house re-sounded with singing, laughter, whistling, tramping of heavy boots, and riotous scufflings. Half-grown boys came to the door and crooked their fingers at the children, who ran out, and were soon heard in the midst of the fun.

"Don't s'pose you've heard from Ed?" Mrs. Smith shook her head. "He'll turn up some day, when you ain't lookin' for 'm." The good

old soul had said that so many times that poor Mrs. Smith derived
no comfort from it any longer.

"Liz heard from Al the other day. He's comin' some day this week.
Anyhow, they expect him."

"Did he say anything of——"

"No, he didn't," Mrs. Gray admitted. "But then it was only a
short letter, anyhow. Al ain't much for writin', anyhow.—But come
out and see my new cheese. I tell yeh, I don't believe I ever had better luck in my life. If Ed should come, I want you should take him
up a piece of this cheese."

It was beyond human nature to resist the influence of that noisy,
hearty, loving household, and in the midst of the singing and laughing [121/122] the wife forgot her anxiety, for the time at least, and
laughed and sang with the rest.

About eleven o'clock a wagon-load more drove up to the door,
and Bill Gray, the widow's oldest son, and his whole family, from
Sand Lake Coolly, piled out amid a good-natured uproar. Every one
talked at once, except Bill, who sat in the wagon with his wrists on
his knees, a straw in his mouth, and an amused twinkle in his blue
eyes.

"Ain't heard nothin' o' Ed, I s'pose?" he asked in a kind of bellow.
Mrs. Smith shook her head. Bill, with a delicacy very striking in
such a great giant, rolled his quid in his mouth, and said:

"Didn't know but you had. I hear two or three of the Sand Lake
boys are comin'. Left New Orleenes some time this week. Didn't
write nothin' about Ed, but no news is good news in such cases,
mother always says."

"Well, go put out yer team," said Mrs. Gray, "an' go'n bring me
in some taters, an', Sim, you go see if you c'n find some corn. Sadie,
you put on the water to bile. Come now, hustle yer boots, all o' yeh.
If I feed this yer crowd, we've got to have some raw materials. If y'
think I'm goin' to feed yeh on pie—you're just mightily mistaken."

The children went off into the field, the girls put dinner on to
boil, and then went to change their dresses and fix their hair. "Somebody might come," they said.

"Land sakes, *I hope* not! I don't know where in time I'd set 'em,
'less they'd eat at the second table," Mrs. Gray laughed, in pretended
dismay.

The two older boys, who had served their time in the army, lay
out on the grass before the house, and whittled and talked desulto-
rily about the war and the crops, and planned buying a threshing-
machine. The older girls and Mrs. Smith helped enlarge the table
and put on the dishes, talking all the time in the cheery, incoherent,
and meaningful way a group of such women have,—a conversation to

be taken for its spirit rather than for its letter, though Mrs. Gray at last got the ear of them all and dissertated at length on girls. [122/123]

"Girls in love ain' no use in the whole blessed week," she said. "Sundays they're a-lookin', down the road, expectin' he'll *come*. Sunday afternoons they can't think o' nothin' else, 'cause he's *here*. Monday morning's they're sleepy and kind o' dreamy and slimpsy, and good f'r nothin' on Tuesday and Wednesday. Thursday they git absent-minded, an' begin to look off toward Sunday agin, an' mope aroun' and let the dishwater git cold, right under their noses. Friday they break dishes, an' go off in the best room an' snivel, an' look out o' the winder. Saturdays they have queer spurts o' workin' like all p'ssessed, an' spurts o' frizzin' their hair. An' Sunday they begin it all over agin."

The girls giggled and blushed, all through this tirade from their mother, their broad faces and powerful frames anything but suggestive of lackadaisical sentiment. But Mrs. Smith said:

"Now, Mrs. Gray, I hadn't ought to stay to dinner. You've got——"

"Now you set right down! If any of them girls' beaus comes, they'll have to take what's left, that's all. They ain't s'posed to have much appetite, nohow. No, you're goin' to stay if they starve, an' they ain't no danger o' that."

At one o'clock the long table was piled with boiled potatoes, cords of boiled corn on the cob, squash and pumpkin pies, hot biscuit, sweet pickles, bread and butter, and honey. Then one of the girls took down a conch-shell from a nail, and going to the door, blew a long, fine, free blast, that showed there was no weakness of lungs in her ample chest.

Then the children came out of the forest of corn, out of the creek, out of the loft of the barn, and out of the garden.

"They come to their feed f'r all the world just like the pigs when y' holler 'poo-ee!' See 'em scoot!" laughed Mrs. Gray, every wrinkle on her face shining with delight.

The men shut up their pack-knives, and surrounded the horse-trough to souse their faces in the cold, hard water, and in a few moments the table was filled with a merry crowd, and a row of wistful-eyed youngsters circled the kitchen wall, where they stood first on one leg and then on the other, in impatient hunger. [123/124]

"Now pitch in, Mrs. Smith," said Mrs. Gray, presiding over the table. "You know these men critters. They'll eat every grain of it, if yeh give 'em a chance. I swan, they're made o' India-rubber, their stomachs is, I know it."

"Haf to eat to work," said Bill, gnawing a cob with a swift, circular motion that rivalled a corn-sheller in results.

"More like workin' to eat," put in one of the girls, with a giggle. "More eat 'n work with you."

"*You* needn't say anything, Net. Any one that'll eat seven ears——"

"I didn't, no such thing. You piled your cobs on my plate."

"That'll do to tell Ed Varney. It won't go down here where we know yeh."

"Good land! Eat all yeh want! They's plenty more in the fiel's, but I can't afford to give you young uns tea. The tea is for us women-folks, and 'specially f'r Mis' Smith an' Bill's wife. We're a-goin' to tell fortunes by it."

One by one the men filled up and shoved back, and one by one the children slipped into their places, and by two o'clock the women alone remained around the débris-covered table, sipping their tea and telling fortunes.

As they got well down to the grounds in the cup, they shook them with a circular motion in the hand, and then turned them bottom-side-up quickly in the saucer, then twirled them three or four times one way, and three or four times the other, during a breathless pause. Then Mrs. Gray lifted the cup, and, gazing into it with profound gravity, pronounced the impending fate.

It must be admitted that, to a critical observer, she had abundant preparation for hitting close to the mark, as when she told the girls that "somebody was comin'." "It's a man," she went on gravely. "He is cross-eyed——"

"Oh, you hush!" cried Nettie.

"He has red hair, and is death on b'iled corn and hot biscuit."

The others shrieked with delight.

"But he's goin' to get the mitten, that red-headed feller is, for I see another feller comin' up behind him." [124/125]

"Oh, lemme see, lemme see!" cried Nettie.

"Keep off," said the priestess, with a lofty gesture. "His hair is black. He don't eat so much, and he works more."

The girls exploded in a shriek of laughter, and pounded their sister on the back.

At last came Mrs. Smith's turn, and she was trembling with excitement as Mrs. Gray again composed her jolly face to what she considered a proper solemnity of expression.

"Somebody is comin' to *you*," she said, after a long pause. "He's got a musket on his back. He's a soldier. He's almost here. See?"

She pointed at two little tea-stems, which really formed a faint suggestion of a man with a musket on his back. He had climbed nearly to the edge of the cup. Mrs. Smith grew pale with excitement. She trembled so she could hardly hold the cup in her hand as she gazed into it.

"It's Ed," cried the old woman. "He's on the way home. Heavens an' earth! There he is now!" She turned and waved her hand out toward the road. They rushed to the door to look where she pointed.

A man in a blue coat, with a musket on his back, was toiling slowly up the hill on the sun-bright, dusty road, toiling slowly, with bent head half hidden by a heavy knapsack. So tired it seemed that walking was indeed a process of falling. So eager to get home he would not stop, would not look aside, but plodded on, amid the cries of the locusts, the welcome of the crickets, and the rustle of the yellow wheat. Getting back to God's country, and his wife and babies!

Laughing, crying, trying to call him and the children at the same time, the little wife, almost hysterical, snatched her hat and ran out into the yard. But the soldier had disappeared over the hill into the hollow beyond, and, by the time she had found the children, he was too far away for her voice to reach him. And, besides, she was not sure it was her husband, for he had not turned his head at their shouts. This seemed so strange. Why didn't he stop to rest at his old neighbor's house? Tortured by hope and doubt, she hurried up the coolly as fast as she could push the baby wagon, the [125/126] blue-coated figure just ahead pushing steadily, silently forward up the coolly.

When the excited, panting little group came in sight of the gate they saw the blue-coated figure standing, leaning upon the rough rail fence, his chin on his palms, gazing at the empty house. His knapsack, canteen, blankets, and musket lay upon the dusty grass at his feet.

He was like a man lost in a dream. His wide, hungry eyes devoured the scene. The rough lawn, the little unpainted house, the field of clear yellow wheat behind it, down across which streamed the sun, now almost ready to touch the high hill to the west, the crickets crying merrily, a cat on the fence near by, dreaming, unmindful of the stranger in blue——

How peaceful it all was. O God! How far removed from all camps, hospitals, battle lines. A little cabin in a Wisconsin coolly, but it was majestic in its peace. How did he ever leave it for those years of tramping, thirsting, killing?

Trembling, weak with emotion, her eyes on the silent figure, Mrs. Smith hurried up to the fence. Her feet made no noise in the dust and grass, and they were close upon him before he knew of them. The oldest boy ran a little ahead. He will never forget that figure, that face. It will always remain as something epic, that return of the private. He fixed his eyes on the pale face covered with a ragged beard.

"Who *are* you, sir?" asked the wife, or, rather, started to ask, for he turned, stood a moment, and then cried:

"Emma!"

"Edward!"

The children stood in a curious row to see their mother kiss this bearded, strange man, the elder girl sobbing sympathetically with her mother. Illness had left the soldier partly deaf, and this added to the strangeness of his manner.

But the youngest child stood away, even after the girl had recognized her father and kissed him. The man turned then to the baby, and said in a curiously unpaternal tone: [126/127]

"Come here, my little man; don't you know me?" But the baby backed away under the fence and stood peering at him critically.

"My little man!" What meaning in those words! This baby seemed like some other woman's child, and not the infant he had left in his wife's arms. The war had come between him and his baby —he was only a strange man to him, with big eyes; a soldier, with mother hanging to his arm, and talking in a loud voice.

"And this is Tom," the private said, drawing the oldest boy to him. *"He'll* come and see me. *He* knows his poor old pap when he comes home from the war."

The mother heard the pain and reproach in his voice and hastened to apologize.

"You've changed so, Ed. He can't know yeh. This is papa, Teddy; come and kiss him—Tom and Mary do. Come, won't you?" But Teddy still peered through the fence with solemn eyes, well out of reach. He resembled a half-wild kitten that hesitates, studying the tones of one's voice.

"I'll fix him," said the soldier, and sat down to undo his knapsack, out of which he drew three enormous and very red apples. After giving one to each of the older children, he said:

"Now I guess he'll come. Eh, my little man? Now come see your pap."

Teddy crept slowly under the fence, assisted by the overzealous Tommy, and a moment later was kicking and squalling in his father's arms. Then they entered the house, into the sitting room, poor, bare, art-forsaken little room, too, with its rag carpet, its square clock, and its two or three chromos and pictures from *Harper's Weekly* pinned about.

"Emma, I'm all tired out," said Private Smith, as he flung himself down on the carpet as he used to do, while his wife brought a pillow to put under his head, and the children stood about munching their apples.

"Tommy, you run and get me a pan of chips, and Mary, you get the tea-kettle on, and I'll go and make some biscuit."

And the soldier talked. Question after question he poured forth about the crops, the cattle, the renter, the neighbors. He slipped [127/128] his heavy government brogan shoes off his poor, tired, blistered feet, and lay out with utter, sweet relaxation. He was a free man again, no longer a soldier under a command. At supper he stopped once, listened and smiled. "That's old Spot. I know her voice. I s'pose that's her calf out there in the pen. I can't milk her to-night, though. I'm too tired. But I tell you, I'd like a drink of her milk. What's become of old Rove?"

"He died last winter. Poisoned, I guess." There was a moment of sadness for them all. It was some time before the husband spoke again, in a voice that trembled a little.

"Poor old feller! He'd a' known me half a mile away. I expected him to come down the hill to meet me. It 'ud 'a' been more like comin' home if I could 'a' seen him comin' down the road an' waggin' his tail, an' laughin' that way he has. I tell yeh, it kind o' took hold o' me to see the blinds down an' the house shut up."

"But, yeh see, we—we expected you'd write again 'fore you started. And then we thought we'd see you if you *did* come," she hastened to explain.

"Well, I ain't worth a cent on writin'. Besides, it's just as well yeh didn't know when I was comin'. I tell you, it sounds good to hear them chickens out there, an' turkeys, an' crickets. Do you know they don't have just the same kind o' crickets down South? Who's Sam hired t' help cut yer grain?"

"The Ramsey boys."

"Looks like a good crop; but I'm afraid I won't do much gettin' it cut. This cussed fever an' ague has got me down pretty low. I don't know when I'll get rid of it. I'll bet I've took twenty-five pounds of quinine if I've taken a bit. Gimme another biscuit. I tell yeh, they taste good, Emma. I ain't had anything like it——Say, if you'd 'a hear'd me braggin' to the' boys about your butter 'n' biscuits I'll bet your ears 'ud 'a' burnt."

The private's wife colored with pleasure. "Oh, you're always a-bragging' about your things. Everybody makes good butter."

"Yes; old lady Snyder, for instance."

"Oh, well, she ain't to be mentioned. She's Dutch."

"Or old Mis' Snively. One more cup o' tea, Mary. That's my [128/129] girl! I'm feeling better already. I just b'lieve the matter with me is, I'm *starved*."

This was a delicious hour, one long to be remembered. They were like lovers again. But their tenderness, like that of a typical American family, found utterances in tones, rather than in words. He was praising her when praising her biscuit, and she knew it. They grew soberer when he showed where he had been struck, one ball burning

the back of his hand, one cutting away a lock of hair from his temple, and one passing through the calf of his leg. The wife shuddered
to think how near she had come to being a soldier's widow. Her
waiting no longer seemed hard. This sweet, glorious hour effaced it
all.

Then they rose, and all went out into the garden and down to the
barn. He stood beside her while she milked old Spot. They began to
plan fields and crops for next year.

His farm was weedy and encumbered, a rascally renter had run
away with his machinery (departing between two days), his children
needed clothing, the years were coming upon him, he was sick and
emaciated, but his heroic soul did not quail. With the same courage
with which he had faced his Southern march he entered upon a still
more hazardous future.

Oh, that mystic hour! The pale man with big eyes standing there
by the well, with his young wife by his side. The vast moon swinging
above the eastern peaks, the cattle winding down the pasture slopes
with jangling bells, the crickets singing, the stars blooming out sweet
and far and serene; the katydids rhythmically calling, the little turkeys crying querulously, as they settled to roost in the poplar tree
near the open gate. The voices at the well drop lower, the little ones
nestle in their father's arms at last, and Teddy falls asleep there.

The common soldier of the American volunteer army had returned. His war with the South was over, and his fight, his daily running fight with nature and against the injustice of his fellowmen,
was begun again. [129]

FRANK NORRIS

The Octopus

. . . THE EVENING BEFORE, when the foreman had blown his whistle at six o'clock, the long line of ploughs had halted upon the instant, and the drivers, unharnessing their teams, had taken them back to the division barns—leaving the ploughs as they were in the furrows. But an hour after daylight the next morning the work was resumed. After breakfast, Vanamee, riding one horse and leading the others, had returned to the line of ploughs together with the other drivers. Now he was busy harnessing the team. At the division blacksmith shop—temporarily put up—he had been obliged to wait while one of his lead horses was shod, and he had thus been delayed quite five minutes. Nearly all the other teams were harnessed, the drivers on their seats, waiting for the foreman's signal.

"All ready here?" inquired the foreman, driving up to Vanamee's team in his buggy.

"All ready, sir," answered Vanamee, buckling the last strap.

He climbed to his seat, shaking out the reins, and turning about, looked back along the line, then all around him at the landscape inundated with the brilliant glow of the early morning.

The day was fine. Since the first rain of the season, there had been no other. Now the sky was without a cloud, pale blue, delicate, luminous, scintillating with morning. The great brown earth turned a huge flank to it, exhaling the moisture of the early dew. The atmosphere, washed clean of dust and mist, was translucent as [121/122] crystal. Far off to the east, the halls on the other side of Broderson Creek stood out against the pallid saffron of the horizon as flat and as sharply outlined as if pasted on the sky. The campanile of the ancient Mission of San Juan seemed as fine as frost work. All about between the horizons, the carpet of the land unrolled itself to infinity. But now it was no longer parched with heat, cracked and warped by a merciless sun, powdered with dust. The rain had done its work;

From Frank Norris, *The Octopus: A Story of California* (Garden City, N.Y.: Doubleday & Company, Inc., n.d.), pp. 121–128. First published in 1901.

not a clod that was not swollen with fertility, not a fissure that did not exhale the sense of fecundity. One could not take a dozen steps upon the ranches without the brusque sensation that underfoot the land was alive; aroused at last from its sleep, palpitating with the desire of reproduction. Deep down there in the recesses of the soil, the great heart throbbed once more, thrilling with passion, vibrating with desire, offering itself to the caress of the plough, insistent, eager, imperious. Dimly one felt the deep-seated trouble of the earth, the uneasy agitation of its members, the hidden tumult of its womb, demanding to be made fruitful, to reproduce, to disengage the eternal renascent germ of Life that stirred and struggled in its loins.

The ploughs, thirty-five in number, each drawn by its team of ten, stretched in an interminable line, nearly a quarter of a mile in length, behind and ahead of Vanamee. They were arranged, as it were, *en échelon,* not in file—not one directly behind the other, but each succeeding plough its own width farther in the field than the one in front of it. Each of these ploughs held five shears, so that when the entire company was in motion, one hundred and seventy-five furrows were made at the same instant. At a distance, the ploughs resembled a great column of field artillery. Each driver was in his place, his glance alternating between his horses and the foreman nearest at hand. Other foremen, in their [122/123] buggies or buckboards, were at intervals along the line, like battery lieutenants. Annixter himself, on horseback, in boots and campaign hat, a cigar in his teeth, overlooked the scene.

The division superintendent, on the opposite side of the line, galloped past to a position at the head. For a long moment there was a silence. A sense of preparedness ran from end to end of the column. All things were ready, each man in his place. The day's work was about to begin.

Suddenly, from a distance at the head of the line came the shrill trilling of a whistle. At once the foreman nearest Vanamee repeated it, at the same time turning down the line, and waving one arm. The signal was repeated, whistle answering whistle, till the sounds lost themselves in the distance. At once the line of ploughs lost its immobility, moving forward, getting slowly under way, the horses straining in the traces. A prolonged movement rippled from team to team, disengaging in its passage a multitude of sounds—the click of buckles, the creak of straining leather, the subdued clash of machinery, the cracking of whips, the deep breathing of nearly four hundred horses, the abrupt commands and cries of the drivers, and, last of all, the prolonged, soothing murmur of the thick brown earth turning steadily from the multitude of advancing shears.

The ploughing thus commenced, continued. The sun rose higher. Steadily the hundred iron hands kneaded and furrowed and stroked the brown, humid earth, the hundred iron teeth bit deep into the Titan's flesh. Perched on his seat, the moist living reins slipping and tugging in his hands, Vanamee, in the midst of this steady confusion of constantly varying sensation, sight interrupted by sound, sound mingling with sight, on this swaying, vibrating seat, quivering with the prolonged thrill of the earth, lapsed to a sort of pleasing numbness, [123/124] in a sense, hypnotized by the weaving maze of things in which he found himself involved. To keep his team at an even, regular gait, maintaining the precise interval, to run his furrows as closely as possible to those already made by the plough in front—this for the moment was the entire sum of his duties. But while one part of his brain, alert and watchful, took cognizance of these matters, all the greater part was lulled and stupefied with the long monotony of the affair.

The ploughing, now in full swing, enveloped him in a vague, slow-moving whirl of things. Underneath him was the jarring, jolting, trembling machine; not a clod was turned, not an obstacle encountered, that he did not receive the swift impression of it through all his body, the very friction of the damp soil, sliding incessantly from the shiny surface of the shears, seemed to reproduce itself in his finger-tips and along the back of his head. He heard the horse-hoofs by the myriads crushing down easily, deeply, into the loam, the prolonged clinking of trace-chains, the working of the smooth brown flanks in the harness, the clatter of wooden hames, the champing of bits, the click of iron shoes against pebbles, the brittle stubble of the surface ground crackling and snapping as the furrows turned, the sonorous, steady breaths wrenched from the deep, labouring chests, strap-bound, shining with sweat, and all along the line the voices of the men talking to the horses. Everywhere there were visions of glossy brown backs, straining, heaving, swollen with muscle; harness streaked with specks of froth, broad, cup-shaped hoofs, heavy with brown loam, men's faces red with tan, blue overalls spotted with axle-grease; muscled hands, the knuckles whitened in their grip on the reins, and through it all the ammoniacal smell of the horses, the bitter reek of perspiration of beasts and men, the aroma of warm leather, the scent of dead stubble—and stronger [124/125] and more penetrating than everything else, the heavy, enervating odour of the upturned, living earth.

At intervals, from the tops of one of the rare, low swells of the land, Vanamee overlooked a wider horizon. On the other divisions of Quien Sabe the same work was in progress. Occasionally he could see another column of ploughs in the adjoining division—sometimes

so close at hand that the subdued murmur of its movements reached
his ear; sometimes so distant that it resolved itself into a long, brown
streak upon the grey of the ground. Farther off to the west on the
Osterman ranch other columns came and went, and, once, from the
crest of the highest swell on his division, Vanamee caught a distant
glimpse of the Broderson ranch. There, too, moving specks indicated
that the ploughing was under way. And farther away still, far off
there beyond the fine line of the horizons, over the curve of the
globe, the shoulder of the earth, he knew were other ranches, and
beyond these others, and beyond these still others, the immensities
multiplying to infinity.

Everywhere throughout the great San Joaquin, unseen and un-
heard, a thousand ploughs up-stirred the land, tens of thousands of
shears clutched deep into the warm, moist soil.

It was the long stroking caress, vigorous, male, powerful, for
which the Earth seemed panting. The heroic embrace of a multitude
of iron hands, gripping deep into the brown, warm flesh of the land
that quivered responsive and passionate under this rude advance, so
robust as to be almost an assault, so violent as to be veritably brutal.
There, under the sun and under the speckless sheen of the sky, the
wooing of the Titan began, the vast primal passion, the two world-
forces, the elemental Male and Female, locked in a colossal embrace,
at grapples in the throes of an infinite desire, at [125/126] once terrible and divine, knowing no law, untamed, savage, natural, sublime.

From time to time the gang in which Vanamee worked halted on
the signal from foreman or overseer. The horses came to a stand-
still, the vague clamour of the work lapsed away. Then the minutes
passed. The whole work hung suspended. All up and down the line
one demanded what had happened. The division superintendent
galloped past, perplexed and anxious. For the moment, one of the
ploughs was out of order, a bolt had slipped, a lever refused to work,
or a machine had become immobilized in heavy ground, or a horse
had lamed himself. Once, even, toward noon, an entire plough was
taken out of the line, so out of gear that a messenger had to be sent
to the division forge to summon the machinist.

Annixter had disappeared. He had ridden farther on to the other
divisions of his ranch, to watch the work in progress there. At twelve
o'clock, according to his orders, all the division superintendents put
themselves in communication with him by means of the telephone
wires that connected each of the division houses, reporting the condition of the work, the number of acres covered, the prospects of
each plough traversing its daily average of twenty miles.

At half-past twelve, Vanamee and the rest of the drivers ate their
lunch in the field, the tin buckets having been distributed to them

that morning after breakfast. But in the evening, the routine of the previous day was repeated, and Vanamee, unharnessing his team, riding one horse and leading the others, returned to the division barns and bunk-house.

It was between six and seven o'clock. The half-hundred men of the gang threw themselves upon the supper the Chinese cooks had set out in the shed of the eating-house, long as a bowling alley, unpainted, crude, [126/127] the seats benches, the table covered with oilcloth. Overhead a half-dozen kerosene lamps flared and smoked.

The table was taken as if by assault; the clatter of iron knives upon the tin plates was as the reverberation of hail upon a metal roof. The ploughmen rinsed their throats with great draughts of wine, and, their elbows wide, their foreheads flushed, resumed the attack upon the beef and bread, eating as though they would never have enough. All up and down the long table, where the kerosene lamps reflected themselves deep in the oilcloth cover, one heard the incessant sounds of mastication, and saw the uninterrupted movement of great jaws. At every moment one or another of the men demanded a fresh portion of beef, another pint of wine, another half-loaf of bread. For upwards of an hour the gang ate. It was no longer a supper. It was a veritable barbecue, a crude and primitive feasting, barbaric, homeric.

But in all this scene Vanamee saw nothing repulsive. Presley would have abhorred it—this feeding of the People, this gorging of the human animal, eager for its meat. Vanamee, simple, uncomplicated, living so close to nature and the rudimentary life, understood its significance. He knew very well that within a short half-hour after this meal the men would throw themselves down in their bunks to sleep without moving, inert and stupefied with fatigue, till the morning. Work, food, and sleep, all life reduced to its bare essentials, uncomplex, honest, healthy. They were strong, these men, with the strength of the soil they worked, in touch with the essential things, back again to the starting point of civilization, coarse, vital, real, and sane.

For a brief moment immediately after the meal, pipes were lit, and the air grew thick with fragrant tobacco smoke. On a corner of the dining-room table, a [127/128] game of poker was begun. One of the drivers, a Swede, produced an accordion; a group on the steps of the bunk-house listened, with alternate gravity and shouts of laughter, to the acknowledged story-teller of the gang. But soon the men began to turn in, stretching themselves at full length on the horse blankets in the racklike bunks. The sounds of heavy breathing increased steadily, lights were put out, and before the afterglow had faded from the sky, the gang was asleep. [128]

ROBERT FROST

Mowing

THERE WAS NEVER a sound beside the wood but one,
And that was my long scythe whispering to the ground.
What was it it whispered? I knew not well myself;
Perhaps it was something about the heat of the sun,
Something, perhaps, about the lack of sound—
And that was why it whispered and did not speak.
It was no dream of the gift of idle hours,
Or easy gold at the hand of fay or elf:
Anything more than the truth would have seemed too weak
To the earnest love that laid the swale in rows,
Not without feeble-pointed spikes of flowers
(Pale orchises), and scared a bright green snake.
The fact is the sweetest dream that labor knows.
My long scythe whispered and left the hay to make. [25]

From *Complete Poems of Robert Frost* (New York: Henry Holt & Company, 1949),
p. 25.

ANDREW LYTLE

——•—•——

The Hind Tit

ON A CERTAIN Saturday, a group of countrymen squatted and lay
about the Rutherford County court-house yard, three-quarters of a
century after Abner L. extended his invitation to Van Buren. One
remarked to the others that "as soon as a farmer begins to keep
books, he'll go broke shore as hell."

Let us take him as a type and consider the life of his household
before and after he made an effort to industrialize it. Let us set his
holdings at two hundred acres, more or less—a hundred in cultivation, sixty in woods and pasture, and forty in waste land, too rocky
for cultivation but offering some pasturage. A smaller acreage would
scarcely justify a tractor. And that is a very grave consideration for a
man who lives on thirty or fifty acres. If the pressure becomes too
great, he will be forced to sell out and leave, or remain as a tenant
or hand on the large farm made up of units such as his. This example, is taken, of course, with the knowledge that the problem on any
two hundred acres is never the same: the richness of the soil, its
qualities, the neighborhood, the distance from market, the climate,
water, and a thousand such things make the life on every farm distinctly individual.

The house is a dog-run with an ell running to the rear, the
kitchen and dining-room being in the ell, if the family does not eat in
the kitchen; and the sleeping-rooms in the main part of the house.
The dog-run is a two- or four-crib construction with an open space
between, the whole covered by one roof. The run or trot gets its
name from the hounds passing through from the front to the rear. It
may or may not have a floor, according to the taste or pride of the
occupant. This farmer will have it floored, because his grandfather,
as he prospered, closed in the dog-run with doors, making it into a
hall; added porches front and rear, weather-boarded the logs, and

From Andrew Nelson Lytle, "The Hind Tit," in *I'll Take My Stand: The South
and the Agrarian Tradition* by Twelve Southerners (New York: Harper & Brothers,
1930), pp. 217–234.

ceiled the two half-story [217/218] rooms. His grandfather belonged to that large number of sturdy freemen who owned from three to five hundred acres of land and perhaps a slave or two in better days. But owning a few slaves did not make him a planter. He and his sons worked alongside them in the fields. Of farmers so situated in the South there was one to every twelve and one-tenth of free population.

There is a brick walk running from the porch to a horse block, lined on either side with hardy buttercups. From the block a road marked off by tall cedars goes out to the pike gate, two hundred yards away. The yard is kept grazed down by sheep, and occasionally the stock is turned in, when the pastures are burned in a drought. The house needs paint, but the trees are whitewashed around the base of the trunks to keep insects off and to give a neat appearance to the yard.

Over the front doorway is a horseshoe, turned the right way to bring luck to all who may pass beneath its lintel. The hall is almost bare, but scrubbed clean. At the back is a small stairway leading to the half-story. This is where the boys sleep, in their bachelorhood definitely removed from the girls. To the left is the principal room of the house. The farmer and his wife sleep there in a four-poster, badly in need of doing over; and here the youngest chillurn sleep on pallets made up on the floor.

The large rock fireplace is the center of the room. The home-made hickory chairs are gathered in a semicircle about it, while on the extreme left of the arc is a rough hand-made rocker with a sheep-skin bottom, shiny from use, and its arms smooth from the polishing of flesh, reserved [218/219] always for "mammy," the tough leather-skinned mother of the farmer. Here she sets and rocks and smokes near enough for the draught to draw the smoke up the chimney. On the mantel, at one end, is dry leaf tobacco, filling the room with its sharp, pungent odor. A pair of dog-irons rests on the hearth, pushed against the back log and holding up the ends of the sticks which have burnt in two and fallen among the hot ashes. The fire is kept burning through the month of May to insure good crops, no matter how mild and warm its days turn out to be. The top rock slab is smoked in the middle where for generations the wind has blown suddenly down the chimney, driving heavy gusts to flatten against the mantel and spread out in the room. A quilting-farme is drawn into the ceiling, ready to be lowered into the laps of the women-folks when the occasion demands, although it is gradually falling into disuse. Beneath it, spreading out from the center of the floor, a rag rug covers the wide pine boards which, in turn, cover the rough-hewn puncheons that sufficed during pioneer days. From this room, or rather, from the hearth of this room, the life of the dwelling moves.

If this is the heart of the house, the kitchen is its busiest part. The old, open fireplace has been closed in since the war, and an iron range has taken its place. This much machinery has added to the order of the establishment's life without disrupting it. Here all the food is prepared, and the canning and preserving necessary to sustain the family during the winter is done.

The cooking is a complicated art, requiring mastery over all its parts to burden the table with victuals that can be [219/220] relished. Each meal is a victory over nature, a suitable union between the general principles of cookery and the accident of preparation. The fire must be kept at the right temperature (without a thermometer), or the bread won't rise; too much lard, or too little, will spoil the pastry; and since the test of all cooking is the seasoning, which can never be reduced to exact rules but is partly intuitive, too many pinches of salt may ruin the dish. The farmer's wife learns to satisfy the tastes of her particular family, but she can never set two meals on the table exactly alike. She never overcomes nature; her victories are partial, but very satisfying, for she knows her limitations.

The kitchen leads out to the back ell-shaped porch. Upon its banister, or, if there is no banister, upon the wash-table, a bucket of water and its gourd, a tin pan, soap, and towel wait to serve the morning toilet. The towel will hang on a folding rack fixed to the wall. This rack may also serve long strings of red peppers drying in the air. A bell-post rises up near the kitchen to ring the boys in from the fields at dinner-time. In the back, behind the kitchen, is the smokehouse and several outhouses. Iron kettles for washing tilt to one side in the ashes of an old fire, some distance away. An ash-hopper made from a hollow log, no longer in use, lies up against the buggy-house, having gone the way of the kitchen fireplace. The lye for soap- and hominy-making is now bought in town.

Convenient to the kitchen is the woodpile, made of different-sized sticks, some for the stove, split and cut to the right length, and some for the fireplaces, back logs and front sticks. The wood has been cut in the early fall, just [220/221] as the sap begins to go down, not too early and not too late, but just at the right time, so that the outer surface will be dry and will catch quick, while the inside remains sappy and hard, burning slowly. It takes a great deal of study and intelligence to keep the fires going steadily.

Before dawn the roosters and the farmer feel the tremendous silence, chilling and filling the gap between night and day. He gets up, makes the fires, and rings the rising bell. He could arouse the family with his voice, but it has been the custom to ring the bell; so every morning it sounds out, taking its place among the other bells

in the neighborhood. Each, according to his nature, gets up and prepares for the day: the wife has long been in the kitchen when the
boys go to the barn; some of the girls help her, while the farmer
plans the morning work and calls out directions.

One or two of the girls set out with their milk-pails to the barn,
where the cows have been kept overnight. There is a very elaborate
process to go through with in milking. First, the cow must be fed to
occupy her attention; next, the milker kneels or sits on a bucket and
washes the bag which will have gotten manure on it during the
night (she kneels to the right, as this is the strategic side; the cow's
foot is somehow freer on the left). After the bag is clean, the milking
begins. There is always a variation to this ritual. When the calf is
young, the cow holds back her milk for it; so the calf is allowed to
suck a little at first, some from each teat, loosening the milk with
uniformity, and then is pulled off and put in a stall until his time
comes. There is one way to pull a calf off, and only one. He must be
held by the ears and the tail at the same time, for only [221/222] in
this manner is he easily controlled. The ears alone, or the tail alone,
is not enough.

This done, the milking begins. The left hand holds the pail, while
the right does the work, or it may be the reverse. The hand hits the
bag tenderly, grabs the teat, and closes the fingers about it, not altogether, but in echelon. The calf is then let out for his share. If he is
young and there are several cows, it will be all that is left, for careful
milkers do not strip the cow until the calf is weaned. The strippings
are those short little squirts which announce the end, and they are
all cream.

The milk is next brought back to the house, strained, and put in
the well to cool. This requires a very careful hand, because if it happens to spill, the well is ruined. The next step is to pour up the old
milk and let it turn—that is, sour—for churning. Some will be set
aside to clabber for the mammy whose teeth are no longer equal to
tougher nourishment. What she does not eat is given to the young
chickens or to the pigs.

After breakfast the farmer's wife, or one of the girls, does the
churning. This process takes a variable length of time. If the milk is
kept a long time before it is poured up, the butter is long in coming.
Sometimes witches get in the churn and throw a spell over it. In that
case a nickel is dropped in to break the charm. The butter, when it
does come, collects in small, yellow clods on top. These clods are separated from the butter-milk and put in a bowl where the rest of the
water is worked out. It is then salted, molded, and stamped with
some pretty little design. After this is done, it is set in the well or the
spring to cool for the table. [222/223] The process has been long, to

some extent tedious, but profitable, because insomuch as it has taken time and care and intelligence, by that much does it have a meaning.

Industrialism gives an electric refrigerator, bottled milk, and dairy butter. It takes a few minutes to remove it from the ice to the table, while the agrarian process has taken several hours and is spread out over two or three days. Industrialism saves time, but what is to be done with this time? The milkmaid can't go to the movies, read the sign-boards, and go play bridge all the time. In the moderate circumstances of this family, deprived of her place in the home economy, she will be exiled to the town to clerk all day. If the income of the family can afford it, she remains idle, and therefore miserable.

The whole process has been given in detail as an example of what goes on in every part of an agrarian life. The boys, coming in to breakfast, have performed in the same way. Every morning the stock must be fed, but there is always variety. They never shuck the same ears of corn, nor do they find the mules in the small part of the stall, nor the hogs in the same attitudes, waiting to be slopped. The buckets of milk did not move regularly from cow to consumer as raw material moves through a factory. The routine was broken by other phenomena. Breakfast intervened. One morning the cow might kick the pail over, or the milkmaid might stumble over a dog, or the cow come up with a torn udder. It is not the only task she performs, just as feeding the stock is not the only task done by the boys. The day of each member of the family is filled with a mighty variety. [223/224]

After the morning work is over, the family gathers about the breakfast table. Thanks are returned and the meal is served, one of the daughters or the mother waiting on the table; and then, without undue haste, the men go to the fields and the women about their dishes. If it is spring, the women can be of great help in the garden. Very likely the cut-worms will be after the young corn. The cut-worm does not like heat. If some one gets into the garden before the sun gets hot, the worm can be found under a clod near the top of the ground and mashed. In another hour he will have gone far below the surface. It is imperative to go at the right time, for of all the thousands of insects and varmints on the land, he has the distinction of his own habits. By learning these habits, and not those of some other pest, can he be overcome.

Before going to the fields the farmer consults the signs. If the smoke from the chimney is blown to the ground, there will be rain. Lightning in the north early in the night means rain before morning. If there is enough blue in the sky to make the Dutchman a pair of breeches, the weather will turn fair. Lightning in the south is a sign of drought. If the moon lies on its back, it is holding water; it is tilted so that the water can run out, the season will be dry. Charms, signs, and omens are folk attempts to understand and predict natural phenomena. They are just as useful and necessary to an aggrarian economy as the same attempts which come from the chemist's laboratory in an industrial society, and far wiser, because they understand their inadequacy, while the hypotheses of science do not.

According to these signs the work is hard or leisurely. [224/225] If the fish are biting, the boys might knock off a day and go fishing, or hunting. Their father has not begun to keep books, so their time is their own.

At eleven o'clock the dinner bell rings. The ploughmen take out and come to the house. So regular is this ritual that a mule on the farm of Gen. Joseph E. Johnston's quartermaster used to square his feet in the furrow and answer the bell with a long, loud bray. Nor was anybody ever able to make him, by beating or pleading, plough a step farther. The teams are watered and put into their stalls, where so many ears of corn are shucked into the troughs, and a section of hay is thrown into the racks.

If the corn is low in the crib, the boys are likely to chuck carefully, keeping their eyes open for the king snake. This snake is worth ten cats as a ratter, and careful, economical farmers always throw one in their cribs if one is to be found. But not only as a ratter is he valuable. He makes war on all poisonous snakes and drives them from his presence. His invincibility is believed to be due to his knowledge of snake grass, an antidote for poison; for after bouts in which he has been bitten by venomous snakes, he has been seen to wiggle toward this grass and chew it. There is only one time of the year when he is to be avoided. He goes blind in August; and, feeling his defenseless condition, he will leg you—that is, charge and wrap his strong body about your leg, squeezing and bruising it.

The midday meal, like all the meals in the country, has a great deal of form. It is, in the first place, unhurried. Diners accustomed to the mad, bolting pace of cafeterias will grow nervous at the slow performance of a country [225/226] table. To be late is a very grave matter, since it is not served until everybody is present. But only some accident, or unusual occurrence, will detain any member of the family, for dinner is a social event of the first importance. The family are together with their experiences of the morning to relate; and merriment rises up from the hot, steaming vegetables, all set about the table, small hills around the mountains of meat at the ends, a heaping plate of fried chicken, a turkey, a plate of guineas, or a one-year ham, spiced, and if company is there, baked in wine. A plate of bread is at each end of the table; a bowl of chitterlings has been set at the father's elbow; and pigs' feet for those that like them.

And they eat with eighteenth-century appetites. There is no puny piddling with the victuals, and fancy tin-can salads do not litter the table. The only salad to be seen on a country table is sallet, or turnip greens, or if further explanation is necessary, the tops of turnips cut off and cooked with a luscious piece of fat meat. It has the appearance of spinach; but, unlike this insip slime, sallet has character, like the life of the farmer at the head of the table. The most important part of this dish is its juice, the pot licker, a rich green liquid, indescribable except as a pot-licker green. Mixed with corn bread, it has no equal. Particularly is it fine for teething babies. If the baby is weaned in the dark of the moon and fed a little pot licker, he will pass through the second summer without great trouble. This will not relieve the pain of cutting. To do that a young rabbit must be killed, its head skinned, and the raw flesh rubbed on the gums. If this [226/227] fails, tie a spray of alderberries around its neck, or hang a mole's foot. But sallet will do everything but cut the pain.

His table, if the seasons allow, is always bountiful. The abundance of nature, its heaping dishes, its bulging-breasted fowls, deep-yellow butter and creamy milk, fat beans and juicy corn, and its potatoes flavored like pecans, fill his dining-room with the satisfaction of well-being, because he has not yet come to look upon his produce at so many cents a pound, or his corn at so much a dozen. If nature gives bountifully to his labor, he may enjoy largely.

The dishes of food are peculiarly relished. Each dish has particular meaning to the consumer, for everybody has had something to do with the long and intricate procession from the ground to the table. Somebody planted the beans and worked them. Somebody else staked them and watched them grow, felt anxious during the early spring drought, gave silent thanksgiving when a deep-beating rain soaked into the crusty soil, for the leaves would no longer take the yellow shrivel. A townsman can never understand the significance of rain, nor why an agrarian will study the signs with so much care and often with so much pain, for to him it has no immediate connection. The worst it can do him is to interrupt a picnic, and the best to beat from the asphalt of its streets and its tall buildings for a few moments the enervating heat peculiar to such places. The fullness of meaning that rain and the elements extend to the farmer is all contained in a mess of beans, a plate of potatoes, or a dish of sallet. When the garden first comes in, this meaning is explicit. If the yield has been large and rich, it will be openly and pridefully commented upon; if the garden has [227/228] burned and it has lost its succulence to the sun, some will remark that sorrier beans have been seen, while others, more resentful of nature's invincible and inscrutable

ways, will answer that better, also, have been seen. But aside from
some such conservative expression, in its formal tone masking a violent passion, no other comment will be made. And as the enjoyment of the garden's produce becomes more regular, this particular
meaning which the dishes at a country table has for its diners settles
into the subconscious and becomes implicit in the conduct of the
household.

The description of this particular board is by no means general.
Just as no two farms are managed alike, so no two tables will be set
alike. It is better than most, and slightly changed from ante-bellum
days. It is more stable, as it has had a century in which to harden its
form. But this form, troubled by the dualism, is less strict than it
would have been if nothing had happened to disturb the direction
of its growth. This farmer, being a Tennessean, perhaps has some
advantage over other Southwesterns except Kentuckians of a tradition less shaken during the hard years. Tennessee has never been
given over to any one money crop. It has looked upon its land to
sustain its culture, and from the beginning has diversified according
to its needs. Serving as a furnishing state to the cotton regions, when
these regions were overturned, it naturally stood the shock better
than they. In consequence the table will be more formal, its meals
better, than in those places where the small upland farmer moved
down upon the segments of the broken plantations. He can never
have the same respect for the sow-belly and [228/229] corn-meal
furnished him by the merchant, and actually a large body of these
farmers in Alabama, Mississippi, Georgia, South Carolina, and West
Tennessee did not vary a great deal this diet, as he could for the
vegetables and meat brought to the table by his own hand.

After the midday meal is over the family takes a rest; then the
men go back to the fields and the women to those things yet to be
done, mending clothes, darning, knitting, canning, preserving, washing or ironing or sewing. By sundown they are gathered about the
supper table, and afterward set before the fire if it is winter, or upon
the porch in warmer weather. One of the boys will get out his guitar
and play "ballets" handed down from father to son, some which
have originated in the new country, some which have been brought
over from the Old World and changed to fit the new locale. Boys
from the neighborhood drop into court, and they will jine in, or
drive away with the gals in hug-back buggies. If they are from another neighborhood, they are sure to be rocked or shot at on the way
over or on the way home.

If the gathering is large enough, as it is likely to be when crops
are laid by, it will turn into a play-party. Most of these games practiced by the plain people have maintained the traditions brought

from England and Scotland, while the townsmen lost their knowledge of them in a generation. For example, "The Hog Drovers" is a version of the English folk-game, "The Three Sailors." The Southern country, being largely inland, could only speculate upon the [229/230] habits of sailors, but they knew all about the hog drovers. Every year droves of razorbacks, with their eyelids sewed together to hinder them from wandering off into the woods, were driven ten or eleven miles a day toward the Eastern markets. They would be stopped at private farms along the route, where pens had been put up to receive them, to feed. The drovers, nomadic and as careless as sailors, could not be made to keep promises. Parents, therefore, were careful of their daughters.

The game comes from, and is a copy of, the life of the people. A boy seats himself upon a chair in the middle of the room with a gal in his lap. He is the head of the house, and she is his daughter. The other gals are seated around the walls, waiting their turns; while the boys, representing the hog drovers, enter two abreast in a sort of a jig, singing the first stanza:

> "Hog drovers, hog drovers, hog drovers we air,
> A-courtin yore darter so sweet and so fair,
>   Can we git lodgin' here, oh, here,
>   Can we git er-lodgin' here?"

They stop in front of the old man, and he answers:

> "Oh, this is my darter that sets by my lap,
> And none o' you pig-stealers can git her from pap,
>   And you can't git lodgin' here, oh, here,
>   And you can't git er-lodgin' here."

The boys then jig about the chair, singing:

> "A good-lookin' darter, but ugly yoreself—
> We'll travel on further and sit on the shelf,
>   And we don't want lodgin' here, oh, here,
>   And we don't want er-lodgin' here." [230/231]

They jig around the room, then return. The old man relents. Possibly it has as its genesis a struggle between greed and the safety of his daughter's virtue:

> "Oh, this is my darter that sets by my lap,
> And Mr. *So-and-so* can git her from pap
>   If he'll put another one here, oh, here,
>   If he'll put another one here."

The boy who is named jigs to one of the gals, brings her to the old man, takes his darter to the rear of the line, and the game starts

over. After every couple has been paired off, they promenade all and
seek buggies or any quiet place suitable for courting.

This and other games, "Fly in the Buttermilk," "Shoot the Buffalo," "Under the Juniper Tree," will fill an evening and break the
order of their lives often enough to dispel monotony, making holi-
days a pleasure; and not so frequent nor so organized that they become a business, which means that games have become self-con-
scious, thus defeating the purpose of all playing. As they play they
do not constantly remind one another that they are having a good
time. They have it.

Besides these play-parties people pleasured themselves in other
ways. There were ice-cream socials, old-time singings, like the Sacred
Harp gatherings, political picnics and barbecues, and barn dances.
All of these gatherings which bring the neighborhood together in a
social way are unlike the "society" of industrialism. Behind it some
ulterior purpose always lurks. It becomes another province of Big
Business and is invaded by hordes of people who, unable [231/232]
to sell themselves in the sterner marts, hope to catch their prey in his
relaxed moments and over the tea tables make connections which
properly belong to the office. This practice prostitutes society, for individuals can mingle socially from no motive except to enjoy one another's company.

The songs of the Sacred Harp, like negro spirituals, are without
accompaniment. The tune is pitched by the leader in the neighborhood schoolhouse under the shadows of oil-lamps. There is a grand
meeting at the county seat once a year, and here the neighborhoods
sing against each other and in unison under one general leader, who
always remembers to turn the meeting over to each district leader
for one song. This is a privilege jealously looked after; and if anyone is by chance overlooked, he will rise and make himself known.
These songs of the Sacred Harp are songs of an agrarian people, and
they will bind the folk-ways which will everywhere else go down before canned music and canned pleasure.

At the square dances, unlike round dancing, the stage is set for
each individual to show the particularity of his art. Each couple is
"out" in turn, swinging every other couple separately, ending up at
"home" when the whole line swings "partners," and then "corners."
In this way a very fine balance is reached between group and individual action. Everybody is a part of the dance all the time, but a
very particular part some of the time. There are no wall-flowers, no
duty dances, no agonizing over popularity, and the scores of such
things which detract from free enjoyment at the round dancings.
"First lady out" means that she [232/233] must step, cheat, and
swing and show her superiority over the ladies who will follow; and

likewise with the gentlemen. And the prompter, the one who calls the "figgers" (which happens still to be the proper English pronunciation of figure), is an artist and wit whose disappearance will leave the world much the poorer. Such calls as

> "Swing the gal you love best;
> Now cheat and swing."

> "Partners to yore places
> Like mules to the traces."

and from Mississippi,

> "Women swing hard, men swing harder,
> Swing that gal with the buckskin garter."

are metaphors and imperatives with full connotation for the dancers, and in an agrarian society will be as applicable a hundred years hence. But so will the fiddlers' tunes, "Leather Breeches," "Rats in the Meal Barrel," "Frog Mouth," "Guinea in the Pea Patch," "Arkansas Traveler," "Cotton-eyed Joe," "No Supper Tonight," "Hell Amongst the Yearlings," "Got a Chaw of Tobaccy from a Nigger," "All My Candy's Gone," and "Katy, Bar the Door." With a list of such dances as a skeleton, if all other records were lost, some future scholar could reconstruct with a common historical accuracy the culture of this people.

Before the farmer decided to keep books, the structure of his neighborhood culture had not been moved, and his sons and daughters, and he and the old woman, were a part of these things. Even mammy, if the rheumaticks had not frozen her jints, would put on her hickory-staved bonnet, [233/234] a fresh-starched apron, and mount the waggin with the rest and drive to the singing and lift her cracked voice as the leader "h'isted" the tune, or at the barbecue pat her feet in time with the whining fiddle and think of better days when she and her old man balanced to "Cairo ladies, show yoreself," or "Jenny, the Flower of Kildare," until the sweat poured from her strong back, gluing the gray linen dress to her shoulders and ballooning it in places with air caught in the swing. [234]

ELIZABETH MADOX ROBERTS

On the Mountainside

THERE WAS a play-party at the schoolhouse at the bottom of the cove. Newt Reddix waited outside the house, listening to the noises as Lester Hunter, the teacher, had listened to them—a new way for Newt. Sound at the bottom of a cove was different from sound at the top, he noticed, for at the top voices spread into a wide thinness. Before Lester came, Newt had let his ears have their own way of listening. Sounds had then been for but one purpose—to tell him what was happening or what was being said. Now the what of happenings and sayings was wrapped about with some unrelated feelings or prettiness, or it stood back beyond some heightened qualities.

"Listen!" Lester had said to him one evening, standing outside a house where a party was going [3/4] forward. "Listen!" And there were footsteps and outcries of men and women, happy cries, shrill notes of surprise and pretended anger, footsteps on rough wood, unequal intervals, a flare of fiddle playing and a tramp of dancing feet. Down in the cove the sounds from a party were different from those that came from a house on the side of a hill, the cries of men bent and disturbed, distorted by the place, by the sink and rise of land. While he listened, the knowledge that Lester Hunter would soon go out of the country, the school term being over, brought a loneliness to his thought.

He went inside the schoolhouse and flung his hat on the floor beside the door; he would take his part now in the playing. His hat was pinned up in front with a thorn and was as pert a hat as any of those beside the door, and no one would give it dishonor. The schoolteacher was stepping about in the dance, turning Corie Yancey, and the fiddle was scraping the top of a tune. For him the entire party was filled with the teacher's impending departure.

"Ladies change and gents the same," the fiddler called, his voice unblended with the tune he played. Newt fell into place when an

From Elizabeth Madox Roberts, *The Haunted Mirror* (New York: The Viking Press, 1932), pp. 3–25.

older man withdrew in his favor and gave him Ollie Mack [4/5] for his partner. The teacher danced easily, bent to the curve of the music, neglectful and willing, giving the music the flowing lightness of his limp body.

Newt wanted to dance as the teacher did, but he denied himself and kept the old harsh gesture, pounding the floor more roughly now and then with a deeply accented step. He wanted to tread the music lightly, meeting it halfway, but he would not openly imitate anybody. While he danced he was always, moment by moment, aware of the teacher, aware of him standing to wait his turn, pulling his collar straight, pushing his hands into the pockets of his coat, looking at Ollie Mack when she laughed, looking full into her face with pleasure, unafraid. The teacher had given an air to the dance, and had made it, for him, more bold in form, more like itself or more true to its kind, more gentle in courtesy. Lester had come from one of the low counties of the rolling plain where the curving creeks of the Pigeon River spread slowly, winding broadly to gather up many little rills. Newt had learned somewhere, in his own blood, to hate the lower country for its pleasantness. There the fields rolled out smoothly and the soil was deep. The grass of any roadside was blue-grass [5/6] mingled, perhaps, with rich weeds. Fat cattle, fine beasts, ate in the mythical pastures. Smooth roads ran between the farms. Dancing, shaking his body stiffly with the beat of the fiddle, Newt saw that Lester took his partner's hand lightly, that he gave equal courtesy to all the women, calling them ladies. He wanted to be as the teacher was, but he could not. The dance drawing to an end, he realized again that in two days more the teacher would go, for he had set his head upon some place far away, down in the settlements, among the lower counties from which he had come six months earlier.

There was pie for a treat, baked by Marthy Anne Sands and brought to the schoolhouse in a great hickory basket. Standing about eating the pie, all were quiet, regretting the teacher's going. Newt wove a variant path in and out among them, hearing the talk of the older men and women.

"My little tad, the least one, Becky, is plumb bereft over 'im," one said, a woman speaking.

"Last year at the school there wasn't hardly anybody would go, and look at this. I had to whop Joel to make him stay on the place one day to feed and water the property whilst I had to go. Hit [6/7] appears like Joel loves book-sense since Les Hunter come up the mountain."

"What makes you in such a swivet to go nohow?" one asked.

"Did you come up the gorge to borrow fire you're in such a swivet to get on?"

"There's a big meeten over to Kitty's branch next light moon.
Why don't you stay? No harm in you to be broguen about a small
spell."

"You could loafer around a spell and wait for the meeten."

"Big meeten. And nohow the meeten needs youens to help sing."

"What's he in such a swivet to go off for?"

"I got to go. I got to see the other end of the world yet."

"What's he a-sayen?"

"I got to go to the other end of the world."

"That's too far a piece."

"There surely undoubtedly is a right smart piece to go."

"He could stay a spell at my place and welcome. I'd be real proud
to have him stay with my folks a spell. And Nate, he'd keep youens a
week, that I right well know. Youens could loafer around awhile as
well as not." [7/8]

"He always earns his way and more, ever since he kem up the
mountain, always earns his keep, anyhow."

"I've got to go. I'm bound for the other end of this old globe. I'm
obliged all the same, but I got a heap to see yet. I'm bound to go."

Newt plowed the corn in the rocky field above the house where he
lived, one horse to the plow, or he hoed where the field lay steepest.
The teacher was gone now. On Sunday Newt would put on his clean
shirt his mother had washed on Friday, and climb up the gorge to
the head of the rise and meet there Tige English and Jonathan
Evans. Then they would go to see Lum Baker's girls. He would contrive to kiss each girl before the night fell and Lum would cry out:
"Come on, you gals now, and milk the cow brutes." Or sometimes
they would go down the way to see Corie Yancey and Ollie Mack.
To Newt all the place seemed still since the teacher had left, idle, as
if it had lost its uses and its future. Going to the well for water he
would stare at the winch, at the soft rot of the bucket, at the stones
inside the well curb, or he would listen [8/9] intently to the sounds
as the vessel struck the water or beat against the stones.

The noises gave him more than the mere report of a bucket falling into a well to get water; they gave him some comprehension of
all things that were yet unknown. The sounds, rich with tonality, as
the bucket struck the water, rang with some strange sonority and
throbbed with a beat that was like something he could not define,
some other, unlike fiddle playing but related to it in its unlikeness.
A report had come to him from an outside world and a suspicion of
more than he could know in his present state haunted him. He cried
out inwardly for the answer, or he looked about him and listened,

remembering all that he could of what Lester Hunter had taught—capitals of countries, seaports, buying and selling, nouns, verbs, numbers multiplied together to make other numbers. Now he looked intently and listened. He detected a throb in sound, but again there was a beat in the hot sun over a moist field. One day he thought that he had divined a throb in the numbers as he counted, a beat in the recurrences of kinds, but this evaded him. He listened and looked at the well happenings, at the house wall, [9/10] at the rail fence, at the barn, at the hills going upward toward the top of the gorge.

On every side were evasions. These sights and sounds could not give him enough; they lay flat against the air; they were imbedded within his own flesh and were sunk into his own sense of them. He would stare at the green and brown moss on the broken frame of the well box and stare again at the floating images in the dark of the well water. The rope would twine over the axle as he turned the wooden handle, and the rounds of the rope would fall into orderly place, side by side, as he knew too casually and too well. Since the teacher had gone the place had flattened to an intolerable staleness that gave out meager tokens of withheld qualities and beings—his mother leaning from the door to call him to dinner, his sister dragging his chair to the table and setting his cup beside his place, the old dog running out to bark at some varmint above in the brush. He could hardly separate the fall of his own bare foot from the rock door-step over which he had walked since he could first walk at all. His thirst and his water to drink were one now. His loneliness, as he sat to rest at noon beside the fence, merged and was identified with the still [10/11] country from brush-grown slope to brush-grown slope.

His father began to clear a new patch below the house; they grubbed at the roots all day when the corn was laid by. One morning in September, when the sun, moving south, was just getting free of Rattlesnake Hill, it came to him that he would go down to the settlements, that he would go to Merryman. All summer he had known that there was a school at Merryman, but he had not thought to go there, for he had no money. It came to him as a settled fact that he would go there and look at the place. Three high ridges with numberless breaks and gorges intervened; he had heard this said by men who knew or had heard of what lay beyond. The determination to set forth and the wish to go came to him at one instant. "My aim, hit's to go there," he said. "I lay off to do that—there, like I say."

He remembered the teacher more clearly at this moment, saw

him in a more sharply detailed picture; his own breath jerked
deeply inward as he was himself related, through his intended departure, to the picture. Hunter was remembered cutting wood for the
schoolhouse fire, sweethearting the girls and turning them lightly in
the dance, or [11/12] sitting by the fire at night, reading his book,
holding the page low to the blaze. He was remembered hallooing
back up the mountain the day he left, his voice calling back as he
went down the ridge and he himself answering until there was not
even a faint hollow whoopee to come up the slope. By the fire Newt
had often taken Hunter's book into his hands, but he could never
read the strange words nor in any way know what they meant when
they were read, for they had stood four-square and hostile against
his understanding. His father's voice would fall dully over the slow
clearing: "You could work on this here enduren the while that I cut
the corn patch."

He knew that he would go. His determination rejected the clearing, knowing that he would be gone before the corn was ready to
cut. It rejected the monotonous passing of the days, the clutter of
feet on the stones by the door, the dull, inconspicuous corn patch
above. He would walk, taking the short cut over the mountains.
Two ridges to go and then there would be a road for his feet, some
one had said. He announced his plan to his father one day while
they leaned over their grub hoes. There was no willigness offered,
but his mind was set, and three days later he had established his
[12/13] plan. His mother had washed his shirts clean and had
rolled them into a bundle with his spare socks, and she had baked
him bread and a joint of ham. She and his sister stood by the doorway weeping after he had driven back the dog and had shouted his
goodbye.

It was a mid-afternoon and the sun beat down into the cove where
he traveled. He worked his way through the thick-set laurel, struggling to keep his bundle tied to his shoulders where the brush stood
most dense.

The dry clatter of the higher boughs came to his ears, but it was
so mingled with the pricking snarls of the twigs on his face that the
one sense was not divided from the other. "This durned ivy," he said
when the laurel held him back. He matched his strength against
boughs or he flashed his wits against snarls and rebounds, hot and
weary, tingling with sweat and with the pricking twigs. Pushed back
at one place where he tried to find an opening, he assailed another
and then another, throwing all his strength angrily against the brush
and tearing himself through the mesh with *god-damns* of relief. A
large shaded stone that bulged [13/14] angrily out of the mountain-

side gave him a space of rest. He stretched himself on the slanting
rock, his face away from the sun, and lay for an hour, thinking nothing, feeling the weariness as it beat heavily upon his limbs.

"I'm bodaciously tired," he said, after a long period of torpor.
"Could I come by a spring branch, I'd drink me a whole durned
quart of it."

Another tree-grown mountain arose across the cove, misty now in
the afternoon and in the first haze of autumn, and beyond lay other
blue mountains, sinking farther and farther into the air. Back of
him it was the same; he had been on the way two weeks now. Before
him he knew each one would be dense with laurel until he came to
the wagon road. He took to the pathless way after his hour of rest,
going forward. When the sun was setting behind Bee Gum Mountain, he saw a house down in the cove, not far as the crow would fly
but the distance of two hours' going for him. When he saw the cabin
he began to sing, chanting:

> Right hands across and howdy-do,
> Left and back and how are you.
>
> Oh, call up yo' dog, oh, call up yo' dog,
> Ring twang a-whoddle lanky day. [14/15]

The sight of the house quickened his desire for Merryman and the
cities and counties in the settlements, and this desire had become
more definite in his act of going. His wish was for sure, quick gestures and easy sayings that would come from the mouth as easily as
breath. There were for him other things, as yet unrelated to any one
place—men playing ball with a great crowd to watch, all the crowd
breaking into a laugh at one time; men racing fine horses on a hard,
smooth track; music playing; men having things done by machinery;
lovely girls not yet imagined; and things to know beyond anything
he could recall, and not one of them too fine or too good for him.
He sang as he went down the slope, his song leaping out of him. He
had heard it said that the lights of Merryman could be seen from
Coster Ridge on a clear night, and Coster was now visible standing
up in the pale air, for a man had pointed him the way that morning.
Singing, he set himself toward the house at the bottom of the cove.

Night was falling when he called "Hello" at the foot of Bee Gum
Mountain. The man of the house asked his name and told his own,
making him welcome. Supper was over, but the host, whose name
was Tom Bland, ordered Nance, his [15/16] woman, to give the
stranger a snack of biscuit bread and bacon, and this Newt ate sitting beside the fire. Another stranger was sitting in the cabin, an old
man who kept very still while Nance worked with the utensils, his
dim eyes looking into the fire or eyeing Newt, who stared back and

searched the looks of the stranger. Then Tom told Nance how they would sleep that night, telling her to give the old man her place in the bed beside himself.

"You could get in bed along with the young ones," he said to her. "The boy here, he could sleep on a shakedown alongside the fireplace."

From gazing into the fire the old stranger would fall asleep, but after a moment he would awake, opening dim, ashamed eyes that glanced feebly at Newt, faintly defying him. Then Nance put some children to bed, her own perhaps, and sat quietly in the corner of the hearth, her hands in her lap. Newt had looked at the host, acquainting himself with him. He was a strong man, far past youth, large boned and broad-muscled. His heavy feet scraped on the floor when he moved from his chair to the water bucket on the window sill. Newt saw that he on his side had been silently searching out the old stranger. After a while the host and the old man began to talk, Tom speaking first.

"There's a sight of travel now."

"Hit's a moven age."

Between each speech there was a slow pause as each saying was carefully probed before the reply was offered.

Tom said: "Two in one night, and last week there was one come by." And then after a while he asked: "Where might youens be bound for, stranger?"

"I'm on my way back," the man said.

There was a long season of quiet. The ideas were richly interspersed with action, for Nance softly jolted back and forth in her chair, her bare feet tapping lightly on the boards of the floor.

"You been far?" Tom asked.

"I been a right far piece. I been to the settle-ments in Froman county, and then I been to the mines around Tateville and Beemen."

Newt bit nervously at his knuckles and looked at the man, taking from him these signs of the world. The fire burned low, and breaking the long silence Tom said once or twice: "There's a sight of travel now." Newt looked at the old man's feet in their patched shoes, feet that had walked the [17/18] streets in towns. Indefinite wonders touched the man's feet, his crumpled knees, and his crooked hands that were spread on his lap.

Then Tom said: "Froman, I reckon that's a prime good place to be now."

"Hit may be so, but I wouldn't be-nasty my feet with the dust of hit no longer. Nor any other place down there. I'm on my way back."

The old man's voice quavered over his words toward the close of this speech, and after a little while he added, his voice lifted: "Hit's a far piece back, but a man has a rather about where he'd like to be." Finally, he spoke in great anger, his arm raised and his hand threatening: "I've swat my last drop of sweat in that-there country and eat my last meal's victuals. A man has a rather as to the place he likes to be."

This thought lay heavily over the fireplace, shared by all but uncomprehended by Nance, whose skin was rich with blood and life. She sat complacently rocking back and forth in her small chair.

After the long quiet which surrounded this thought the old man began to speak softly, having spent his passion: "I'm on my way back. I been in a study a long time about goen back but seems like [18/19] I couldn't make hit to go. Work was terrible pressen. But now I'm on my way back where I was borned and my mammy and pappy before me. I was a plumb traitor to my God when I left the mountains and come to the settle-ments. Many is the day I'd study about that-there and many is the night I lay awake to study about the way back over Coster Ridge, on past Bear Mountain, past Hog Run, past Little Pine Tree, up and on past Louse Run, up, then on over Long Ridge and up into Laurel, into Grady Creek and on up the branch, past the Flat Rock, past the saw-mill, past the grove of he-balsams, and then the smoke a comen outen the chimney and the door open and old Nomie's pup a-comen down the road to meet me. I'd climb the whole way whilst I was a-layen there, in my own mind I would, and I'd see the ivy as plain as you'd see your hand afore your face, and the coves and the he-balsams. In my own mind I'd go back, a step at a time, Coster, Bear Mountain and the Bee Gum, Little Pine Tree, Louse Run, Grady, and I'd see the rocks in the way to go, and a log stretched out in my way maybe. I wouldn't make hit too easy to go. Past Bear Mountain, past Hog Run and the cove, scratchen my way through ivy brush. Then I'd [19/20] come to myself and there I'd be, a month's travel from as much as a sight of the Flat Rock, and I'd groan and shake and turn over again. I was a traitor to my God."

Nance laid a little stick on the fire, with a glance at Tom, he allowing it without protest. Then she sat back in her stiff chair with a quick movement, her bare feet light on the boards. The old man was talking again.

"Where my mammy was borned before me and her manny and daddy before again. And no water in all Froman or Tateville but dead pump waters, no freestone like you'd want. How could a man expect to live? Many's the night I've said, could I be on the shady

side of the Flat Rock, up past the saw-mill, up past the grove of he-
balsams, where the spring branch runs out over the horse-shoe rock,
and could I get me one drink of that-there cold crystal water I'd ask
ne'er thing more of God Almighty in life."

"I know that-there very spring branch," Newt now said. He was
eager to enter the drama of the world, and his time now had come.
"I know that-there very place. You come to a rock set on end
[20/21] and a hemlock bush set off to the right, she-balsams all off
to the left like."

"Mankind, that's just how hit's set. I believe you been right
there!"

"A mountain goes straight up afore you as you stand, say this-here
is the spring, and the water comes out and runs off over a horse-shoe
rock."

"Mankind, that's just how hit's set. I do believe you know that-
there very place. You say hit's there just the same?"

"I got me a drink at that-there very spring branch Tuesday 'twas a
week ago."

"You drank them waters!" And then he said after a period of wonder: "To think you been to that very spring branch! You been
there!"

"We can burn another stick," Tom said, as if in honor of the
strange event, and Nance mended the fire again. Outside Newt
heard dogs howling far up the slope and some small beast cried.

"To think you been there! You are a-setten right now in hearen of
my voice and yet a Tuesday 'twas a week ago you was in the spot I
call home. Hit's hard to study over. You come down the mountain
fast. That country is powerful hard goen."

"Yes, I come right fast."[21/22]

"I couldn't make hit back in twice the time and more. Hard goen
it was. What made you travel so hard, young man?"

"I'm a-maken hit toward the settle-ments."

"And what you think to find in the settle-ments, God knows!
What you think to see, young man?"

"Learnen. I look to find learnen in the settle-ments."

In the pause that followed the old man gazed at the hearth as if
he were looking into time, into all qualities, and he fell momentar-
ily asleep under the impact of his gaze. But presently he looked at
Newt and said: "And to think you tasted them waters Tuesday
'twas a week ago!"

"You come to a rock set on end, and here's the hemlock off to the
right like, and here to the left goes the gorge."

The old man was asleep, his eyes falling away before the fire. But
he waked suddenly and said with kindling eyes, his hand uplifted:

"You come from there at a master pace, young man, come from the place I hope to see if God Almighty sees fitten to bless me afore I lay me down and die. You walked, I reckon, right over the spot I pined to see a many is the year, God knows, and it was nothing to you, but take care, the places you [22/23] knowed when you was a little shirt-tail boy won't go outen your head or outen your recollections."

Then he said, another outbreak after a long pause, his hand again uplifted: "I reckon you relish learnen, young man, and take a delight in hit, and set a heap of store by the settle-ments. But the places you knowed when you was a little tad, they won't go outen your remembrance. Your insides is made that way, and made outen what you did when you was a shirt-tail boy, and you'll find it's so. Your dreams of a night and all you pine to see will go back. You won't get shed so easy of hit. You won't get shed."

Newt looked into the fire and a terror grew into his thought. He saw minutely the moss on the well curb and the shapes in which it grew, and saw the three stones that lay beside the well, that lifted his feet out of the mud. The sound made by the bucket in the well as it rocked from wall to wall, as it finally struck the water, rolled acutely backward into his inner hearing. He saw the rope twine over the beam as he turned the wooden handle, drawing the full bucket to the top. Three long steps then to the door of the house, the feel of the filled bucket drawing at his arm. Up the loft ladder to his room, his hands drawing up his [23/24] body, the simple act of climbing, of emerging from some lower place to a higher, and he was buried in the act, submerged in a deep sense of it.

"You may go far and see a heap of life," the old stranger said, slowly, defiantly prophetic, "you may go far, but mark me as I say it, the places you knowed when you was a little tad will be the strongest in your remembrance. It's true, whoever you are and whatever land you come from. Your whole insides is made outen what you done first."

Newt saw in terror what he saw as he gazed into the sinking embers. His mother calling him from the house door, calling him to come to his dinner, her hand uplifted to the door frame. His sister, a little girl, dragging his chair in place and pushing his cup up against the plate. His tears for them dimmed the fire to a vague, red, quivering glow. The floating images in the dark of the well water, the bright light of the sky in the middle as a picture in a frame, and his own head looking into the heart of the picture—these were between him and the fire, moving more inwardly and dragging himself with them as they went. He was bereft, divided, emptied of his every wish, and he gazed at the fire, scarcely seeing it.

There was moving in the room, figures making [24/25] a dim passage of shadows behind him. Presently he knew that the old man had gone to his sleeping place and that Nance was spreading quilts on the floor to the side of the fireplace. Her strong body was pleasant to sense as she flung out the covers and pulled them into line, and a delight in the strange room, the strange bed, welled over him. His breath was then set to a fluted rhythm as he drew suddenly inward a rich flood of air, a rhythm flowing deeply until it touched the core of his desire for the settlements, laid an amorous pulse on his determination to go there. Learning was the word he cherished and kept identified with his quickened breath. He remembered that the lights of Merryman and the settlements would be brightly dusted over the low valley when he reached Coster.

By the end of the week he would, his eager breath told him, be looking down on to the farther valleys. [25]

3

The Yeoman and the American Political Character

WHILE THE PLACE of agriculture in the wealth of nations was an issue that caused much debate in Europe during the eighteenth century, in America the issue became complexly and inextricably interwoven in the very political fabric of the nation. It is most clearly seen in the early party battle, following the creation of the Constitution, between the Federalist and Agrarian forces led respectively by Hamilton and Jefferson. The Federalists, on the one hand, favored a strong, highly centralized federal government, controlled by a propertied few, with the support of commercial and industrial expansion. The Republicans, on the other hand, favored a reliance on local government, under the leadership of a natural aristocracy of talent and virtue, with a primarily agrarian national economy based on small, independent farmers and landholders. The one viewed man as basically selfish, perverse, corrupt, and in need of an authoritarian control, while the other viewed him as rational, trustworthy, perfectible, and in need of minimal authority.

Both Hamilton and Jefferson were willing to concede that agriculture and industrialism were important components of the national economy; the question was which was to receive government patronage or to become the dominant form of activity that would engage the majority of the laboring populace. It is to this issue that the letters and essays included here by Jefferson, Franklin, Hamilton, Taylor, and Cooper speak. The tensions of their debate were to reverberate down to and beyond the Civil War, and while Jefferson's democratic theories were largely to prevail in the political sphere, Hamilton's industrial program was to prevail in the economic sphere as America realized the extent of its natural resources and looked to capitalism to exploit them. George Fitzhugh, the vigorous and influential pro-slavery exponent, suggests in some excerpts from *Canni-*

107

bals All! the extent to which the Northern industrial society and
the agrarian South were alienated before the war, and offers interesting sidelights in his unusual defense of the slave system as one in
which white men are freed from the, to him, odious tasks of agricultural labor, and in which a humane form of socialism is practiced.

A matter of primary importance in Jeffersonian agrarian thought
was the matter of property. To the agrarians, as to John Locke before them, land was the common stock of society and a man's right
to title and ownership could result only from occupancy and use. By
use, they meant the land was to be rendered productive by cultivation, by the mixing of sweat and labor with the soil. This application of the philosophy of natural rights to land tenure led to the
theory that the working landholder had a right to special protection
by the state. The small farm was the best foundation for economic
security and fostered the virtues of independence and self-reliance.
Thus, for Jefferson, the farmers were "the most precious part of the
state." To James Fenimore Cooper, property was the foundation of
civilization—"its existence and security are indispensable to social
improvement"—although its rights may be abused, if for example it
becomes the sole test for franchise. In the same spirit, Whitman declared in *Democratic Vistas,* "The true gravitation-hold of liberalism
in the United States will be a more universal ownership of property," and the future of national unity rests upon "the safety and endurance of the aggregate of its middling property owners." Andrew
Carnegie, one of America's most successful industrialists, was a firm
advocate of the sanctity of American property and declared in
Triumphant Democracy, "To say the soil is owned and cultivated by
the people is to dispel all doubts as to the stability, the peace, and
the prosperity of the State." Attempting to prove in that book that
republican institutions were superior to monarchical in success and
prosperity, Carnegie gathered together sufficient statistics on agriculture in the 1880's to paint a rosy picture of American farming and
paid homage to the agrarian art, "the prime divinity of the Republic."

To Henry George, however, the concept of private property in the
land was at the root of the obvious inequality, the great disparity
between progress and poverty, that he observed in late nineteenth-
century America despite Carnegie's assurance of prosperity. George
agreed with Jefferson in his desire for equal rights for all and special
privileges for none, but while he believed that man has a natural
right to inhabit the earth, the privilege of private ownership, combined with the increasing value of land, led to the propagation of a
new breed of owners—absentee landholders who dealt in land speculation and reaped the profits of unearned increment from rent,

mortgage interest, and property resale value. George's solution, offered in his book *Progress and Poverty,* was a very ingenious but overly simple one: declare all land common property, permit the individuals who now claim land to retain possession of it, and then appropriate by taxation the rent and unearned increment that accrues to them by virtue of their possession. This is his theory of the single tax—the abolition of all taxation, save that on land values, which he felt would prove sufficient to support the government and remove the gravest cause of economic injustice. George's proposal never earned a trial, but others were equally aware of the drab, tragic lives of those who lived under the economic serfdom imposed by greedy land speculators, as was Garland in his powerful short story "Under the Lion's Paw," which argues the case for the agricultural victims of unearned increment more eloquently than George's entire book.

George's diagnosis of the problem of the farmers in 1879 pointed to but one of the many problems they were facing in the decades following the Civil War. While farm acreage doubled in America between 1860 and 1900, and science and technology was applied to agricultural improvement, the small farmers were unable to compete with the larger combines, and many perished in the face of soil exhaustion, staple crop overproduction, a decline in financial self-sufficiency, and inadequate legislative protection. In an attempt to help themselves, several Southern and Western farmers' associations began in 1889 to merge in the organization of a third political party —the People's, or later Populist Party. While it attracted a degree of support from industrial labor, with whom it hoped for a political alliance, it remained primarily a sectional agrarian organization and failed to succeed in the political arena. Two excellent documents which reflect the Populist mind and spirit are Nelson A. Dunning's "Introductory History" in his *Farmer's Alliance History* and the Populist Party platform drawn up at Omaha in 1892, largely written by the colorful, eloquent reformer and author of Utopian novels, Ignatius Donnelly.

The most notable statement in support of an agrarian economy in this century was issued on the eve of the Depression in 1930 by a group of twelve Southerners, which included some of the finest creative talents in modern literature, in their symposium *I'll Take My Stand.* Among the Southern Agrarians were John Crowe Ransom, Donald Davidson, Allen Tate, Robert Penn Warren, Andrew Lytle, and Stark Young, themselves forming a brilliant nucleus of American writers. Aware of the devotion to materialism, science, and technology in the national culture, they felt that the South had the potential for resisting the domination of the machine by maintaining an agricultural economy. Although the Old South was backward in some respects, they said, it had nurtured a society in which spiritual and aesthetic experience was possible, and this because of its agrarian heritage. In such a life, they believed, might be found the needed corrective for American materialism and pursuit of progress without humanistic values. Thus, as poets and citizens, the Southern Agrarians spoke out, as Davidson reports in his brief history of the group, for "the rehabilitation of the farmer," for "legislation that will deprive the giant corporation of its privilege of irresponsibility," and for "a revision of our political framework that will permit regional governments to function adequately." In this group, Jefferson had his latest agrarian disciples, who even in the phraseology of their common "Statement of Principles" reflected the spirit of the Jeffersonian style: "The theory of agrarianism is that the culture of the soil is the best and most sensitive of vocations, and that therefore it should have the economic preference and enlist the maximum number of workers." While the movement had little impact on the nation's economic or political life, in their common and later separate creative endeavors, its members did achieve a recognition of the importance of a sense of humanistic values and traditions in modern culture and reaffirmed the aesthetic and spiritual needs of man. They also issued an early forewarning of the development of alarming trends in our industrial society towards conformity, alienation, and dehumanization, which later social analysts have confirmed.

As the nation entered the Depression era, conditions of life and labor on the farm grew worse: farmers were plagued with unemployment, poor housing, ill health, insufficient education, and general insecurity. There was a continuing decrease in the proportion of operating owners and a sharp increase in the proportion of sharecroppers and tenant farmers. In some states in 1937, as much as four-fifths of the cultivated land was in the hands of landlords and mortgage holders. Something of the tragedy of the farmer's plight is captured in Sherwood Anderson's poignant sketch "Blue Smoke," especially as it affected tobacco growers in the South. Many rural politicians attempted to build careers by courting the farmers' support with promises of relief. Such a man was the colorful, clever Louisiana demagogue Huey P. Long, whose Share-the-Wealth program promised to make "Every Man a King" with a guaranteed minimum income of $5,000 for each family. His stock in trade was an earthy, boisterous, coarse appeal to the rural rednecks, and he threatened to play it right into the White House before an assassin stopped him with a bullet. Whether he really had the problems of the common man at heart is an unresolvable puzzle, although he achieved some good ends with the most corrupt means.

The one man who emerged during the Depression to provide immediate aid to the nation and the farmer was Franklin D. Roosevelt. Placing top priority on the condition of the independent farmer, Roosevelt provided aid on an unprecedented scale with the subsidy of crop prices, programs of credit, crop insurance, market controls, soil conservation, tariffs, and import quotas. In his message to Congress on farm tenancy on February 16, 1937, Roosevelt harked back to the Jeffersonian concept of the small family farm as essential to the development of the best democratic virtues:

> The American dream of the family-sized farm, owned by the family which operates it, has become more and more remote. . . . When fully half the total farm population of the United States no longer can feel secure, when millions of our people have lost their roots in the soil, action to provide security is imperative, and will generally be approved.

While Roosevelt shared Jeffersons' ardent concern for and confidence in the common man, and enacted effective legislation to restore his economic security, he violated the early statesman's principle that the best government is the one which governs least. The elaborate bureaucracy and welfare programs he found necessary to achieve his goals created a powerful federal authority more akin to what Hamilton desired. For good or ill, Roosevelt established trends in our economic and political life which are not likely to be counteracted in our time.

Throughout our political history, the yeoman has played an influential role, and the proposition still persists that the survival of the democratic state requires the preservation of the small, independent, family-operated farm, that both democracy and the agricultural community are dependent on each other and face the common threats of industrialism and collectivism. That this idea remains with us is attributable to the profound influence of Jefferson, for whom agrarianism and democracy were synonymous, and for whom the family farm was the most perfect expression of the American way of life.

THOMAS JEFFERSON

Letters

TO JEAN BAPTISTE SAY

WASHINGTON, February 1, 1804.

DEAR SIR,—I have to acknowledge the receipt of your obliging letter, and with it, of two very interesting volumes on Political Economy. These found me engaged in giving the leisure moments I rarely find, to the perusal of Malthus' work on population, a work of sound logic, in which some of the opinions of Adam Smith, as well as of the economists, are ably examined. I was pleased, on turning to some chapters where you treat the same questions, to find his opinions corroborated by yours. I shall proceed to the reading of your work with great pleasure. In the meantime, the present conveyance, by a gentleman of my family going to Paris, is too safe to hazard a delay in making my acknowledgments for this mark of attention, and for having [1/2] afforded to me a satisfaction, which the ordinary course of literary communications could not have given me for a considerable time.

The differences of circumstance between this and the old countries of Europe, furnish differences of fact whereon to reason, in questions of political economy, and will consequently produce sometimes a difference of result. There, for instance, the quantity of food is fixed, or increasing in a slow and only arithmetical ratio, and the proportion is limited by the same ratio. Supernumerary births consequently add only to your mortality. Here the immense extent of uncultivated and fertile lands enables every one who will labor, to marry young, and to raise a family of any size. Our food, then, may increase geometrically with our laborers, and our births, however multiplied, become effective. Again, there the best distribution of labor is supposed to be that which places the manufacturing hands

From *The Writings of Thomas Jefferson,* edited by Andrew A. Lipscomb and Albert Ellery Bergh, Library Edition (Washington: Thomas Jefferson Memorial Association of the United States, 1904), XI, 1–3, 55–56, alongside the agricultural; so that the one part shall feed both, and the other part furnish both with clothes and other comforts. Would that be best here? Egoism and first appearances say yes. Or would it be better that all our laborers should be employed in agriculture? In this case a double or treble portion of fertile lands would be brought into culture; a double or treble creation of food be produced, and its surplus go to nourish the now perishing births of Europe, who in return would manufacture and send us in exchange our clothes and other [2/3] comforts. Morality listens to this, and so invariably do the laws of nature create our duties and interests, that when they seem to be at variance, we ought to suspect some fallacy in our reasonings. In solving this question, too, we should allow its just weight to the moral and physical preference of the agricultural, over the manufacturing, man. My occupations permit me only to ask questions. They deny me the time, if I had the information, to answer them. Perhaps, as worthy the attention of the author of the *Traité d'Economie Politique,* I shall find them answered in that work. If they are not, the reason will have been that you wrote for Europe; while I shall have asked them because I think for America. Accept, Sir, my respectful salutations, and assurances of great consideration. [3]

TO MR. LITHSON

WASHINGTON, January 4, 1805

DEAR SIR,—Your favor of December 4th has been duly received. Mr. Duane informed me that he meant to publish a new edition of the Notes on Virginia, and I had in contemplation some particular alterations which would require little time to make. My occupations by no means permit me at this time to revise the text, and make those changes in it which I should now do. I should in that case certainly qualify several expressions in the nineteenth chapter, which have been construed differently from what they were intended. I had under my eye, when writing, the manufacturers of the great cities in the old countries, at the time present, with whom the want of food and clothing necessary to sustain life, has begotten a depravity of morals, a dependence and corruption, which renders them an undesirable accession to a country whose morals are sound. My expressions looked forward to the time when our own great cities would get into the same state. But they have been quoted as if meant for the present time here. As yet our manufacturers are as much at their ease, as independent and moral as our agricultural inhabitants, and they will continue so as long as there are vacant lands for them to

resort to; because whenever it shall be attempted by the other classes
to reduce them to the minimum of subsistence, they will quit their
trades and go to laboring the earth. A [55/56] first question is,
whether it is desirable for us to receive at present the dissolute and
demoralized handicraftsmen of the old cities of Europe? A second
and more difficult one is, when even good handicraftsmen arrive
here, is it better for them to set up their trade, or go to the culture
of the earth? Whether their labor in their trade is worth more than
their labor on the soil, increased by the creative energies of the
earth? Had I time to revise that chapter, this question should be discussed, and other views of the subject taken, which are presented by
the wonderful changes which have taken place here since 1781, when
the Notes on Virginia were written. Perhaps when I retire, I may
amuse myself with a serious review of this work; at present it is out
of the question. Accept my salutations and good wishes. [56]

BENJAMIN FRANKLIN

The Internal State of America; Being a True Description of the Interest and Policy of That Vast Continent, 1799

THERE IS a tradition, that, in the planting of New England, the first settlers met with many difficulties and hardships as is generally the case when a civilized people attempt establishing themselves in a wilderness country. Being piously dispos'd, they sought relief from heaven, by laying their wants and distresses before the Lord, in frequent set days of fasting and prayer. Constant meditation and discourse on these subjects kept their minds gloomy and discontented; and, like the children of Israel, there were many dispos'd to return to that Egypt, which persecution had induc'd them to abandon. At length, when it was proposed in the assembly to proclaim another fast, a farmer of plain sense rose, and remark'd, that the inconveniencies they suffer'd, and concerning which they had so often weary'd heaven with their complaints, were not so great as they [116/117] might have expected, and were diminishing every day, as the colony strengthen'd; that the earth began to reward their labour, and to furnish liberally for their subsistence; and the seas and rivers were full of fish, the air sweet, the climate healthy; and, above all, that they were there in the full enjoyment and liberty, civil and religious. He therefore thought, that reflecting and conversing on these subjects would be more comfortable, as tending more to make them contented with their situation; and that it would be more becoming the gratitude they ow'd to the Divine Being, if, instead of a fast, they should proclaim a thanksgiving. His advice was taken; and from that day to this they have, in every year, observ'd circumstances of public felicity sufficient to furnish employment for a *Thanksgiving Day;* which is therefore constantly ordered and religiously observed.

From *The Writings of Benjamin Franklin,* edited by Albert Henry Smyth (New York: The Macmillan Company, 1907), X, 116–122.

I see in the public papers of different states frequent complaints of *hard times, deadness of trade, scarcity of money,* &c. It is not my intention to assert or maintain, that these complaints are intirely without foundation. There can be no country or nation existing, in which there will not be some people so circumstanced, as to find it hard to gain a livelihood; people who are not in the way of any profitable trade, and with whom money is scarce, because they have nothing to give in exchange for it; and it is always in the power of a small number to make a great clamour. But let us take a cool view of the general state of our affairs, and perhaps the prospect will appear less gloomy than has been imagined.

The great business of the continent is agriculture. For one artisan, or merchant, I suppose, we have at least 100 [117/118] farmers, by far the greatest part cultivators of their own fertile lands, from whence many of them draw, not only the food necessary for their subsistance, but the materials of their clothing, so as to have little occasion for foreign supplies; while they have a surplus of productions to dispose of, whereby wealth is gradually accumulated. Such has been the goodness of Divine Providence to these regions, and so favourable the climate, that, since the three or four years of hardship in the first settlement of our fathers here, a famine or scarcity has never been heard of among us; on the contrary, tho' some years may have been more, and others less plentiful, there has always been provision enough for ourselves, and quantity to spare for exportation. And altho' the crops of last year were generally good, never was the farmer better paid for the part he can spare commerce, as the published price-currents abundantly testify. The lands he possesses are also continually rising in value with the increase of population; and, on the whole, he is enabled to give such good wages to those who work for him, that all who are acquainted with the old world must agree, that in no part of it are the labouring poor so well fed, well cloth'd, well lodg'd, and well paid, as in the United States of America.

If we enter the cities, we find, that, since the Revolution, the owners of houses and lots of ground have had their interest vastly augmented in value; rents have risen to an astonishing height, and thence encouragement to encrease building, which gives employment to an abundance of workmen, as does also the encreas'd luxury and splendor of living of the inhabitants, thus made richer. These work-men all demand and obtain much higher wages than any [118/119] other part of the world would afford them, and are paid in ready money. This rank of people therefore do not, or ought not, to complain of hard times; and they make a very considerable part of the city inhabitants.

At the distance I live from our American fisheries, I cannot speak of them with any certainty; but I have not heard, that the labour of the valuable race of men employ'd in them is worse paid, or that they meet with less success, than before the Revolution. The whalemen indeed have been depriv'd of one market for their oil; but another, I hear, is opening for them, which it is hoped may be equally advantageous; and the demand is constantly encreasing for their spermaceti candles, which therefore bear a much higher price than formerly.

There remain the merchants and shopkeepers. Of these, tho' they make but a small part of the whole nation, the number is considerable, too great indeed for the business they are employ'd in: for the consumption of goods in every country, has its limits; the faculties of the people, that is, their ability to buy and pay, being equal only to a certain quantity of merchandize. If merchants calculate amiss on this proportion, and import too much, they will of course find the sale dull for the overplus, and some of them will say, that trade languishes. They should, and doubtless will, grow wiser by experience, and import less. If too many artificers in town, and farmers from the country, flattering themselves with the idea of leading easier lives, turn shopkeepers, the whole natural quantity of business divided among them all may afford too small a share for each, and occasion complaints, that trading is dead; these may also suppose, that it is owing to scarcity of money, [119/120] while, in fact, it is not so much from the fewness of buyers, as from the excessive number of sellers, that the mischief arises; and, if every shop-keeping farmer and mechanic would return to the use of his plough and working-tools, there would remain of widows, and other women, shop-keepers sufficient for that business, which might then afford them a comfortable maintenance.

Whoever has travelled thro' the various parts of Europe, and observed how small is the proportion of people in affluence or easy circumstances there, compar'd with those in poverty and misery; the few rich and haughty landlords, the multitude of poor, abject, and rack'd tenants, and the half-paid and half-starv'd ragged labourers; and views here the happy mediocrity, that so generally prevails throughout these states, where the cultivator works for himself, and supports his family in decent plenty, will, methinks, see abundant reason to bless Divine Providence for the evident and great difference in our favour, and be convinc'd, that no nation that is known to us enjoys a greater share of human felicity.

It is true, that in some of the states there are parties and discords; but let us look back, and ask if we were ever without them? Such will exist wherever there is liberty; and perhaps they help to preserve it. By the collision of different sentiments, sparks of truth are struck out, and political light is obtained. The different factions, which at present divide us, aim all at the publick good; the differences are only about the various modes of promoting it. Things, actions, measures, and objects of all kinds, present themselves to the minds of men in such a variety of lights, that it is not possible we should all think alike at the same time on [120/121] every subject, when hardly the same man retains at all times the same ideas of it. Parties are therefore the common lot of humanity; and ours are by no means more mischievous or less beneficial than those of other countries, nations, and ages, enjoying in the same degree the great blessing of political liberty.

Some indeed among us are not so much griev'd for the present state of our affairs, as apprehensive for the future. The growth of luxury alarms them, and they think we are from that alone in the high road to ruin. They observe, that no revenue is sufficient without economy, and that the most plentiful income of a whole people from the natural productions of their country may be dissipated in vain and needless expences, and poverty be introduced in the place of affluence. This may be possible. It however rarely happens; for there seems to be in every nation a greater proportion of industry and frugality, which tend to enrich, than of idleness and prodigality, which occasion poverty; so that upon the whole there is a continual accumulation. Reflect what Spain, Gaul, Germany, and Britain were in the time of the Romans, inhabited by people little richer than our savages, and consider the wealth they at present possess, in numerous well-built cities, improv'd farms, rich moveables, magazines stor'd with valuable manufactures, to say nothing of plate, jewels, and ready money; and all this, notwithstanding their bad, wasteful, plundering governments, and their mad, destructive wars; and yet luxury and extravagant living have never suffered much restraint in those countries. Then consider the great proportion of industrious frugal farmers inhabiting the interior part of these American states, and of whom the body of our nation [121/122] consists; and judge whether it is probable the luxury of our seaports can be sufficient to ruin such a country. If the importation of foreign luxuries could ruin a people, we should probably have been ruin'd long ago; for the British nation claim'd a right, and practis'd it, of importing among us, not only the superfluities of their own production, but those of every nation under heaven; we bought and consum'd them, and yet we fluorish'd and grew rich. At present, our independent governments may do what we could not then do, discourage by heavy duties, or prevent by prohibitions, such importations, and thereby grow richer; if, indeed, which may admit of dispute, the desire of adorning ourselves with fine cloaths, possessing fine furniture, with good houses, &c., is not, by strongly inciting to labour and industry, the occasion of producing a greater value, than is consum'd in the gratification of that desire.

The agriculture and fisheries of the United States are the great sources of our encreasing wealth. He that puts a seed into the earth is recompens'd, perhaps, by receiving twenty out of it; and he who draws a fish out of our waters, draws up a piece of silver.

Let us (and there is no doubt but we shall) be attentive to these, and then the power of rivals, with all their restraining and prohibiting acts, cannot much hurt us. We are the sons of the earth and seas, and, like Antaeus, if, in wrestling with Hercules, we now and then receive a fall, the touch of our parents will communicate to us fresh strength and ability to renew the contest. Be quiet and thankful.
[122]

ALEXANDER HAMILTON

Report on Manufactures

COMMUNICATED TO THE HOUSE OF REPRESENTATIVES, DECEMBER 5, 1791

THE SECRETARY of the Treasury, in obedience to the order of the House of Representatives, of the 15th day of January, 1790, has applied his attention, at as early a period as his other duties would permit, to the subject of Manufactures, and particularly to the means of promoting such as will tend to render the United States independent on foreign nations for military and other essential supplies; and he there-upon respectfully submits the following report:

The expediency of encouraging manufactures in the United States, which was not long since deemed very questionable, appears at this time to be pretty generally admitted. The embarrassments which have obstructed the progress of our external trade, have led to serious reflections on the necessity of enlarging the sphere of our domestic commerce. The restrictive regulations, which, in foreign markets, abridge the vent of the increasing surplus of our agricultural produce, serve to beget an earnest desire that a more extensive demand for that surplus may be created at home; and the complete success which has rewarded manufacturing enterprise in some valuable branches, conspiring with the promising symptoms which attend some less mature essays in others, justify a hope that the obstacles to the growth of this [70/71] species of industry are less formidable than they were apprehended to be, and that it is not difficult to find, in its further extension, a full indemnification for any external disadvantages, which are or may be experienced, as well as an accession of resources, favorable to national independence and safety.

There are still, nevertheless, respectable patrons of opinions unfriendly to the encouragement of manufactures. The following are, substantially, the arguments by which these opinions are defended:

From *The Works of Alexander Hamilton,* edited by Henry Cabot Lodge, Federal Edition (New York and London: G. P. Putnam's Sons, 1904), IV, 70–73, 83–86.

"In every country (say those who entertain them) agriculture is the most beneficial and productive object of human industry. This position, generally if not universally true, applies with peculiar emphasis to the United States, on account of their immense tracts of fertile territory, uninhabited and unimproved. Nothing can afford so advantageous an employment for capital and labor, as the conversion of this extensive wilderness into cultivated farms. Nothing, equally with this, can contribute to the population, strength, and real riches of the country.

"To endeavor, by the extraordinary patronage of government, to accelerate the growth of manufactures, is, in fact, to endeavor, by force and art, to transfer the natural current of industry from a more to a less beneficial channel. Whatever has such a tendency, must necessarily be unwise; indeed, it can hardly ever be wise in a government to attempt to give a direction to the industry of its citizens. This, under the quick-sighted guidance of private interest, will, if left to itself, infallibly find its own way to the most profitable employment; and it is by such employment, [71/72] that the public prosperity will be most effectually promoted. To leave industry to itself, therefore, is, in almost every case, the soundest as well as the simplest policy.

"This policy is not only recommended to the United States, by considerations which affect all nations; it is, in a manner, dictated to them by the imperious force of a very peculiar situation. The smallness of their population compared with their territory; the constant allurements to emigration from the settled to the unsettled parts of the country; the facility with which the less independent condition of an artisan can be exchanged for the more independent condition of a farmer;—these, and similar causes, conspire to produce, and, for a length of time, must continue to occasion, a scarcity of hands for manufacturing occupation, and dearness of labor generally. To these disadvantages for the prosecution of manufactures, a deficiency of pecuniary capital being added, the prospect of a successful competition with the manufactures of Europe, must be regarded as little less than desperate. Extensive manufacturers can only be the offspring of a redundant, at least of a full, population. Till the latter shall characterize the situation of this country, 't is vain to hope for the former.

"If, contrary to the natural course of things, an unseasonable and premature spring can be given to certain fabrics, by heavy duties, prohibitions, bounties, or by other forced expedients, this will only be to sacrifice the interests of the community to those of particular classes. Besides the misdirection of [72/73] labor, a virtual monopoly will be given to the persons employed on such fabrics; and an enhancement of price, the inevitable consequence of every monop-

oly, must be defrayed at the expense of the other parts of society. It
is far preferable, that those persons should be engaged in the cultivation of the earth, and that we should procure, in exchange for its
productions, the commodities with which foreigners are able to supply us in greater perfection and upon better terms."

This mode of reasoning is founded upon facts and principles
which have certainly respectable pretensions. If it had governed the
conduct of nations more generally than it has done, there is room to
suppose that it might have carried them faster to prosperity and
greatness than they have attained by the pursuit of maxims too
widely opposite. Most general theories, however, admit of numerous
exceptions, and there are few, if any, of the political kind, which do
not blend a considerable portion of error with the truths they incul-
cate. . . . [73/83]

To affirm that the labor of the manufacturer is unproductive, because he consumes as much of the produce of land as he adds value
to the raw material which he manufactures, is not better founded
than it would be to affirm that the labor of the farmer, which furnishes materials to the manufacturer, is unproductive, because he
consumes an equal value of manufactured articles. Each furnishes a
certain portion of the produce of his labor to the other, and each
destroys a corresponding portion of the produce of the labor of the
other. In the meantime, the [83/84] maintenance of two citizens, instead of one, is going on; the State has two members instead of one;
and they, together, consume twice the value of what is produced
from the land.

If, instead of a farmer and artificer, there were a farmer only, he
would be under the necessity of devoting a part of his labor to the
fabrication of clothing and other articles, which he would procure of
the artificer, in the case of their being such a person; and of course
he would be able to devote less labor to the cultivation of his farm,
and would draw from it a proportionately less product. The whole
quantity of production, in this state of things, in provisions, raw
materials, and manufactures, would certainly not exceed in value
the amount of what would be produced in provisions and raw materials only, if there were an artificer as well as a farmer.

Again, if here were both an artificer and a farmer, the latter
would be left at liberty to pursue exclusively the cultivation of his
farm. A greater quantity of provisions and raw materials would, of
course, be produced, equal, at least, as has been already observed, to
the whole amount of the provisions, raw materials, and manufactures, which would exist on a contrary supposition. The artificer, at
the same time, would be going on in the production of manufactured commodities, to an amount sufficient, not only to repay the

farmer, in those commodities, for the provisions and materials which were procured from him, but to furnish the artificer himself with a supply of similar commodities for his own use. Thus, then, there would be two [84/85] quantities or values in existence, instead of one; and the revenue and consumption would be double, in one case, what it would be in the other.

If, in place of both of these suppositions, there were supposed to be two farmers and no artificer, each of whom applied a part of his labor to the culture of land and another part to the fabrication of manufactures; in this case, the portion of the labor of both, bestowed upon land, would produce the same quantity of provisions and raw materials only, as would be produced by the entire sum of the labor of one, applied in the same manner; and the portion of the labor of both, bestowed upon manufactures, would produce the same quantity of manufactures only, as would be produced by the entire sum of the labor of one, applied in the same manner. Hence, the produce of the labor of the two farmers would not be greater than the produce of the labor of the farmer and artificer; and hence it results, that the labor of the artificer is as positively productive as that of the farmer, and as positively augments the revenue of the society.

The labor of the artificer replaces to the farmer that portion of his labor with which he provides the materials of exchange with the artificer, and which he would otherwise have been compelled to apply to manufactures; and while the artificer thus enables the farmer to enlarge his stock of agricultural industry, a portion of which he purchases for his own use, he also supplies himself with the manufactured articles of which he stands in need. He does still more. Besides this equivalent, which he gives for the portion of agricultural labor consumed by him, [85/86] and this supply of manufactured commodities for his own consumption, he furnishes still a surplus, which compensates for the use of the capital advanced, either by himself or some other person, for carrying on the business. This is the ordinary profit of the stock employed in the manufactory, and is, in every sense, as effective an addition to the income of the society as the rent of land.

The produce of the labor of the artificer, consequently, may be regarded as composed of three parts: one, by which the provisions for his subsistence and the materials for his work are purchased of the farmer; one, by which he supplies himself with manufactured necessaries; and a third, which constitutes the profit on the stock employed. The two last portions seem to have been overlooked in the system which represents manufacturing industry as barren and unproductive.

In the course of the preceding illustrations, the products of equal quantities of the labor of the farmer and artificer have been treated as if equal to each other. But this is not to be understood as intending to assert any such precise equality. It is merely a manner of expression, adopted for the sake of simplicity and perspicuity. Whether the value of the produce of the labor of the farmer be somewhat more or less than that of the artificer, is not material to the main scope of the argument, which, hitherto, has only aimed at showing that the one, as well as the other, occasions a positive augmentation of the total produce and revenue of the society. [86]

JOHN TAYLOR

Arator

NO. 3. THE POLITICAL STATE OF AGRICULTURE

IN COLLECTING the causes which have contributed to the miserable agricultural state of the country, as it is a national calamity of the highest magnitude, we should be careful not to be blinded by partiality for our customs or institutions, nor corrupted by a disposition to flatter ourselves or others. I shall begin with those of a political nature. These are a secondary providence, which govern unseen the great interests of society; and if agriculture is bad and languishing in a country and climate, where it may be good and prosperous, no doubt remains with me, that political institutions have chiefly perpetrated the evil; just as they decide the fate of commerce.

The device of subjecting it to the payment of bounties to manufacturing, is an institution of this kind. This device is one item in every system for rendering governments too strong for nations. Such an object never was and never can be effected, except by factions legally created at the publick expense. The wealth transferred from the nation to such factions, devotes them to the will of the government, by which it is bestowed. They must render the service for which it was given, or it would be taken away. It is unexceptionably given to support a government against a nation, or one faction against another. Armies, loaning, banking, and an intricate treasury system, endowing a government with the absolute power of applying publick money, under the cover of nominal checks, are other devices of this kind. Whatever strength or wealth a government and its legal factions acquire by law, is taken from a nation; and whatever is taken from a nation, weakens and impoverishes that interest, which composes the majority. There, political oppression in every form must finally fall, however it may oscillate during the period of tran-

From John Taylor. *Arator, Being a Series of Agricultural Essays, Practical and Political*, Fifth Edition, Revised and Enlarged (Petersburg, Va.: Whitworth & Yancey, 1818), pp. 19–21, 192–196. First published in 1813.

125

sit from a good to a bad government, so as sometimes to scratch [19/20] factions. Agriculture being the interest covering a great majority of the people of the United States, every device for getting money or power, hatched by a fellow-feeling or common interest, between a government and its legal creatures, must of course weaken and impoverish it.—Desertion, for the sake of reaping without labour, a share in the harvest of wealth and power, bestowed by laws at its expense, thins its ranks; an annual tribute to these legal factions, empties its purse; and poverty debilitates both its soil and understanding.

The device of protecting duties, under the pretext of encouraging manufactures, operates like its kindred, by creating a capitalist interest, which instantly seizes upon the bounty taken by law from agriculture; and instead of doing any good to the actual workers in wood, metals, cotton or other substances, it helps to rear up an aristocratical order, at the expense of the workers in earth, to unite with governments in oppressing every species of useful industry.

The products of agriculture and manufacturing, unshackled by law, would seek each for themselves, the best markets through commercial channels, but these markets would hardly ever be the same; protecting duties tie travellers together, whose business and interest lie in different directions. This ligature upon nature, will, like all unnatural ligatures, weaken or kill. The best markets of our agriculture lie in foreign countries, whilst the best markets of our manufactures are at home.—Our agriculture has to cross the ocean, and encounter a competition with foreign agriculture on its own ground. Our manufactures meet at home a competition with foreign manufactures. The disadvantages of the first competition, suffice to excite all the efforts of agriculture to save her life; the advantages of the second suffice gradually to bestow a sound constitution on manufacturing. But the manufacture of an aristocratical interest, under the pretext of encouraging work of a very different nature, may reduce both manufacturers and husbandmen, as Strickland says, is already effected in the case of the latter, to the "lowest state of degradation."

This degradation could never have been seen by a [20/21] friend to either, who could afterwards approve of protecting duties. Let us take the article of wheat to unfold an idea of the disadvantages which have produced it. If wheat is worth 16s. sterling in England the 70 lb. the farmers sell it here at about 6s. sterling.—American agriculture then meets English agriculture in a competition, compelling her to sell at little more than one third of the price obtained by her rival. But American manufactures take the field against English on very different terms. These competitors meet in the United States. The American manufactures receive first, a bounty equal to the freight, commission and English taxes, upon their English rivals; and secondly, a bounty equal to our own necessary imposts. Without protecting duties, therefore, the American manufacturer gets for the same article, about 25 per cent, more, and the American agriculturalist about 180 per cent. less, than their English rivals. Protecting duties added to these inequalities, may raise up an order of masters for actual manufacturers, to intercept advantages too enormous to escape the vigilance of capital, impoverish husbandmen, and aid in changing a fair to a fradulent government; but they will never make either of these intrinsically valuable classes richer, wiser or freer. [21]

NO 60. THE RIGHTS OF AGRICULTURE

It is lamentable to confess, that this, to be a true, must be almost a negative number. This most useful and virtuous interest, enjoys no rights, except in the United States; and there it enjoys no exclusive rights, whilst the few in which it shares are daily contracted by the various arts of ambition and avarice. Every where else, agriculture is a slave; here she is only a dupe. Abroad she is condemned by avowed force to feed voluptuousness, avarice and ambition; here, she is deluded by flattery and craft, during fits of joy or of fury, to squander her property, to mortgage her labourers, and to shackle her freedom. Abroad, she suffers contempt, and is sensible of her degradation; here, she is a blind Quixote, mounted on a wooden horse, and persuaded by the acclamations of her foes, that she is soaring to the stars, whilst she is ready to tumble into the dust.

Privileges are rearing by laws all around at her expense, and whilst she is taught to believe that they will only take from her a few inconsiderable slips, they will at length draw a spacious circumvallation, within which will gradually grow up a power, beyond her control. Tricks, as well as inventions, are daily fortified with legal bulwarks, called charters, to transfer her wealth, and to secure frauds against her efforts. Capital in every form, save that of agriculture, is fed by taxes and by bounties, which she must pay; whilst not a single bounty is paid to her by capital in any form; and instead of being favoured with some prizes in the lottery of society, she pays most, and is rewarded herself by the blanks of underwriting the projects of statesmen, and bearing the burdens of government. [192/193]

The use of society, is to secure the fruits of his own industry and talents to each associator. Its abuse consists in artifice or force, for transferring those fruits from some partners to others. Of this abuse, that interest covering the majority of partners is the victim. And the difficulty of discriminating laws, transferring such fruits for the benefit of society, from those having in view the gratification of avarice and ambition, produces a sympathy and combination between these distinct kinds of law. As the members of the government, and members of legal frauds, both extract power and income from the majority, they are apt to coalesce; and each party to favour the designs of its ally, in their operations upon the common enemy. Hence governments love to create exclusive rights, and exclusive rights cling to governments. The ligament of parent and child, binds them together, and the power creating these abuses, must make them props for its support, or instruments for its subversion. Its election between these alternatives is certain, and society is thus unavoidably thrown into two divisions. One containing all those who pay, and the other those who receive contributions, required either for publick use, or to foster private avarice or ambition. Good government is graduated by this latter kind of contribution thus unfortunately allied to the former. The highest amount constitutes the worst, and the lowest, the best possible species of government. But as both are drawn from the majority of every society, whenever the agricultrual interest covers that majority, this interest is the victim of the coalition; and as it almost universally does cover this majority, the agricultural interest is almost universally its slaves.

The consequences to agriculture will be demonstrated by converting this coalition between government and its creatures, or of all who receive tolls given by law, into a political pope, and placing in his mouth an address to agriculture, in a parody of Ernulphus's form of excommunication.

"May you be taxed in your land, your slaves, your houses, your carriages, your horses, your clothing, your liquors, your coffee, your tea, and your salt. May you be taxed by banks, by protecting duties, by embargoes, [193/194] and by charters of a thousand different forms. May the exemption of your exports from taxation be removed, and may you then be taxed through your wheat, your corn, your tobacco, your cotton, your rice, your indigo, your sugar, your hemp, your live stock, your beef, your pork, your tar, pitch and turpentine, your onions, your cheese, and your potatoes. May you be taxed for the support of government, or to enrich exclusive or chartered interests, through every article you import, and through every article you export, by duties called protecting, but intended to take away your constitutional protection against taxation for the benefit of capitalists. May you be taxed through every article produced by your labour or necessary to your subsistence, comfort and pleasure, by exercises [excises]. And whilst every species of your products, and of you consumptions are thus taxed, may your capital, being visible, be moreover taxed in various modes. May all these taxes whether plain or intricate, (after deducting the small sum necessary to produce the genuine end of society) be employed in enriching capitalists, and buying soldiers, placemen and contractors, to make you submissive to usurpations, and as quiet under your burthens, as a martyr tied to the stake, under the flames. After you have been taxed as far as you can pay, may you by the bounty of God Almighty be moreover mortgaged up to your value or credit, for the benefit of the said coalition of capitalists. And finally, may none of this good and useful coalition, to whom is given the wealth of this world, as the kindgom of heaven is to the pope and his clergy, be taxed in their stock or principal held under any law or charter whatsoever; nor in their capital employed in any manufacture of speculation, nor in any profit drawn from such principal stock or capital; nor thro' any of their sinecures, salaries, contracts or incomes; but on the contrary, may such stock, principal, capital, profits, salaries, contracts, and sinecures, be constantly fostered by bounties in various injurious forms, to be paid by you, you damned dirty working, productive bitch, agriculture." Throughout the world, agriculture, like one of Ernulphus's contrite excommunicants, responds, amen, to this pious invocation. [194/195]

Throughout the world, agriculture has enjoyed, and in England, continues to enjoy, one of the rights in which she has a share in the United States; that of a voice in elections.—And throughout the world, this right has been unable to shield her against an anathema, which prescribes for her as perfect a hell, as the formula of Ernulphus prescribes for his heretick. Let the agricultural interest of the United States, pause here and look around. Is a blind confidence in a right so universally ineffectual, a sufficient safeguard for its freedom and happiness? To me it seems, that an interest can never be long free, which blindly confides in a coalition, whose object it is to draw from that interest, power and wealth. That the major interest must be as cunning, as wise and as watchful, as the minor, or that the minor interest will enslave it. And that agriculture must as attentively keep her eyes upon the coalition, to avoid its operations upon her, as the coalition does upon agriculture, for the purpose of transferring to its members portions of her power and wealth, whenever she slumbers.

Hence have arisen the political suggestions to be found in these essays. I cannot discern much good in an improvement of agriculture, to get luxury, voluptuousness and tyranny for a few, and wretchedness for a multitude.—The best cultivated country in the world, abounds most in paupers and thieves. Agriculture must be a politician to avoid this fate; and those who ridicule her pretensions to knowledge in this science, intend by persuading her to repose in a blind confidence, built upon the frail right of election, to expose her to it. How can she even judiciously elect, if she cannot or will not judge of publick measures, by the light of her own interest?

The moral consequence of this supineness of ignorance, is, that social happiness gradually becomes the dependant of a minority, and of course it is provided for, by continually subtracting from the happiness of a majority. The visible immorality of this, demonstrates the virtue, as well as wisdom of suggestions designed to obstruct it.

The remaining right in which agriculture participates, in common with all other interests, having any thing to [195/196] export, is bestowed by the constitutional prohibition of duties upon exports. This right originated in state jealousies, and not from a disposition to favour agriculture, but yet it is her best security, for the preservation of that portion of our government, which will longest be sensible of her elective influence; and its relinquishment will be the most fatal wound which can be inflicted on her. The coalition I have described will try every art in her most unguarded moments, to snatch it from her, and it will be the last relinquishment it will need. To determine whether her elective influence can bear further wounds, let agriculture re-survey the legislation of our whole term of independence, and compare the catalogues she may select, of laws for creating or fostering privileges and exclusive interests, with those for fostering herself; and let this comparison form the criterion for ascertaining her legislative influence. Thus only can she judiciously increase this influence, if it has settled too low, or diminish it, if it has raised too high. There is no fair mode of judging, except by these legislative acts. To infer, that the agricultural interest influences legislatures, because it chiefly elects them, would be like inferring, that the French nation influences the tribunate, because they wholly elect it. Let agriculture therefore hold fast the solitary security she enjoys in common with her industrious associates, against the ambitions of usurpers, and the avarice of capitalists, not be deluded into the absurd notion, that it is wise to relinquish the only peculium of industry, for the sake of some temporary operation upon foreign nations, inevitably resulting upon herself in the form of retaliation, whilst the protection of exports against taxation, will be gone forever. [196]

JAMES FENIMORE COOPER

The American Democrat

ON PROPERTY

As PROPERTY is the base of all civilization, its existence and security are indispensable to social improvement. Were it possible to have a community of property, it would soon be found that no one would toil, but that men would be disposed to be satisfied with barely enough for the supply of their physical wants, since none would exert themselves to obtain advantages solely for the use of others. The failure of all attempts to form communities, even on a small scale, with a common interest, goes to prove this. Where there is a rigid equality of condition, as well as of rights, that condition must necessarily be one of a low scale of mediocrity, since it is impossible to elevate those who do not possess the requisite qualities any higher. Thus we see that the societies, or religious sects, in which a community of property prevails, are content with merely supplying the wants of life, knowing little or nothing of its elegancies, refinements, or mental pleasures. These communities, moreover, possess an outlet for their idle and dissolute, by resorting to expulsion, a remedy that society itself cannot apply.

The principle of individuality, or to use a less winning term, of selfishness, lies at the root of all voluntary [135/136] human exertion. We toil for food, for clothes, for houses, lands, and for property, in general. This is done, because we know that the fruits of our labor will belong to ourselves, or to those who are most dear to us. It follows, that all which society enjoys beyond the mere supply of its first necessities, is dependant on the rights of property.

It is not known that man exists anywhere without establishing rules for the protection of property. Even insects, reptiles, beasts and birds, have their several possessions, in their nests, dens and supplies.

From James Fenimore Cooper, *The American Democrat, or Hints on the Social and Civic Relations of the United States of America* (Cooperstown: H. & E. Phinney, 1838), pp. 135–141, 168–171.

So completely is animal exertion, in general, whether in man or beast, dependant on the enjoyment of this right, under limitations which mark their several conditions, that we may infer that the rights of property, to a certain extent, are founded in nature. The food obtained by his toil, cannot be taken from the mouth of man, or beast, without doing violence to one of the first of our natural rights. We apply the term of robber, or despoiler, to the reptile or bird, that preys on the aliment of another animal, as well as to the human thief. So long as natural justice is admitted to exist, the party assailed, in such cases, has a right to defend his own.

The rights of property become artificial and extended, as society becomes civilized. In the savage state the land is without owners, property consisting in the hut, the food, and the arms used in war and in the chase. In pastoral, or semi-barbarous states, use gives claims, not to individuals, but to tribes, and flocks are pastured on grounds that belong to one entire community, but to that one only. Private property is composed of cattle, sheep, tents, horses, camels, with the common claims to share in the common fields. [136/137]

Civilization has established various, and in some cases, arbitrary and unjust distinctions, as pertaining to the rights of property. These are abuses, the tendency of man being to convert into curses things that Providence designed to prove benefits. Still, most of the ordinances of civilized society, that are connected with this interest, are founded in reason, and ought to be rigidly maintained.

The first great principle connected with the rights of property, is its inviolability in all cases in which the laws leave it in possession of the proprietor. Every child should be taught to respect the sanctity of his neighbour's house, garden, fields and all that is his. On those parts of another's possessions, where it is permitted to go, he should go with care not to abuse the privilege, and from those parts which he is forbidden to use, he should religiously abstain. The child that is properly impressed in infancy, with the rights of property, is in little danger of committing theft in after life, or, in any other manner of invading that which is the just possession of another.

The doctrine that any one "may do what he please with his own," however, is false. One may do with his own, whatever the laws and institutions of his country allow, and no more. One may even respect the letter, and yet violate the spirit of those laws and institutions, committing a moral, if not a legal offence, in so doing. Thus, he, who would bring his money to bear upon the elections of a country like this, abuses his situation, unless his efforts are confined to fair and manly discussions before the body of the people.

In nations where the mass have no political rights, means have been found to accumulate power by the aid of wealth. The pretence has been that none but the rich have a stake in society. Every man who has [137/138] wants, feelings, affections and character, has a stake in society. Of the two, perhaps, the necessities of men are a greater corrective of political abuses, than their surplus means. Both may lead to evil, beyond a doubt, but, as laws which are framed by all, must be tolerably impartial and general in their operation, less danger arises from the rule of the former, than from the rule of the latter. When property rules, it rules alone; but when the poor are admitted to have a voice in government, the rich are never excluded. Such is the nature of man, that all exclusive power is uniformly directed to exclusive purposes. Property always carries with it a portion of indirect political influence, and it is unwise, and even dangerous, to strengthen this influence by adding to it constitutional privileges; the result always being to make the strong stronger, and the weak weaker.

On the other hand, all who love equal justice, and, indeed, the safety of free institutions, should understand that property has its rights, and the necessity of rigidly respecting them. It is the right of the possessor of property to be placed on an equal footing with all his fellow citizens, in every respect. If he is not to be exalted on account of his wealth, neither is he to be denounced. In this country, it is the intention of the institutions, that money should neither increase nor lessen political influence.

There are habits that belong to every condition of life. The man of hereditary wealth, is usually a man of leisure, and he little understands the true spirit of democracy, who supposes that such a man is not to enjoy the tastes and inclinations, which are the fruits of leisure and cultivation, without let or hindrance. Democracy leaves every man the master of his acts and time, his tastes and habits, so long as he discharges his duty to the publick, and respects the [138/ 139] laws. He who declaims against another for holding himself aloof from general association, arrogates to himself a power of censure that he does not rightly possess, and betrays his own consciousness of inferiority. Men of really high social station never make this complaint, for they are above jealousy; and they who do, only discover a feeling that is every way removed from the manliness and spirit of true independence.

One may certainly be purse-proud, and of all the sources of human pride, mere wealth is the basest and most vulgar minded. Real gentlemen are almost invariably above this low feeling, and they who attribute habits, that have their rise in sentiment, tastes, knowledge and refinement, to such a cause, usually make the mistake of letting their own ignorance of the existence of motives so elevated, be known. In a word, if the man of property has no more personal legal immunities, than the man who has none, neither has he fewer. He is privileged to use his own means, under the general regulations of society, in the pursuit of his own happiness, and they who would interfere with him, so far from appreciating liberty, are ignorant of its vital principles.

If left to itself, unsupported by factitious political aid, but sufficiently protected against the designs and rapacity of the dishonest, property is an instrument of working most of the good that society enjoys. It elevates a national character, by affording the means of cultivating knowledge and the tastes; it introduces all above barbarism into society; and it encourages and sustains laudable and useful efforts in individuals. Like every other great good, its abuses are in proportion to its benefits.

The possessor of property is not, half the time, as much the object of envy as the needy imagine, for its [139/140] corrupting influence endangers eternal peace. Great estates are generally of more benefit to the community than to their owners. They bring with them anxiety, cares, demands, and, usually, exaggerated notions, on the part of the publick, of the duties of the rich. So far from being objects of envy, their possessors are oftener the subjects of commiseration; he who has enough for his rational wants, agreeably to his habits and education, always proving the happier man.

The possessions of new families are commonly exaggerated in the publick mind, while those of long established families are as commonly diminished.

A people that deems the possession of riches its highest source of distinction, admits one of the most degrading of all influences to preside over its opinions. At no time, should money be ever ranked as more than a means, and he who lives as if the acquisition of property were the sole end of his existence, betrays the dominion of the most sordid, base, and grovelling motive, that life offers.

Property is desirable as the ground work of moral independence, as a means of improving the faculties, and of doing good to others, and as the agent in all that distinguishes the civilized man from the savage.

Property has been made the test of political rights, in two distinct forms. It has been *represented,* and it has been established as a *qualification.* The *representation* of property is effected in two modes; first, by giving the proprietor more votes than one, according to the number and situation of his freeholds; and, secondly, by raising the test of qualification so high, as to exclude all but the affluent from the franchise. The first was the English system, previously to the recent changes; the last, is the actual system of France. [140/141]

A government founded on the representation of property, however direct or indirect, is radically vicious, since it is a union of two of the most corrupting influences to which man is subject. It is the proper business of government to resist the corruptions of money, and not to depend on them.

To a qualification of property, if placed so low as to embrace the great majority of the people, there is no very serious objection, though better tests might, perhaps, be devised. Residence, character, information, and fixed relations with society, ought to be added to this qualification; and it might be better, even, could they be made entirely to supersede it. In local governments, or those of towns and villages, which do little more than control property, a low property qualification is the true test of the franchise, though even in these cases, it might be well to add information and character. [141]

ON COMMERCE

Commerce, in a general sense, is trade, but it is also usual to apply the word particularly to the traffick between nations. Navigation is not commerce, but a means of conducting commerce.

Commerce is merely an incident of civilized society, though there is always a strong disposition in commercial communities to treat it as a principal. The interests of commerce, in a general sense, depend on certain great principles, which ought always to be respected; but, as these interests, by their nature, are also liable to be influenced by the constant vicissitudes arising out of the fluctuations of trade, there is a strong disposition in those connected with commerce, to sacrifice all governing rules, to protect the interests of the day. This disposition is common to man, but it is more active in merchants, on account of the magnitude and precarious nature of the risks they run. The agriculturist who loses a crop, suffers an injury, more or less serious, that another year will repair; but the merchant who loses his adventures, is usually ruined. [168/169]

It follows, that a community governed by men in trade, or which is materially influenced by men in trade, is governed without any fixed principles, every thing being made to yield to the passing interests of the hour, those interests being too engrossing to admit of neglect, or postponement.

It is a mistake to suppose commerce favorable to liberty. Its tendency is to a monied aristocracy, and this, in effect, has always been the polity of every community of merchants. Commerce is an enemy of despotic power in the hands of a prince, of church influence, and of hereditary aristocracies, from which facts it has obtained its reputation of sustaining freedom; but, as a class, merchants will always be opposed to the control of majorities.

The true office of commerce is to facilitate exchanges of articles between men, to the amount that their wants and interests require; but as every transfer of property leaves a profit with the merchant, he has a disposition to increase his gains, by pushing his transactions beyond the just limits of trade. This disposition is best checked by the penalties of bankruptcies, but, in a country like this, in which no such penalty exists, the consequence is to produce an unbroken succession of commercial reverses, that affect the value of all the property in the nation, almost periodically.

Commerce is entitled to a complete and efficient protection in all its legal rights, but the moment it presumes to control a country, or to substitute its fluctuating expedients for the high principles of natural justice that ought to lie at the root of every political system, it should be frowned on, and rebuked.

The merchant who is the immediate agent in paying the duties on goods, has no more claims than another, as the money eventually comes from the [169/170] pocket of the consumer, and the factor is amply paid for his services in his profits.

All legislation affecting the currency, commerce and banking, in a country like this, ought to be limited, as far as circumstances will allow, to general and simple provisions, the nature of the institutions forbidding the interference that is elsewhere practised with advantage. A familiar example will show our meaning. In all commercial communities there is a commercial mart, or a capital, where exchanges are effected, cargoes disposed of in gross, and where all the great interests of trade concentrate, as the blood flows to and from the heart. In identified governments, like that of England, for instance, legislation may respect this natural tendency to concentration in commerce, and enact laws for its especial benefit and protection. Thus an English law may have an especial relation to the interests of London, as the mart that regulates the entire currency of the kingdom. But, on the other hand, in a government like that of America, there is a principle of diffusion, which requires that the legislation should be general in its application. New York and New Orleans, for instance, regulate the currency and exchanges of the whole country; but congress cannot pass a law to aid these legitimate efforts of trade, since any legislation that should favor New York at the expense of Philadelphia, in appearances even, would be opposed to the controlling principle of the compact. It follows, that the interference of the government with all such questions, in this country, should be unfrequent and cautious, since it possesses a power to injure, with very little power to benefit.

The real merchant is a man of a high pursuit, and has need of great general knowledge, much firmness of character, and of far-sighted views, to succeed in his objects. He is a principal agent in extending knowledge [170/171] and civilization, and is entitled to a distinguished place in the scale of human employments. But the mere factor, who is the channel of communication between the producer and the consumer, in what is called a regular trade, has no more claims to this character, than the clerk who copies a treaty has a claim to be considered a negotiator. [171]

GEORGE FITZHUGH

Cannibals All!

SLAVERY—ITS EFFECT ON THE FREE

BEATEN at every other quarter, we learn that a distinguished writer at the North, is about to be put forward by the Abolitionists, to prove that the influence of slavery is deleterious on the whites who own no slaves.

Now, at first view it elevates those whites; for it makes them not the bottom of society, as at the North—not the menials, the hired day laborer, the work scavengers and scullions—but privileged citizens, like Greek and Roman citizens, with a numerous class far beneath them. In slave society, one white man does not lord it over another; for all are equal in privilege, if not in wealth; and the poorest would not become a menial—hold your horse, and then extend his hand or his hat for a gratuity, were you to proffer him the wealth of the Indies. The menial, the exposed and laborious, and the disgraceful occupations are all filled by slaves. But filled they must be by someone, and in free society, half of its members are employed in occupations that are not considered or treated as respectable. Our slaves till the land, do the coarse and hard labor on our roads and canals, sweep our [320/321] streets, cook our food, brush our boots, wait on our tables, hold our horses, do all hard work, and fill all menial offices. Your freemen at the North do the same work and fill the same offices. The only difference is, we love our slaves, and we are ready to defend, assist and protect them; you hate and fear your white servants, and never fail, as a moral duty, to screw down their wages to the lowest, and to starve their families, if possible, as evidence of your thrift, economy and management—the only English and Yankee virtues.

In free society, miscalled freemen fulfill all the offices of slaves for less wages than slaves, and are infinitely less liked and cared for by

From George Fitzhugh, *Cannibals All! or Slaves Without Masters* (Richmond, Va.: Adolphus Morris, Publisher, 1857), pp. 320–322, 335–340.

138

their superiors than slaves. Does this elevate them and render them happy?

The trades, the professions, the occupations that pay well, and whose work is light, is reserved for freemen in slave society. Does this depress them?

The doctor, the lawyer, the mechanic, the dentist, the merchant, the overseer, every trade and profession, in fact, live from the proceeds of slave labor at the South. They divide the profits with the owner of the slaves. He has nothing to pay them except what his slaves make. But you Yankees and Englishmen more than divide the profits—you take the lion's share. You make more money from our cotton, and tobacco, and sugar, and indigo, and wheat, and corn, and rice, than we make ourselves. [321/322] You live by slave labor —would perish without it—yet you abuse it. Cut off England and New England from the South American, East and West India and our markets, from which to buy their food, and in which to sell their manufactures, and they would starve at once. You live by our slave labor. It elevates your whites as well as ours, by confining them, in a great degree, to skillful, well-paying, light, and intellectual employments—and it feeds and clothes them. Abolish slavery, and you will suffer vastly more than we, because we have all the lands of the South, and can *command* labor as you do, and a genial soil and climate, that require less labor. But while in the absence of slavery, we would support ourselves, we should cease to support you. We would neither send you food and clothing, nor buy your worse than useless notions. [322]

DEFICIENCY OF FOOD IN FREE SOCIETY

THE NORMAL state of free society is a state of famine. Agricultural labor is the most arduous, least respectable, and worst paid of all labor. Nature and philosophy teach all who can to avoid and escape from it, and to pursue less laborious, more respectable, and more lucrative employments. None work in the field who can help it. Hence free society is in great measure dependent for its food and clothing on slave society. Western Europe and New England get their cotton, sugar, and much of their bread and meat from the South, from Cuba, Russia, Poland, and Turkey. After all, the mass of their population suffers continual physical want. McCulloch informs us in his edition of Adam Smith, "that the better sort of Irish laborers eat meat once a month, or once in six months; the lowest order never. The better class of English laborers eat meat twice or three times a week." Now no Southern negro would believe this if you were to swear to it. Yet it is a very favorable account of those laborers. The Irish rarely eat bread, and the English peasantry have wholly inadequate allowance [335/336] of it. On the Continent, the peasantry generally live on fruits, nuts and olives, and other things, which our slaves do not seek as food at all, but as mere condiments to give a relish to their meat and bread. Agriculture is the proper pursuit of slaves, to be superintended and directed, however, by freemen. Its profits are inadequate to the support of separate families of laborers, especially of white laborers in cold climates, whose wants are greater than those of negroes at the South. The expenses of families are greatly lessened where slavery associates a large number under a common head, or master, and their labor is rendered more efficient and productive.

This is the great idea of the Socialists, and it is a truer one than the "every-man-for-himself" doctrine of the political economists. Free society is in great measure fed and clothed by slave society, which it pays for in worthless baubles, fashionable trifles, and deleterious luxuries;—without which, slave society would do much better. Everyone should study the census of the Union, in order to see how dependent the Northeast is on slave labor, and how trifling are her agricultural products.

The profits of slave farming enure chiefly to the advantage of Western Europe and our North. Practical men, therefore, at the North, so far from going to work to abolish slavery, are bringing daily a larger supply of slaves into the slave market, [336/337] than ever was brought before. Add the Coolies of Asia and apprentices from Africa to the old negro slave trade, and the annual supply of new slaves exceeds by far that of any other period.

The Abolitionists will probably succeed in dissolving the Union, in involving us in civil and fratricidal war, and in cutting off the North from its necessary supply of food and clothing; but they should recollect that whilst they are engaged in this labor of love, Northern and English merchants are rapidly extending and increasing slavery, by opening daily markets for the purchase and sale of Coolies, apprentices, and Africans.

The foreign slave trade is not necessary for the supply of the slave markets. The increase of the present slaves, if humanely treated, would suffice to meet that demand. But Africans and Coolies cost less than the rearing of slaves in America, and the trade in them, whenever carried on, induces masters to work their old slaves to death and buy new ones from abroad.

The foreign slave trade, especially the Coolie trade, is the most inhuman pursuit in which man ever engaged. Equally inhuman to the victims which it imports, and to the old slaves, whose treatment and condition it renders intolerably cruel. By directing philanthropy and public opinion in a false direction, the Abolitionists have become the most efficient propagandists of slavery and the slave trade. And [337/338] slavery, such as it exists in pursuance of the foreign slave trade, shocks our sense of humanity quite as much as that of the most sensitive Abolitionists.

Since writing thus far, we met with the following in the *Charleston Mercury:*

WHEAT IN MASSACHUSETTS.—The deficiency in the production of wheat in Massachusetts alone, in 1855, for the consumption of her inhabitants, was 3,915,550 bushels; and of Indian corn, 3,420,675 bushels (*without allowing any thing for the consumption of corn by cattle*).

In 1850, the deficiency in the production of wheat in all the New England States, was equal to 1,691,502 barrels of flour; and to 3,464,675 bushels of corn (*without allowing any thing for the consumption by cattle*).

This is 327,185 barrels more than was exported of domestic flour from all of the United States to foreign countries during the year ending 30th June, 1855, and 87,000 more barrels than was exported both of domestic and foreign flour from the United States for the same period.

We conclude, from our examination of the census, that the grain and potatoes made in New England would about feed her cattle, horses, hogs, and sheep—leaving none for her inhabitants. We lately compared carefully the census of Massachusetts and North Carolina, and found, in round numbers, that according to population, North Carolina produced [338/339] annually ten times as much of human food as Massachusetts—but that Massachusetts balanced the account by producing annually ten times as many paupers and criminals as North Carolina. We also discover that the want of food in the one State and its abundance in the other, tells on the duration of human life. The morality in Massachusetts is nearly double that in North Carolina. We infer that there is ten times as much of human happiness in North Carolina as in Massachusetts. The census gives no account of the infidels and the Isms—of them there are none in North Carolina, and Massachusetts may boast that she rivals Germany, France, and Western New York in their production.

Really, it is suicidal folly in New England to talk of disunion and setting up for herself. She does not possess the elements of separate nationality. She is intelligent and wealthy; but her wealth is cosmopolitan—her poverty indigenous. Her commerce, her manufactures, and moneyed capital, constitute her wealth. Disunion would make these useless and unprofitable at home, and they would be transferred immediately to other States and Nations.

North Carolina might well set up for herself, for she can produce all the necessaries and comforts and luxuries of life within herself, and has Virginia between herself and danger on the one side, [339/340] and an inaccessible sea coast on the other. But we of Virginia, being a border State, would be badly situated in case of disunion, and mean to cling to it as long as honor permits. Besides, Virginia loves her nearest sister, Pennsylvania, and cannot bear the thought of parting company with her.

> Tecum obeam lubens![1][340]
> Tecum vivere amem!

[1] "With thee I fain would live, with thee I'd gladly die." Horace, *Odes*, III, ix, 24.

WALT WHITMAN

Democratic Vistas

THE TRUE gravitation-hold of liberalism in the United States will be a more universal ownership of property, general homesteads, general comfort—a vast, intertwining reticulation of wealth. As the human frame, or, indeed, any object in this manifold universe, is best kept together by the simple miracle of its own cohesion, and the necessity, exercise and profit thereof, so a great and varied nationality, occupying millions of square miles, were firmest held and knit by the principle of the safety and endurance of the aggregate of its middling property owners. So that, from another point of view, ungracious as it may sound, and a paradox after what we have been saying, democracy looks with suspicious, ill-satisfied eye upon the very poor, the ignorant, and on those out of business. She asks for men and women with occupations, well-off, owners of houses and acres, and with cash in the bank—and with some cravings for literature, too; and must have them, and hastens to make them. Luckily, the seed is already well-sown, and has taken ineradicable root.* [221/222]

Huge and mighty are our days, our republican lands—and most in their rapid shiftings, their changes, all in the interest of the cause.

---

* For fear of mistake, I may as well distinctly specify, as cheerfully included in the model and standard of these Vistas, a practical, stirring, worldly, money-making, even materialistic character. It is undeniable that our farms, stores, offices, dry-goods, coal and groceries, enginery, cash-accounts, trades, earnings, markets, &c., should be attended to in earnest, and actively pursued, just as if they had a real permanent existence. I perceive clearly that the extreme business energy, and this almost maniacal appetite for wealth prevalent in the United States, are parts of amelioration and progress, indispensably needed to prepare the very results I demand. My theory includes riches, and the getting of riches, and the amplest products, power, activity, inventions, movements, &c. Upon them, as upon substrata, I raise the edifice design'd in these Vistas.

From Walt Whitman, *Complete Prose Works* (Philadelphia: David McKay, Publisher, 1892), pp. 221–223, 236–237. First published in 1871.

As I write this particular passage, (November, 1868,) the din of disputation rages around me. Acrid the temper of the parties, vital the pending questions. Congress convenes; the President sends his message; reconstruction is still in abeyance; the nomination and the contest for the twenty-first Presidential draw close, with loudest threat and bustle. Of these, and all the like of these, the eventuations I know not; but well I know that behind them, and whatever their eventuations, the vital things remain safe and certain, and all the needed work goes on. Time, with soon or later superciliousness, disposes of Presidents, Congressmen, party platforms, and such. Anon, it clears the stage of each and any mortal shred that thinks itself so potent to its day; and at and after which, (with precious, golden exceptions once or twice in a century,) all that relates to sir potency is flung to moulder in a burial-vault, and no one bothers himself the least bit about it afterward. But the People ever remain, tendencies continue, and all the idiocratic transfers in unbroken chain go on.

In a few years the dominion-heart of America will be far inland, toward the West. Our future national capital may not be where the present one is. It is possible, nay likely, that in less than fifty years, it will migrate a thousand or two miles, will be re-founded, and every thing belonging to it made on a different plan, original, far more superb. The main social, political, spine-character of the States will probably run along the Ohio, Missouri and Mississippi rivers, and west and north of them, including Canada. Those regions, with the group of powerful brothers toward the Pacific, (destined to the mastership of that sea and its countless paradises of islands,) will compact and settle the traits of America, with all the old retain'd, but more expanded, grafted on newer, hardier, purely native stock. A giant growth, composite from the rest, getting their contribution, absorbing it, to make it more illustrious. From the north, intellect, the sun of things, also the idea of unswayable justice, anchor [222/223] amid the last, the wildest tempests. From the south the living soul, the animus of good and bad, haughtily admitting no demonstration but its own. While from the west itself comes solid personality, with blood and brawn, and the deep quality of all-accepting fusion.

Political democracy, as it exists and practically works in America, with all its threatening evils, supplies a training-school for making first-class men. It is life's gymnasium, not of good only, but of all. We try often, though we fall back often. A brave delight, fit for freedom's athletes, fills these arenas, and fully satisfies, out of the action in them, irrespective of success. Whatever we do not attain, we at any rate attain the experiences of the fight, the hardening of the strong campaign, and throb with currents of attempt at least. Time is ample. Let the victors come after us. Not for nothing does evil play its part among us. Judging from the main portions of the history of the world, so far, justice is always in jeopardy, peace walks amid hourly pit-falls, and of slavery, misery, meanness, the craft of tyrants and the credulity of the populace in some of their protean forms, no voice can at any time say, They are not. The clouds break a little, and the sun shines out—but soon and certain the lowering darkness falls again, as if to last forever. Yet is there an immortal courage and prophecy in every sane soul that cannot, must not, under any circumstances, capitulate. *Vive*, the attack—the perennial assault! *Vive*, the unpopular cause—the spirit that audaciously aims —the never-abandon'd efforts, pursued the same amid opposing proofs and precedents. . . . [223/236]

Of course, in these States, for both man and woman, we must entirely recast the types of highest personality from what the oriental, feudal, ecclesiastical worlds bequeath us, and which yet possess the imaginative and esthetic fields of the United States, pictorial and melodramatic, not without use as studies, but making sad work, and forming a strange anachronism upon the scenes and exigencies around us. Of course, the old undying elements remain. The task is, to successfully adjust them to new combinations, our own days. Nor is this so incredible. I can conceive a community, to-day and here, in which, on a sufficient scale, the perfect personalities, without noise meet; say in some pleasant western settlement or town, where a couple of hundred best men and women, of ordinary worldly status, have by luck been drawn together, with nothing extra of genius or wealth, but virtuous, chaste, industrious, cheerful, resolute, friendly and devout. I can conceive such a community organized in running order, powers judiciously delegated—farming, building, trade, courts, mails, schools, elections, all attended to; and then the rest of life, the main thing, freely branching and blossoming in each individual, and bearing golden fruit. I can see there, in every young and old man, after his kind, and in every woman after hers, a true personality, develop'd, exercised proportionately in [236/237] body, mind, and spirit. I can imagine this case as one not necessarily rare or difficult, but in buoyant accordance with the municipal and general requirements of our times. And I can realize in it the culmination of something better than any stereotyped *eclat* of history or poems. Perhaps, unsung, undramatized, unput in essays or biographies—perhaps even some such community already exists, in Ohio, Illinois, Missouri, or somewhere, practically fulfilling itself, and thus outvying, in cheapest vulgar life, all that has been hitherto shown in best ideal pictures.

In short, and to sum up, America, betaking herself to formative action, (as it is about time for more solid achievement, and less windy promise,) must, for her purposes, cease to recognize a theory of character grown of feudal aristocracies, or form'd by merely literary standards, or from any ultramarine, full-dress formulas of culture, polish, caste, &c., and must sternly promulgate her own new standard, yet old enough, and accepting the old, the perennial elements, and combining them into groups, unities, appropriate to the modern, the democratic, the west, and to the practical occasions and needs of our own cities, and of the agricultural regions. Ever the most precious is the common. Ever the fresh breeze of field, or hill, or lake, is more than any palpitation of fans, though of ivory, and redolent with perfume; and the air is more than the costliest perfumes. [237]

HENRY GEORGE

Of Property in Land in the United States

IN THE EARLIER stages of civilization we see that land is everywhere regarded as common property. And, turning from the dim past to our own times, we may see that natural perceptions are still the same, and that when placed under circumstances in which the influence of education and habit is weakened, men instinctively recognize the equality of right to the bounty of nature.

The discovery of gold in California brought together in a new country men who had been used to look on land as the rightful subject of individual property, and of whom probably not one in a thousand had ever dreamed of drawing any distinction between property in land and property in anything else. But, for the first time in the history of the Anglo-Saxon race, these men were brought into contact with land from which gold could be obtained by the simple operation of washing it out.

Had the land with which they were thus called upon to deal been agricultural, or grazing, or forest land, of peculiar richness; had it been land which derived peculiar value from its situation for commercial purposes; or by reason of the water power which it afforded, or even had it contained rich mines of coal, iron or lead, the land system to which they had been used would have been applied, and it would have been reduced to private ownership in large tracts, as even the pueblo lands of San Francisco (really the most valuable in the State), which by Spanish law had been set apart to furnish homes for the future residents of that city, were reduced, without any protest worth speaking of. But the novelty of the case broke through habitual ideas, and threw men back upon first principles, and it was by common consent declared that this gold-bearing land [346/347] should remain common property, of which no one might take more

From Henry George, *Progress and Poverty: An Inquiry into the Cause of Industrial Depressions, and of Increase of Want with Wealth, the Remedy,* Fourth Edition (New York: D. Appleton and Company, 1882), pp. 346–354. First published in 1879.

than he could reasonably use, or hold for a longer time than he continued to use it. This perception of natural justice was acquiesced in
by the General Government and the courts, and while placer mining
remained of importance, no attempt was made to overrule this rever-
sion to primitive ideas. The title to the land remained in the Government, and no individual could acquire more than a possessory
claim. The miners in each district fixed the amount of ground an
individual could take and the amount of work that must be done to
constitute use. If this work were not done, any one could re-locate
the ground. Thus, no one was allowed to forestall or to lock up natural resources. Labor was acknowledged as the creator of wealth, was
given a free field, and secured in its reward. The device would not
have assured complete equality of rights under the conditions that
in most countries prevail; but under the conditions that there and
then existed—a sparse population, an unexplored country, and an
occupation in its nature a lottery, it secured substantial justice. One
man might strike an enormously rich deposit, and others might
vainly prospect for months and years, but all had an equal chance.
No one was allowed to play the dog in the manger with the bounty
of the Creator. The essential idea of the mining regulations was to
prevent forestalling and monopoly. Upon the same principle are
based the mining laws of Mexico; and the same principle was
adopted in Australia, in British Columbia, and in the diamond
fields of South Africa, for it accords with natural perceptions of justice.

With the decadence of placer mining in California, the accustomed idea of private property finally prevailed in the passage of a
law permitting the patenting of mineral lands. The only effect is to
lock up opportunities—to give the owner of mining ground the
power of saying that no one else may use what he does not choose to
use himself. And there are many cases in which mining ground is
thus withheld from use of speculative purposes, just as valuable
[347/348] building lots and agricultural land are withheld from
use. But while thus preventing use, the extension to mineral land of
the same principle of private ownership which marks the tenure of
other lands, has done nothing for the security of improvements. The
greatest expenditures of capital in opening and developing mines—
expenditures that in some cases amounted to millions of dollars—
were made upon possessory titles.

Had the circumstances which beset the first English settlers in
North America been such as to call their attention *de novo* to the
question of land ownership, there can be no doubt that they would
have reverted to first principles, just as they reverted to first principles in matters of government; and individual land ownership

would have been rejected, just as aristocracy and monarchy were rejected. But while in the country from which they came this system had not yet fully developed itself, nor its effects been fully felt, the fact that in the new country an immense continent invited settlement prevented any question of the justice and policy of private property in land from arising. For in a new country, equality seems sufficiently assured if no one is permitted to take land to the exclusion of the rest. At first no harm seems to be done by treating this land as absolute property. There is plenty of land left for those who choose to take it, and the slavery that in a later stage of development necessarily springs from the individual ownership of land is not felt.

In Virginia and to the South, where the settlement had an aristocratic character, the natural complement of the large estates into which the land was carved was introduced in the shape of negro slaves. But the first settlers of New England divided the land as, twelve centuries before, their ancestors had divided the land of Britain, giving to each head of a family his town lot and his seed lot, while beyond lay the free common. So far as concerned the great proprietors whom the English kings by letters patent endeavored to create, the settlers saw clearly enough the injustice of the attempted monopoly, and none of these [348/349] proprietors got much from their grants; but the plentifulness of land prevented attention from being called to the monopoly which individual land ownership, even when the tracts are small, must involve when land becomes scarce. And so it has come to pass that the great republic of the modern world has adopted at the beginning of its career an institution that ruined the republics of antiquity; that a people who proclaim the inalienable rights of all men to life, liberty, and the pursuit of happiness have accepted without question a principle which, in denying the equal and inalienable right to the soil, finally denies the equal right to life and liberty; that a people who, at the cost of a bloody war have abolished chattel slavery, yet permit slavery in a more widespread and dangerous form to take root.

The continent has seemed so wide, the area over which population might yet pour so vast, that familiarized by habit with the idea of private property in land, we have not realized its essential injustice. For not merely has this background of unsettled land prevented the full effect of private appropriation from being felt, even in the older sections, but to permit a man to take more land than he could use, that he might compel those who afterwards needed it to pay him for the privilege of using it, has not seemed so unjust when others in their turn might do the same thing by going further on. And more than this, the very fortunes that have resulted from the appropriation of land, and that have thus really been drawn from taxes levied upon the wages of labor, have seemed, and have been heralded, as prizes held out to the laborer. In all the newer States, and even to a considerable extent in the older ones, our landed aristocracy is yet in its first generation. Those who have profited by the increase in the value of land have been largely men who began life without a cent. Their great fortunes, many of them running up high into the millions, seem to them, and to many others, as the best proofs of the justice of existing social conditions in rewarding prudence, foresight, industry, and thrift; whereas, the truth is that these fortunes are but the gains of monopoly, [349/350] and are necessarily made at the expense of labor. But the fact that those thus enriched started as laborers hides this, and the same feeling which leads every ticket holder in a lottery to delight in imagination in the magnitude of the prizes has prevented even the poor from quarreling with a system which thus made many poor men rich.

In short, the American people have failed to see the essential injustice of private property in land, because as yet they have not felt its full effects. This public domain—the vast extent of land yet to be reduced to private possession, the enormous common to which the faces of the energetic were always turned, has been the great fact that, since the days when the first settlements began to fringe the Atlantic Coast, has formed our national character and colored our national thought. It is not that we have eschewed a titled aristocracy and abolished primogeniture; that we elect all our officers from School Director up to President; that our laws run in the name of the people, instead of in the name of a prince; that the State knows no religion, and our judges wear no wigs—that we have been exempted from the ills that Fourth of July orators used to point to as characteristic of the effete despotisms of the Old World. The general intelligence, the general comfort, the active invention, the power of adaptation and assimilation, the free, independent spirit, the energy and hopefulness that have marked our people, are not causes, but results—they have sprung from unfenced land. This public domain has been the transmuting force which has turned the thriftless, unambitious European peasant into the self-reliant Western farmer; it has given a consciousness of freedom even to the dweller in crowded cities, and has been a well-spring of hope even to those who have never thought of taking refuge upon it. The child of the people, as he grows to manhood in Europe, finds all the best seats at the banquet of life marked "taken," and must struggle with his fellows for the crumbs that fall, without one chance in a thousand of forcing or sneaking his way to a seat. In America, whatever his condition, there has always been the consciousness [350/351] that the public domain lay behind him; and the knowledge of this fact, acting and reacting, has penetrated our whole national life, giving it to generosity and independence, elasticity and ambition. All that we are proud of in the American character; all that makes our conditions and institutions better than those of older countries, we may trace to the fact that land has been cheap in the United States, because new soil has been open to the emigrant.

But our advance has reached the Pacific. Further west we cannot go, and increasing population can but expand north and south and fill up what has been passed over. North, it is already filling up the valley of the Red River, pressing into that of the Saskatchewan and pre-empting Washington Territory; south, it is covering Western Texas and taking up the arable valleys of New Mexico and Arizona.

The republic has entered upon a new era, an era in which the monopoly of the land will tell with accelerating effect. The great fact which has been so potent is ceasing to be. The public domain is almost gone—a very few years will end its influence, already rapidly failing. I do not mean to say that there will be no public domain. For a long time to come there will be millions of acres of public lands carried on the books of the Land Department. But it must be remembered that the best part of the continent for agricultural purposes is already overrun, and that it is the poorest land that is left. It must be remembered that what remains comprises the great mountain ranges, the sterile deserts, the high plains fit only for grazing. And it must be remembered that much of this land which figures in the reports as open to settlement is unsurveyed land, which has been appropriated by possessory claims or locations which do not appear until the land is returned as surveyed. California figures on the books of the Land Department as the greatest land State of the Union, containing nearly 100,000,000 acres of public land—something like one-twelfth of the whole public domain. Yet so much of this is covered by railroad grants or held in the way of which I have spoken; so much consists of untillable mountains [351/352] or plains which require irrigation, so much is monopolized by locations which command the water, that as a matter of fact it is difficult to point the immigrant to any part of the State where he can take up a farm on which he can settle and maintain a family, and so men, weary of the quest, end by buying land or renting it on shares. It is not that there is any real scarcity of land in California—for, an empire in herself, California will some day maintain a population as large as that of France—but appropriation has got ahead of the settler and manages to keep just ahead of him.

Some twelve or fifteen years ago the late Ben Wade of Ohio said, in a speech in the United States Senate, that by the close of this century every acre of ordinary agricultural land in the United States would be worth $50 in gold. It is already clear that if he erred at all, it was in overstating the time. In the twenty-one years that remain of the present century, if our population keeps on increasing at the rate which it has maintained since the institution of the government, with the exception of the decade which included the civil war, there will be an addition to our present population of something like forty-five millions, an addition of some seven millions more than the total population of the United States as shown by the census of 1870, and nearly half as much again as the present population of Great Britain. There is no question about the ability of the United States to support such a population and many hundreds of millions more, and, under proper social adjustments, to support them in increased comfort; but in view of such an increase of population, what becomes of the unappropriated public domain. Practically there will soon cease to be any. It will be a very long time before it is all in use; but it will be a very short time, as we are going, before all that men can turn to use will have an owner.

But the evil effects of making the land of a whole people the exclusive property of some, do not wait for the final appropriation of the public domain to show themselves. [352/353] It is not necessary to contemplate them in the future; we may see them in the present. They have grown with our growth, and are still increasing.

We plow new fields, we open new mines, we found new cities; we drive back the Indian and exterminate the buffalo; we girdle the land with iron roads and lace the air with telegraph wires; we add knowledge to knowledge, and utilize invention after invention; we build schools and endow colleges; yet it becomes no easier for the masses of our people to make a living. On the contrary, it is becoming harder. The wealthy class is becoming more wealthy; but the poorer class is becoming more dependent. The gulf between the employed and the employer is growing wider; social contrasts are becoming sharper; as liveried carriages appear, so do barefooted children. We are becoming used to talk of the working classes and the propertied classes; beggars are becoming so common that where it was once thought a crime little short of highway robbery to refuse food to one who asked for it, the gate is now barred and the bulldog loosed, while laws are passed against vagrants which suggest those of Henry VIII.

We call ourselves the most progressive people on earth. But what is the goal of our progress, if these are its wayside fruits?

These are the results of private property in land—the effects of a principle that must act with increasing and increasing force. It is not that laborers have increased faster than capital; it is not that population is pressing against subsistence; it is not that machinery has

made "work scarce"; it is not that there is any real antagonism between labor and capital—it is simply that land is becoming more
valuable; that the terms on which labor can obtain access to the natural opportunities which alone enable it to produce, are becoming
harder and harder. The public domain is receding and narrowing.
Property in land is concentrating. The proportion of our people
who have no legal right to the land on which they live is becoming
steadily larger.

Says the New York *World:* "A non-resident proprietary, [353/354]
like that of Ireland, is getting to be the characteristic of large farming districts in New England, adding yearly to the nominal value of
leasehold farms; advancing yearly the rent demanded, and steadily
degrading the character of the tenantry." And the *Nation,* alluding
to the same section, says: "Increased nominal value of land, higher
rents, fewer farms occupied by owners; diminished product; lower
wages; a more ignorant population; increasing number of women
employed at hard, outdoor labor (surest sign of a declining civilization), and a steady deterioration in the style of farming—these are
the conditions described by a cumulative mass of evidence that is
perfectly irresistible."

The same tendency is observable in the new States, where the
large scale of cultivation recalls the latifundia that ruined ancient
Italy. In California a very large proportion of the farming land is
rented from year to year, at rates varying from a fourth to even half
the crop.

The harder times, the lower wages, the increasing poverty percep-
tible in the United States are but results of the natural laws we have
traced—laws as universal and as irresistible as that of gravitation. We
did not establish the republic when, in the face of principalities and
powers, we flung the declaration of the inalienable rights of man; we
shall never establish the republic until we practically carry out that
declaration by securing to the poorest child born among us an equal
right to his native soil! We did not abolish slavery when we ratified
the Fourteenth Amendment; to abolish slavery we must abolish private property in land! Unless we come back to first principles, unless
we recognize natural perceptions of equity, unless we acknowledge
the equal right of all to land, our free institutions will be in vain,
our common schools will be in vain; our discoveries and inventions
will but add to the force that presses the masses down! [354]

HAMLIN GARLAND

Under the Lion's Paw

IT WAS the last of autumn and first day of winter coming together. All day long the ploughmen on their prairie farms had moved to and fro in their wide level fields through the falling snow, which melted as it fell, wetting them to the skin—all day, notwithstanding the frequent squalls of snow, the dripping, desolate clouds, and the muck of the furrows, black and tenacious as tar.

Under their dripping harness the horses swung to and fro silently, with that marvellous uncomplaining patience which marks the horse. All day the wild geese, honking wildly, as they sprawled side-wise down the wind, seemed to be fleeing from an enemy behind, and with neck outthrust and wings extended, sailed down the wind, soon lost to sight.

Yet the ploughman behind his plough, though the snow lay on his ragged great-coat, and the cold clinging mud rose on his heavy boots, fettering him like gyves, whistled in the very beard of the gale. As day passed, the snow, ceasing to melt, lay along the ploughed land, and lodged in the depth of the stubble, till on each slow round the last furrow stood out black and shining as jet between the ploughed land and the gray stubble.

When night began to fall, and the geese, flying low, began to alight invisibly in the near corn-field, Stephen Council was still at work "finishing a land." He rode on his sulky plough when going with the wind, but walked when facing it. Sitting bent and cold but cheery under his slouch hat, he talked encouragingly to his four-in-hand.

"Come round there, boys!—Round agin! We got t' finish this land. Come in there, Dan! *Stiddy*, Kate,—stiddy! None o' y'r tantrums, Kittie. It's purty tuff, but got a be did. *Tchk! tchk!* Step along, Pete! Don't let Kate git y'r single-tree on the wheel. *Once* more!" [130/131]

From Hamlin Garland, *Main-Travelled Roads* (New York and London: Harper & Brothers, n.d.), pp. 130–144. First published in 1891.

They seemed to know what he meant, and that this was the last round, for they worked with greater vigor than before.

"Once more, boys, an' then, sez I, oats an' a nice warm stall, an' sleep f'r all."

By the time the last furrow was turned on the land it was too dark to see the house, and the snow was changing to rain again. The tired and hungry man could see the light from the kitchen shining through the leafless hedge, and he lifted a great shout, "Supper f'r a half a dozen!"

It was nearly eight o'clock by the time he had finished his chores and started for supper. He was picking his way carefully through the mud, when the tall form of a man loomed up before him with a premonitory cough.

"Waddy ye want?" was the rather startled question of the farmer.

"Well, ye see," began the stranger, in a depreciating tone, "we'd like t' git in f'r the night. We've tried every house f'r the last two miles, but they hadn't any room f'r us. My wife's jest about sick, 'n' the children are cold and hungry——"

"Oh, y' want 'o stay all night, eh?"

"Yes, sir; it 'ud be a great accom——"

"Waal, I don't make it a practice t' turn anybuddy way hungry, not on sech nights as this. Drive right in. We ain't got much, but sech as it is——"

But the stranger had disappeared. And soon his steaming, weary team, with drooping heads and swinging single-trees, moved past the well to the block beside the path. Council stood at the side of the "schooner" and helped the children out—two little half-sleeping children—and then a small woman with a babe in her arms.

"There ye go!" he shouted jovially, to the children. "*Now* we're all right! Run right along to the house there, an' tell Mam' Council you wants sumpthin' t' eat. Right this way, Mis'—keep right off t' the right there. I'll go an' git a lantern. Come," he said to the dazed and silent group at his side.

"Mother," he shouted, as he neared the fragrant and warmly lighted kitchen, "here are some wayfarers an' folks who need [131/132] sumpthin' t' eat an' a place t' snooze." He ended by pushing them all in.

Mrs. Council, a large, jolly, rather coarse-looking woman, took the children in her arms. "Come right in, you little rabbits. 'Most asleep, hey? Now here's a drink o' milk f'r each o' ye. I'll have s'm tea in a minute. Take off y'r things and set up t' the fire."

While she set the children to drinking milk, Council got out his lantern and went out to the barn to help the stranger about his team, where his loud, hearty voice could be heard as it came and went between the haymow and the stalls.

The woman came to light as a small, timid, and discouraged-looking woman, but still pretty, in a thin and sorrowful way.

"Land sakes! An' you've travelled all the way from Clear Lake t'-day in this mud! Waal! waal! No wonder you're all tired out. Don't wait f'r the men, Mis'——" She hesitated, waiting for the name.

"Haskins."

"Mis' Haskins, set right up to the table an' take a good swig o' tea whilst I make y' s'm toast. It's green tea, an' it's good. I tell Council as I git older I don't seem to enjoy Young Hyson n'r Gunpowder. I want the reel green tea, jest as it comes off'n the vines. Seems t' have more heart in it, some way. Don't s'pose it has. Council says it's all in m' eye."

Going on in this easy way, she soon had the children filled with bread and milk and the woman thoroughly at home, eating some toast and sweet-melon pickles, and sipping the tea.

"See the little rats!" she laughed at the children. "They're full as they can stick now, and they want to go to bed. Now, don't git up, Mis' Haskins; set right where you are an' let me look after 'em. I know all about young ones, though I'm all alone now. Jane went an' married last fall. But, as I tell Council, it's lucky we keep our health. Set right there, Mis' Haskins; I won't have you stir a finger."

It was an unmeasured pleasure to sit there in the warm, homely kitchen, the jovial chatter of the housewife driving out and holding at bay the growl of the impotent, cheated wind. [132/133]

The little woman's eyes filled with tears which fell down upon the sleeping baby in her arms. The world was not so desolate and cold and hopeless, after all.

"Now I hope. Council won't stop out there and talk politics all night. He's the greatest man to talk politics an' read the *Tribune*— How old is it?"

She broke off and peered down at the face of the babe.

"Two months 'n' five days," said the mother, with a mother's exactness.

"Ye don't say! I want 'o know! The dear little pudzy-wudzy!" she went on, stirring it up in the neighborhood of the ribs with her fat forefinger.

"Pooty tough on 'oo to go gallivant'n' 'cross lots this way——"

"Yes, that's so; a man can't lift a mountain," said Council, entering the door. "Mother, this is Mr. Haskins, from Kansas. He's been eat up 'n' drove out by grasshoppers."

"Glad t' see yeh!—Pa, empty that wash-basin 'n' give him a chance t' wash."

Haskins was a tall man, with a thin, gloomy face. His hair was a reddish brown, like his coat, and seemed equally faded by the wind and sun, and his sallow face, though hard and set, was pathetic somehow. You would have felt that he had suffered much by the line of his mouth showing under his thin, yellow mustache.

"Hain't Ike got home yet, Sairy?"

"Hain't seen 'im."

"W-a-a-l, set right up, Mr. Haskins; wade right into what we've got; 'taint much, but we manage to live on it—she gits fat on it," laughed Council, pointing his thumb at his wife.

After supper, while the women put the children to bed, Haskins and Council talked on, seated near the huge cooking-stove, the steam rising from their wet clothing. In the Western fashion Council told as much of his own life as he drew from his guest. He asked but few questions, but by and by the story of Haskins' struggles and defeat came out. The story was a terrible one, but he told it quietly, seated with his elbows on his knees, gazing most of the time at the hearth. [133/134]

"I didn't like the looks of the country, anyhow," Haskins said, partly rising and glancing at his wife. "I was ust t' northern Ingyannie, where we have lots o' timber 'n' lots o' rain, 'n' I didn't like the looks o' that dry prairie. What galled me the worst was goin' s' far away acrosst so much fine land layin' all through here vacant."

"And the 'hoppers eat ye four years, hand runnin', did they?"

"Eat! They wiped us out. They chawed everything that was green. They jest set around waitin' f'r us to die t' eat us, too. My God! I ust t' dream of 'em sittin' 'round on the bedpost, six feet long, workin' their jaws. They eet the fork-handles. They got worse 'n' worse till they jest rolled on one another, piled up like snow in winter. Well, it ain't no use. If I was t' talk all winter I couldn't tell nawthin'. But all the while I couldn't help thinkin' of all that land back here that nobuddy was usin' that I ought 'o had 'stead o' bein' out there in that cussed country."

"Waal, why didn't ye stop an' settle here?" asked Ike, who had come in and was eating his supper.

"Fer the simple reason that you fellers wantid ten 'r fifteen dollars an acre fer the bare land, and I hadn't no money fer that kind o' thing."

"Yes, I do my own work," Mrs. Council was heard to say in the pause which followed. "I'm a gettin' purty heavy t' be on m' laigs all day, but we can't afford t' hire, so I keep rackin' around somehow, like a foundered horse. S' lame—I tell Council he can't tell how lame I am, f'r I'm jest as lame in one laig as t' other." And the good soul laughed at the joke on herself as she took a handful of flour and dusted the biscuit-board to keep the dough from sticking.

"Well, I hain't *never* been very strong," said Mrs. Haskins. "Our folks was Canadians an' small-boned, and then since my last child I hain't got up again fairly. I don't like t' complain. Tim has about all he can bear now—but they was days this week when I jest wanted to lay right down an' die."

"Waal, now, I'll tell ye," said Council, from his side of the stove, silencing everybody with his good-natured roar, "I'd go down and [134/135] *see* Butler, *anyway*, if I was you. I guess he'd let you have his place purty cheap; the farm's all run down. He's ben anxious t' let t' somebuddy next year. It 'ud be a good chance fer you. Anyhow, you go to bed and sleep like a babe. I've got some ploughing t' do, anyhow, an' we'll see if somethin' can't be done about your case. Ike, you go out an' see if the horses is all right, an' I'll show the folks t' bed."

When the tired husband and wife were lying under the generous quilts of the spare bed, Haskins listened a moment to the wind in the eaves, and then said, with a slow and solemn tone,

"There are people in this world who are good enough t' be angels, an' only haff t' die to *be* angels."

II

Jim Butler was one of those men called in the West "land poor." Early in the history of Rock River he had come into the town and started in the grocery business in a small way, occupying a small building in a mean part of the town. At this period of his life he earned all he got, and was up early and late sorting beans, working over butter, and carting his goods to and from the station. But a change came over him at the end of the second year, when he sold a lot of land for four times what he paid for it. From that time forward he believed in land speculation as the surest way of getting rich. Every cent he could save or spare from his trade he put into land at forced sale, or mortgages on land, which were "just as good as the wheat," he was accustomed to say.

Farm after farm fell into his hands, until he was recognized as one of the leading landowners of the county. His mortgages were scattered all over Cedar County, and as they slowly but surely fell in he sought usually to retain the former owner as tenant.

He was not ready to foreclose; indeed, he had the name of being one of the "easiest" men in the town. He let the debtor off again and again, extending the time whenever possible.

"I don't want y'r land," he said. "All I'm after is the int'rest on my money—that's all. Now, if y' want 'o stay on the farm, why, [135/136] I'll give y' a good chance. I can't have the land layin' vacant." And in many cases the owner remained as tenant.

In the meantime he had sold his store; he couldn't spend time in it; he was mainly occupied now with sitting around town on rainy days smoking and "gassin' with the boys," or in riding to and from his farms. In fishing-time he fished a good deal. Doc Grimes, Ben Ashley, and Cal Cheatham were his cronies on these fishing excursions or hunting trips in the time of chickens or partridges. In winter they went to Northern Wisconsin to shoot deer.

In spite of all these signs of easy life Butler persisted in saying he "hadn't enough money to pay taxes on his land," and was careful to convey the impression that he was poor in spite of his twenty farms. At one time he was said to be worth fifty thousand dollars, but land had been a little slow of sale of late, so that he was not worth so much.

A fine farm, known as the Higley place, had fallen into his hands in the usual way the previous year, and he had not been able to find a tenant for it. Poor Higley, after working himself nearly to death on it in the attempt to lift the mortgage, had gone off to Dakota, leaving the farm and his curse to Butler.

This was the farm which Council advised Haskins to apply for; and the next day Council hitched up his team and drove down to see Butler.

"You jest let *me* do the talkin'," he said. "We'll find him wearin' out his pants on some salt barrel somew'ers; and if he thought you *wanted* a place he'd sock it to you hot and heavy. You jest keep quiet; I'll fix 'im."

Butler was seated in Ben Ashley's store telling fish yarns when Council sauntered in casually.

"Hello, But; lyin' agin, hey?"

"Hello, Steve! How goes it?"

"Oh, so-so. Too dang much rain these days. I thought it was goin' t' freeze up f'r good last night. Tight squeak if I get m' ploughin' done. How's farmin' with *you* these days?"

"Bad. Ploughin' ain't half done." [136/137]

"It 'ud be a religious idee f'r you t' go out an' take a hand y'rself."

"I don't haff to," said Butler, with a wink.

"Got anybody on the Higley place?"

"No. Know of anybody?"

"Waal, no; not eggsackly. I've got a relation back t' Michigan who's ben hot an' cold on the idee o' comin' West f'r some time. *Might* come if he could get a good lay-out. What do you talk on the farm?"

"Well, I d' know. I'll rent it on shares or I'll rent it money rent."

"Waal, how much money, say?"

"Well, say ten per cent, on the price—two-fifty."

"Wall, that ain't bad. Wait on 'im till 'e thrashes?"

Haskins listened eagerly to this important question, but Council was coolly eating a dried apple which he had speared out of a barrel with his knife. Butler studied him carefully.

"Well, knocks me out of twenty-five dollars interest."

"My relation'll need all he's got t' git his crops in," said Council, in the same, indifferent way.

"Well, all right; *say* wait," concluded Butler.

"All right; this is the man. Haskins, this is Mr. Butler—no relation to Ben—the hardest-working man in Cedar County."

On the way home Haskins said: "I ain't much better off. I'd like that farm; it's a good farm, but it's all run down, an' so 'm I. I could make a good farm of it if I had half a show. But I can't stock it n'r seed it."

"Waal, now, don't you worry," roared Council in his ear. "We'll pull y' through somehow till next harvest. He's agreed t' hire it ploughed, an' you can earn a hundred dollars ploughin' an' y' c'n git the seed o' me, an' pay me back when y' can."

Haskins was silent with emotion, but at last he said, "I ain't got nothin' t' live on."

"Now, don't you worry 'bout that. You jest make your headquarters at ol' Steve Council's. Mother'll take a pile o' comfort in havin' y'r wife an' children 'round. Y' see, Jane's married off lately, [137/138] an' Ike's away a good 'eal, so we'll be darn glad t' have y' stop with us this winter. Nex' spring we'll see if y' can't git a start agin." And he chirruped to the team, which sprang forward with the rumbling, clattering wagon.

"Say, looky here, Council, you can't do this. I never saw——" shouted Haskins in his neighbor's ear.

Council moved about uneasily in his seat and stopped his stammering gratitude by saying: "Hold on, now; don't make such a fuss over a little thing. When I see a man down, an' things all on top of 'm, I jest like t' kick 'em off an' help 'm up. That's the kind of religion I got, an' it's about the *only* kind."

They rode the rest of the way home in silence. And when the red light of the lamp shone out into the darkness of the cold and windy night, and he thought of this refuge for his children and wife, Haskins could have put his arm around the neck of his burly companion and squeezed him like a lover. But he contented himself with saying, "Steve Council, you'll git y'r pay f'r this some day."

"Don't want any pay. My religion ain't run on such business principles."

The wind was growing colder, and the ground was covered with a white frost, as they turned into the gate of the Council farm, and the children came rushing out, shouting, "Papa's come!" They hardly looked like the same children who had sat at the table the night before. Their torpidity, under the influence of sunshine and Mother Council, had given way to a sort of spasmodic cheerfulness, as insects in winter revive when laid on the hearth.

III

Haskins worked like a fiend, and his wife, like the heroic woman that she was, bore also uncomplainingly the most terrible burdens. They rose early and toiled without intermission till the darkness fell on the plain, then tumbled into bed, every bone and muscle aching with fatigue, to rise with the sun next morning to the same round of the same ferocity of labor.

The eldest boy drove a team all through the spring, ploughing [138/139] and seeding, milked the cows, and did chores innumerable, in most ways taking the place of a man.

An infinitely pathetic but common figure—this boy on the American farm, where there is no law against child labor. To see him in his coarse clothing, his huge boots, and his ragged cap, as he staggered with a pail of water from the well, or trudged in the cold and cheerless dawn out into the frosty field behind his team, gave the city-bred visitor a sharp pang of sympathetic pain. Yet Haskins loved his boy, and would have saved him from this if he could, but he could not.

By June the first year the result of such Herculean toil began to show on the farm. The yard was cleaned up and sown to grass, the garden ploughed and planted, and the house mended.

Council had given them four of his cows.

"Take 'em an' run 'em on shares. I don't want 'o milk s' many. Ike's away s' much now, Sat'd'ys an' Sund'ys, I can't stand the bother anyhow."

Other men, seeing the confidence of Council in the newcomer, had sold him tools on time; and as he was really an able farmer, he soon had round him many evidences of his care and thrift. At the advice of Council he had taken the farm for three years, with the privilege of re-renting or buying at the end of the term.

"It's a good bargain, an' y' want 'o nail it," said Council. "If you have any kind ov a crop, you c'n pay y'r debts, an' keep seed an' bread."

The new hope which now sprang up in the heart of Haskins and his wife grew almost as a pain by the time the wide field of wheat began to wave and rustle and swirl in the winds of July. Day after day he would snatch a few moments after supper to go and look at it.

"Have ye seen the wheat t'-day, Nettie?" he asked one night as he rose from supper.

"No, Tim, I ain't had time."

"Well, take time now. Le's go look at it."

She threw an old hat on her head—Tommy's hat—and looking [139/140] almost pretty in her thin, sad way, went out with her husband to the hedge.

"Ain't it grand, Nettie? Just look at it."

It was grand. Level, russet here and there, heavy-headed, wide as a lake, and full of multitudinous whispers and gleams of wealth, it stretched away before the gazers like the fabled field of the cloth of gold.

"Oh, I think—I *hope* we'll have a good crop, Tim; and oh, how good the people have been to us!"

"Yes; I don't know where we'd be t'-day if it hadn't ben f'r Council and his wife."

"They're the best people in the world," said the little woman, with a great sob of gratitude.

"We'll be in the field on Monday sure," said Haskins, gripping the rail on the fences as if already at the work of the harvest.

The harvest came, bounteous, glorious, but the winds came and blew it into tangles, and the rain matted it here and there close to the ground, increasing the work of gathering it threefold.

Oh, how they toiled in those glorious days! Clothing dripping with sweat, arms aching, filled with briers, fingers raw and bleeding, backs broken with the weight of heavy bundles, Haskins and his man toiled on. Tommy drove the harvester, while his father and a hired man bound on the machine. In this way they cut ten acres every day, and almost every night after supper, when the hand went to bed, Haskins returned to the field shocking the bound grain in the light of the moon. Many a night he worked till his anxious wife came out at ten o'clock to call him into rest and lunch.

At the same time she cooked for the men, took care of the children, washed and ironed, milked the cows at night, made the butter, and sometimes fed the horses and watered them while her husband kept at the shocking.

No slave in the Roman galleys could have toiled so frightfully and lived, for this man thought himself a free man, and that he was working for his wife and babes.

When he sank into his bed with a deep groan of relief, too tired to change his grimy, dripping clothing, he felt that he was getting [140/141] nearer and nearer to a home of his own, and pushing the wolf of want a little farther from his door.

There is no despair so deep as the despair of a homeless man or woman. To roam the roads of the country or the streets of the city, to feel there is no rood of ground on which the feet can rest, to halt weary and hungry outside lighted windows and hear laughter and song within,—these are the hungers and rebellions that drive men to crime and women to shame.

It was the memory of this homelessness, and the fear of its coming again, that spurred Timothy Haskins and Nettie, his wife, to such ferocious labor during that first year.

IV

"'M, yes; 'm, yes; first-rate," said Butler, as his eye took in the neat garden, the pig-pen, and the well-filled barnyard. "You're gitt'n' quite a stock around yeh. Done well, eh?"

Haskins was showing Butler around the place. He had not seen it for a year, having spent the year in Washington and Boston with Ashley, his brother-in-law, who had been elected to Congress.

"Yes, I've laid out a good deal of money durin' the last three years. I've paid out three hundred dollars f'r fencin'."

"Um—h'm! I see, I see," said Butler, while Haskins went on:

"The kitchen there cost two hundred; the barn ain't cost much in money, but I've put a lot o' time on it. I've dug a new well, and I —"

"Yes, yes, I see. You've done well. Stock worth a thousand dollars," said Butler, picking his teeth with a straw.

"About that," said Haskins, modestly. "We begin to feel's if we was gitt'n' a home f'r ourselves; but we've worked hard. I tell you we begin to feel it, Mr. Butler, and we're goin' t' begin to ease up purty soon. We've been kind o' plannin' a trip back t' *her* folks after the fall ploughin's done."

"*Eggs-actly!*" said Butler, who was evidently thinking of something else. "I suppose you've kind o' calc'lated on stayin' here three years more?" [141/142]

"Well, yes. Fact is, I think I c'n buy the farm this fall, if you'll give me a reasonable show."

"Um—m! What do you call a reasonable show?"

"Well, say a quarter down and three years' time."

Butler looked at the huge stacks of wheat, which filled the yard, over which the chickens were fluttering and crawling, catching grasshoppers, and out of which the crickets were singing innumerably. He smiled in a peculiar way as he said, "Oh, I won't be hard on yeh. But what did you expect to pay f'r the place?"

"Why, about what you offered it for before, two thousand five hundred, or *possibly* three thousand dollars," he added quickly, as he saw the owner shake his head.

"This farm is worth five thousand and five hundred dollars," said Butler, in a careless and decided voice.

"What!" almost shrieked the astounded Haskins. "What's that? Five thousand? Why, that's double what you offered it for three years ago."

"Of course, and it's worth it. It was all run down then; now it's in good shape. You've laid out fifteen hundred dollars in improvements, according to your own story."

"But *you* had nothin' t' do about that. It's my work an' my money."

"You bet it was; but it's my land."

"But what's to pay me for all my——"

"Ain't you had the use of 'em?" replied Butler, smiling calmly into his face.

Haskins was like a man struck on the head with a sandbag; he couldn't think; he stammered as he tried to say: "But—I never'd git the use—You'd rob me! More'n that: you agreed—you promised that I could buy or rent at the end of three years at——"

"That's all right. But I didn't say I'd let you carry off the improvements, nor that I'd go on renting the farm at two-fifty. The land is doubled in value, it don't matter how; it don't enter into the question; an' now you can pay me five hundred dollars a year rent, or take it on your own terms at fifty-five hundred, or—git out."
[142/143]

He was turning away when Haskins, the sweat pouring from his face, fronted him, saying again:

"But *you've* done nothing to make it so. You hain't added a cent. I put it all there myself, expectin' to buy. I worked an' sweat to improve it. I was workin' for myself an' babes——"

"Well, why didn't you buy when I offered to sell? What y' kickin' about?"

"I'm kickin' about payin' you twice f'r my own things,—my own fences, my own kitchen, my own garden."

Butler laughed. "You're too green t' eat, young feller. *Your* improvements! The law will sing another tune."

"But I trusted your word."

"Never trust anybody, my friend. Besides, I didn't promise not to do this thing. Why, man, don't look at me like that. Don't take me for a thief. It's the law. The reg'lar thing. Everybody does it."

"I don't care if they do. It's stealin' jest the same. You take three thousand dollars of my money—the work o' my hands and my wife's." He broke down at this point. He was not a strong man mentally. He could face hardship, ceaseless toil, but he could not face the cold and sneering face of Butler.

"But I don't take it," said Butler, coolly "All you've got to do is to go on jest as you've been a-doin', or give me a thousand dollars down, and a mortgage at ten per cent on the rest."

Haskins sat down blindly on a bundle of oats near by, and with staring eyes and drooping head went over the situation. He was under the lion's paw. He felt a horrible numbness in his heart and limbs. He was hid in a mist, and there was no path out.

Butler walked about, looking at the huge stacks of grain, and pulling now and again a few handfuls out, shelling the heads in his hands and blowing the chaff away. He hummed a little tune as he did so. He had an accommodating air of waiting.

Haskins was in the midst of the terrible toil of the last year. He was walking again in the rain and the mud behind his plough; he felt the dust and dirt of the threshing. The ferocious husking-time, with its cutting wind and biting, clinging snows, lay hard upon [143/144] him. Then he thought of his wife, how she had cheerfully cooked and baked, without holiday and without rest.

"Well, what do you think of it?" inquired the cool, mocking, insinuating voice of Butler.

"I think you're a thief and a liar!" shouted Haskins, leaping up. "A black-hearted houn'!" Butler's smile maddened him; with a sudden leap he caught a fork in his hands, and whirled it in the air. "You'll never rob another man, damn ye!" he grated through his teeth, a look of pitiless ferocity in his accusing eyes.

Butler shrank and quivered, expecting the blow; stood, held hypnotized by the eyes of the man he had a moment before despised—a man transformed into an avenging demon. But in the deadly hush between the lift of the weapon and its fall there came a gush of faint, childish laughter and then across the range of his vision, far away and dim, he saw the sun-bright head of his baby girl, as with the pretty, tottering run of a two-year-old, she moved across the grass of the dooryard. His hands relaxed: the fork fell to the ground; his head lowered.

"Make out y'r deed an' mor'gage, an' git off'n my land, an' don't ye never cross my line agin; if y' do, I'll kill ye."

Butler backed away from the man in wild haste, and climbing into his buggy with trembling limbs drove off down the road, leaving Haskins seated dumbly on the sunny pile of sheaves, his head sunk into his hands. [144]

ANDREW CARNEGIE

———•—•———

Triumphant Democracy

AGRICULTURE

*And they shall beat their swords into plough-
shares, and their spears into pruninghooks: nation shall not lift up sword against nation, neither
shall they learn war any more.* ISAIAH

WE TALK of our commerce, and we boast of our manufactures, but
the products of the soil are more important than both combined.

While commerce employs 2,900,000, and manufactures and mining 6,000,000, by far the largest corps of the industrial army—
10,700,000—tills the soil. Fortunate indeed for the country that so
great a proportion of its people are farmers and live in the country,
close to nature, among birds and bees and flowers and the golden
grain and the scent of the hay, and with the complaining brooks
that make the meadows green; where the morning sun can be seen as
it comes forth, and the glorious picture of its setting can be wor-
shipped every evening. This is the life that produces contented, so-
ber-minded, good-natured, fair and independent men. The rural democracy is the controlling force which shields the nation from the
"falsehood of extremes."

To say that the soil is owned and cultivated by the people is to
dispel all doubts as to the stability, the peace, and the prosperity of
the State.

In 1887, the latest date for which returns are available, the principal nations of the world stand in the following [247/248] order in
the value of their agricultural and pastoral products: The Republic
heads the procession with nearly $4,000,000,000, having marched in

From Andrew Carnegie, *Triumphant Democracy: Sixty Years' March of the
Republic,* Revised Edition, Based on the Census of 1890 (New York: Charles
Scribner's Sons, 1893), pp. 247–254.

little more than a century from the foot to the head of the column. Russia, with her immense area and one hundred millions of population, follows at a respectful distance with about $2,800,000,000; then comes La Belle France, with $2,300,000,000, have recently passed Germany in the race, which comes next with $2,120,000,000; then Austria-Hungary with $1,655,000,000, the harvest of her extensive corn lands and plains; and sixth in order comes the beautiful isle of the sea, small but mighty, Britain, with $1,255,000,000, a prodigious sum for her small area, proving how mother earth responds to proper cultivation. Italy, Spain, Australia, and Canada follow, but their united product is not quite two-thirds that of the Republic.

Comparing these figures with those of 1880, we are struck with the fact that, with the exception of the United States, no country shows much increase in its agricultural products. All have apparently about reached their capacity. The agricultural products of the Republic, on the other hand, were rated in 1880 at only three thousand million dollars; in 1887, as we have seen, they amounted to four thousand millions, an increase of thirty-three per cent in seven years. She is fast becoming the granary of the world. No other region seems able to export any greatly increasing quantity of food products to supply the deficiencies of Europe.

Ceres is indeed the prime divinity of the Republic. To her shrine is attracted the largest number of worshippers, and their homage is rewarded by her sweetest smiles and her most gracious favors. [248/249]

No victory of peace was so long deferred, or so complete when it came, as the conquest of the soil. A hundred years ago agriculture was in little better condition all over the world than it was a thousand years before. Indeed it has been boldly asserted that the Greeks, Romans, Egyptians, and Assyrians cultivated their soil better than any portion of the earth was tilled even a century ago. The alternation of crops was almost unknown; the fields exhausted by frequent repetition of the same crop were allowed to lie fallow, as in the time of Moses. Drainage, where practised, was of the rudest kind; and in the sodden ground crops were thin and poor in quality, and unhealthy as food. Farming implements were of the most primitive type. The plough generally used was little better than that of Virgil's time, and only scratched the ground. The sower, with basket suspended by a cord round the neck, walked over the field throwing handfuls of grain on each side, as described in the parable, and as shown even now by pictures in rural almanacs. The reaping-hook, almost as old as the hills on which waved the ripened corn, was the only means of cutting it; while only the "thresher's weary flingin'-

tree" of Burns enabled the farmer to separate the grain from the straw.

In breeding and rearing cattle, progress had been equally insignificant. The quality of food given to cattle was so bad that attention to breeding alone availed little in improving stock. The average weight of oxen and sheep sold in Smithfield market has more than doubled since the middle of the last century, a result to be ascribed to improved feeding quite as much as to increased care in breeding. [249/250]

The primitive condition of agriculture in America a century and a quarter ago is well illustrated in the following extract from a work by the Swedish traveller, Kalm. Speaking of the James River colonists, he says:

> "They make scarce any manure for their corn fields, but when one piece of ground has been exhausted by continual cropping, clear and cultivate another piece of fresh land, and when that is exhausted proceed to a third. Their cattle are allowed to wander through the woods and uncultivated grounds, where they are half starved, having long ago extirpated almost all the annual grasses by cropping them too early in the spring, before they had time to form their flowers or to shed their seeds."

And the imperfect feeding caused the cattle to diminish in size generation by generation, till they grew so stunted and small as to be appropriately called "runts."

The advance made in agriculture and cattle-raising during the last half century has been prodigious; and much of it is due either to the creation by American inventive genius of mechanical appliances, or to enforced European inventiveness resulting from American competition. From the earliest times American statesmen have directed their energies to the advancement of agricultural arts. Washington, with a burden of care such as has been the lot of few, found time to superintend agricultural operations and experiments. The importance of agriculture to civilization formed the text of his last annual message to Congress; and the last elaborate production of his pen, written only a week before his death, was a long letter to the manager of his farms, containing thirty-two folio sheets of directions for their cultivation during several succeeding years. Most of Washington's successors to the Presidency gave personal attention to [250/251] agriculture. One of the most distinguished of them, Mr. Jefferson, invented the hill-side plough; and Adams, Calhoun, Clay, and Webster forgot the anxieties of statesmanship in the peaceful pursuits of the farm. Beginning thus early, the advancement of agriculture has continued to be the first care of American statesmen and the American people, with the result that the Republic leads the world to-day not only in amount of agricultural products, but in excellence of agricultural machinery.

One-fourth of the total wealth of America is employed in the ownership and cultivation of the soil, and that is about the proportion which agriculture contributes to the industrial produce. Statistics for 1830 being untrustworthy, comparisons cannot safely be made with so early a period; but taking the figures of the census of 1850, which was very complete, we find that in the short space of forty years the amount of improved land more than trebled. The following table shows the extent and regularity of the progress made:

	1850	1860	1870	1880	1890
Total acres in farm	293,560,614	407,212,538	407,735,041	536,081,835	580,000,000
Acres improved	113,032,614	163,110,720	188,921,099	284,771,042	348,000,000
Number of farms	1,449,073	2,044,077	2,659,985	4,008,907	4,650,000
Average size of farms	203	199	153	134	125

It will be seen that the tendency is toward smaller rather than larger farms. Notwithstanding the gigantic holdings which have been the fashion in recent years in some of the northwestern States, the average farm has fallen in size from two hundred and three acres in 1850 to one hundred and thirty-four acres in 1880, and probably to one hundred and twenty-five acres or less at the present [251/252] time. As this result has been reached under a system of absolute freedom, we are justified in assuming that the cultivation of holdings small enough to be worked by one family without employing help is found to be the condition best fitted for survival. When I was in the Northwest upon the huge estates there, sagacious agriculturists in the district predicted that the small farmer, upon his eighty, or, at the most, one hundred and sixty, acres, would eventually drive out the great capitalists who had undertaken to farm thousands of acres by the labor of others; and the disintegration of these immense holdings has already begun. This is most cheering, for it is manifestly better for the State that a race of citizens, each his own master and landlord, should inhabit the land and each call a small portion of it his own, than that one man should be lord over thousands of acres and hundreds of farm laborers. Political and economical ends fortunately unite in this the grandest of all branches of industry in the nation. The centralization which seems inseparable from manufacturing is not, we may console ourselves, to invade the realms of agriculture. The State is still to rest in security upon the millions who possess and cultivate the soil divided into small farms. Such citizens are the very life-blood of the Republic.

In view of the fact that the land is going more and more into the hands of the people in smaller and smaller areas, what are we to think of men like Henry George, who are constantly proclaiming that the land is going into the hands of the few? It is usually added that the rich are becoming richer and the poor poorer. This statement is equally untrue, for every source of proof bearing upon the assertion is known to tell just the opposite, and that [252/253] wealth was never being so rapidly distributed among the masses; that of the returns of labor and capital, never did so large a proportion go to labor and so small a share to capital. But in refuting this statement we have not, unfortunately, the means of giving exact figures, although of its incorrectness there can be no doubt. In regard to the land, however, we have the exact figures. There is no trustworthy source of information other than the census. It cannot be so far wrong as to report a steady decrease in the size of agricultural holdings during every decade from 1850, when the first figures were obtained, to 1890, during which period the average holding has fallen from two hundred and three acres to one hundred and twenty-five. We have evidence of similar distribution of land among the people in most of the leading countries of the world. Here, then, is the truth, both in regard to wealth and land, under present conditions: the poor are becoming richer and the rich poorer, and the land is going more and more into the hands of the masses of the people every day.

The improved land in 1880 was but fifteen per cent of the total area, but even then, according to Mulhall, it produced thirty per cent of the grain of the world. The capital invested in farms and farming was $10,600,000,000 (£2,120,000,000), being more than three times as much as that invested in manufacturing, the next largest industry. At present, the proportion is doubtless less, since manufactures have increased at a more rapid rate than agriculture. The difference between "acres in farms" and "acres improved" is that the former includes about thirty-five per cent of natural woodland, which, although owned by the farmer, has not yet been cleared for crops. [253/254] In the newly settled States of the West it also includes a considerable but rapidly decreasing extent of land covered with a luxuriant growth of native grass, but as yet unploughed. It will therefore be seen that the productive acreage of the country may be, and no doubt soon will be, largely increased by the present farmers, independently of any increase in the number of farms.

It was considered wonderful at the beginning of the century to look back to sixty-five thousand square miles that had been brought under cultivation. Between 1850 and 1860, however, one hundred and seventy-seven thousand square miles had been turned into farms, and between 1870 and 1880 over two hundred thousand square miles. Thus in ten years territory larger than Britain, and almost equal in extent to the entire area of France or Germany, was added to the farm area in America, and still the work goes on. During the last ten years the sales of public lands exceeded one hundred and ninety million acres, or three hundred thousand square miles, one-tenth the area of the country—an area fifty per cent greater than that of the German Empire. In Dakota alone the new farms in 1883 exceeded six million acres—one-third of all Scotland. It is very clear that the Americans are likely to remain the great agricultural people of the world. [254]

NELSON A. DUNNING

The Farmers' Alliance

INTRODUCTORY HISTORY

ARISTOCRATIC IDEAS, backed up by intelligence and refinement, may serve a good purpose in toning down the untamed spirit, and broadening the nature of a native American; but when this station in society is reached through the medium of a bank account, human nature revolts, and the average person becomes disgusted. This spirit of avarice, or desire to make money, has become the bane of our social relations, and threatens the perpetuity of the government itself. The desire for wealth is increased as the power and privileges which it brings become more clearly understood. When the brains of a Webster or a Calhoun must wait unnoticed in the anteroom, while the plethoric pocket-book of some conscienceless speculator, monopolist, or trickster, brings to its owner the privileges of the parlor, [3/4] and the softest seat at the feast, intelligence and moral rectitude will always be at a discount, while fraud and corruption will bring a premium. In order that such conditions may exist, some portions of the people must suffer. This becomes a self-evident truth to all who will give the matter even the least consideration. The possession of wealth may be assumed, as a rule, to bring about the differences that are seen in society, and, because of this, becomes the essential object for which a large portion of our people are contending.

It is evident that all cannot be rich, and it is also true that none should be poor because of economic conditions. All economists agree that labor is the sole producer of wealth. If this proposition be true, it might be proper to ask: Why does not the producer of this wealth possess it, after production? What intervening cause steps in between the producer and this wealth, and prevents his owning and enjoying what his brain and brawn have created? No one seems to question the right or justice of each individual enjoying the fruits of his own

From Nelson A. Dunning, *The Farmers' Alliance History and Agricultural Digest* (Washington, D.C.: The Alliance Publishing Co., 1891), pp. 3–9.

labor. But the recognition of this right does not prevent the separation of production and possession, nor does it indicate a remedy for the evil. The idea of labor in production, at the present time, is associated with only a portion of our people. It represents, under the prevailing ideas of society, an undesirable condition, from which all, or nearly all, seek to be freed. The man or woman does not live who desires to labor every day in every year of their whole sojourn upon earth. Such a desire would be unnatural, a sin against the future, and a libel upon the past. Nine-tenths of the labor performed at the present time is done with the belief that this hard labor will bring about future ease and comfort. But when these efforts are honestly and earnestly continued for a series of years, and the anticipated reward does not come, and the plain fact is demonstrated that labor brings no reward, some give up in despair, while others determine to ascertain the cause, if possible.

It was to satisfy the American farmer that his calling had either become obsolete, or his environment unnatural, that agricultural organizations, for political or economic purposes, were brought into existence. Up to 1860 the economic privileges of the farmer were somewhat near a parity with other [4/5] branches of productive industry. The systematic spoliation of the present was, to a large extent, practically unknown. Special laws and privileges, which operated directly against the national interests of agriculture, existed only in a mild degree. At that period immense fortunes were almost unknown, and aristocracy was confined to the better educated and more refined. Neither poverty nor crime existed in the same proportion as now, and the general trend of events was toward conservatism in all economic conditions. Moderate fortunes, moderate sized farms, and moderate business enterprises, were not only the rule of the times, but were maintained under the protecting care of society's consent. Of course there were exceptions, but not in the offensive and disturbing sense in which they now exist. All must admit that the parasitic age had not begun at this date, and that labor in production paid less tribute than at the present time. Emerson says: "The glory of the farmer is that, in the division of labors, it is his part to create. All trade rests at last on his primitive activity. He stands close to Nature; he obtains from the earth the bread and the meat. The food which was not he causes to be." It is because of the truth contained in this statement that the farmer complains. It is because he simply creates for others, with but a feeble voice, if any, in determining the measure of his remuneration, that he has at last been compelled to enter an earnest protest. Willing as he is to create, and anxious to serve all other classes with the fruits of his industry and skill, yet the farmer has learned, by sad experience, that his toil has gone unrequited, and his anxiety has been construed into servility. The American farmer, in his present condition, is a living example of the folly and disaster which inevitably follow, where one class of citizens permits another class to formulate and administer all economic legislation. In other words, he is the victim of misplaced confidence, and has at last undertaken to regain his lost advantages and rights. The late Civil War gave an impetus to all productive labor. All efforts in that direction were profitable for a time, and the business of agriculture was looked upon with much favor. Vast sums of money were expended in the purchase and improvement of farming lands, and the success of that branch of industry seemed assured. The war ended in the [5/6] spring of 1865, and that year closed amid universal prosperity in the North, East, and West. The people were out of debt, all labor was employed, and all the conditions which wait upon a prosperous and industrious people were seen on every hand.

The people of the South had begun the task of repairing the ravages of war and rebuilding their shattered fortunes with a determination which admitted of no failure, and the whole country echoed with the busy hum of industry. During the year which followed, these conditions continued, but in the latter part of 1867 a change was observed. It had been brought about quietly. No one seemed to know how, but the effects were none the less positive. Agriculture was the first to feel this changed condition, and undertook to counteract it by a closer economy and increased production. The first compelled the manufacturer to curtail his production or lessen its value. Either course reduced the remuneration of the laborer, and compelled him to purchase less or buy cheaper. This reacted upon the farmer. The second overstocked the market, and reduced the price of the whole product, and enabled those who could to dictate their own terms. This condition has obtained among the farmers to the present time. In the vain endeavor to extricate themselves from their surroundings, having faith in the prospect of better times, the farmers borrowed money on note or mortgage to tide them over, only to find that the future brought no relief. This dark cloud of debt and disappointment hung lower and lower each succeeding year, until the storm of 1873 swept over the country, leaving in its course the wrecks of many thousand financial disasters.

In 1867 the first agricultural organization of promise appeared in the Grange, or Patrons of Husbandry. This organization sought to better the condition of the farmer by eliminating the so-called middleman,—the merchant or dealer. It assumed that the profit, which lodged somewhere between the producer and the consumer, was the cause of nearly all the disaster that waited upon agricultural effort.

This idea took hold of the people, and the result was an immense organization, with every promise of success. The experiment, aside from its educational results, was almost an entire failure.

Since this time the causes which have depressed agriculture [6/7] have been discovered, throughout the length and breadth of the land, by those who were interested, those who sympathized, to be the politician and the demagogue; but the discovery produced little or no effect. It remained for the farmer himself, after several ineffectual attempts, to solve the problem, and in so doing challenge the respect and admiration of the thinking world. The solution of this question, and the demand for its enactment into law, have no parallel in all history. It is an uprising of the conservative element of the people, the brain and brawn of the nation. It is a protest against present conditions; a protest against the unequal distribution of the profits arising from labor in production; a protest against those economic methods which give to labor a bare living, and make capital the beneficiary of all life's pleasures and comforts. It is a protest against continual toil on the one hand, and continual ease and comfort on the other. It is a protest against forced economy, debt, and privation to the producer, and peace, plenty, happiness, and prosperity to the non-producer.

The farmers have learned the secret, that organization, unity of action, and continuity of purpose, on their part, will in the end unite all sections, enrich all communities, and make every citizen equal before just laws. Intelligence to organize, fellow-feeling enough to unite, and manhood sufficient to stand firm, are the necessary requirements to bring this about. Organization is now the order of the day. It is the motive power that rules and guides the world. Without it the best of causes will not succeed, while with it the worse cause may prosper for a time. In the great struggle of life, as society is now constituted, organized evil must be met with organized good; organized greed with organized equity. In the combination of kindred forces lie the astonishing results of modern undertakings.

Individual enterprises are at a discount in the commercial world for many reasons. The individual may die and the whole business pass necessarily into the hands of those less competent to direct; or the individual may make a false move and thereby jeopardize the entire venture through an error in his single judgment; or, again, he may fall under the influence of bad habits and wreck the business through neglect or fast living. All these contingencies are impossible with an organization [7/8] properly constituted. Members of the organization may die, but the organization continues. The aggregate business intelligence of the whole membership is used, and not the single ideas of one. Organizations go on, live on; gathering experience which is stored up; gathering special information which is safely put away; increasing in wealth of which the outside world has no knowledge; using their power when least expected, and for objects that require years of patient waiting and calculation to perfect and mature. These considerations not only recommend a system of organization to all progressive minds, but make them absolutely necessary for success in modern business. One thing is certain,—organization as a factor of our modern civilization has come to stay. It cannot be eliminated, but may be, to a greater or less extent, confined in its operation within legitimate bounds. Its benefits will be sought under all conditions and by all classes of people, and those who ignore its power or underestimate its strength are sure to have cause for regret in the end.

The difficulty of organization among farmers is not wholly confined to a want of information, but shows itself in neighborhood factions of numerous kinds, individual or local jealousies, family or political differences, and a multitude of other insignificant but annoying obstructions that have to be avoided, smoothed over, or settled. These are never met with among men who organize from a business standpoint. The farmers, as a class, have been betrayed in almost everything, with a regularity truly astonishing. They have struggled against all odds, and have submitted to the result with a fortitude absolutely wonderful, but the time has come when something must be done. Some united action is demanded in defence of their own rights, and the maintenance of agriculture. This fact is too plain and too imperative to be longer ignored. It is a question now between liberty and serfdom, and must be decided without delay. Some will ask: What shall we organize for? For the same reasons that our enemies do; for individual benefits through combined effort. Organize to watch them, to consider their motives, and, if possible, checkmate their designs, when aimed at you or your business. This is a selfish world, and they who fail to realize this fact are quite sure to find it out [8/9] when too late. Organize for better laws; for through legislation comes prosperity or adversity.

During the past quarter of a century, the farmers of this country have labored, and others have made the laws. What has been the result? The non-producer has thrived while the producer has grown poor. Not only have the non-producers organized against the farmers, but almost all other producers. There is hardly a manufactured product, or ever a raw material, that is not subject to the guidance of an organization or combination of the whole, excepting the products of the farm. This means the spoliation of all who cannot meet this force with similar power. That being true, the farmer becomes the easy prey of all, and receives the treatment his own neglect brings upon him. All non-producers are the avowed enemies of producers, and should be so considered in all propositions of economics. When they organize, it is for the purpose of increasing their strength, which in turn makes them a correspondingly more dangerous enemy, and increases the necessity of stronger defence. In the vast amount of national legislation of the past twenty-five years, there is not one single act which was passed in the interest of the farmer. Search through the whole mass, and not one will be found that was introduced, passed, and put upon the statute books, for the sole benefit of agriculture. Until this is changed, and labor in production is made to bring a reward, industry is useless and economy is folly. [9]

NATIONAL PEOPLE'S PARTY PLATFORM

——◆———

ASSEMBLED upon the 116th anniversary of the Declaration of Independence, the People's Party of America, in their first national convention, involving upon their action the blessing of Almighty God, put forth in the name and on behalf of the people of this country, the following preamble and declaration of principles:

PREAMBLE

The conditions which surround us best justify our co-operation; we meet in the midst of a nation brought to the verge of moral, political, and material ruin. Corruption dominates the ballot-box, the Legislatures, the Congress, and touches even the ermine of the bench. The people are demoralized; most of the States have been compelled to isolate the voters at the [280/281] polling places to prevent universal intimidation and bribery. The newspapers are largely subsidized or muzzled, public opinion silenced, business prostrated, homes covered with mortgages, labor impoverished, and the land concentrating in the hands of capitalists. The urban workmen are denied the right to organize for self-protection, imported pauperized labor beats down their wages, a hireling standing army, unrecognized by our laws, is established to shoot them down, and they are rapidly degenerating into European conditions. The fruits of the toil of millions are boldly stolen to build up colossal fortunes for a few, unprecedented in the history of mankind; and the possessors of those, in turn, despite the Republic and endanger liberty. From the same prolific womb of governmental injustice we breed the two great classes—tramps and millionaires.

The national power to create money is appropriated to enrich bondholders; a vast public debt payable in legal tender currency has been funded into gold-bearing bonds, thereby adding millions to the burdens of the people.

From Thomas Hudson McKee, *The National Conventions and Platforms of all Political Parties 1789 to 1904*, Fifth Edition, Revised and Enlarged (Baltimore: The Friedenwald Company, 1904), pp. 280–285.

Silver, which has been accepted as coin since the dawn of history, has been demonetized to add to the purchasing power of gold by de creasing the value of all forms of property as well as human labor, and the supply of currency is purposely abridged to fatten usurers, bankrupt enterprise, and enslave industry. A vast conspiracy against mankind has been organized on two continents, and it is rapidly taking possession of the world. If not met and overthrown at once it forebodes terrible social convulsions, the destruction of civilization, or the establishment of an absolute despotism.

We have witnessed for more than a quarter of a century the struggles of the two great political parties for power and plunder, while grievous wrongs have been inflicted upon the suffering people. We charge that the controlling influences dominating both these parties have permitted the existing dreadful conditions to develop without serious effort to prevent or restrain them. Neither do they now promise us any substantial reform. They have agreed together to ignore, in the coming campaign, every issue but one. They propose to drown the outcries of a plundered people with the uproar of a sham battle over the tariff, so that capitalists, corporations, national banks, rings, trusts, watered stock, the demonetization of silver and the oppressions of the usurers may all be lost sight of. They propose to sacrifice our homes, lives, and [281/282] children on the altar of mammon; to destroy the multitude in order to secure corruption funds from the millionaires.

Assembled on the anniversary of the birthday of the nation, and filled with the spirit of the grand general and chief who established our independence, we seek to restore the government of the Republic to the hands of "the plain people," with which class it origi- nated. We assert our purposes to be identical with the purposes of the National Constitution; to form a more perfect union and establish justice, insure domestic tranquility, provide for the common defence, promote the general welfare, and secure the blessings of liberty for ourselves and our posterity.

We declare that this Republic can only endure as a free government while built upon the love of the whole people for each other and for the nation; that it cannot be pinned together by bayonets; that the civil war is over, and that every passion and resentment which grew out of it must die with it, and that we must be in fact, as we are in name, one united brotherhood of free men.

Our country finds itself confronted by conditions for which there is no precedent in the history of the world; our annual agricultural productions amount to billions of dollars in value, which must, within a few weeks or months, be exchanged for billions of dollars' worth of commodities consumed in their production; the existing currency supply is wholly inadequate to make this exchange; the results are falling prices, the formation of combines and rings, the impoverishment of the producing class. We pledge ourselves that if given power we will labor to correct these evils by wise and reasonable legislation, in accordance with the terms of our platform.

We believe that the power of government—in other words, of the people—should be expanded (as in the case of the postal service) as rapidly and as far as the good sense of an intelligent people and the teachings of experience shall justify, to the end that oppression, injustice, and poverty shall eventually cease in the land.

While our sympathies as a party of reform are naturally upon the side of every proposition which will tend to make men intelligent, virtuous, and temperate, we nevertheless regard these questions, important as they are, as secondary to the great issues now pressing for solution, and upon which not only our individual prosperity but the very existence of free institutions depend; and we ask all men to first help us to determine whether we are to have a republic to administer before we differ as to the conditions upon which it is to be [282/283] administered, believing that the forces of reform this day organized will never cease to move forward until every wrong is remedied and equal rights and equal privileges securely established for all the men and women of this country.

PLATFORM

We declare, therefore—

First.—That the union of the labor forces of the United States this day consummated shall be permanent and perpetual; may its spirit enter into all hearts for the salvation of the Republic and the uplifting of mankind.

Second.—Wealth belongs to him who creates it, and every dollar taken from industry without an equivalent is robbery. "If any will not work, neither shall he eat." The interests of rural and civic labor are the same; their enemies are identical.

Third.—We believe that the time has come when the railroad corporations will either own the people or the people must own the railroads, and should the government enter upon the work of owning and managing all railroads, we should favor an amendment to the Constitution by which all persons engaged in the government service shall be placed under a civil-service regulation of the most rigid character, so as to prevent the increase of the power of the national administration by the use of such additional government employees.

FINANCE.—We demand a national currency, safe, sound, and flexible, issued by the general government only, a full legal tender for all debts, public and private, and that without the use of banking corporations, a just, equitable, and efficient means of distribution direct to the people, at a tax not to exceed 2 per cent per annum, to be provided as set forth in the sub-treasury plan of the Farmer's Alliance, or a better system; also by payments in discharge of its obligations for public improvements.

1. We demand free and unlimited coinage of silver and gold at the present legal ratio of 16 to 1.

2. We demand that the amount of circulating medium be speedily increased to not less than $50 per capita.

3. We demand a graduated income tax.

4. We believe that the money of the country should be kept as much as possible in the hands of the people, and hence we demand that all State and national revenues shall be limited to the necessary expenses of the government, economically and honestly administered.

5. We demand that postal savings banks be established by the [283/284] government for the safe deposit of the earnings of the people and to facilitate exchange.

TRANSPORTATION.—Transportation being a means of exchange and a public necessity, the government should own and operate the railroads in the interest of the people. The telegraph, telephone, like the post-office system, being a necessity for the transmission of news, should be owned and operated by the government in the interest of the people.

LAND.—The land, including all the natural sources of wealth, is the heritage of the people, and should not be monopolized for speculative purposes, and alien ownership of land should be prohibited. All land now held by railroads and other corporations in excess of their actual needs, and all lands now owned by aliens should be reclaimed by the government and held for actual settlers only.

EXPRESSION OF SENTIMENTS

Your Committee on Platform and Resolutions beg leave unanimously to report the following:

Whereas, Other questions have been presented for our consideration, we hereby submit the following, not as a part of the Platform of the People's Party, but as resolutions expressive of the sentiment of this Convention:

1. *Resolved,* That we demand a free ballot and a fair count in all

elections, and pledge ourselves to secure it to every legal voter without Federal intervention, through the adoption by the States of the unperverted Australian or secret ballot system.

2. *Resolved,* That the revenue derived from a graduated income tax should be applied to the reduction of the burden of taxation now levied upon the domestic industries of this country.

3. *Resolved,* That we pledge our support to fair and liberal pensions to ex-Union soldiers and sailors.

4. *Resolved,* That we condemn the fallacy of protecting American labor under the present system, which opens our ports to the pauper and criminal classes of the world and crowds out our wage-earners; and we denounce the present ineffective laws against contract labor, and demand the further restriction of undesirable emigration.

5. *Resolved,* That we cordially sympathize with the efforts of organized workingmen to shorten the hours of labor, and demand a rigid enforcement of the existing eight-hour law on Government work, and ask that a penalty clause be added to the said law.

6. *Resolved,* That we regard the maintenance of a large standing army of mercenaries, known as the Pinkerton system, as a menace to our liberties, and we demand its abolition; and we condemn the recent invasion of the Territory of Wyoming by the hired assassins of plutocracy, assisted by Federal officers. [284/285]

7. *Resolved,* That we commend to the favorable consideration of the people and the reform press the legislative system known as the initiative and referendum.

8. *Resolved,* That we favor a constitutional provision limiting the office of President and Vice-President to one term, and providing for the election of Senators of the United States by a direct vote of the people.

9. *Resolved,* That we oppose any subsidy or national aid to any private corporation for any purpose.

10. *Resolved,* That this convention sympathizes with the Knights of Labor and their righteous contest with the tyrannical combine of clothing manufacturers of Rochester, and declare it to be the duty of all who hate tyranny and oppression to refuse to purchase the goods made by the said manufacturers, or to patronize any merchants who sell such goods. [285]

TWELVE SOUTHERNERS

———•·•———

A Statement of Principles

THE AUTHORS contributing to this book are Southerners, well acquainted with one another and of similar tastes, though not necessarily living in the same physical community, and perhaps only at this moment aware of themselves as a single group of men. By conversation and exchange of letters over a number of years it had developed that they entertained many convictions in common, and it was decided to make a volume in which each one should furnish his views upon a chosen topic. This was the general background. But background and consultation as to the various topics were enough; there was to be no further collaboration. And so no single author is responsible for any view outside his own article. It was through the good fortune of some deeper agreement that the book was expected to achieve its unity. All the articles bear in the same sense upon the book's title-subject: all tend to support a Southern way of life against what may be called the American or prevailing way; and all as much as agree that the best terms in which to represent the distinction are contained in the phrase, Agrarian *versus* Industrial.

*   *   *

But after the book was under way it seemed a pity if the contributors, limited as they were within their special subjects [ix/x] should stop short of showing how close their agreements really were. On the contrary, it seemed that they ought to go on and make themselves known as a group already consolidated by a set of principles which could be stated with a good deal of particularity. This might prove useful for the sake of future reference, if they should undertake any further joint publication. It was then decided to prepare a general introduction for the book which would state briefly the common convictions of the group. This is the statement. To it every one of the contributors in this book has subscribed.

From Twelve Southerners, *I'll Take My Stand: The South and the Agrarian Tradition* (New York: Harper & Brothers Publishers, 1930), pp. ix–xx.

*   *   *

Nobody now proposes for the South, or for any other community in this country, an independent political destiny. That idea is thought to have been finished in 1865. But how far shall the South surrender its moral, social, and economic autonomy to the victorious principle of Union? That question remains open. The South is a minority section that has hitherto been jealous of its minority right to live its own kind of life. The South scarcely hopes to determine the other sections, but it does propose to determine itself, within the utmost limits of legal action. Of late, however, there is the melancholy fact that the South itself has wavered a little and shown signs of wanting to join up behind the common or American industrial ideal. It is against that tendency that this book is written. The younger Southerners, who are being converted frequently to the industrial gospel, must come back to the support of the Southern tradition. They must be persuaded to look very critically at the [x/xi] advantages of becoming a "new South" which will be only an undistinguished replica of the usual industrial community.

*   *   *

But there are many other minority communities opposed to industrialism, and wanting a much simpler economy to live by. The communities and private persons sharing the agrarian tastes are to be found widely within the Union. Proper living is a matter of the intelligence and the will, does not depend on the local climate or geography, and is capable of a definition which is general and not Southern at all. Southerners have a filial duty to discharge to their own section. But their cause is precarious and they must seek alliances with sympathetic communities everywhere. The members of the present group would be happy to be counted as members of a national agrarian movement.

*   *   *

Industrialism is the economic organization of the collective American society. It means the decision of society to invest its economic resources in the applied sciences. But the word science has acquired a certain sanctitude. It is out of order to quarrel with science in the abstract, or even with the applied sciences when their applications are made subject to criticism and intelligence. The capitalization of the applied sciences has now become extravagant and uncritical; it has enslaved our human energies to a degree now clearly felt to be burdensome. The apologists of industrialism do not like to meet this charge directly; so they often [xi/xii] take refuge in saying that they are devoted simply to science! They are really devoted to the applied sciences and to practical production. Therefore it is necessary to employ a certain skepticism even at the expense of the Cult of Science, and to say, It is an Americanism, which looks innocent and disinterested, but really is not either.

* * *

The contribution that science can make to a labor is to render it easier by the help of a tool or a process, and to assure the laborer of his perfect economic security while he is engaged upon it. Then it can be performed with leisure and enjoyment. But the modern laborer has not exactly received this benefit under the industrial regime. His labor is hard, its tempo is fierce, and his employment is insecure. The first principle of a good labor is that it must be effective, but the second principle is that it must be enjoyed. Labor is one of the largest items in the human career; it is a modest demand to ask that it may partake of happiness.

* * *

The regular act of applied science is to introduce into labor a labor-saving device or a machine. Whether this is a benefit depends on how far it is advisable to save the labor. The philosophy of applied science is generally quite sure that the saving of labor is a pure gain, and that the more of it the better. This is to assume that labor is an evil, that only the end of labor or the material product is good. On this assumption labor becomes mercenary and servile, and it is no wonder if many forms of modern labor are accepted [xii/xiii] without resentment though they are evidently brutalizing. The act of labor as one of the happy functions of human life has been in effect abandoned, and is practiced solely for its rewards.

* * *

Even the apologists of industrialism have been obliged to admit that some economic evils follow in the wake of the machines. These are such as overproduction, unemployment, and a growing inequality in the distribution of wealth. But the remedies proposed by the apologists are always homeopathic. They expect the evils to disappear when we have bigger and better machines, and more of them. Their remedial programs, therefore, look forward to more industrialism. Sometimes they see the system righting itself spontaneously and without direction: they are Optimists. Sometimes they rely on the benevolence of capital, or the militancy of labor, to bring about a fairer division of the spoils: they are Coöperationists or Socialists. And sometimes they expect to find super-engineers, in the shape of Boards of Control, who will adapt production to consumption and regulate prices and guarantee business against fluctuations: they are

Sovietists. With respect to these last it must be insisted that the true Sovietists or Communists—if the term may be used here in the European sense—are the Industrialists themselves. They would have the government set up an economic super-organization, which in turn would become the government. We therefore look upon the Communist menace as a menace indeed, but not as a Red one; because it is simply according to the blind drift of our industrial [xiii/xiv] development to expect in America at last much the same economic system as that imposed by violence upon Russia in 1917.

*   *   *

Turning to consumption, as the grand end which justifies the evil of modern labor, we find that we have been deceived. We have more time in which to consume, and many more products to be consumed. But the tempo of our labors communicates itself to our satisfactions, and these also become brutal and hurried. The constitution of the natural man probably does not permit him to shorten his labor-time and enlarge his consuming-time indefinitely. He has to pay the penalty in satiety and aimlessness. The modern man has lost his sense of vocation.

*   *   *

Religion can hardly expect to flourish in an industrial society. Religion is our submission to the general intention of a nature that is fairly inscrutable; it is the sense of our rôle as creatures within it. But nature industrialized, transformed into cities and artificial habitations, manufactured into commodities, is no longer nature but a highly simplified picture of nature. We receive the illusion of having power over nature, and lose the sense of nature as something mysterious and contingent. The God of nature under these conditions is merely an amiable expression, a superfluity, and the philosophical understanding ordinarily carried in the religious experience is not there for us to have. [xiv/xv]

*   *   *

Nor do the arts have a proper life under industrialism, with the general decay of sensibility which attends it. Art depends, in general, like religion, on a right attitude to nature; and in particular on a free and disinterested observation of nature that occurs only in leisure. Neither the creation nor the understanding of works of art is possible in an industrial age except by some local and unlikely suspension of the industrial drive.

*   *   *

The amenities of life also suffer under the curse of a strictly-business or industrial civilization. They consist in such practices as manners, conversation, hospitality, sympathy, family life, romantic love —in the social exchanges which reveal and develop sensibility in human affairs. If religion and the arts are founded on right relations of man-to-nature, these are founded on right relations of man-to-man.

*   *   *

Apologists of industrialism are even inclined to admit that its actual processes may have upon its victims the spiritual effects just described. But they think that all can be made right by extraordinary educational efforts, by all sorts of cultural institutions and endowments. They would cure the poverty of the contemporary spirit by hiring experts to instruct it in spite of itself in the historic culture. But salvation is hardly to be encountered on that road. The trouble with the life-pattern is to be located at its economic base, and we cannot rebuild it by pouring in soft materials [xv/xvi] from the top. The young men and women in colleges, for example, if they are already placed in a false way of life, cannot make more than an inconsequential acquaintance with the arts and humanities transmitted to them. Or else the understanding of these arts and humanities will but make them the more wretched in their own destitution.

*   *   *

The "Humanists" are too abstract. Humanism, properly speaking, is not an abstract system, but a culture, the whole way in which we live, act, think, and feel. It is a kind of imaginatively balanced life lived out in a definite social tradition. And, in the concrete, we believe that this, the genuine humanism, was rooted in the agrarian life of the older South and of other parts of the country that shared in such a tradition. It was not an abstract moral "check" derived from the classics—it was not soft material poured in from the top. It was deeply founded in the way of life itself—in its tables, chairs, portraits, festivals, laws, marriage customs. We cannot recover our native humanism by adopting some standard of taste that is critical enough to question the contemporary arts but not critical enough to question the social and economic life which is their ground.

*   *   *

The tempo of the industrial life is fast, but that is not the worst of it; it is accelerating. The ideal is not merely some set form of industrialism, with so many stable industries, but industrial progress, or an incessant extension of industrialization. It never proposes a specific goal; it initiates the [xvi/xvii] infinite series. We have not merely capitalized certain industries; we have capitalized the laboratories and inventors, and undertaken to employ all the labor-saving devices that come out of them. But a fresh labor-saving device introduced into an industry does not emancipate the laborers in that industry so much as it evicts them. Applied at the expense of agriculture, for example, the new processes have reduced the part of the population supporting itself upon the soil to a smaller and smaller fraction. Of course no single labor-saving process is fatal; it brings on a period of unemployed labor and unemployed capital, but soon a new industry is devised which will put them both to work again, and a new commodity is thrown upon the market. The laborers were sufficiently embarrassed in the meantime, but, according to the theory, they will eventually be taken care of. It is now the public which is embarrassed; it feels obligated to purchase a commodity for which it had expressed no desire, but it is invited to make its budget equal to the strain. All might yet be well, and stability and comfort might again obtain, but for this: partly because of industrial ambitions and partly because the repressed creative impulse must break out somewhere, there will be a stream of further labor-saving devices in all industries, and the cycle will have to be repeated over and over. The result is an increasing disadjustment and instability.

*   *   *

It is an inevitable consequence of industrial progress that production greatly outruns the rate of natural consumption. To overcome the disparity, the producers, disguised as the [xvii/xviii] pure idealists of progress, must coerce and wheedle the public into being loyal and steady consumers, in order to keep the machines running. So the rise of modern advertising—along with its twin, personal salesmanship—is the most significant development of our industrialism. Advertising means to persuade the consumers to want exactly what the applied sciences are able to furnish them. It consults the happiness of the consumer no more than it consulted the happiness of the laborer. It is the great effort of a false economy of life to approve itself. But its task grows more difficult every day.

*   *   *

It is strange, of course, that a majority of men anywhere could ever as with one mind become enamored of industrialism: a system that has so little regard for individual wants. There is evidently a kind of thinking that rejoices in setting up a social objective which has no relation to the individual. Men are prepared to sacrifice their private dignity and happiness to an abstract social ideal, and without asking whether the social ideal produces the welfare of any individual man whatsoever. But this is absurd. The responsibility of men is for their own welfare and that of their neighbors; not for the hypothetical welfare of some fabulous creature called society.

* * *

Opposed to the industrial society is the agrarian, which does not stand in particular need of definition. An agrarian society is hardly one that has no use at all for industries, for [xviii/xix] professional vocations, for scholars and artists, and for the life of cities. Technically, perhaps, an agrarian society is one in which agriculture is the leading vocation, whether for wealth, for pleasure, or for prestige—a form of labor that is pursued with intelligence and leisure, and that becomes the model to which the other forms approach as well as they may. But an agrarian regime will be secured readily enough where the superfluous industries are not allowed to rise against it. The theory of agrarianism is that the culture of the soil is the best and most sensitive of vocations, and that therefore it should have the economic preference and enlist the maximum number of workers.

* * *

These principles do not intend to be very specific in proposing any practical measures. How may the little agrarian community resist the Chamber of Commerce of its county seat, which is always trying to import some foreign industry that cannot be assimilated to the life-pattern of the community? Just what must the Southern leaders do to defend the traditional Southern life? How may the Southern and the Western agrarians unite for effective action? Should the agrarian forces try to capture the Democratic party, which historically is so closely affiliated with the defense of individualism, the small community, the state, the South? Or must the agrarians—even the Southern ones—abandon the Democratic party to its fate and try a new one? What legislation could most profitably be championed by the powerful agrarians in the Senate of the United States? What anti-industrial measures might promise [xix/xx] to stop the advances of industrialism, or even undo some of them, with the least harm to those concerned? What policy should be pursued by the educators who have a tradition at heart? These and many other questions are of the greatest importance, but they cannot be answered here.

For, in conclusion, this much is clear: If a community, or a section, or a race, or an age, is groaning under industrialism, and well aware that it is an evil dispensation, it must find the way to throw it off. To think that this cannot be done is pusillanimous. And if the whole community, section, race, or age thinks it cannot be done, then it has simply lost its political genius and doomed itself to impotence. [xx]

DONALD DAVIDSON

"I'll Take My Stand": A History

IN THE AUTUMN of 1930 I was one of twelve Southerners who made an avowal of their concern for the destiny of the South. This avowal took the form of a book of essays, preceded by a statement of principles, the whole under the title: *I'll Take My Stand: The South and the Agrarian Tradition*. For certain obvious reasons it seems proper to review the origin and history of this adventure in social criticism. Among those reasons is the desire—I trust, a pardonable one—to have one true account of the book's history appear as a matter of record. It is with this purpose that I now write. But it should be understood that my expression is not the result of any new and systematic collaboration by the twelve original contributors. I am depending upon my own memory and am giving my own interpretation. When I use the first person plural, I do so for convenience only, and no presumption is intended.

In publishing *I'll Take My Stand* we were hardly so aspiring as to look for a great deal of support outside the South; but within our own section we took for granted that we might speak as Southerners. We thought that our fellow-Southerners would grasp without laborious explanation the terms of our approach to Southern problems; and that the argument, which was certain to follow, would proceed within [301/302] a range of assumptions understood and accepted by all. We welcomed the argument, since we felt that all parties would benefit by a free public discussion, of a sort unknown in the South since antebellum days. Such a discussion has taken place.

Yet with due respect to the able critics, whether of South or North, who have praised or blamed, seriously or jokingly, I beg leave to point out that the discussion of *I'll Take My Stand*, although it has continued briskly over a period of nearly five years, has been somewhat less profitable than it might have been, because the contending parties have too often argued in different terms. So

From Donald Davidson, "'I'll Take My Stand': A History," *American Review*, V (Summer, 1935), 301–321. Reprinted with the kind permission of the author.

far as the South was concerned, we were not altogether right in assuming that we could speak as Southerners to Southerners. For all
that some of our critics and we had in common in the way of premises, we might as well have been addressing Mr. Henry Ford or Mr.
Granville Hicks. No doubt we should have spared ourselves many
surprises if we had corrected our manuscripts accordingly. But let
that pass! Between these critics and ourselves is a gap of misunderstanding which in times like these ought not to be left yawning.

To our critics (if I may judge by their pronouncements), industrialism in 1930 was a foregone conclusion, an impregnable system
moving inexorably on a principle of economic determinism and already dominating the United States and the South. It had evils,
which might be softened by humanitarian devices; but its possibiliti-
ties for good outbalanced the evil. Mr. Gerald Johnson, for one,
spoke of "a glittering civilization" that ought to arise in an industrialized South. It is easy to imagine the pictures in his mind
[302/303] of a wealthy, urbanized South, plentifully equipped with
machines, hospitals, universities, and newspaper literates as alert as
he is. The pictures of agrarianism were correspondingly bleak. To
such critics, agrarianism suggested doomed farmers eaten up with
hookworm, brutal labour from sunrise to sunset, or at best an idealized plantation life vanishing or utterly gone; or, so far as agrarianism meant agriculture in the strict sense, it signified a snappy com-
mercialized occupation, making large-scale use of machines and
scientific agronomy. When we championed agrarianism, they were
amused and incredulous, if not disgusted, and therefore the tone of
their discussion was often one of scornful levity.

It was easy enough, and sometimes exciting, to meet such levity
with the retort called for under the circumstances. It would be easy
now to inquire in all seriousness whether industrial civilization still
glitters. But since we, no less than our critics, underestimated the
speed and the thoroughness of the industrial collapse, I put this
question, too, aside. Such uncomplimentary exchanges get nowhere,
since they leave the premises of argument untouched. We did not
and we do not think of industrialism and agrarianism in the terms
that our critics have used. For their part, they have been unable to
see the purposes of *I'll Take My Stand* in the proper context. It is
that context which I wish to describe.

I'll Take My Stand was intended to be a book of principles and
ideas, offering, with whatever implications it might have for America in general, a philosophy of Southern life rather than a detailed
programme. It was based upon historical analysis and [303/304]
contemporary observation. It was not a handbook of farming or economics. It was not a rhapsody on Pickett's Charge and the Old Plan-

tation. It was first of all a book for mature Southerners of the late nineteen-twenties, in the so-called New South—Southerners who, we trusted, were not so far gone in modern education as to require, for the act of comprehension, coloured charts, statistical tables, graphs, and journalistic monosyllables, but were prepared to use intelligence and memory.

In so far as it might benefit by an historical approach, the book needs to be considered against the background of 1929 and the years previous when it was being germinated and planned, and not, as it has been interpreted, against the background of Mr. Hoover's failure, the depression, and the New Deal. If we could have foreseen these events, we would have contrived to make the essays point clearly the moral that was even then implicit in them. But we were not, like the Prophet Moses, aware of any impending plagues to which we could refer for confirmation. In those years industrial commercialism was rampant. In no section were its activities more blatant than in the South, where old and historic communities were crawling on their bellies to persuade some petty manufacturer of pants or socks to take up his tax-exempt residence in their midst. This industrial invasion was the more disturbing because it was proceeding with an entire lack of consideration for its results on Southern life. The rural population, which included at least two-thirds of the total Southern population, was being allowed to drift into poverty and was being viewed with social disdain. [304/305] Southern opinion, so far as it was articulate, paid little serious attention to such matters. The older liberals of the Walter Hines Page school still believed in the easy humanitarianism of pre-World War days. The younger liberals were damning the Fundamentalists, and rejoicing in the efforts of the sociological missionaries who were arriving almost daily from the slum-laboratories of Chicago and New York. The business interests were taking full advantage of the general dallying with superficial issues.

I do not know at what precise moment the men who contributed to *I'll Take My Stand* arrived at the notion of making their views public. I do know that as individuals, observing and thinking separately, they arrived at the same general conclusions at about the same time. Although some of us were intimate friends, we had recently been scattered and had been writing in widely different fields. I remember that we were greatly and very pleasantly surprised, when we first approached the Southern topic, to find ourselves in hearty agreement. Each had been cherishing his notions in solitude, hardly expecting them to win the approval of the determined moderns who were his friends. But if we who had been so far separated and so differently occupied could so easily reach an understanding,

were there not many other Southerners, fully as apprehensive and
discontented as ourselves, who would welcome a forthright assertion
of principles? These must be Southern principles, we felt, for the
only true salvation of the South had to come from within—there had
been already too much parasitic reliance on external counsel. But
the principles must also be relevant to the new circumstances.
[305/306] What were the right Southern principles in the late nineteen-twenties?

Of course we never imagined that Southern principles, once defined, would apply just as benevolently in New York City as some
wise men thought that Eastern metropolitan principles would apply
in the South. We never dreamed of carrying across the line some
kind of Southern crusade to offset the Northern push which at our
own doors was making noises like a Holy War. In only one contin-
gency (which at that time seemed remote enough) could we possibly
conceive that Southern principles might have a national meaning.
Whoever or whatever was to blame for the condition of American
civilization in those days—and there were malcontents even in the
North who were asking such embarrassing questions—certainly the
South was not in any responsible sense the author of that condition.
The characteristic American civilization of the nineteen-twenties
had been produced under Northern auspices. It was the result of a
practically undisturbed control over American affairs that the North
had enjoyed since its victory at Appomattox, and of a fairly deliberate and consistent exclusion of Southern views. If ever it should
occur to the people of the North that that exclusion was a defect—if
ever Southern opinions should again be as hospitably entertained as
were Mr. Jefferson's and Mr. Madison's in other days, then Southern
principles would again have a meaning beyond the borders of the
South.

The idea of publishing a book dealing with the Southern situation went back perhaps as far as 1925 and certainly had begun to
take shape by 1928. For it was American industrialism of the boom
period that [306/307] disturbed us, no less than the later spectacle
of industrial disorder. Before even a prospectus could be outlined, a
great deal of discussion and correspondence was necessary. A sketch
of what we had been doing just before the publication of *I'll Take
My Stand* may be worth noting, since it indicates the diversity of interests from which we were drawn to focus on a single project. Tate
had been in France, finishing his biography of Jefferson Davis and
writing poetry and literary criticism. Ransom had been at work
upon *God Without Thunder*, a study of religion and science. Wade
had been writing a biography of John Wesley. Owsley was continuing the historical research that grew out of his *State Rights in the*

Confederacy and that was to lead to his *King Cotton Diplomacy*. Nixon, who had just left Vanderbilt for Tulane, had been studying the Populist movement and the problem of the tenant farmer. Warren was at Oxford; he had published a biography of John Brown. Lytle had been in the East, writing plays and acting. Lanier had been teaching at New York University and doing research in the psychology of race. Kline had just received a Master of Arts degree in English at Vanderbilt University. I was attempting to edit a book page and to follow the curious tergiversations that modernism produced among the rising Southern writers. As for the other two contributors (who were not of the "Nashville group"), Stark Young, in addition to dramatic criticism, had written some excellent novels on Southern themes which at that time were none too well appreciated; and John Gould Fletcher, in England, had turned to social criticism in *The Two* [307/308] *Frontiers,* a comparative study of Russia and America.

Most of us had a good deal of cosmopolitanism in our systems, the result of travel or residence abroad or of prolonged absorption in literature, pedagogy, or technical research. Those of us who had written poetry and criticism were painfully aware of the harsh constriction that modern life imposes on the artist. We were rebellious that such constriction should operate upon Southern artists—or, for that matter, upon any artist; and some of us had written essays asking why this should be so. All of us, I think, were turning with considerable relief from the shallow social criticism and tortured art of the nineteen-twenties to the works of the new historians and biographers who were somehow avoiding both the complaisance of the old Southern liberals and the dissociated cynicism of the younger ones. In their perfectly objective restatement of Southern history and American history we found new cause for our growing distrust of the scorn that was being volleyed at the "backward" South. What the historians said was in all really important points at startling variance with the assumptions of social critics and the "social workers" whose procedure was based on big-city attitudes. Suddenly we realized to the full what we had long been dimly feeling, that the Lost Cause might not be wholly lost after all. In its very backwardness the South had clung to some secret which embodied, it seemed, the precise elements out of which its own reconstruction—and possibly even the reconstruction of America—might be achieved. With American civilization, ugly and visibly bent on ruin, before our eyes, why should we not explore this secret? [308/309]

We were the more inclined to this course because of a natural loyalty to the South which the events of the nineteen-twenties had warmed and quickened. This was our first and most enduring point of agreement. That loyalty had both combative and sentimental aspects, I am sure. We were and are devoted to the South in spite of its defects, because it is our country, as our mother is our mother. But we have never been in the false and uncritical position attributed to us by some interpreters, of invariably preferring Southern things merely because they are Southern. For the record let it be noted that no more drastic criticisms of Southern life and affairs, past and present, can be found than in some of the books and essays of Owsley and Tate; and they, with Wade and others, have on occasion been denounced by Southern organizations for their "disloyalty." We never believed that one could be a good Southerner by simply drinking mint-juleps or by remarking sententiously on the admirable forbearance of Lee after Appomattox.

Such were our guiding motives. The search for Southern principles was a more deliberate affair, and doubtless had a good deal in it of that rationalization which is so often condemned and so generally indulged in. I am sure that at first we did not do much thinking in strictly economic terms. Uppermost in our minds was our feeling of intense disgust with the spiritual disorder of modern life—its destruction of human integrity and its lack of purpose; and, with this, we had a decided sense of impending fatality. We wanted a life which through its own conditions and purposefulness would engender naturally (rather [309/310] than by artificial stimulation), order, leisure, character, stability, and that would also, in the larger sense, be aesthetically enjoyable. What history told us of the South, what we knew of it by experience, now freshened by conscious analysis, and what we remembered of the dignity and strength of the generation that fought the Confederate War (for most of us were old enough to have received indelible impressions from survivors who never in anything but a military sense surrendered)—all this drove us straight to the South and its tradition. The good life we sought was once embodied here, and it lingered yet. Even in its seeming decline it contrasted sharply with the mode of life that we feared and disliked. The pertinent essays and reviews which we wrote before the appearance of *I'll Take My Stand* all had this central theme. Readers who wish to look for them will find them in *Harper's Magazine, The Forum,* the *Sewanee Review,* the *Nation,* the *New Republic,* the *Mississippi Valley Historical Review,* and elsewhere.

As we thought and talked further, we realized that the good life of the Old South, in its best period, and the life of our own South so far as it was still characteristic, was not to be separated from the agrarian tradition which was and is its foundation. By this route we came at last to economics and so found ourselves at odds with the prevailing schools of economic thought. These held that economics determines life and set up an abstract economic existence as the governor of man's effort. We believed that life determines economics, or ought to do so, and that economics is no more than an instrument, around the [310/311] use of which should gather many more motives than economic ones. The evil of industrial economics was that it squeezed all human motives into one narrow channel and then looked for humanitarian means to repair the injury. The virtue of the Southern agrarian tradition was that it mixed up a great many motives with the economic motive, thus enriching it and reducing it to a proper subordination.

Therefore the agrarian tradition was necessarily defined as "a way of life" from which originated, among other things, an economy. In *I'll Take My Stand* we did not enlarge upon the technical features of the economy, which could wait for a later description, but we treated other features of the Southern tradition at elaborate length and in broad contrast with the hostile industrial conceptions. The times seemed to call for just this emphasis, but I can see now that it puzzled our critics, who had somehow learned to think of "agrarian" in the strictly occupational terms used by newspapers and professional economists. Though it undoubtedly took too much for granted in our readers, the definition was sufficient for our immediate purposes. To us it signified a complete order of society based ultimately upon the land. It presupposed several kinds of farmers and endless varieties of other occupations. The elements of such a society had always existed in the South. They must now be used and improved upon if people were to remain their own masters and avoid the consequences of an industrial order which we could already see was headed toward communism or fascism.

The large-scale plantation had been an important [311/312] part of the older Southern life, but we were rather critical of the plantation, both because we felt its rôle had been over-emphasized and sentimentalized, and because we were interested in correcting, for the modern South, the abuses of the plantation system. We thought the rôle of the small farmer, or yeoman farmer, had been very much underestimated. We were concerned with the fate of the tenant farmer, with rural towns and communities, and with their importance in setting the tone of Southern life, even in the cities. We wished that the greatest possible number of people might enjoy the integrity and independence that would come with living upon their own land. Therefore we tended to push the large plantation into the background of consideration and to argue the case of the yeoman farmer. In this we followed Jefferson; but where the political rôle of the South was concerned we followed Calhoun, for it was the obvious, if regrettable, duty of the South to continue to defend itself against an aggressive, exploiting North.

Yet undeniable as our nostalgia for old times may have been—and quite justified—we had no intention of drawing a mellow and pretty picture of an idealized past. We leaned rather far in the other direction. Certainly Lytle's essay, "The Hind Tit," was aimed to show the merits of an agrarian life even in its roughest and most backwoodsy state. We were determined, furthermore, to make the broadest possible application of the general theory, and therefore we planned and secured essays that discussed religion, education, manners, the theory of progress, the race problem, the historical background, the arts, the problem [312/313] of the college graduate. Only one of the essays dealt with economics specifically. One essay outlined the general argument of the book, and like several of the other essays included a close negative analysis of industrialism, which we took pains to define rather carefully. We did not, of course, mean that the term industrialism should include any and every form of industry and every conceivable use of machines; we meant giant industrialism, as a force dominating every human activity: as the book says, "the decision of society to invest its economic resources in the applied sciences."

From the outset we had to deal with the problem of who the contributors ought to be. This finally resolved itself into the problem of who could be trusted to approach the issues as we saw them. A few of us, at Nashville, had enjoyed the benefits of long friendship and much discussion. We knew each other's minds, but we needed help. A memorandum in my file indicates that we planned the volume to be "deliberately partisan" to an extent which would exclude certain kinds of contributors: "sentimental conservatives whose sectionalism is of an extreme type" and "progressives whose liberalism is of an 'uplift' type." My note further says: "The volume will emphasize trans-Appalachian Southern thought and will therefore have a minority of contributors (if any at all) from the Atlantic states." But the names of possible contributors as recorded in this prospectus suggest how catholic our intention, or how great our innocence of mind, was in those days. Besides some names of the actual contributors, it includes the following: William E. Dodd, Broadus Mitchell, Newbell Niles [313/314] Puckett, W. W. Alexander, Julia Peterkin, G. B. Winton, Grover Hall, Louis Jaffee, Julian Harris, Judge Finis Garrett, Chancellor James H. Kirkland. To these were later added the names of Gerald Johnson, Stringfellow Barr, John Peale Bishop. But of the persons named only two were actually solicited—Gerald Johnson and Stringfellow Barr; and both declined, Mr. Johnson

with a curt jocular quip, Mr. Barr after a friendly exchange of correspondence which seemed at first to indicate his adherence.

Perhaps these rebuffs discouraged us from a wider solicitation. At
any rate the contributors finally agreed upon came into the book
largely because, by reason of close acquaintance, this or that person
felt they could be counted on and could presume to approach them.
Even then, for the sake of unity, we felt obliged to draw up the
"Statement of Principles" printed as an introduction. Each contribu-
tor was asked to approve these principles and to offer suggestions of
his own. The "statement" was revised several times. Nearly all of the
contributors had something to suggest, and most of the suggestions
were duly embodied. Finally, it represented composite opinion, arrived at after much trouble. The actual phrasing was the work of
Ransom, except for some passages and sentences here and there. I remember one last-minute change of wording. The second paragraph
originally began: "Nobody now proposes for the South, or for any
other community in this country, an independent political destiny.
That idea was finished in 1865." The latter sentence was changed to
read, "That idea *is thought to have been* finished in 1865."
[314/315]

There was no editor in the usual sense; the book was a joint undertaking. However, some of us at Nashville acted as an informal
steering committee and were obliged to hold many consultations
more or less editorial. One hotly argued editorial difficulty arose not
long before the book was scheduled to appear. Tate, Warren, and
Lytle held that the title ought to be changed from *I'll Take My
Stand* to *A Tract Against Communism*. Over against this suggestion,
which had good reason in it, was the embarrassing fact that the book
was practically ready for issue. The following extract from a letter
by Tate, written immediately after this incident, is prophetic of
what was in store for us: "It is over now. Your title triumphs. And I
observe that Alexander [of the Nashville *Tennesseean*] today on
the basis of the title defines our aims as an 'agrarian revival' and re-
duces our real aims to nonsense. These are, of course, an agrarian
revival in the full sense, but by not making our appeal through the
title to ideas, we are at the mercy of all the Alexanders—for they
need only to draw portraits of us plowing or cleaning the spring to
make hash of us before we get a hearing."

Tate was exactly right as to what would happen, though he now
says: "It would have happened anyway." In the contentious months
that followed, when we argued with all objectors who were worth
arguing with, such portraits or far worse ones were drawn. We had
virtually dared our contemporaries to debate with us the question,
then more or less tabooed, of whether the new industrialism was as

good for the South as was claimed. With due allowance for various friendly receptions and a generous allotment of [315/316] newspaper space which certainly gave us a hearing of a sort, it seems worth while to record a few samples of the raillery, not always good-humoured, with which our contemporaries greeted us. They begged to remind us of ox-carts and outdoor privies, and inquired whether we ever used porcelain bathtubs. If we admired agrarianism, what were we doing in libraries, and why were we not out gee-hawing? Had we ever tried to "make money" on a farm? Did we want to "turn the clock back" and retreat into "a past that never was"?

The Chattanooga *News,* although it complimented us with a series of very lengthy editorials, dubbed us "the Young Confederates," smiled indulgently over our "delightful economic absurdities," and said: "This quixotic tilting of literary lances against industrialization smacks of the counsel of despair." The Macon *Telegraph,* famous liberal newspaper that carries on its masthead a quotation from Mill's "Essay on Liberty," tore into the book, even before it was published, with all the savagery of the Chicago *Tribune's* best South-baiting editorials. Under the sarcastic title, "Lee, We Are Here!" the *Telegraph* began its insinuations thus: "One of the strangest groups to flourish in the South is the Neo-Confederates. This socially reactionary band does not come out of Atlanta—hatch of the Ku Klux Klan and the Supreme Kingdom—but appears to have its headquarters in Nashville." Later, with the book in hand, the *Telegraph* represented it as "a nostalgic cult owning a basis no more serious than sentiment," "an amusing patter-song," "a high spot in the year's hilarity." The New Orleans *Tribune* quoted with [316/317] avowed relish some phrases which the New York *Times* had editorially applied to the book: "a boy's Froissart of tales," "twelve Canutes," "worn-out romanticism."

A few critics, but only a very few, were more serious-minded and friendly. Some of these, oddly enough, were Eastern critics, who had lived at close quarters with industrialism and learned to dislike it; and in the end an Eastern magazine, THE AMERICAN REVIEW, gave us both understanding and hospitality of a sort we have never received, for example, from the *Virginia Quarterly Review.* And among Southern critics, it was a notable fact that our most consistent newspaper support came from Birmingham, the South's most highly industrialized city; from John Temple Graves II, of the Birmingham *News.*

Since we are not thin-skinned, we have managed to survive a curious notoriety of the sort that tempts friends to smile askance and tap their foreheads significantly. But our publishers practically dropped the book, no sooner than it was issued.

To the more sober charge that the agrarian proposals were not accompanied by a specific programme we have always been disposed to give heed. We had not attempted to frame any positive set-up for industry under an agrarian economy, and even our programme for the farm was not much particularized in the book itself. To an eminent and friendly Tennesseean, who deprecated our lack of a political programme, one of us answered that we represented "a body of principles looking for a party," and he was thereupon invited to run for Governor on an agrarian ticket. The truth is that *I'll Take My Stand* [317/318] was by necessity a general study, preliminary to a specific application which we hoped the times would permit us, with others, to work out slowly and critically. The emergencies of 1930 and later years made such deliberate procedure impossible. But even when the book was in press we should have been pleased to add the very specific proposals which were, in fact, made public during the debates sponsored by various newspapers and educational institutions. Ransom, for example, throughout 1930 and 1931 argued for a kind of subsistence farming (hardly of the later Rooseveltian model) and for government policies which would bring about a wide distribution of owned land. He has later developed these proposals in magazine articles and pamphlets. In fact most of the contributors, through whatever media have been open to them, in recent years have pushed the principles of agrarianism far beyond the point represented in *I'll Take My Stand* and have made proposals about as specific as could be expected from men who do not have the good fortune to be members of Congress or of the Brain Trust. These may be viewed as a substitute, however inadequate, for a second volume of *I'll Take My Stand,* which through causes beyond our control we have not been able to publish.

Since my purpose here is expository rather than argumentative, I will do no more than indicate the direction of agrarian proposals. Most of them have been fully stated by Frank Owsley in his recent article, "The Pillars of Agrarianism" (THE AMERICAN REVIEW, March 1935). We consider the rehabilitation of the farmer as of first importance to the South, the basis of all good remedial procedure; and we therefore [318/319] favour a definite policy of land conservation, land distribution, land ownership. At the risk of appearing socialistic to the ignorant, we favour legislation that will deprive the giant corporation of its privilege of irresponsibility, and that will control or prevent the socially harmful use of labour-saving (or labour-evicting) machinery. We advocate the encouragement of handicrafts, or of modified handicrafts with machine tools. In this connection, we believe that the only kind of new industry the South can now afford to encourage is the small industry which produces fine goods involving craftsmanship and art. We oppose the introduction of "mass-producing" industries that turn out coarse goods and cheap gadgets. We favour the diversion of public and private moneys from productive to non-productive uses—as for example to the arts—that over-accumulation of invested capital may be forestalled. We hold very strongly for a revision of our political framework that will permit regional governments to function adequately; and that will enable the national government to deal sensibly with issues in which the interests of regions are irreconcilable, or prevent the kind of regional exploitation, disguised as paternalism, now being practised on the South. That is to say, we favour a true Federalism and oppose Leviathanism, as ruinous to the South and eventually fatal to the nation.

It may be said of such proposals that they are not at all points peculiar to the Southern Agrarians, but are held by persons of various bias, some of whom may lean to an industrial point of view. I am sure this observation would be correct. The so-called Agrarians [319/320] are not a neatly organized band of conspirators. They are individuals united in a common concern but differing among themselves as to ways and means. They hope that their concern for the South, and to some extent their approach to Southern problems, is shared by many persons. They are conscious that many other minds than theirs are busy with these problems. They would be glad, as the book states, to be counted as members of a national agrarian movement.

Nevertheless, it is fair to emphasize at least two points of fundamental difference between the agrarian approach and others. We are interested in a way of life that will restore economics, among other things, rather than in an economics that promises merely to restore bare security, on hazardous terms, while leaving untouched the deep corruptions that render the security hardly capable of being enjoyed or nobly used. For this reason we are obliged to regard the Roosevelt Administration with a mixture of approval and distrust, for its approach, to the Southern situation especially, is too much of the latter order. At times President Roosevelt and his advisers seem to be governed by only two motives: the economic and the humanitarian. They propose to repair our faltering economic system and to guarantee a modicum of comfort to the human casualties of our false way of life. But they are doing nothing to repair the false way of life. Rather they seem to want to crystallize it in all its falsity. We believe that no permanent solution of our troubles can be found in that way. Complication will be heaped upon complication, until we shall be destroyed in the end from sheer moral impotence. But that is hard to explain to people who [320/321] insist in believing that labour can be benefited only by the invention of machinery and the promotion of labour unions, or who do not admit that the same human will which builds skyscrapers can also abandon them.

The second point of difference is one on which we would make few concessions, or none. Undoubtedly the South is a part of modern economy. Who could deny that? We should nevertheless insist that the South still has liberty to determine what its rôle will be with relation to that economy; and that that liberty ought not to be abrogated by the South or usurped by others. Unless the South can retain that power of decision, it can retain little of what may be, in any good sense, Southern. Above all, it cannot keep its self-respect or ever have the confidence in its own genius which is the greatest moral necessity of a living people. [321]

HUEY P. LONG

——•—•——

Every Man a King

COTTON REDUCTION PLAN—POTLIKKER EPISODE

IN THE late summer of 1931 it became apparent that there would be a tremendous cotton surplus in the United States. I proposed that no cotton should be planted in the United States in 1932, and that thereby the farmer, in possession of his 1931 crop, might reap for this one crop a price much in excess of what he would get for two crops, should one be raised in 1932.

The plan and suggestion met with such immediate favorable response that the Louisiana Legislature, meeting in special session, unanimously passed favorably upon the plan in both houses. The plan was later adopted by the Legislature of South Carolina. It was desired by the farmers of Texas, Alabama, Georgia and Arkansas, and might have been passed in all of those states, had it not been that the Governor of Texas threatened to veto the law should it be passed by the Texas Legislature.

We are now watching the farm relief plans. None will succeed permanently except one which balances production with consumption, and no plan is capable of accomplishing that, save and except that which has been prescribed in the Scripture, which is "to let the land lie barren in the days of surplus," the plan which I proposed.

When I saw hard times ahead in this country, I undertook to encourage the people of the South, and, for that matter, of the United States, to raise gardens [263/264] and to feed themselves and their children food products which they might not have the money to buy in days of stress. I began the propaganda with regard to potlikker and corn pone, which can be fed to a family for a few cents per week and the whole family kept strong and healthy.

Potlikker is the juice that remains in a pot after greens or other vegetables are boiled with proper seasoning. The best seasoning is a

From Huey P. Long, *Every Man a King: The Autobiography of Huey P. Long* (Chicago: Quadrangle Books, 1964), pp. 263–265. First published in 1933.

piece of salt fat pork, commonly referred to as "dry salt meat" or "side meat." If a pot be partly filled with well-cleaned turnip greens and turnips (the turnips should be cut up), with a half-pound piece of the salt pork, and then with water, and boiled until the greens and turnips are cooked reasonably tender, then the juice remaining in the pot is the delicious, invigorating, soul-and-body-sustaining pot-likker. The turnips and greens, or whatever other vegetable is used, should be separated from the juice; that is, the potlikker should be taken as any other soup and the greens eaten as any other food.

Corn pone is made simply of meal, mixed with a little salt and water, made into a pattie and baked until it is hard.

It has always been the custom to eat corn pone with potlikker. Most people crumble the corn pone into the potlikker. The blend is an even tasting food.

But, with the progress of education, the coming of "style," and the change of the times, I concluded that refinement necessitated that corn pone be "dunked" in the potlikker, rather than crumbled in the old-fashioned way. So I suggested that those sipping of potlikker should hold the corn pone in the left hand and [264/265] the spoon in the right, sip of the soup one time, then dip the corn pone in the potlikker and bite the end of the bread. My experience showed this to be an improvement over the crumbling.

But upon my undertaking not only to advertise and to bring about a wider use and distribution of potlikker and corn pone, but also to introduce a more elegant method of eating this delectable concoction, I met with opposition, first State-wide, then nation-wide, later international.

When Franklin D. Roosevelt, the present President of the United States, sent his telegram to the Atlanta Constitution, lining up his forces with the crumblers, I compromised—I compromised with all foes on the basis that it would be a commendable pursuit to eat pot-likker with corn pone, whether it be done by crumbling or by dunking.

But the serious strain here is that the health of the entire nation would be marvelously improved if people would boil their vegetables and eat the juice left after such vegetables are removed from the kettle, as there are in these foods properties such as iron, manganese, and others which are needed for health and complexion, sound bodies and minds, and "the perfect 36." [265]

SHERWOOD ANDERSON

——•◆•——

Blue Smoke

YOU BEGIN with the ground—Ground lugs—Bright lugs—Yellow red—Long red—Short red and tips.

The big tobacco warehouse and sales-room is at the edge of a town over the Virginia line in Tennessee. There are these big tobacco warehouses and sales-rooms in a dozen towns within a morning's truck-driving distance of the town from which I write, and there are tobacco farmers in town from over in Virginia, from North Carolina, from Kentucky, and even from South Carolina.

A learned man at the post office in one of these towns told me that this Southern Appalachian country is one of the oldest in the world. He says he got it out of a book. He says that is the reason why the hills are soft and round. The towns are tucked away in the valleys in the hills. From the hilltops there are little white towns with many church spires.

A man from within ten miles of this town may take his tobacco to a Virginia or South Carolina town, and a man from far over in Kentucky may try his luck here. The towns scream on billboards along the highways. The towns shout, "TAKE [87/88] YOUR TOBACCO TO GREENVILLE." "TRY ABINGDON." "ASHEVILLE, THE BEST TOBACCO MARKET IN THE SOUTH."

The towns want the market. The merchants hunger for it. In Asheville, two years ago, a merchant explained to me. That year the banks began cracking up down there. "If we hadn't got a pretty good tobacco market we'd have been done for," he said. The market may be important to the merchant, eager for the farmer's money, but it's ten times as important to the little tobacco raisers. They come into town filled with what the economists call "income expectancy."

What happens to them here, at this market, is the turning point of the year.

From Sherwood Anderson, *Puzzled America* (New York and London: Charles Scribner's Sons, 1935), pp. 87–99.

To many of them it means a year's income, all they will get. The kids need shoes and maybe a new suit or dress. And there is the "old woman," the tobacco farmer's wife. Just because she is called the "old woman" doesn't mean she is old. She is usually long and lean as is her "old man." This is still the hill country, little farms tucked away in little valleys in the hills—"hollers," they call them.

"Where's your place, Luther?"

I am not going to try to write in the dialect of the country. [88/89]

"Why, I'm a Scott County man. It's in Scratchgravel Holler." He's a Virginian, that one. He has come over here into Tennessee, to try his luck in this Tennessee market. The native Virginian never locates himself by a town. He doesn't say, "I'm from over near Lynchburg, or Charlottesville," as a Middle-Western man would. He says, "I'm from Grayson, or Scott, or Albemarle," naming his county. I remember a Virginia Floyd County woman who had married into Augusta County. "How are you, Mrs. Greer?" I asked. "I'm just common," she said, "except I'm honing for Floyd." It's good. It's a land, not a town attachment.

The men stand wistfully in the road before the tobacco market. Some of them have come to the market alone, others have brought their families. The tobacco farmer rarely has a truck of his own to bring his tobacco to market. "I'm too small a feller for that," he explains. He may own a Model T Ford. You can't haul much tobacco in that.

So he goes in with a half a dozen neighbors and they hire a truck to do the hauling—John's tobacco, Jim's, Luther's, Fred's. "A little feller like I am can't put out much, maybe one acre, or two, or three."

"It's really a woman's crop," John says. [89/90] "You've got to mess and mess with it, all year long." He stands before the warehouse, where the selling is going on. Luther and Jim and Fred stand with him. Fred has had a few shots of moon. You can smell it on him. He keeps slapping Jim on the back and laughing, rather foolishly. He says two of his kids, little fellers, put out half an acre for themselves. He helped them. They are both boys, and one of them wants a bicycle and the other some red-top boots. A man named Love comes up. "Hello, Love," Fred says, and I am a bit startled. "Is that really your name?" I want to ask. Love is built like another Abraham Lincoln. He has a long, scrawny neck, and there are bright red spots on his cheeks. "Look out or tuberculosis will get you," I think. He stands and spits on the ground. He is suspicious of me.

"You ain't a government man, are you?"

Formerly, in these hills, among these hill men, to admit you were a government man, that you had anything to do with government— to say the least, it was somewhat dangerous.

But times have changed. They have changed fast in the last year. There is a curious, wistful looking toward government now. Government becomes, to these little men, grubbing in the earth in these little valleys, curiously the Almost God. [90/91]

Personified in Mr. Roosevelt. They are nice about it, but it has its connotations. These little farmers have been stripped naked by the money-changers time and again. I suspect that these men could be made into brown or black or silver shirts easily enough. They hunger for leadership, and are looking to government and to Franklin D. Roosevelt with a curious boyish faith. "We can't do it by ourselves," they keep saying. They feel dimly that the big tobacco and cigarette companies are the common enemy. "We can't handle 'em. Government's got to help us or we're lost." Government at Washington is something far away and outside local county and state government, "the law."

"Look out. Here comes the law." A short fat man, a deputy sheriff, walks past us.

The men keep speaking of Roosevelt. "Ain't going to blame him for nothing he can't do." As though to say—"don't expect too much." There is this curious sweetness, humility, in these common men. A man going about among them, as I am doing just now, keeps asking himself, "Why does any one want to cheat them or hurt them?"

Most of the tobacco in this country is raised in small patches, one or two or three or at the most five acres. It is Burley tobacco. It's an exacting crop. You work at it all through the year. Now [91/92] the tobacco is going to market and the farmer who has just sold his crop will go home from here to burn over his seed bed for next year's crop.

For the seed bed he'll try to find a little patch of new rich ground, usually at the edge of the woods. The ground for the seed bed needs to be rich, so he selects the new ground, and if it isn't rich enough, he piles on the manure or the fertilizer.

Then he burns it over, puts on some dry litter and burns it off. The seed goes in and he takes a trip to town and buys strips of cheese-cloth to spread over the patch. Soon now you will see the little white patches over these hills.

Hoeing and cultivating and working all through the year. In the spring the fields blossom with a mass of lovely white bloom, a sight to see. You leave a few blossoms for next year's seed plants, but all the rest of the blossoms you take off. Fred says he nips his out with his fingers, but Luther says he uses a knife.

Then there is the harvest. It's a ticklish matter getting this crop in. When it comes to the sales warehouse, the sale floor, everything counts for you or against you. What you want, to get the price, is the great wide thin bright yellow tobacco leaves. Leaves can be so easily spotted and spoiled. [92/93] They can dry too fast or too slow. If they are seasoned just right they will be soft, like soft silk.

But to get them that way is a job. It takes the skill and the know-how. As I have already said, it begins at the ground. You break off the lower leaves, bind them together into a "hand." That's your "ground lugs." You won't get so much for your ground lugs. The rains have washed up onto the leaves. They are discolored where they have touched the ground. They will be coarse and spotty. Then come your "bright lugs," your "yellow red," your "long red." Here's your money tobacco, if it's cured right. Your "tips," at the very top of the plant are likely to be small, broken and spotty. They will go off at a low price. They will make snuff or cheap smoking tobacco.

When you have cut your tobacco you build racks in the field and let it hang out to dry. That is to get your fine yellow color.

Then into the barn. You want a barn the rain can't get into but that lets in plenty of air.

Now comes the grading, time to have an eye in your head, to have feel in your fingers. Fred says, "Can't one man in ten grade tobacco. It's like picking a new dress for a woman."

Now the tobacco goes into the sales warehouse. [93/94] It is carefully piled, each grade in a separate basket, and now come the buyers, the auctioneer and the pin hookers.

The pin hookers are a special breed. Some of them do nothing else but this all through the year. They work two months and rest ten. The big rush in the tobacco market lasts through January and February. The pin hooker is a man who knows his tobacco. He lives and bets on his knowledge. He is a man often who never raised a stalk of tobacco in his life, but he is a trader, and a sharp one. He knows his tobacco, and he knows his Fred, his Luther, Jim, and Tom. Life is a poker game for him.

The tobacco market is a kind of fair. Every one comes. The great, roomy warehouse is out at the edge of town near the railroad.

The patent medicine man has come, and the horse trader is here. There are long lines of trucks waiting for their turn to get tobacco on to the floor. The warehouse is owned by a private company. It takes off a percentage for every pound of tobacco sold. When there is a big market a farmer may be two or three days getting his crop on to the sales floor. He has brought a basket of food from home, and often at night he and the old woman and the kids sleep on the tobacco in the truck. [94/95]

Then, during the daytime you walk about and watch the sale. Hope. Hope. Hope. There are only four or five big tobacco companies in America, and each has its buyer here. The buyers are young, shrewd, fast-thinking, clever.

The men go to the sales floor and come back. The tobacco is stacked in long rows. Now they are selling Tom Whistler's baskets. How indifferent the buyers appear! Can they know what this means to Tom? You have been in a hospital and have seen a surgeon cut a man's arm off. It's like that. Each buyer puts his arm into the basket and jerks out a hand of the tobacco. He holds it up to the light, feels the leaves, throws the hand back into the basket.

"Eight-fifty."

"Nine."

That is Tom Whistler standing over there with his wife and kids. This sale is to decide everything for him. This is his year's income. Will the wife get a new dress, the kids new shoes? Will he have money to pay his taxes? I saw a tall man sitting on top of his basket after the buyers had passed. He put his face down in his hands and cried. Love pointed him out to me.

"Fred got four cents for his crop last year," Love says to me. "Did Fred cry? No! Fred went [95/96] out and got a bottle of moon and that night he got pie-eyed."

The tobacco industry is a big, regulated, controlled industry. But the little farmers feel it isn't controlled for them. Some of them talk about it as they stand in the warehouse and in the street, waiting.

The pin hooker moves about among them. He goes to a farmer whose crop has not yet been sold. He tempts the farmer. Some few of the farmers, the smart ones, those who know how to cure and grade their tobacco, know as much as the pin hooker. Others are unfortunate. "A lot of us are pretty dumb," Fred says. The pin hooker makes a flat offer. If he sees a basket he thinks is badly graded, he will go to the farmer, buy it and regrade it. There are the pin hookers who work outside and the floor pin hookers. I stood on the floor on a day when tobacco took a sharp jump upward. A pin hooker wearing a fancy vest and with a big cigar in his mouth came and spoke to me. "I shaved off eight hundred bucks today," he said. By a little sharp trading he had managed to make more in a few hours that morning than Fred or Luther or Love had made by a month of work in the field.

The tobacco raisers, standing about in the warehouse [96/97] and in the street outside, keep talking about government. Men are going through the country now signing them up. The crop is to be cut sharply next year. Government is going to try taking a hand at control in their favor. "It has to begin at the ground, like raising tobacco," Love says. You can't tell these men that prices paid on the floor—in spite of the auctioneer, each company is represented by its own buyer—you can't convince them that the big companies don't fix the price.

Luther, who is more skillful than the others and gets a better

price for his tobacco, has a radio and he tells the others what he
hears coming through the air at night when he is at home. He
speaks about individualism, explaining to the others. "It means
something what they call the New Deal. It means that people have
got to be made to quit cutting each other's throats. Individualism
means that—the devil take the hindermost. We're the hindermost,"
he says and grins.

On the floor of the great warehouses the sales go on. Men with
hand trucks are wheeling away the sold baskets. In another warehouse across the street men are at work packing the tobacco into
great hogsheads. A long train of tobacco-loaded cars will leave here
tonight. This tobacco, now being sold, may not get to the user for
years. It [97/98] will be handled and rehandled, cured and recured,
sorted, graded, tested, treated.

There is a constant hubbub, the cry of the auctioneer, the quick
bark of the buyers. The shrewd-eyed pin hookers move from group
to group. In the street the patent medicine man keeps talking. "You
got hookworms, I tell you."

And now look, it is Fred's turn. The auctioneer and the buyers
have come to his baskets. We all go into the warehouse to stand
watching, and Fred draws a little away. His old woman, a thin-
cheeked one of thirty, already with six kids—they get married young
in the mountains—the kids are clinging to her skirts. There is fear in
her eyes, in Fred's eyes, and even in the eyes of the children. "You
get out of here," Fred says gruffly, and she takes the smallest of the
children into her arms and, followed by the others, goes reluctantly
away. Fred has spoken gruffly to her, but there is something else back
of the gruffness in his voice. He has already had two or three drinks
of moon. "You take now your eighteen- or your twenty-cent tobacco
—a man can live," Jim says, "but your five- or your six-cent stuff—it's
starvation."

Fred walks a little away and I see him standing by the wall. He
takes a bottle from his hip pocket and has himself another shot. His
best tobacco, his [98/99] bright lugs, bring nine cents, but all the
rest of it, two-thirds of his crop, goes for two and three cents.

Jim Luther, and Tom do not look at Fred. Luther spits on the
floor. Jim steps over and pulls a hand of tobacco out of a nearby basket. "This is pretty good," he says to me. He spreads one of the yellow leaves out over his big hand. "You see, it has been cured right.
See how thin it is. Like silk, ain't it?"

The men stand looking at me, and I am suddenly ashamed of my
city clothes. Jim, Luther, and Tom all wear patched clothes. Their
overalls are patched, and all have long, thin, sun-tanned, wind-bit-
ten faces. "You ain't a government man, are you?" Love asks me

again. "Because if you are, you had better tell government they got to keep on helping us what they can."

"We've got pretty puny, trying to help ourselves," Jim says, and they all turn and walk away out of the warehouse and into the street. [99]

FRANKLIN D. ROOSEVELT

———◦———

President's Message to Congress:
Farm Tenancy

THE WHITE HOUSE, *February 16, 1937*

To the Congress of the United States:

I transmit herewith for the information of the Congress the report of the Special Committee on Farm Tenancy.

The facts presented in this report reveal a grave problem of great magnitude and complexity. The American dream of the family-size farm, owned by the family which operates it, has become more and more remote. The agricultural ladder, on which an energetic young man might ascend from hired man to tenant to independent owner, is no longer serving its purpose.

Half a century ago one of every four farmers was a tenant. Today, two of every five are tenants, and on some of our best farm lands seven of every ten farmers are tenants. All told, they operate land and buildings valued at $11,000,000,000.

For the past 10 years, the number of new tenants every year has been about 40,000. Many tenants change farms every 2 or 3 years, and apparently one out of three changes farms every year. The agricultural [25/26] ladder, for these American citizens, has become a treadmill.

At the same time, owners of family-size farms have been slipping down. Thousands of farmers commonly considered owners are as insecure as tenants. The farm owner-operator's equity in his property is, on the average, 42 percent, and in some of our best farming sections is as little as one-fifth.

When fully half the total farm population of the United States no longer can feel secure, when millions of our people have lost

From *Farm Tenancy: Report of the President's Committee,* Prepared under the Auspices of the National Resources Committee (Washington, D.C.: United States Government Printing Office, 1937), pp. 25–26.

their roots in the soil, action to provide security is imperative, and will be generally approved.

A problem of such magnitude is not solved overnight, nor by any one limited approach, nor by the Federal Government alone. While aggravated by the depression, the tenancy problem is the accumulated result of generations of unthinking exploitation of our agricultural resources, both land and people. We can no longer postpone action. We must begin at once with such resources of manpower, money, and experience as are available, and with such methods as will call forth the cooperative effort of local, State, and Federal agencies of Government, and of landlords quite as much as tenants. In dealing with the problem of relief among rural people during the depression, we have already accumulated information and experience which will be of great value in the long-time program. It will be wise to start the permanent program on a scale commensurate with our resources and experience, with the purpose of later expanding the program to a scale commensurate with the magnitude of the problem as rapidly as our experience and resources will permit.

The Special Committee on Farm Tenancy emphasizes the necessity for action of at least four types: First, action to open the door of ownership to tenants who now have the requisite ability and experience, but who can become owners only with the assistance of liberal credit, on long terms, and technical advice; second, modest loans, with the necessary guidance and education to prevent small owners from slipping into tenancy, and to help the masses of tenants, croppers, and farm laborers at the very bottom of the agricultural ladder increase their standards of living, achieve greater security, and begin the upward climb toward landownership; third, the retirement by public agencies of land proved to be unsuited for farming, and assistance to the families living thereon in finding homes on good land; fourth, cooperation with State and local agencies of government to improve the general leasing system. These activities, which bear such close relation to each other, should furnish a sound basis for the beginning of a program for improving the present intolerable condition of the lowest income farm families.

The Committee has very properly emphasized the importance of health and education in any long-time program for correcting the evils from which this large section of our population suffers. Attention is also called to the part which land speculation has played in bringing insecurity into the lives of rural families, and to the necessity for eliminating sharp fluctuations in land value due to speculative activity in farm lands.

The attack on the problem of farm tenancy and farm security is a logical continuation of the agricultural program this administration has been developing since March 4, 1933. Necessarily, whatever program the Congress devises will have to be closely integrated with existing activities for maintaining farm income and for conserving and improving our agricultural resources.

Obviously, action by the States alone and independently cannot cure the widespread ill. A Nation-wide program under Federal leadership and with the assistance of States, counties, communities, and individuals is the only solution. Most Americans believe that our form of government does not prohibit action on behalf of those who need help.

FRANKLIN D. ROOSEVELT [26]

4

The Weeds in the Garden: Dissent and Disillusionment

NOT ALL American writers have been convinced that the agrarian tradition is valid, that reality measures up to its assumptions about human nature, society, or agricultural life and activity. In 1775, the anonymous author of a survey of colonial agriculture called *American Husbandry* noted that "the American planters and farmers are in general the greatest slovens in Christendom." George Washington expressed an opinion in a letter to Arthur Young written in 1791, "that the aim of the farmers in this country, if they can be called farmers, is, not to make the most they can from the land, which is, or has been cheap, but the most of the labour, which is dear; the consequence of which has been, much ground has been scratched over and none cultivated or improved as it ought to have been." The obstacles of a wide variety of climates and soils, and the lack of experience and sometimes aptitude of the early American farmer often did conspire to make his efforts appear backward.

Along with the general portrait of the husbandman as an honest, noble champion of individualism, there has also existed in American literature an obverse portrait of the poor white farmer as a lazy, shiftless, uncouth member of a mongrel race. William Byrd of Westover initiated this brutish character with his sketches of the idle lubberlanders observed in North Carolina during his survey of the disputed boundary line between that state and Virginia. Although Byrd was reacting partly out of his aristocratic sensitivities, and partly out of the cultivated tradition in Virginia that North Carolina was but a refuge for social malcontents and runaways, he fathered a long-continuing series of descriptions of poor white degenerates, extending through nineteenth-century Southern literature, the humor of the Old Southwest, and local color fiction, down to the present with Erskine Caldwell's lustful and depraved sharecroppers.

There were those in the nineteenth century who became disillusioned with the agrarian life when they attempted to put it into practice for idealistic rather than practical reasons. The second quarter of the century saw the growth of numerous short-lived experiments in communal living, with both religious and secular philosophical bases. Many of the Utopian experimenters recognized the significance of agriculture to their endeavors and honored it as an occupation of great practical and moral consequence. What happened, however, when the city-bred, manicured, sensitive hands of the study-room idealists were placed to the harsh plow and blistering hoe was another matter. Nathaniel Hawthorne, who usually saw the darker side of human nature and was cynical of the high-minded Utopians and Transcendentalists, provided in *The Blithedale Romance* a fictionalized account of his brief infatuation with the Brook Farm experiment in Massachusetts in 1841. A. Bronson Alcott founded the short-lived society Fruitlands in 1842, where all members were to share the agricultural labors and subsist on a vegetarian diet. His daughter, Louisa May Alcott, provided a good-humored account of this agrarian failure in her story "Transcendental Wild Oats." Henry David Thoreau, always the practical experimenter, tester, and prover of the transcendental theories issued from the safe studies of Emerson and others, tried to live out the ideal pattern of the agrarian during a portion of his stay at Walden. He concluded that the reported virtues of the farmer's existence are largely mythical and that in the total natural scheme, the husbandman is of little import: "We are wont to forget that the sun looks on our cultivated fields and on the prairies and forests without distinction. They all reflect and absorb his rays alike, and the former make but a small part of the glorious picture which he beholds in his daily course."

Thorstein Veblen and H. L. Mencken became impatient with the farmer in this century for other reasons. To Veblen, the farmer was attempting to continue to live according to an illusioned, outmoded view of his significance in modern industrial society, and his insistence upon his virtuous independence was but a way of concealing his basically selfish regard only for his own welfare. He accuses him of disguising his nature as a greedy absentee landlord, acquiring more land than he can cultivate, and seeking "to come in for as much of a free income at the cost of the rest of the community as the law would allow." These same themes are developed with rhetorically inspired abuse and ill humor, and much less mercy, by H. L. Mencken in his sarcastic attack on "The Husbandman," as "a tedious brand of ignoramus, a cheap rogue and hypocrite, the eternal Jack of the human pack." All the basic and historically revered principles of agrarianism are reviewed by Mencken and refuted in possibly the most severe criticism delivered in this country.

A great discrepancy between the ideal and the real became evident to many with the development of the sharecropper and tenant-farmer systems, which by the 1930's had involved many underprivileged agriculturalists in a state of perpetual physical, intellectual, and emotional bondage. In his autobiographical book *Lanterns on the Levee,* the eloquent Mississippi poet and latter-day agrarian William Alexander Percy described the development of these systems as the necessary response of the South after the Civil War to the economic problems of Reconstruction. He defended sharecropping, if honestly administered, as "one of the best systems ever devised to give security and a chance for profit to the simple and the unskilled." But in their poignant, impressionistic prose and photographic essay on the lives of several typical Alabama sharecropper families of the late 1930's, *Let Us Now Praise Famous Men,* novelist James Agee and journalist Walker Evans recorded testimony of the tragic effect it could have on human lives when unjustly administered.

Perhaps the only defense that can be offered to the dissenters in the American garden of Eden is the one offered by Percy, when he says that if there is any failure in the sharecropping system, "the failure is in human nature." Sidney Lanier put it most aptly in one of his dialect poems, in the concluding line which serves as a title: "Thar's more in the man than thar is in the land." And if a myth is the expression of the general beliefs, the ethos of a social class or nation, it should be judged not according to its correspondence to reality but its facility for the expression of an accepted truth among a people of a particular time and place. The myth of the agrarian life serves this function admirably.

WILLIAM BYRD

———•———

History of the Dividing Line Between Virginia and North Carolina: Run in the Year 1728

March 25, 1728

THE AIR was chill'd this morning with a smart north-west wind, which favour'd the Dismalites in their dirty march. They return'd by the path they had made in coming out, and with great industry arriv'd in the evening at the spot where the line had been discontinued.

After so long and laborious a journey, they were glad to repose themselves on their couches of cypress-bark, where their sleep was as sweet as it wou'd have been on a bed of Finland down.

In the mean time, we who stay'd behind had nothing to do, but to make the best observations we cou'd upon that part of the country. The soil of our landlord's plantation, tho' none of the best, seem'd more fertile than any thereabouts, where the ground is near as sandy as the desarts of Affrica, and consequently barren. The road leading from thence to Edenton, being in distance about 27 miles, lies upon a ridge call'd Sandy-Ridge, which is so wretchedly poor that it will not bring potatoes.

The pines in this part of the country are of a different species from those grown in Virginia: their bearded leaves are much longer and their cones much larger. Each cell contains a seed of the size and figure of a black-ey'd pea, which shedding in November, is very good mast for hogs, and fattens them in a short time. [74/75]

The smallest of these pines are full of cones, which are 8 or 9 inches long, and each affords commonly 60 or 70 seeds. This kind of

From *The Writings of "Colonel William Byrd of Westover in Virginia Esqr."*, edited by John Spencer Bassett (New York: Doubleday, Page & Co., 1901), pp. 74–76, 240–242. First published in 1841.

mast has the advantage of all other, by being more constant, and less liable to be nippt by the frost, or eaten by the caterpillars. The trees also abound more with turpentine, and consequently yield more tarr, than either the yellow or the white pine; and for the same reason make more durable timber for building. The inhabitants hereabouts pick up knots of lightwood in abundance, which they burn into tar, and then carry it to Norfolk or Nansimond for a market. The tar made in this method is the less valuable, because it is said to burn the cordage, tho' it is full as good for all other uses, as that made in Sweden and Muscovy.

Surely there is no place in the world where the inhabitants live with less labour than in N Carolina. It approaches nearer to the description of Lubberland than any other, by the great felicity of the climates, the easiness of raising provisions, and the slothfulness of the people.

Indian corn is of so great increase, that a little pains will subsist a very large family with bread, and then they may have meat without any pains at all, by the help of the low grounds, and the great variety of mast that grows on the high-land. The men, for their parts, just like the Indians, impose all the work upon the poor women. They make their wives rise out of their beds early in the morning, at the same time that they lye and snore, till the sun has run one third of his course, and [75/76] disperst all the unwholesome damps. Then, after stretching and yawning for half an hour, they light their pipes, and, under the protection of a cloud of smoak, venture out into the open air; tho', if it happens to be never so little cold, they quickly return shivering into the chimney corner. When the weather is mild, they stand leaning with both their arms upon the corn-field fence, and gravely consider whether they had best go and take a small heat at the hough: but generally find reasons to put it off till another time.

Thus they loiter away their lives, like Solomon's sluggard, with their arms across, and at the winding up of the year scarcely have bread to eat.

To speak the truth, tis a thorough aversion to labor that makes people file off to N Carolina, where plenty and a warm sun confirm them in their disposition to laziness for their whole lives. [76]

November 16, 1728

We gave orders that the horses shou'd pass Roanoak River at Monisep Ford, while most of the baggage was transported in a canoe.

We landed at the plantation of Cornelius Keith, where I beheld the wretchedest scene of poverty I had ever met with in this happy part of the world. The man, his wife and six small children, liv'd in a penn, like so many cattle, without any roof over their heads but that of heaven. And this was their airy residence in the day time, but then there was a fodder stack not far from this inclosure, in which the whole family shelter'd themselves a night's and in bad weather. [240/241]

However, 'twas almost worth while to be as poor as this man was, to be as perfectly contented. All his wants proceeded from indolence, and not from misfortune. He had good land, as well as good health and good limbs to work it, and, besides had a trade very useful to all the inhabitants round about. He cou'd make and set up quern stones very well, and had proper materials for that purpose just at hand, if he cou'd have taken the pains to fetch them.

There is no other kind of mills in those remote parts, and, therefore, if the man wou'd have workt at his trade, he might have liv'd very comfortably. The poor woman had a little more industry, and spun cotton enough to make a thin covering for her own and her children's nakedness.

I am sorry to say it, but idleness is the general character of the men in the southern parts of this colony as well as in North Carolina. The air is so mild, and the soil so fruitful, that very little labour is requir'd to fill their bellies, especially where the woods afford such plenty of game. These advantages discharge the men from the necessity of killing themselves with work, and then for the other article of raiment, a very little of that will suffice in so temperate a climate. But so much as is absolutely necessary falls to the good women's share to provide. They all spin, weave and knit, whereby they make a good shift [241/242] to cloath the whole family; and to their credit be it recorded, many of them do it very completely, and thereby reproach their husbands' laziness in the most inoffensive way, that is to say, by discovering a better spirit of industry in themselves. [242]

NATHANIEL HAWTHORNE

The Blithedale Romance

... I WAS NOW on my legs again. My fit of illness had been an avenue between two existences; the low-arched and darksome doorway, through which I crept out of a life of old conventionalisms, on my hands and knees, as it were, and gained admittance into the freer region that lay beyond. In this respect, it was like death. And, as with death, too, it was good to have gone through it. Not otherwise could I have rid myself of a thousand follies, fripperies, prejudices, habits, and other such worldly dust as inevitably settles upon the crowd along the broad [55/56] highway, giving them all one sordid aspect before noon-time, however freshly they may have begun their pilgrimage in the dewy morning. The very substance upon my bones had not been fit to live with in any better, truer, or more energetic mode than that to which I was accustomed. So it was taken off me and flung aside, like any other worn-out or unseasonable garment; and, after shivering a little while in my skeleton, I began to be clothed anew, and much more satisfactorily than in my previous suit. In literal and physical truth, I was quite another man. I had a lively sense of the exultation with which the spirit will enter on the next stage of its eternal progress, after leaving the heavy burthen of its mortality in an earthly grave, with as little concern for what may become of it as now affected me for the flesh which I had lost.

Emerging into the genial sunshine, I half fancied that the labors of the brotherhood had already realized some of Fourier's predictions. Their enlightened culture of the soil, and the virtues with which they sanctified their life, had begun to produce an effect upon the material world and its climate. In my new enthusiasm, man looked strongly and stately,—and woman, O how beautiful!—and the earth a green garden, blossoming with many-colored delights. Thus Nature, whose laws I had broken in various artificial ways, comported herself towards me as a strict but loving mother, who uses the

From Nathanial Hawthorne, *The Blithedale Romance* (Boston: Ticknor, Reed, and Fields, 1852), pp. 55–64.

rod upon her little boy for his naughtiness, and then gives him a
smile, a kiss, and some pretty playthings, to console the urchin for
her severity.

In the interval of my seclusion, there had been a number of recruits to our little army of saints and martyrs. [56/57] They were
mostly individuals who had gone through such an experience as to
disgust them with ordinary pursuits, but who were not yet so old,
nor had suffered so deeply, as to lose their faith in the better time to
come. On comparing their minds one with another, they often discovered that this idea of a Community had been growing up, in silent and unknown sympathy, for years. Thoughtful, strongly-lined
faces were among them; sombre brows, but eyes that did not require
spectacles, unless prematurely dimmed by the student's lamplight,
and hair that seldom showed a thread of silver. Age, wedded to the
past, incrusted over with a stony layer of habits, and retaining nothing fluid in its possibilities, would have been absurdly out of place
in an enterprise like this. Youth, too, in its early dawn, was hardly
more adapted to our purpose; for it would behold the morning radiance of its own spirit beaming over the very same spots of with-
ered grass and barren sand whence most of us had seen it vanish. We
had very young people with us, it is true,—downy lads, rosy girls in
their first teens, and children of all heights above one's knee;—but
these had chiefly been sent hither for education, which it was one of
the objects and methods of our institution to supply. Then we had
boarders, from town and elsewhere, who lived with us in a familiar
way, sympathized more or less in our theories, and sometimes shared
in our labors.

On the whole, it was a society such as has seldom met together;
nor, perhaps, could it reasonably be expected to hold together long.
Persons of marked individuality—crooked sticks, as some of us might
be called—are not exactly the easiest to bind up into a faggot. But, so
[57/58] long as our union should subsist, a man of intellect and
feeling, with a free nature in him, might have sought far and near
without finding so many points of attraction as would allure him
hitherward. We were of all creeds and opinions, and generally tolerant of all, on every imaginable subject. Our bond, it seems to me,
was not affirmative, but negative. We had individually found one
thing or another to quarrel with in our past life, and were pretty
well agreed as to the inexpediency of lumbering along with the old
system any further. As to what should be substituted, there was
much less unanimity. We did not greatly care—at least, I never did—
for the written constitution under which our millennium had commenced. My hope was, that, between theory and practice, a true and
available mode of life might be struck out; and that, even should we

ultimately fail, the months or years spent in the trial would not have been wasted, either as regarded passing enjoyment, or the experience which makes men wise.

Arcadians though we were, our costume bore no resemblance to the be-ribboned doublets, silk breeches and stockings, and slippers fastened with artificial roses, that distinguish the pastoral people of poetry and the stage. In outward show, I humbly conceive, we looked rather like a gang of beggars, or banditti, than either a company of honest laboring men, or a conclave of philosophers. Whatever might be our points of difference we all of us seemed to have come to Blithedale with the one thrifty and laudable idea of wearing out our old clothes. Such garments as had an airing, whenever we strode a-field! Coats with high collars and with no collars, broad-skirted or swallow-tailed, and with the waist at [58/59] every point between the hip and armpit; pantaloons of a dozen successive epochs, and greatly defaced at the knees by the humiliations of the wearer before his lady-love;—in short, we were a living epitome of defunct fashions, and the very raggedest presentment of men who had seen better days. It was gentility in tatters. Often retaining a scholarlike or clerical air, you might have taken us for the denizens of Grub-street, intent on getting a comfortable livelihood by agricultural labor; or, Coleridge's projected Pantisocracy in full experiment; or, Candide and his motley associates, at work in their cabbage-garden; or anything else that was miserably out at elbows, and most clumsily patched in the rear. We might have been sworn comrades to Falstaff's ragged regiment. Little skill as we boasted in other points of husbandry, every mother's son of us would have served admirably to stick up for a scarecrow. And the worst of the matter was, that the first energetic movement essential to one downright stroke of real labor was sure to put a finish to these poor habiliments. So we gradually flung them all aside, and took to honest homespun and linsey-woolsey, as preferable, on the whole, to the plan recommended, I think, by Virgil,—"*Ara nudus; sere nudus,*"—which, as Silas Foster remarked, when I translated the maxim, would be apt to astonish the women-folks.

After a reasonable training, the yeoman life throve well with us. Our faces took the sunburn kindly; our chests gained in compass, and our shoulders in breadth and squareness; our great brown fists looked as if they had never been capable of kid gloves. The plough, the hoe, the scythe, and the hay-fork, grew familiar to our [59/60] grasp. The oxen responded to our voices. We could do almost as fair a day's work as Silas Foster himself, sleep dreamlessly after it, and awake at daybreak with only a little stiffness of the joints, which was usually quite gone by breakfast-time.

To be sure, our next neighbors pretended to be incredulous as to our real proficiency in the business which we had taken in hand. They told slanderous fables about our inability to yoke our own oxen, or to drive them a-field when yoked, or to release the poor brutes from their conjugal bond at night-fall. They had the face to say, too, that the cows laughed at our awkwardness at milking-time, and invariably kicked over the pails; partly in consequence of our putting the stool on the wrong side, and partly because, taking offence at the whisking of their tails, we were in the habit of holding these natural fly-flappers with one hand, and milking with the other. They further averred that we hoed up whole acres of Indian corn and other crops, and drew the earth carefully about the weeds; and that we raised five hundred tufts of burdock, mistaking them for cabbages; and that, by dint of unskillful planting, few of our seeds ever came up at all, or, if they did come up, it was stern-foremost; and that we spent the better part of the month of June in reversing a field of beans, which had thrust themselves out of the ground in this unseemly way. They quoted it as nothing more than an ordinary occurrence for one or other of us to crop off two or three fingers, of a morning, by our clumsy use of the hay-cutter. Finally, and as an ultimate catastrophe, these mendacious rogues circulated a report that we communitarians were exterminated, to the last man, by severing ourselves asunder [60/61] with the sweep of our own scythes!—and that the world had lost nothing by this little accident.

But this was pure envy and malice on the part of the neighboring farmers. The peril of our new way of life was not lest we should fail in becoming practical agriculturists, but that we should probably cease to be anything else. While our enterprise lay all in theory, we had pleased ourselves with delectable visions of the spiritualization of labor. It was to be our form of prayer and ceremonial of worship. Each stroke of the hoe was to uncover some aromatic root of wisdom, heretofore hidden from the sun. Pausing in the field, to let the wind exhale the moisture from our foreheads, we were to look upward, and catch glimpses into the far-off soul of truth. In this point of view, matters did not turn out quite so well as we anticipated. It is very true that, sometimes, gazing casually around me, out of the midst of my toil, I used to discern a richer picturesqueness in the visible scene of earth and sky. There was, at such moments, a novelty, an unwonted aspect, on the face of Nature, as if she had been taken by surprise and seen at unawares, with no opportunity to put off her real look, and assume the mask with which she mysteriously hides herself from mortals. But this was all. The clods of earth, which we so constantly belabored and turned over and over, were never etherealized into thought. Our thoughts, on the contrary, were fast becoming cloddish. Our labor symbolized nothing, and left us mentally sluggish in the dusk of the evening. Intellectual activity is incompatible with any large amount of bodily exercise. The yeoman and the scholar—the yeoman and the man of finest moral culture, though not the man of [61/62] sturdiest sense and integrity—are two distinct individuals, and can never be melted or welded into one substance.

Zenobia soon saw this truth, and gibed me about it, one evening, as Hollingsworth and I lay on the grass, after a hard day's work.

"I am afraid you did not make a song, to-day, while loading the hay-cart," said she, "as Burns did, when he was reaping barley."

"Burns never made a song in haying-time," I answered, very positively. "He was no poet while a farmer, and no farmer while a poet."

"And, on the whole, which of the two characters do you like best?" asked Zenobia. "For I have an idea that you cannot combine them any better than Burns did. Ah, I see, in my mind's eye, what sort of an individual you are to be, two or three years hence. Grim Silas Foster is your prototype, with his palm of sole-leather and his joints of rusty iron (which all through summer keep the stiffness of what he calls his winter's rheumatize), and his brain of—I don't know what his brain is made of, unless it be a Savoy cabbage; but yours may be cauliflower, as a rather more delicate variety. Your physical man will be transmuted into salt beef and fried pork, at the rate, I should imagine, of a pound and a half a day; that being about the average which we find necessary in the kitchen. You will make your toilet for the day (still like this delightful Silas Foster) by rinsing your fingers and the front part of your face in a little tin-pan of water at the door-step, and teasing your hair with a wooden pocket-comb before a seven-by-nine-inch looking-glass. [62/63] Your only pastime will be to smoke some very vile tobacco in the black stump of a pipe."

"Pray, spare me!" cried I. "But the pipe is not Silas's only mode of solacing himself with the weed."

"Your literature," continued Zenobia, apparently delighted with her description, "will be the Farmer's Almanac; for I observe our friend Foster never gets so far as the newspaper. When you happen to sit down, at odd moments, you will fall asleep, and make nasal proclamation of the fact, as he does; and invariably you must be jogged out of a nap, after supper, by the future Mrs. Coverdale, and persuaded to go regularly to bed. And on Sundays, when you put on a blue coat with brass buttons, you will think of nothing else to do, but to go and lounge over the stone walls and rail fences, and stare at the corn growing. And you will look with a knowing eye at oxen, and will have a tendency to clamber over into pig-sties, and feel of

the hogs, and give a guess how much they will weigh after you shall
have stuck and dressed them. Already I have noticed you begin to
speak through your nose, and with a drawl. Pray, if you really did
make any poetry to-day, let us hear it in that kind of utterance!"

"Coverdale has given up making verses now," said Hollingsworth,
who never had the slightest appreciation of my poetry. "Just think
of him penning a sonnet with a fist like that! There is at least this
good in a life of toil, that it takes the nonsense and fancy-work out
of a man, and leaves nothing but what truly belongs to him. If a
farmer can make poetry at the plough-tail, it must be because his nature insists on it; and if that be the case, let him make it, in Heav-
en's name!" [63/64]

"And how is it with you?" asked Zenobia, in a different voice; for
she never laughed at Hollingsworth, as she often did at me. "You, I
think, cannot have ceased to live a life of thought and feeling."

"I have always been in earnest," answered Hollingsworth. "I have
hammered thought out of iron, after heating the iron in my heart!
It matters little what my outward toil may be. Were I a slave at the
bottom of a mine, I should keep the same purpose, the same faith in
its ultimate accomplishment, that I do now. Miles Coverdale is not
in earnest, either as a poet or a laborer."

"You give me hard measure, Hollingsworth," said I, a little hurt. "I
have kept pace with you in the field; and my bones feel as if I had
been in earnest, whatever may be the case with my brain!"

"I cannot conceive," observed Zenobia, with great emphasis,—and,
no doubt, she spoke fairly the feeling of the moment,—"I cannot
conceive of being so continually as Mr. Coverdale is within the
sphere of a strong and noble nature, without being strengthened and
ennobled by its influence!"

This amiable remark of the fair Zenobia confirmed me in what I
had already begun to suspect, that Hollingsworth, like many other
illustrious prophets, reformers and philanthropists, was likely to
make at least two proselytes among the women to one among the
men. Zenobia and Priscilla! These, I believe (unless my unworthy
self might be reckoned for a third), were the only disciples of his
mission; and I spent a great deal of time, uselessly, in trying to con-
jecture what Hollingsworth meant to do with them—and they with
him! [64]

LOUISA MAY ALCOTT

Transcendental Wild Oats:
A Chapter from an Unwritten Romance

ON THE FIRST day of June, 184–, a large wagon, drawn by a small horse and containing a motley load, went lumbering over certain New England hills, with the pleasing accompaniments of wind, rain, and hail. A serene man with a serene child upon his knee was driving, or rather being driven, for the small horse had it all his own way. A brown boy with a William Penn style of countenance sat beside him, firmly embracing a bust of Socrates. Behind them was an energetic-looking woman, with a benevolent brow, satirical mouth, and eyes brimful of hope and courage. A baby reposed upon her lap, a mirror leaned against her knee, and a basket of provisions danced about at her feet, as she struggled with a large, unruly umbrella. Two blue-eyed little girls, with hands full of childish treasures, sat under one old shawl, chatting happily together.

In front of this lively party stalked a tall, sharp-featured man, in a long blue cloak; and a fourth small girl trudged along beside him through the mud as if she rather enjoyed it.

The wind whistled over the bleak hills; the rain fell in a despondent drizzle, and twilight began to fall. But the calm man gazed as tranquilly into the fog as if he beheld a radiant bow of promise spanning the gray sky. The cheery woman tried to cover every one but herself with the big umbrella. The brown boy pillowed his head on the bald pate of Socrates and slumbered peacefully. The little girls sang lullabies to their dolls in soft, maternal murmurs. The sharp-nosed pedestrian marched steadily on, with the blue cloak streaming out behind him like a banner; and the lively infant splashed through the puddles with a ducklike satisfaction pleasant to behold.

From Louisa May Alcott, "Transcendental Wild Oats," *The Independent*, XXV (December 18, 1873), 1569–1571.

Thus these modern pilgrims journeyed hopefully out of the old world, to found a new one in the wilderness.

The editors of *The Transcendental Tripod* had received from Messrs. Lion & Lamb (two of the aforesaid pilgrims) a communication from which the following statement is an extract: —

"We have made arrangements with the proprietor of an estate of about a hundred acres which liberates this tract from human ownership. Here we shall presecute our effort to initiate a Family in harmony with the primitive instincts of man.

"Ordinary secular farming is not our object. Fruit, grain, pulse, herbs, flax, and other vegetable products, receiving assiduous attention, will afford ample manual occupation, and chaste supplies for the bodily needs. It is intended to adorn the pastures with orchards, and to supersede the labor of cattle by the spade and the pruning-knife.

"Consecrated to human freedom, the land awaits the sober culture of devoted men. Beginning with small pecuniary means, this enterprise must be rooted in a reliance on the succors of an ever-bounteous Providence, whose vital affinities being secured by this union with uncorrupted field and unworldly persons, the cares and injuries of a life of gain are avoided.

"The inner nature of each member of the Family is at no time neglected. Our plan contemplates all such disciplines, cultures, and habits as evidently conduce to the purifying of the inmates.

"Pledged to the spirit alone, the founders anticipate no hasty or numerous addition to their numbers. The kingdom of peace is entered only through the gates of self-denial; and felicity is the test and the reward of loyalty to the unswerving law of Love."

This prospective Eden at present consisted of an old red farmhouse, a dilapidated barn, many acres of meadow-land, and a grove. Ten ancient apple-trees were all the "chaste supply" which the place offered as yet; but, in the firm belief that plenteous orchards were soon to be evoked from their inner consciousness, these sanguine founders had christened their domain Fruitlands.

Here Timon Lion intended to found a colony of Latter Day Saints, who, under his patriarchal sway, should regenerate the world and glorify his name forever. Here Abel Lamb, with the devoutest faith in the high ideal which was to him a living truth, desired to plant a Paradise, where Beauty, Virtue, Justice, and Love might live happily together, without the possibility of a serpent entering in. And here his wife, unconverted but faithful to the end, hoped, after many wanderings over the face of the earth, to find rest for herself and a home for her children.

"There is our new abode," announced the enthusiast, smiling with a satisfaction quite undamped by the drops dripping from his hat-brim, as they turned at length into a cart-path that wound along a steep hillside into a barren-looking valley.

"A little difficult of access," observed his practical wife, as she endeavored to keep her various household gods from going overboard with every lurch of the laden ark.

"Like all good things. But those who earnestly desire and patiently seek will soon find us," placidly responded the philosopher from the mud, through which he was now endeavoring to pilot the much-enduring horse.

"Truth lies at the bottom of a well, Sister Hope," said Brother Timon, pausing to detach his small comrade from a gate, whereon she was perched for a clearer gaze into futurity.

"That's the reason we so seldom get at it, I suppose," replied Mrs. Hope, making a vain clutch at the mirror, which a sudden jolt sent flying out of her hands.

"We want no false reflections here," said Timon, with a grim smile, as he crunched the fragments under foot in his onward march.

Sister Hope held her peace, and looked wistfully through the mist at her promised home. The old red house with a hospitable glimmer at its windows cheered her eyes; and, considering the weather, was a fitter refuge than the sylvan bowers some of the more ardent souls might have preferred.

The new-comers were welcomed by one of the elect precious,—a regenerate farmer, whose idea of reform consisted chiefly in wearing white cotton raiment and shoes of untanned leather. This costume, with a snowy beard, gave him a venerable, and at the same time a somewhat bridal appearance.

The goods and chattels of the Society not having arrived, the weary family reposed before the fire on blocks of wood, while Brother Moses White regaled them with roasted potatoes, brown bread and water, in two plates, a tin pan, and one mug; his table service being limited. But, having cast the forms and vanities of a depraved world behind them, the elders welcomed hardship with the enthusiasm of new pioneers, and the children heartily enjoyed this foretaste of what they believed was to be a sort of perpetual picnic.

During the progress of this frugal meal, two more brothers appeared. One a dark, melancholy man, clad in homespun, whose peculiar mission was to turn his name hind part before and use as few words as possible. The other was a bland, bearded Englishman, who expected to be saved by eating uncooked food and going without clothes. He had not yet adopted the primitive costume, however; but contented himself with meditatively chewing dry beans out of a basket.

"Every meal should be a sacrament, and the vessels used should be beautiful and symbolical," observed Brother Lamb, mildly, righting the tin pan slipping about on his knees. "I priced a silver service when in town, but it was too costly; so I got some graceful cups and vases of Britannia ware."

"Hardest things in the world to keep bright. Will whiting be allowed in the community?" inquired Sister Hope, with a housewife's interest in labor-saving institutions.

"Such trivial questions will be discussed at a more fitting time," answered Brother Timon, sharply, as he burnt his fingers with a very hot potato. "Neither sugar, molasses, milk, butter, cheese, nor flesh are to be used among us, for nothing is to be admitted which has caused wrong or death to man or beast."

"Our garments are to be linen till we learn to raise our own cotton or some substitute for woollen fabrics," added Brother Abel, blissfully basking in an imaginary future as warm and brilliant as the generous fire before him.

"Haou abaout shoes?" asked Brother Moses, surveying his own with interest.

"We must yield that point till we can manufacture an innocent substitute for leather. Bark, wood, or some durable fabric wll be invented in time. Meanwhile, those who desire to carry out our idea to the fullest extent can go barefooted," said Lion, who liked extreme measures.

"I never will, nor let my girls," murmured rebellious Sister Hope, under her breath.

"Haou do you cattle'ate to treat the ten-acre lot? Ef things ain't 'tended to right smart, we shan't hev no crops," observed the practical patriarch in cotton.

"We shall spade it," replied Abel, in such perfect good faith that Moses said no more, though he indulged in a shake of the head as he glanced at hands that had held nothing heavier than a pen for years. He was a paternal old soul and regarded the younger men as promising boys on a new sort of lark.

"What shall we do for lamps, if we cannot use any animal substance? I do hope light of some sort is to be thrown upon the enterprise," said Mrs. Lamb, with anxiety, for in those days kerosene and camphene were not, and gas unknown in the wilderness.

"We shall go without till we have discovered some vegetable oil or wax to serve us," replied Brother Timon, in a decided tone, which caused Sister Hope to resolve that her private lamp should be always trimmed, if not burning.

"Each member is to perform the work for which experience, strength, and taste best fit him," continued Dictator Lion. "Thus drudgery and disorder will be avoided and harmony prevail. We shall rise at dawn, begin the day by bathing, followed by music, and then a chaste repast of fruit and bread. Each one finds congenial occupation till the meridian meal; when some deep-searching conversation gives rest to the body and development to the mind. Healthful labor again engages us till the last meal, when we assemble in social communion, prolonged till sunset, when we retire to sweet repose, ready for the next day's activity."

"What part of the work do you incline to yourself?" asked Sister Hope, with a humorous glimmer in her keen eyes.

"I shall wait till it is made clear to me. Being in preference to doing is the great aim, and this comes to us rather by a resigned willingness than a willful activity, which is a check to all divine growth," responded Brother Timon.

"I thought so." And Mrs. Lamb sighed audibly, for during the year he had spent in her family Brother Timon had so faithfully carried out his idea of "being, not doing," that she had found his "divine growth" both an expensive and unsatisfactory process.

Here her husband struck into the conversation, his face shining with the light and [1569/1570] joy of the splendid dreams and high ideals hovering before him.

"In these steps of reform, we do not rely so much on scientific reasoning or physiological skill as on the spirit's dictates. The greater part of man's duty consists in leaving alone much that he now does. Shall I stimulate with tea, coffe, or wine? No. Shall I consume flesh? Not if I value health. Shall I subjugate cattle? Shall I claim property in any created thing? Shall I trade? Shall I adopt a form of religion? Shall I interest myself in politics? To how many of these questions—could we ask them deeply enough and could they be heard as having relation to our eternal welfare—would the response be 'Abstain'?"

A mild snore seemed to echo the last word of Abel's rhapsody, for Brother Moses had succumbed to mundane slumber and sat nodding like a massive ghost. Forest Absalom, the silent man, and John Pease, the English member, now departed to the barn; and Mrs. Lamb led her flock to a temporary fold, leaving the founders of the "Consociate Family" to build castles in the air till the fire went out and the symposium ended in smoke.

The furniture arrived next day, and was soon bestowed; for the principal property of the community consisted in books. To this rare

library was devoted the best room in the house, and the few busts
and pictures that still survived many flittings were added to beautify
the sanctuary, for here the family was to meet for amusement, instruction, and worship.

Any housewife can imagine the emotions of Sister Hope, when she
took possession of a large, dilapidated kitchen, containing an old
stove and the peculiar stores out of which food was to be evolved for
her little family of eleven. Cakes of maple sugar, dried peas and
beans, barley and hominy, meal of all sorts, potatoes, and dried
fruit. No milk, butter, cheese, tea, or meat appeared. Even salt was
considered a useless luxury and spice entirely forbidden by these lovers of Spartan simplicity. A ten years' experience of vegetarian vaga-
ries had been good training for this new freak, and her sense of the
ludicrous supported her through many trying scenes.

Unleavened bread, porridge, and water for breakfast; bread,
vegetables, and water for dinner; bread, fruit, and water for supper
was the bill of fare ordained by the elders. No teapot profaned that
sacred stove, no gory steak cried aloud for vengeance from her chaste
gridiron; and only a brave woman's taste, time, and temper were
sacrificed on that domestic altar.

The vexed question of light was settled by buying a quantity of
bayberry wax for candles; and, on discovering that no one knew how
to make them, pine knots were introduced, to be used when absolutely necessary. Being summer, the evenings were not long, and the
weary fraternity found it no great hardship to retire with the birds.
The inner light was sufficient for most of them. But Mrs. Lamb re-
belled. Evening was the only time she had to herself, and while the
tired feet rested the skilful hands mended torn frocks and little
stockings, or anxious heart forgot its burden in a book.

So "mother's lamp" burned steadily, while the philosophers built
a new heaven and earth by moonlight; and through all the meta-
physical mists and philanthropic pyrotechnics of that period Sister
Hope played her own little game of "throwing light," and none but
the moths were the worse for it.

Such farming probably was never seen before since Adam delved.
The band of brothers began by spading garden and field; but a few
days of it lessened their ardor amazingly. Blistered hands and aching
backs suggested the expediency of permitting the use of cattle till
the workers were better fitted for noble toil by a summer of the new
life.

Brother Moses brought a yoke of oxen from his farm,—at least, the
philosophers thought so till it was discovered that one of the animals
was a cow; and Moses confessed that he "must be let down easy, for
he couldn't live on garden sarse entirely."

Great was Dictator Lion's indignation at this lapse from virtue. But time pressed, the work must be done; so the meek cow was permitted to wear the yoke and the recreant brother continued to enjoy forbidden draughts in the barn, which dark proceeding caused the children to regard him as one set apart for destruction.

The sowing was equally peculiar, for, owing to some mistake, the three brethren, who devoted themselves to this graceful task, found when about half through the job that each had been sowing a different sort of grain in the same field; a mistake which caused much perplexity, as it could not be remedied; but, after a long consultation and a good deal of laughter, it was decided to say nothing and see what would come of it.

The garden was planted with a generous supply of useful roots and herbs; but, as manure was not allowed to profane the virgin soil, few of these vegetable treasures ever came up. Purslane reigned supreme, and the disappointed planters ate it philosophically, deciding that Nature knew what was best for them, and would generously supply their needs, if they could only learn to digest her "sallets" and wild roots.

The orchard was laid out, a little grafting done, new trees and vines set, regardless of the unfit season and entire ignorance of the husbandmen, who honestly believed that in the autumn they would reap a bounteous harvest.

Slowly things got into order, and rapidly rumors of the new experiment went abroad, causing many strange spirits to flock thither, for in those days communities were the fashion and transcendentalism raged wildly. Some came to look on and laugh, some to be supported in poetic idleness, a few to believe sincerely and work heartily. Each member was allowed to mount his favorite hobby and ride it to his heart's content. Very queer were some of the riders, and very rampant some of the hobbies.

One youth, believing that language was of little consequence if the spirit was only right, startled new-comers by blandly greeting them with "Good-morning, damn you," and other remarks of an equally mixed order. A second irrepressible being held that all the emotions of the soul should be freely expressed, and illustrated his theory by antics that would have sent him to a lunatic asylum, if, as an unregenerate wag said, he had not already been in one. When his spirit soared, he climbed trees and shouted; when doubt assailed him, he lay upon the floor and groaned lamentably. At joyful periods, he raced, leaped, and sang; when sad, he wept aloud; and when a great thought burst upon him in the watches of the night, he crowed like a jocund cockerel, to the great delight of the children and the great annoyance of the elders. One musical brother fiddled whenever so moved, sang sentimentally to the four little girls, and put a music-box on the wall when he hoed corn.

Brother Pease ground away at his uncooked food, or browsed over the farm on sorrel, mint, green fruit, and new vegetables. Occasionally he took his walks abroad, airily attired in an unbleached cotton *poncho,* which was the nearest approach to the primeval costume he was allowed to indulge in. At midsummer he retired to the wilderness, to try his plan where the woodchucks were without prejudices and huckleberrybushes were hospitably full. A sunstroke unfortunately spoilt his plan, and he returned to semi-civilization a sadder and wiser man.

Forest Absalom preserved his Pythagorean silence, cultivated his fine dark locks, and worked like a beaver, setting an excellent example of brotherly love, justice, and fidelity by his upright life. He it was who helped overworked Sister Hope with her heavy washes, kneaded the endless succession of batches of bread, watched over the children, and did the many tasks left undone by the brethren, who were so busy discussing and defining great duties that they forgot to perform the small ones.

Moses White placidly plodded about, "chorin' raound," as he called it, looking like an old-time patriarch, with his silver hair and flowing beard, and saving the community from many a mishap by his thrift and Yankee shrewdness.

Brother Lion domineered over the whole concern; for, having put the most money into the speculation, he was resolved to make it pay, —as if anything founded on an ideal basis could be expected to do so by any but enthusiasts.

Abel Lamb simply revelled in the Newness, firmly believing that his dream was to be beautifully realized and in time not only little Fruitlands, but the whole earth, be turned into a Happy Valley. He worked with every muscle of his body, for *he* was in deadly earnest. He taught with his whole head and heart; planned and sacrificed, preached and prophesied, with a soul full of the purest aspirations, most unselfish purposes, and desires for a life devoted to God and man, too high and tender to bear the rough usage of this world.

It was a little remarkable that only one woman ever joined this community. Mrs. Lamb merely followed wheresoever her husband led,—"as ballast for his balloon," as she said, in her bright way.

Miss Jane Gage was a stout lady of mature years, sentimental, amiable, and lazy. She wrote verses copiously; and had vague yearnings and graspings after the unknown, which led her to believe herself fitted for a higher sphere than any she had yet adorned.

Having been a teacher, she was set to instructing the children in the common branches. Each adult member took a turn at the infants; and, as each taught in his own way, the result was a chronic state of chaos in the minds of these much-afflicted innocents.

Sleep, food, and poetic musings were the desires of dear Jane's life, and she shirked all duties as clogs upon her spirit's wings. Any thought of lending a hand with the domestic drudgery never occurred to her; and when to the question, "Are there any beasts of burden on the place?" Mrs. Lamb answered, with a face that told its own tale, "Only one woman!" the buxom Jane took no shame to herself, but laughed at the joke, and let the stout-hearted sister tug on alone.

Unfortunately, the poor lady hankered after the flesh-pots, and endeavored to stay herself with private sips of milk, crackers, and cheese, and on one dire occasion she partook of fish at a neighbor's table.

One of the children reported this sad lapse from virtue, and poor Jane was publicly reprimanded by Timon.

"I only took a little bit of the tail,"sobbed the penitent poetess.

"Yes, but the whole fish had to be tortured and slain that you might tempt your carnal appetite with that one taste of the tail. Know ye not, consumers of flesh meat, that ye are nourishing the wolf and tiger in your bosoms?"

At this awful question and the peal of laughter which arose from some of the younger brethren, tickled by the ludicrous contrast between the stout sinner, the stern judge, and the naughty satisfaction of the young detective, poor Jane fled from the room to pack her trunk and return to a world where fishes' tails were not forbidden fruit.

Transcendental wild oats were sown broadcast that year, and the fame thereof has not yet ceased in the land; for, futile as this crop seemed to outsiders, it bore an invisible harvest, worth much to those who planted in earnest. As none of the members of this particular community have ever recounted their experiences before, a few of them may not be amiss, since the interest in these attempts has never died out and Fruitlands was the most ideal of all these castles in Spain.

A new dress was invented, since cotton, silk, and wool were forbidden as the product of slave-labor, worm-slaughter, and sheep-robbery. Tunics and trowsers of brown linen were the only wear. The women's skirts were longer, and their straw hat-brims wider than the men's, and this was the only difference. Some persecution lent a charm to the costume, and the long-haired, linen-clad reformers quite enjoyed the mild martyrdom they endured when they left home.

Money was abjured, as the root of all evil. The produce of the land was to supply most of their wants, or be exchanged for the few things they could not grow. This idea had its inconveniences; but self-denial was the fashion, and it was surprising how many things one can do without. When they desired to travel, they walked, if possible, begged the loan of a vehicle, or boldly entered car or coach, and, stating their principles to the officials, took the consequences. Usually their dress, their earnest frankness, and gentle resolution won them a passage; but now and then they met with hard usage, and had the satisfaction of suffering for their principles.

On one of these penniless pilgrimages they took passage on a boat, and, when fare was demanded, artlessly offered to talk, instead of pay. As the boat was well under way and they actually had not a cent, there was no help for it. So Brothers Lion and Lamb held forth to the assembled passengers in their most eloquent style. There must have been something effective in this conversation, for the listeners were moved to take up a contribution for these inspired lunatics, who preached peace on earth and good-will to man so earnestly, with empty pockets. A goodly sum was collected; but when the captain presented it the reformers proved that they were consistent even in their madness, for not a penny would they accept, saying, with a look at the group about them, whose indifference or contempt had changed to interest and respect, "You see how well we get on without money"; and so went serenely on their way, with their linen blouses flapping airily in the cold October wind.

They preached vegetarianism everywhere and resisted all temptations of the flesh, contentedly eating apples and bread at well-spread tables, and much afflicting hospitable hostesses by denouncing their food and taking away their appetites, discussing the "horrors of shambles," the "incorporation of the brute in man," and "on elegant abstinence the sign of a pure soul." But, when the perplexed or offended ladies asked what they should eat, they got in reply a bill of fare consisting of "bowls of sunrise for breakfast," "solar seeds of the sphere," "dishes from Plutarch's chaste table," and other viands equally hard to find in any modern market.

Reform conventions of all sorts were haunted by these brethren, who said many wise things and did many foolish ones. Unfortunately, these wanderings interfered with their harvest at home; but the rule was to do what the spirit moved, so they left their crops to Providence and went a-reaping in wider and, let us hope, more fruitful fields than their own.

Luckily, the earthly providence who watched over Abel Lamb was at hand to glean the scanty crop yielded by the "uncorrupted land," which, "consecrated to human freedom," had received "the sober culture of devout men."

About the time the grain was ready to house, some call of the Oversoul wafted all the men away. An easterly storm was coming up and the yellow stacks were sure to be ruined. Then Sister Hope gathered her forces. Three little girls, one boy (Timon's son), and herself, harnessed to clothes-baskets and Russia-linen sheets, were the only teams she could command; but with these poor appliances the indomitable woman got in the grain and saved food for her young, with the instinct and energy of a mother-bird with a brood of hungry nestlings to feed.

This attempt at regeneration had its tragic as well as comic side, though the world only saw the former.

With the first frosts, the butterflies, who had sunned themselves in the new light through the summer, took flight, leaving the few bees to see what honey they had stored for winter use. Precious little appeared beyond the satisfaction of a few months of holy living.

At first it seemed as if a chance to try holy dying also was to be offered them. Timon, much disgusted with the failure of the scheme, decided to retire to the Shakers, who seemed to be the only successful community going.

"What is to become of us?" asked Mrs. Hope, for Abel was heartbroken at the bursting of his lovely bubble.

"You can stay here, if you like, till a tenant is found. No more wood must be cut, however, and no more corn ground. All I have must be sold to pay the debts of the concern, as the responsibility rests with me," was the cheering reply.

"Who is to pay us for what we have lost? I gave all I had,—furniture, time, strength, six months of my children's lives,—and all are wasted. Abel gave himself body and soul, and is almost wrecked by hard work and disappointment. Are we to have no return for this, but leave to starve and freeze in an old house, with winter at hand, no [1570/1571] money, and hardly a friend left; for this wild scheme has alienated nearly all we had. You talk much about justice. Let us have a little, since there is nothing else left."

But the woman's appeal met with no reply but the old one: "It was an experiment. We all risked something, and must bear our losses as we can."

With this cold comfort, Timon departed with his son, and was absorbed into the Shaker brotherhood, where he soon found that the order of things was reversed, and it was all work and no play.

Then the tragedy began for the forsaken little family. Desolation and despair fell upon Abel. As his wife said, his new beliefs had alienated many friends. Some thought him mad, some unprincipled. Even the most kindly thought him a visionary, whom it was useless to help till he took more practical views of life. All stood aloof, saying: "Let him work out his own ideas, and see what they are worth."

He had tried, but it was a failure. The world was not ready for

Utopia yet, and those who attempted to found it only got laughed at for their pains. In other days, men could sell all and give to the poor, lead lives devoted to holiness and high thought, and, after the persecution was over, find themselves honored as saints or martyrs. But in modern times these things are out of fashion. To live for one's principles, at all costs, is a dangerous speculation; and the failure of an ideal, no matter how humane and noble, is harder for the world to forgive and forget than bank robbery or the grand swindles of corrupt politicians.

Deep waters now for Abel, and for a time there seemed no passage through. Strength and spirits were exhausted by hard work and too much thought. Courage failed when, looking about for help, he saw no sympathizing face, no hand outstretched to help him, no voice to say cheerily,

"We all make mistakes, and it takes many experiences to shape a life. Try again, and let us help you."

Every door was closed, every eye averted, every heart cold, and no way open whereby he might earn bread for his children. His principles would not permit him to do many things that others did; and in the few fields where conscience would allow him to work, who would employ a man who had flown in the face of society, as he had done?

Then this dreamer, whose dream was the life of his life, resolved to carry out his idea to the bitter end. There seemed no place for him here,—no work, no friend. To go begging conditions was as ignoble as to go begging money. Better perish of want than sell one's soul for the sustenance of his body. Silently he lay down upon his bed, turned his face to the wall, and waited with pathetic patience for death to cut the knot which he could not untie. Days and nights went by, and neither food nor water passed his lips. Soul and body were dumbly struggling together, and no word of complaint betrayed what either suffered.

His wife, when tears and prayers were unavailing, sat down to wait the end with a mysterious awe and submission; for in this entire resignation of all things there was an eloquent significance to her who knew him as no other human being did.

"Leave all to God," was his belief; and in this crisis the loving soul clung to this faith, sure that the Allwise Father would not desert this child who tried to live so near to Him. Gathering her children about her, she waited the issue of the tragedy that was being enacted in that solitary room, while the first snow fell outside, untrodden by the footprints of a single friend.

But the strong angels who sustain and teach perplexed and troubled souls came and went, leaving no trace without, but working

miracles within. For, when all other sentiments had faded into dim-
ness, all other hopes died utterly; when the bitterness of death was
nearly over, when body was past any pang of hunger or thirst, and
soul stood ready to depart, the love that outlives all else refused to
die. Head had bowed to defeat, hand had grown weary with too
heavy tasks, but heart could not grow cold to those who lived in its
tender depths, even when death touched it.

"My faithful wife, my little girls,—they have not forsaken me, they
are mine by ties that none can break. What right have I to leave
them alone? What right to escape from the burden and the sorrow I have helped to bring? This duty remains to me, and I must do
it manfully. For their sakes, the world will forgive me in time; for
their sakes, God will sustain me now."

Too feeble to rise, Abel groped for the food that always lay within
his reach, and in the darkness and solitude of that memorable night
ate and drank what was to him the bread and wine of a new communion, a new dedication of heart and life to the duties that were left
him when the dreams fled.

In the early dawn, when that sad wife crept fearfully to see what
change had come to the patient face on the pillow, she found it smiling at her, saw a wasted hand outstretched to her, and heard a feeble
voice cry bravely, "Hope!"

What passed in that little room is not to be recorded except in the
hearts of those who suffered and endured much for love's sake.
Enough for us to know that soon the wan shadow of a man came
forth, leaning on the arm that never failed him, to be welcomed
and cherished by the children, who never forgot the experiences of
that time.

"Hope," was the watchword now; and, while the last logs blazed
on the hearth, the last bread and apples covered the table, the new
commander, with recovered courage, said to her husband,—

"Leave all to God—and me. He has done his part, now I will do
mine."

"But we have no money, dear."

"Yes, we have. I sold all we could spare, and have enough to take
us away from this snowbank."

"Where can we go?"

"I have engaged four rooms at our good neighbor, Lovejoy's.
There we can live cheaply till spring. Then for new plans and a
home of our own, please God."

"But, Hope, your little store won't last long, and we have no
friends."

"I can sew and you can chop wood. Lovejoy offers you the same
pay as he gives his other men; my old friend, Mrs. Truman, will

send me all the work I want; and my blessed brother stands by us to the end. Cheer up, dear heart, for while there is work and love in the world we shall not suffer."

"And while I have my good angel Hope, I shall not despair, even if I wait another thirty years before I step beyond the circle of the sacred little world in which I still have a place to fill."

So one bleak December day, with their few possessions piled on an ox-sled, the rosy children perched atop, and the parents trudging arm in arm behind, the exiles left their Eden and faced the world again.

"Ah, me! my happy dream. How much I leave behind that never can be mine again," said Abel, looking back at the lost Paradise, lying white and chill in its shroud of snow.

"Yes, dear; but how much we bring away," answered brave-hearted Hope, glancing from husband to children.

"Poor Fruitlands! The name was as great a failure as the rest!" continued Abel, with a sigh, as a frostbitten apple fell from a leafless bough at his feet.

But the sigh changed to a smile as his wife added, in a half-tender, half-satirical tone,—

"Don't you think Apple Slump would be a better name for it, dear?" [1571]

ORIGINAL CHARACTERS OF
TRANSCENDENTAL WILD OATS

TIMON LION ....*Charles Lane.*
HIS SON ....*William Lane.*
ABEL LAMB ....*A. Bronson Alcott.*
SISTER HOPE ....*Mrs. Alcott.*
HER DAUGHTERS ....*The Alcott girls.*
JOHN PEASE ....*Samuel Bower.*
FOREST ABSALOM ....*Abram Everett.*
MOSES WHITE ....*Joseph Palmer.*
JANE GAGE ....*Anna Page.*

HENRY DAVID THOREAU

The Bean-Field

MEANWHILE my beans, the length of whose rows, added together, was seven miles already planted, were impatient to be hoed, for the earliest had grown considerably before the latest were in the ground; indeed they were not easily to be put off. What was the meaning of this so steady and self-respecting, this small Herculean labor, I knew not. I came to love my rows, my beans, though so many more than I wanted. They attached me to the earth, and so I got strength like Antaeus. But why should I raise them? Only Heaven knows. This was my curious labor all summer,—to make this portion of the earth's surface, which had yielded only cinquefoil, blackberries, johnswort, and the like, before, sweet wild fruits and pleasant flowers, produce instead this pulse. What shall I learn of beans or beans of me? I cherish them, I hoe them, early and late I have an eye to them; and this is my day's work. It is a fine broad leaf to look on. My auxiliaries are the dews and rains which water this dry soil, and what fertility is in the soil itself, which for the most part is lean and effete. My enemies are worms, cool days, and most of all woodchucks. The last have nibbled for me a quarter of an acre clean. But what right had I to oust johnswort and the rest, and break up their ancient [171/172] herb garden? Soon, however, the remaining beans will be too tough for them, and go forward to meet new foes.

When I was four years old, as I well remember, I was brought from Boston to this my native town, through these very woods and this field, to the pond. It is one of the oldest scenes stamped on my memory. And now to-night my flute has waked the echoes over that very water. The pines still stand here older than I; or, if some have fallen, I have cooked my supper with their stumps, and a new growth is rising all around, preparing another aspect for new infant eyes. Almost the same johnswort springs from the same perennial root in this pasture, and even I have at length helped to clothe that

From *The Writings of Henry David Thoreau,* II: *Walden* (Boston and New York: Houghton, Mifflin Company, 1906), 171–184.

fabulous landscape of my infant dreams, and one of the results of my presence and influence is seen in these bean leaves, corn blades, and potato vines.

I planted about two acres and a half of upland; and as it was only about fifteen years since the land was cleared, and I myself had got out two or three cords of stumps, I did not give it any manure; but in the course of the summer it appeared by the arrowheads which I turned up in hoeing, that an extinct nation had anciently dwelt here and planted corn and beans ere white men came to clear the land, and so, to some extent, had exhausted the soil for this very crop.

Before yet any woodchuck or squirrel had run across the road, or the sun had got above the shrub oaks, while all the dew was on, though the farmers warned me against it,—I would advise you to do all your work if possible while the dew is on,—I began to level the ranks of haughty weeds in my bean-field and throw [172/173] dust upon their heads. Early in the morning I worked barefooted, dabbling like a plastic artist in the dewy and crumbling sand, but later in the day the sun blistered my feet. There the sun lighted me to hoe beans, pacing slowly backward and forward over that yellow gravelly upland, between the long green rows, fifteen rods, the one end terminating in a shrub oak copse where I could rest in the shade, the other in a blackberry field where the green berries deepened their tints by the time I had made another bout. Removing the weeds, putting fresh soil about the bean stems, and encouraging this weed which I had sown, making the yellow soil express its summer thought in bean leaves and blossoms rather than in wormwood and piper and millet grass, making the earth say beans instead of grass,— this was my daily work. As I had little aid from horses or cattle, or hired men or boys, or improved implements of husbandry, I was much slower, and became much more intimate with my beans than usual. But labor of the hands, even when pursued to the verge of drudgery, is perhaps never the worst form of idleness. It has a constant and imperishable moral, and to the scholar it yields a classic result. A very *agricola laboriosus* was I to travellers bound westward through Lincoln and Wayland to nobody knows where; they sitting at their ease in gigs, with elbows on knees, and reins loosely hanging in festoons; I the home-staying, laborious native of the soil. But soon my homestead was out of their sight and thought. It was the only open and cultivated field for a great distance on either side of the road, so they made the most of it; and sometimes the [173/174] man in the field heard more of travellers' gossip and comment than was meant for his ear: "Beans so late! peas so late!"—for I continued to plant when others had begun to hoe,—the ministerial husbandman had not suspected it. "Corn, my boy, for fodder; corn for fodder." "Does he *live* there?" asks the black bonnet of the gray coat; and the hard-featured farmer reins up his grateful dobbin to inquire what you are doing where he sees no manure in the furrow, and recommends a little chip dirt, or any little waste stuff, or it may be ashes or plaster. But here were two acres and a half of furrows, and only a hoe for cart and two hands to draw it,—there being an aversion to other carts and horses,—and chip dirt far away. Fellow-travellers as they rattled by compared it aloud with the fields which they had passed, so that I came to know how I stood in the agricultural world. This was one field not in Mr. Colman's report. And, by the way, who estimates the value of the crop which nature yields in the still wilder fields unimproved by man? The crop of *English* hay is carefully weighed, the moisture calculated, the silicates and the potash; but in all dells and pond-holes in the woods and pastures and swamps grows a rich and various crop only unreaped by man. Mine was, as it were, the connecting link between wild and cultivated fields; as some states are civilized, and others half-civilized, and others savage or barbarous, so my field was, though not in a bad sense, a half-cultivated field. They were beans cheerfully returning to their wild and primitive state that I cultivated, and my hoe played the *Ranz des Vaches* for them. [174/175]

Near at hand, upon the topmost spray of a birch, sings the brown thrasher—or red mavis, as some love to call him—all the morning, glad of your society, that would find out another farmer's field if yours were not here. While you are planting the seed, he cries,— "Drop it, drop it,—cover it up, cover it up,—pull it up, pull it up, pull it up." But this was not corn, and so it was safe from such enemies as he. You may wonder what his rigmarole, his amateur Paganini performances on one string or on twenty, have to do with your planting, and yet prefer it to leached ashes or plaster. It was a cheap sort of top dressing in which I had entire faith.

As I drew a still fresher soil about the rows with my hoe, I disturbed the ashes of unchronicled nations who in primeval years lived under these heavens, and their small implements of war and hunting were brought to the light of this modern day. They lay mingled with other natural stones, some of which bore the marks of having been burned by Indian fires, and some by the sun, and also bits of pottery and glass brought hither by the recent cultivators of the soil. When my hoe tinkled against the stones, that music echoed to the woods and the sky, and was an accompaniment to my labor which yielded an instant and immeasurable crop. It was no longer beans that I hoed, nor I that hoed beans; and I remembered with as much pity as pride, if I remembered at all, my acquaintances who had gone to the city to attend the oratorios. The nighthawk circled

overhead in the sunny afternoons—for I sometimes made a day of it
—like a mote in the eye, or in heaven's eye, falling from time to time
with a swoop [175/176] and a sound as if the heavens were rent,
torn at last to very rags and tatters, and yet a seamless cope remained; small imps that fill the air and lay their eggs on the ground
on bare sand or rocks on the tops of hills, where few have found
them; graceful and slender like ripples caught up from the pond, as
leaves are raised by the wind to float in the heavens; such kindred-
ship is in nature. The hawk is aerial brother of the wave which he
sails over and surveys, those his perfect air-inflated wings answering
to the elemental unfledged pinions of the sea. Or sometimes I
watched a pair of hen-hawks circling high in the sky, alternately
soaring and descending, approaching and leaving one another, as if
they were the embodiment of my own thoughts. Or I was attracted
by the passage of wild pigeons from this wood to that, with a slight
quivering winnowing sound and carrier haste; or from under a rotten stump my hoe turned up a sluggish portentous and outlandish
spotted salamander, a trace of Egypt and the Nile, yet our contemporary. When I paused to lean on my hoe, these sounds and sights I
heard and saw anywhere in the row, a part of the inexhaustible entertainment which the country offers.

On gala days the town fires its great guns, which echo like pop-
guns to these woods, and some waifs of martial music occasionally
penetrate thus far. To me, away there in my bean-field at the other
end of the town, the big guns sounded as if a puffball had burst; and
when there was a military turnout of which I was ignorant, I have
sometimes had a vague sense all the day of some sort of itching and
disease in the horizon, as if some [176/177] eruption would break
out there soon, either scarlatina or canker-rash, until at length some
more favorable puff of wind, making haste over the fields and up the
Wayland road, brought me information of the "trainers." It seemed
by the distant hum as if somebody's bees had swarmed, and that the
neighbors, according to Virgil's advice, by a faint *tintinnabulum*
upon the most sonorous of their domestic utensils, were endeavoring
to call them down into the hive again. And when the sound died
quite away, and the hum had ceased, and the most favorable breezes
told no tale, I knew that they had got the last drone of them all
safely into the Middlesex hive, and that now their minds were bent
on the honey with which it was smeared.

I felt proud to know that the liberties of Massachusetts and of our
fatherland were in such safe keeping; and as I turned to my hoeing
again I was filled with an inexpressible confidence, and pursued my
labor cheerfully with a calm trust in the future.

When there were several bands of musicians, it sounded as if all
the village was a vast bellows, and all the buildings expanded and

collapsed alternately with a din. But sometimes it was a really noble and inspiring strain that reached these woods, and the trumpet that sings of fame, and I felt as if I could spit a Mexican with a good relish,—for why should we always stand for trifles?—and looked round for a woodchuck or a skunk to exercise my chivalry upon. These martial strains seemed as far away as Palestine, and reminded me of a march of crusaders in the horizon, with a slight tantivy and tremulous motion of the elm tree tops which [177/178] overhang the village. This was one of the *great* days; though the sky had from my clearing only the same everlastingly great look that it wears daily, and I saw no difference in it.

It was a singular experience that long acquaintance which I cultivated with beans, what with planting, and hoeing, and harvesting, and threshing, and picking over and selling them,—the last was the hardest of all—I might add eating, for I did taste. I was determined to know beans. When they were growing, I used to hoe from five o'clock in the morning till noon, and commonly spent the rest of the day about other affairs. Consider the intimate and curious acquaintance one makes with various kinds of weeds,—it will bear some iteration in the account, for there was no little iteration in the labor,— disturbing their delicate organizations so ruthlessly, and making such invidious distinctions with his hoe, levelling whole ranks of one species, and sedulously cultivating another. That's Roman wormwood,—that's pigweed,—that's sorrel,—that's piper-grass,—have at him, chop him up, turn his roots upward to the sun, don't let him have a fibre in the shade, if you do he'll turn himself t'other side up and be as green as a leek in two days. A long war, not with cranes, but with weeds, those Trojans who had sun and rain and dews on their side. Daily the beans saw me come to their rescue armed with a hoe, and thin the ranks of their enemies, filling up the trenches with weedy dead. Many a lusty crest-waving Hector, that towered a whole foot above his crowding comrades, fell before my weapon and rolled in the dust. [178/179]

Those summer days which some of my contemporaries devoted to the fine arts in Boston or Rome, and others to contemplation in India, and others to trade in London or New York, I thus, with the other farmers of New England, devoted to husbandry. Not that I wanted beans to eat, for I am by nature a Pythagorean, so far as beans are concerned, whether they mean porridge or voting, and exchanged them for rice; but, perchance, as some must work in fields if only for the sake of tropes and expression, to serve a parable-maker one day. It was on the whole a rare amusement, which, continued too long, might have become a dissipation. Though I gave them no manure, and did not hoe them all once, I hoed them unusually well as far as I went, and was paid for it in the end, "there being in

truth," as Evelyn says, "no compost or lætation whatsoever comparable to this continual motion, repastination, and turning of the
mould with the spade." "The earth," he adds elsewhere, "especially
if fresh, has a certain magnetism in it, by which it attracts the salt,
power, or virtue (call it either) which gives it life, and is the logic of
all the labor and stir we keep about it, to sustain us; all dungings
and other sordid temperings being but the vicars succedaneous to
this improvement." Moreover, this being one of those "worn-out and
exhausted lay fields which enjoy their sabbath," had perchance, as
Sir Kenelm Digby thinks likely, attracted "vital spirits" from the air.
I harvested twelve bushels of beans.

But to be more particular, for it is complained that Mr. Colman
has reported chiefly the expensive experiments of gentlemen farmers, my outgoes were,— [179/180]

For a hoe ....$ 0 54		
Plowing, harrowing, and furrowing 7 50		Too Much.
Beans for seed 3 12½		
Peas " 0 40		
Potatoes " 1 33		
Turnip seed 0 06		
White line for crow fence 0 02		
Horse cultivator and boy three hours 1 00		
Horse and cart to get crop 0 75		
In all $14 72½		

My income was (patremfamilias vendacem, non emacem esse opor-
tet), from

Nine bushels and twelve quarts of beans	
sold $16 94	
Five bushels large potatoes 2 50	
Nine " small 2 25	
Grass 1 00	
Stalks 0 75	
In all $23 44	
Leaving a pecuniary profit, as I have else-	
where said, of ....$ 8 71½	

This is the result of my experience in raising beans: Plant the
common small white bush bean about the first of June, in rows three
feet by eighteen inches apart, being careful to select fresh round and
unmixed seed. First look out for worms, and supply vacancies by
planting anew. Then look out for woodchucks, if it is an exposed
place, for they will nibble off the earliest tender leaves almost clean
as they go; and again, when the young tendrils make their appearance, they have notice of it, [180/181] and will shear them off with

both buds and young pods, sitting erect like a squirrel. But above all harvest as early as possible, if you would escape frosts and have a fair and salable crop; you may save much loss by this means.

This further experience also I gained: I said to myself, I will not plant beans and corn with so much industry another summer, but such seeds, if the seed is not lost, as sincerity, truth, simplicity, faith, innocence, and the like, and see if they will not grow in this soil, even with less toil and manurance, and sustain me, for surely it has not been exhausted for these crops. Alas! I said this to myself; but now another summer is gone, and another, and another, and I am obliged to say to you, Reader, that the seeds which I planted, if indeed they *were* the seeds of those virtues, were wormeaten or had lost their vitality, and so did not come up. Commonly men will only be brave as their fathers were brave, or timid. This generation is very sure to plant corn and beans each new year precisely as the Indians did centuries ago and taught the first settlers to do, as if there were a fate in it. I saw an old man the other day, to my astonishment, making the holes with a hoe for the seventieth time at least, and not for himself to lie down in! But why should not the New Englander try new adventures, and not lay so much stress on his grain, his potato and grass crop, and his orchards,—raise other crops than these? Why concern ourselves so much about our beans for seed, and not be concerned at all about a new generation of men? We should really be fed and cheered if when we met a man we were sure to see that [181/182] some of the qualities which I have named, which we all prize more than those other productions, but which are for the most part broadcast and floating in the air, had taken root and grown in him. Here comes such a subtile and ineffable quality, for instance, as truth or justice, though the slightest amount or new variety of it, along the road. Our ambassadors should be instructed to send home such seeds as these, and Congress help to distribute them over all the land. We should never stand upon ceremony with sincerity. We should never cheat and insult and banish one another by our meanness, if there were present the kernel of worth and friendliness. We should not meet thus in haste. Most men I do not meet at all, for they seem not to have time; they are busy about their beans. We would not deal with a man thus plodding ever, leaning on a hoe or a spade as a staff between his work, not as a mushroom, but partially risen out of the earth, something more than erect, like swallows alighted and walking on the ground:—

> "and as he spake, his wings now and then
> spread, as he meant to fly, then close again,—"

so that we should suspect that we might be conversing with an angel. Bread may not always nourish us; but it always does us good,

it even takes stiffness out of our joints, and makes us supple and
buoyant, when we knew not what ailed us, to recognize any generosity in man or Nature, to share any unmixed and heroic joy.

Ancient poetry and mythology suggest, at least, that husbandry
was once a sacred art; but it is pursued with irreverent haste and
heedlessness by us, our object being [182/183] to have large farms
and large crops merely. We have no festival, nor procession, nor ceremony, not excepting our cattle-shows and so-called Thanksgivings,
by which the farmer expresses a sense of the sacredness of his calling,
or is reminded of its sacred origin. It is the premium and the feast
which tempt him. He sacrifices not to Ceres and the Terrestrial
Jove, but to the infernal Plutus rather. By avarice and selfishness,
and a grovelling habit, from which none of us is free, of regarding
the soil as property, or the means of acquiring property chiefly, the
landscape is deformed, husbandry is degraded with us, and the
farmer leads the meanest of lives. He knows Nature but as a robber.
Cato says that the profits of agriculture are particularly pious or just
(*maximeque pius quaestus*), and according to Varro the old Romans
"called the same earth Mother and Ceres, and thought that they
who cultivated it led a pious and useful life, and that they alone
were left of the race of King Saturn."

We are wont to forget that the sun looks on our cultivated fields
and on the praries and forests without distinction. They all reflect
and absorb his rays alike, and the former make but a small part of
the glorious picture which he beholds in his daily course. In his view
the earth is all equally cultivated like a garden. Therefore we should
receive the benefit of his light and heat with a corresponding trust
and magnanimity. What though I value the seed of these beans, and
harvest that in the fall of the year? This broad field which I have
looked at so long looks not to me as the principal cultivator, but
away from me to influences more genial to it, which [183/184]
water and make it green. These beans have results which are not
harvested by me. Do they not grow for woodchucks partly? The ear
of wheat (in Latin *spica*, obsoletely *speca*, from *spe*, hope) should
not be the only hope of the husbandman; its kernel or grain (*gra-
num*, from *gerendo*, bearing) is not all that it bears. How, then, can
our harvest fail? Shall I not rejoice also at the abundance of the
weeds whose seeds are the granary of the birds? It matters little comparatively whether the fields fill the farmer's barns. The true husbandman will cease from anxiety, as the squirrels manifest no concern whether the woods will bear chestnuts this year or not, and
finish his labor with every day, relinquishing all claim to the produce of his fields, and sacrificing in his mind not only his first but
his last fruits also. [184]

SIDNEY LANIER

Thar's More in the Man Than
Thar Is in the Land

I KNOWED a man, which he lived in Jones,
Which Jones is a county of red hills and stones,
And he lived pretty much by gittin' of loans,
And his mules was nuthin' but skin and bones,
And his hogs was flat as his corn-bread pones,
And he had 'bout a thousand acres o' land.

This man—which his name it was also Jones—
He swore that he'd leave them old red hills and stones
Fur he couldn't make nuthin' but yallerish cotton,
And little o' *that,* and his fences was rotten,
And what little corn he had, *hit* was boughten
And dinged ef a livin' was in the land.

And the longer he swore the madder he got,
And he riz and he walked to the stable lot,
And he hollered to Tom to come thar and hitch
Fur to emigrate somewhar whar land was rich,
And to quit raisin' cock-burrs, thistles and sich,
And a wastin' ther time on the cussed land.

So him and Tom they hitched up the mules,
Pertestin' that folks was mighty big fools
That ud stay in Georgy ther lifetime out,
Jest scratchin' a livin' when all of 'em mought
Git places in Texas whar cotton would sprout
By the time you could plant it in the land. [180/181]

From *Poems of Sidney Lanier,* edited by His Wife, New Edition (New York: Charles Scribner's Sons, 1906), pp. 180–182. First published in the *Georgia Daily,* 1869.

And he driv by a house whar a man named Brown
Was a livin', not fur from the edge o' town,
And he bantered Brown fur to buy his place,
And said that bein' as money was skace,
And bein' as sheriffs was hard to face,
Two dollars an acre would git the land.

They closed at a dollar and fifty cents,
And Jones he bought him a waggin and tents,
And loaded his corn, and his wimmin, and truck,
And moved to Texas, which it tuck
His entire pile, with the best of luck,
To git thar and git him a little land.

But Brown moved out on the old Jones' farm,
And he rolled up his breeches and bared his arm,
And he picked all the rocks from off'n the groun',
And he rooted it up and he plowed it down,
Then he sowed his corn and his wheat in the land.

Five years glid by, and Brown, one day
(Which he'd got so fat that he wouldn't weigh),
Was a settin' down, sorter lazily,
To the bulliest dinner you ever see,
When one o' the children jumped on his knee
And says, "Yan's Jones, which you bought his land."

And thar was Jones, standin' out at the fence,
And he hadn't no waggin, nor mules, nor tents,
Fur he had left Texas afoot and cum
To Georgy to see if he couldn't git sum
Employment, and he was a lookin' as hum-
Ble as ef he had never owned any land. [181/182]

But Brown he axed him in, and he sot
Him down to his vittles smokin' hot,
And when he had filled hisself and the floor
Brown looked at him sharp and riz and swore
That, "whether men's land was rich or poor
Thar was more in the *man* than thar was in the *land*."

MACON, GEORGIA, 1869. [182]

THORSTEIN VEBLEN

The Independent Farmer

THE CASE of the American farmer is conspicuous; though it can scarcely be called singular, since in great part it is rather typical of the fortune which has overtaken the underlying populations throughout Christendom under the dominion of absentee ownership in its later developed phase. Much the same general run of conditions recurs elsewhere in those respects which engage the fearsome attention of these farmers. By and large, the farmer is so placed in the economic system that both as producer and as consumer he deals with business concerns which are in a position to make the terms of the traffic, which it is for him to take or leave. Therefore the margin of benefit that comes to him from his work is commonly at a minimum. He is commonly driven by circumstances over which he has no control, the circumstances being made by the system of absentee ownership and its business enterprise. Yet he is, on the whole, an obstinately loyal supporter of the system of law and custom which so makes the conditions of life for him.

His unwavering loyalty to the system is in part a holdover from that obsolete past when he was the Independent Farmer of the poets; but in part it is also due to the still surviving persuasion that he is on the way, by hard work and shrewd management, to acquire a "competence"; such as will enable him some day to take his due place among the absentee owners of the land and so come in for an easy livelihood at the cost of the rest of the community; and in part it is also due to the persistent [395/396] though fantastic opinion that his own present interest is bound up with the system of absentee ownership, in that he is himself an absentee owner by so much as he owns land and equipment which he works with hired help—always presuming that he is such an owner, in effect or in prospect.

It is true, the farmer-owners commonly are absentee owners to this

From *The Portable Veblen,* edited by Max Lerner (New York: The Viking Press, 1950), pp. 395–406. First published in *Absentee Ownership and Business Enterprise in Recent Times,* 1923.

extent. Farming is team-work. As it is necessarily carried on by current methods in the great farming sections, farm work runs on such a scale that no individual owner can carry on by use of his own personal work alone, or by use of the man-power of his own household alone—which makes him an absentee owner by so much. But it does not, in the common run, make him an absentee owner of such dimensions as are required in order to create an effectual collusive control of the market, or such as will enable him, singly or collectively, to determine what charges the traffic shall bear. It leaves him still effectually in a position to take or leave what is offered at the discretion of those massive absentee interests that move in the background of the market.

Always, of course, the farmer has with him the abiding comfort of his illusions, to the effect that he is in some occult sense the "Independent Farmer," and that he is somehow by way of achieving a competence of absentee ownership by hard work and sharp practice, some day; but in practical effect, as things habitually work out, he is rather to be called a quasi-absentee owner, or perhaps a pseudo-absentee owner, being too small a parcel of absentee ownership to count as such in the outcome. But it is presumably all for the best, or at least it is expedient for business-as-usual, that the farmer should continue to nurse his illusions and go about his [396/397] work; that he should go on his way to complete that destiny to which it has pleased an all-seeing and merciful Providence to call him.

From colonial times and through the greater part of its history as a republic America has been in the main an agricultural country. Farming has been the staple occupation and has employed the greater part of the population. And the soil has always been the chief of those natural resources which the American people have taken over and made into property. Through the greater part of its history the visible growth of the country has consisted in the extension of the cultivated area and the increasing farm output, farm equipment, and farm population. This progressive taking-over and settlement of the farming lands is the most impressive material achievement of the American people, as it is also the most serviceable work which they have accomplished hitherto. It still is, as it ever has been, the people's livelihood; and the rest of the industrial system has in the main, grown up, hitherto, as a subsidiary or auxiliary, adopted to and limited by the needs and the achievements of the country's husbandry. The incentives and methods engaged in this taking-over of the soil, as well as the industrial and institutional consequences that have followed, are accordingly matters of prime consideration in any endeavour to understand or explain the national character and the temperamental bent which underlies it.

The farm population—that farm population which has counted substantially toward this national achievement—have been a ready, capable and resourceful body of workmen. And they have been driven by the incentives already spoken of in an earlier passage as being characteristic of the English-speaking colonial enterprise—individual self-help and cupidity. Except transiently and provisionally, and with doubtful effect, this farm population [397/398] has nowhere and at no time been actuated by a spirit of community interest in dealing with any of their material concerns. Their community spirit, in material concerns, has been quite notably scant and precarious, in spite of the fact that they have long been exposed to material circumstances of a wide-sweeping uniformity, such as should have engendered a spirit of community interest and made for collective enterprise, and such as could have made any effectual collective enterprise greatly remunerative to all concerned. But they still stand sturdily by the timeworn make-believe that they still are individually self-sufficient masterless men, and through good report and evil report they have remained Independent Farmers, as between themselves, which is all that is left of their independence—Each for himself, etc.

Of its kind, this is an admirable spirit, of course; and it has achieved many admirable results, even though the results have not all been to the gain of the farmers. Their self-help and cupidity have left them at the mercy of any organisation that is capable of mass action and a steady purpose. So they have, in the economic respect—and incidentally in the civil and political respect—fallen under the dominion of those massive business interests that move obscurely in the background of the market and buy and sell and dispose of the farm products and the farmers' votes and opinions very much on their own terms and at their ease.

But all the while it remains true that they have brought an unexampled large and fertile body of soil to a very passable state of service, and their work continues to yield a comfortably large food supply to an increasing population, at the same time that it yields a comfortable run of free income to the country's kept classes. It is true, in the end the farm population find [398/399] themselves at work for the benefit of business-as-usual, on a very modest livelihood. For farming is, perhaps necessarily, carried on in severalty and on a relatively small scale, even though the required scale exceeds what is possible on a footing of strict self-ownership of land and equipment by the cultivators; and there is always the pervading spirit of self-help and cupidity, which unavoidably defeats even that degree of collusive mass action that might otherwise be possible. Whereas the system of business interests in whose web the farmers are caught is drawn on a large scale, its units are massive, impersonal, imperturbable and, in effect, irresponsible, under the established order of law and custom, and they are interlocked in an unbreakable framework of common interests.

By and large, the case of America is as the case of the American farm population, and for the like reasons. For the incentives and ideals, the law and custom and the knowledge and belief, on which the farm population has gone about its work and has come to this pass, are the same as have ruled the growth and shaped the outcome for the community at large. Nor does the situation in America differ materially from the state of things elsewhere in the civilised countries, in so far as these others share in the same material civilisation of Christendom.

In the American tradition, and in point of historical fact out of which the tradition has arisen, the farmer has been something of a pioneer. Loosely it can be said that the pioneering era is now closing, at least provisionally and as regards farming. But while the pioneer-farmer is dropping out of the work of husbandry, his pioneer soul goes marching on. And it has been an essential trait of this American pioneering spirit to seize upon so much of the country's natural resources as the enterprising pioneer [399/400] could lay hands on—in the case of the pioneer-farmer, so much of the land as he could get and hold possession of. The land had, as it still has, a prospective use and therefore a prospective value, a "speculative" value as it is called; and the farmer-pioneer was concerned with seizing upon this prospective value and turning it into net gain by the way of absentee ownership, as much as the pioneer-farmer was concerned with turning the fertile soil to present use in the creation of a livelihood for himself and his household from day to day.

Habitually and with singular uniformity the American farmers have aimed to acquire real estate at the same time that they have worked at their trade as husbandmen. And real estate is a matter of absentee ownership, an asset whose value is based on the community's need of this given parcel of land for use as a means of livelihood, and the value of which is measured by the capitalised free income which the owner may expect to come in for by holding it for as high a rental as the traffic in this need will bear. So that the pioneering aim, in American farming, has been for the pioneer-farmers, each and several, to come in for as much of a free income at the cost of the rest of the community as the law would allow; which has habitually worked out in their occupying, each and several, something more than they could well take care of. They have habitually "carried" valuable real estate at the same time that they have worked the soil of so much of their land as they could take care of, in as effectual a manner as they could under these circumstances. They have been cultivators of the main chance as well as of the fertile soil; with the result that, by consequence of this intense and unbroken habituation, the farm population is today imbued with that penny-wise spirit of self-help and cupidity that now [400/401] leaves them and their work and holdings at the disposal of those massive vested interests that know the uses of collusive mass action, as already spoken of above.

But aside from this spiritual effect which this protracted habituation to a somewhat picayune calculation of the main chance has had on the farmers' frame of mind, and aside from their consequent unfitness to meet the businesslike manœuvres of the greater vested interests, this manner of pioneering enterprise which the farmers have habitually mixed into their farming has also had a more immediate bearing on the country's husbandry, and, indeed, on the industrial system as a whole. The common practice has been to "take up" more land than the farmer could cultivate, with his available means, and to hold it at some cost. Which has increased the equipment required for the cultivation of the acres cultivated, and has also increased the urgency of the farmer's need of credit by help of which to find the needed equipment and meet the expenses incident to his holding his idle and semi-idle acres intact. And farm credit has been notoriously usurious. All this has had the effect of raising the cost of production of farm products; partly by making the individual farm that much more unwieldy as an instrument of production, partly by further enforcing the insufficiency and the make-shift character for which American farm equipment is justly famed, and partly also by increasing the distances over which the farm supplies and the farm products have had to be moved.

This last point marks one of the more serious handicaps of American farming, at the same time that it has contributed materially to enforce that "extensive," "superficial," and exhausting character of American farming which has arrested the attention of all foreign observers. In American practice the "farm area" has always [401/402] greatly exceeded the "acreage under cultivation," even after all due allowance is made for any unavoidable inclusion of waste and half-waste acreage within the farm boundaries. Even yet, at the provisional close of the career of the American pioneer-farmer, the actual proportion of unused and half-used land included within and among the farms will materially exceed what the records show, and it greatly exceeds what any inexperienced observer will be able to credit. The period is not long past—if it is past—when, taking one locality with another within the great farming sections of the country, the idle and half-idle lands included in and among the farms equalled the acreage that was fully employed, even in that "extensive" fashion in which American farming has habitually been carried on.

But there is no need of insisting on this high proportion of idle acreage, which none will credit who has not a wide and intimate knowledge of the facts in the case. For more or less—for as much as all intelligent observers will be ready to credit—this American practice has counted toward an excessively wide distribution of the cultivated areas, excessively long distances of transport, over roads which have by consequence been excessively bad—necessarily and notoriously so—and which have hindered communication to such a degree as in many instances to confine the cultivation to such crops as can be handled with a minimum of farm buildings and will bear the crudest kind of carriage over long distances and with incalculable delays. This applies not only to the farm-country's highways, but to its railway facilities as well. The American practice has doubled the difficulty of transportation and retarded the introduction of the more practicable and more remunerative methods of farming; until make-shift and haphazard have in many places become so ingrained in the habits of the farm [402/403] population that nothing but abounding distress and the slow passing of generations can correct it all.[1] At the same time, as an incident by the way, this same excessive dispersion of the farming communities over long distances, helped out by bad roads, has been perhaps the chief factor in giving the retail business communities of the country towns their strangle-hold on the underlying farm population.

And it should surprise no one if a population which has been exposed to unremitting habituation of this kind has presently come to feel at home in it all; so that the bootless chicanery of their self-help is rated as a masterly fabric of axiomatic realities, and sharp practice has become a matter of conscience. In such a community it should

[1] As a side issue to this arrangement of magnificent distances in the fertile farm country, it may be called to mind that the education of the farm children has on this account continually suffered from enforced neglect, with untoward results. And there are those who belive that the noticeably high rate of insanity among farmers' wives in certain sections of the prairie country is traceable in good part to the dreary isolation enforced upon them by this American plan of "country life."

hold true that "An honest man will bear watching," that the common good is a by-word, that "Everybody's business is nobody's business," that public office is a private job, where the peak of aphoristic wisdom is reached in that red-letter formula of democratic politics, "Subtraction, division, and silence." So it has become a democratic principle that public office should go by rotation, under the rule of equal opportunity—equal opportunity to get something for nothing —but should go only to those who value the opportunity highly enough to make a desperate run for it. Here men "run" for office, not "stand" for it. Subtraction is the aim of this pioneer cupidity, not production; and salesmanship is its line of approach, not workmanship; and so, being in no way related quantitatively to a person's workmanlike powers [403/404] or to his tangible performance, it has no "saturation point."[2]

The spirit of the American farmers, typically, has been that of the pioneer rather than the workman. They have been efficient workmen, but that is not the trait which marks them for its own and sets them off in contrast with the common run. Their passion for acquisition has driven them to work, hard and painfully, but they have never been slavishly attached to their work; their slavery has been not to an imperative bent of workmanship and human service, but to an indefinitely extensible cupidity which strives to work when other expedients fail; at least so they say. So they have been somewhat footloose in their attachment to the soil as well as somewhat hasty and shiftless in its cultivation. They have always, in the typical case, wanted something more than their proportionate share of the soil; not because they were driven by a felt need of doing more than

[2] This civilised-man's cupidity is one of those "higher wants of man" which the economists have found to be "indefinitely extensible," and like other spiritual needs it is self-authenticating, its own voucher.

The Latin phrase is *auri sacra fames*, which goes to show the point along the road to civilisation reached by that people. They had reached a realisation of the essentially sacramental virtue of this indefinitely extensible need of more; but the *aurum* in terms of which they visualised the object of their passion is after all a tangible object, with physical limitations of weight and space, such as to impose a mechanical "saturation point" on the appetite for its accumulation. But the civilised peoples of Christendom at large, and more particularly America, the most civilised and most Christian of them all, have in recent times removed this limitation. The object of this "higher want of man" is no longer specie, but some form of credit instrument which conveys title to a run of free income; and it can accordingly have no "saturation point," even in fancy, inasmuch as credit is also indefinitely extensible and stands in quantitative relation to tangible fact.

their fair share of work or because they aimed to give the community more service than would be a fair equivalent of their own livelihood, but with a view to cornering [404/405] something more than their proportion of the community's indispensable means of life and so getting a little something for nothing in allowing their holdings to be turned to account, for a good and valuable consideration.

The American farmers have been footloose, on the whole, more particularly that peculiarly American element among them who derive their traditions from a colonial pedigree. There has always been an easy shifting from country to town, and this steady drift into the towns of the great farming sections has in the main been a drift from work into business. And it has been the business of these country towns—what may be called their business-as-usual—to make the most of the necessities and the ignorance of their underlying farm population. The farmers have on the whole been ready to make such a shift whenever there has been an "opening"; that is to say, they have habitually been ready to turn their talents to more remunerative use in some other pursuit whenever the chance has offered, and indeed they have habitually been ready to make the shift out of husbandry into the traffic of the towns even at some risk whenever the prospect of a wider margin of net gain has opened before their eager eyes.

In all this pursuit of the net gain the farm population and their country-town cousins have carried on with the utmost good nature. The business communities of the country towns have uniformly got the upper hand. But the farmers have shown themselves good losers; they have in the main gracefully accepted the turn of things and have continued to count on meeting with better luck or making a shrewder play next time. But the upshot of it so far has habitually been that the farm population find themselves working for a very modest livelihood [405/406] and the country towns come in for an inordinately wide margin of net gains; that is to say, net gain over necessary outlay and over the value of the services which they render their underlying farm populations.

To many persons who have some superficial acquaintance with the run of the facts it may seem, on scant reflection, that what is said above of the inordinate gains that go to the country towns is a rash overstatement, perhaps even a malicious overstatement. It is not intended to say that the gains *per capita* of the persons currently engaged in business in the country towns, or the gains per cent, on the funds invested, are extraordinarily high; but only that as counted on the necessary rather than the actual cost of the useful work done, and as counted on the necessary rather than the actual number of persons engaged, the gains which go to the business traffic of the country towns are inordinately large.[3] [406]

[3] It may be added, though it should scarcely be necessary, that a good part of the gains which are taken by the country-town business community passes through their hands into the hands of those massive vested interests that move obscurely in the background of the market, and to whom the country towns stand in a relation of feeders, analogous to that in which the farm population stands to the towns. In good part the business traffic of the country towns serves as ways and means of net gain to these business interests in the background. But when all due allowance is made on this and other accounts, and even if this element which may be called net gains in transit be deducted, the statement as made above remains standing without material abatement: the business gains which come to the country towns in their traffic with their underlying farm populations are inordinately large, as counted on the necessary cost and use-value of the service rendered, or on the necessary work done. But whether these gains, in so far as they are "inordinate"—that is in so far as they go in under the caption of Something for Nothing—are retained by the business men of the town or are by them passed on the larger business interests which dominate them, that is an idle difference for all that concerns the fortunes of the underlying farm population or the community at large. In either case it is idle waste, so far as concerns the material well-being of any part of the farm population.

H. L. MENCKEN

The Husbandman

LET THE FARMER, so far as I am concerned, be damned forever-more. To Hell with him, and bad luck to him. He is a tedious fraud and ignoramus, a cheap rogue and hypocrite, the eternal Jack of the human pack. He deserves all that he ever suffers under our economic system, and more. Any city man, not insane, who sheds tears for him is shedding tears of the crocodile.

No more grasping, selfish and dishonest mammal, indeed, is known to students of the *Anthropoidea*. When the going is good for him he robs the rest of us up to the extreme limit of our endurance; when the going is bad he comes bawling for help out of the public till. Has anyone ever heard of a farmer [360/361] making any sacrifice of his own interests, however slight, to the common good? Has anyone ever heard of a farmer practising or advocating any political idea that was not absolutely self-seeking—that was not, in fact, deliberately designed to loot the rest of us to his gain? Greenbackism, free silver, the government guarantee of prices, bonuses, all the complex fiscal imbecilities of the cow State John Baptists—these are the contributions of the virtuous husbandmen to American political theory. There has never been a time, in good seasons or bad, when his hands were not itching for more; there has never been a time when he was not ready to support any charlatan, however grotesque, who promised to get it for him. Only one issue ever fetches him, and that is the issue of his own profit. He must be promised something definite and valuable, to be paid to him alone, or he is off after some other mountebank. He simply cannot imagine himself as a citizen of a commonwealth, in duty bound to give as well as take; he can imagine himself only as getting all and giving nothing.

Yet we are asked to venerate this prehensile moron as the *Ur-burgher*, the citizen *par excellence*, the foundation-stone of the state!

From H. L. Mencken, *A Mencken Chrestomathy* (New York: Alfred A. Knopf, 1949), pp. 360–364. First published in 1924.

And why? Because he produces something that all of us must have—that we must get somehow on penalty of death. And how do we get it from him? By submitting helplessly to his unconscionable black-mailing—by paying him, not under any rule of reason, but in proportion to his roguery and incompetence, and hence to the direness of our need. I doubt that the human race, as a whole, would submit to that sort of high-jacking, year in and year out, from any other necessary class of men. But the farmers carry it on incessantly, without challenge or reprisal, and the only thing that keeps them from reducing us, at intervals, to actual famine is their own imbecile knavery. They are all willing and eager to pillage us by starving us, but they can't do it because they can't resist attempts to swindle each other. Recall, for example, the case of the cotton-growers in the South. Back in the 1920s they agreed among themselves to cut down the cotton acreage in order to inflate the price—and instantly every party to the agreement began planting *more* cotton in order to profit by the abstinence of his neighbors. That abstinence being wholly imaginary, the [361/362] price of cotton fell instead of going up—and then the entire pack of scoundrels began demanding assistance from the national treasury—in brief, began demanding that the rest of us indemnify them for the failure of their plot to blackmail us.

The same demand is made sempiternally by the wheat farmers of the Middle West. It is the theory of the zanies who perform at Washington that a grower of wheat devotes himself to that banal art in a philanthropic and patriotic spirit—that he plants and harvests his crop in order that the folks of the cities may not go without bread. It is the plain fact that he raises wheat because it takes less labor than any other crop—because it enables him, after working no more than sixty days a year, to loaf the rest of the twelve months. If wheat-raising could be taken out of the hands of such lazy *fellahin* and organized as the production of iron or cement is organized, the price might be reduced by two-thirds, and still leave a large profit for *entrepreneurs*. But what would become of the farmers? Well, what rational man gives a hoot? If wheat went to $10 a bushel tomorrow, and all the workmen of the cities became slaves in name as well as in fact, no farmer in this grand land of freedom would consent voluntarily to a reduction of as much as $1/8$ of a cent a bushel. "The greatest wolves," said E. W. Howe, a graduate of the farm, "are the farmers who bring produce to town to sell." Wolves? Let us not insult *Canis lupus*. I move the substitution of *Hyæna hyæna*.

Meanwhile, how much truth is in the common theory that the husbandman is harassed and looted by our economic system, that the men of the cities prey upon him—specifically, that he is the chronic victim of such devices as the tariff, railroad regulation, and

the banking system? So far as I can make out, there is none whatever. The net effect of our present banking system is that the money
accumulated by the cities is used to finance the farmers, and that
they employ it to blackmail the cities. As for the tariff, is it a fact
that it damages the farmer, or benefits him? Let us turn for light to
the worst tariff act ever heard of in human history: that of 1922. It
put a duty of 30 cents a bushel on wheat, and so barred out Cana-
dian wheat, and gave the American farmer a vast and unfair advantage. For months running the difference in the price of wheat on the
two sides [362/363] of the American-Canadian border—wheat raised
on farms not a mile apart—ran from 25 to 30 cents a bushel. Danish
butter was barred out by a duty of 8 cents a pound—and the American farmer pocketed the 8 cents. Potatoes carried a duty of 50 cents a
hundredweight—and the potato-growers of Maine, eager to mop up,
raised such an enormous crop that the market was glutted, and they
went bankrupt, and began bawling for government aid. High duties
were put, too, upon meats, upon cheese, upon wool—in brief, upon
practically everything that the farmer produced. But his profits were
taken from him by even higher duties upon manufactured goods,
and by high freight rates? Were they, indeed? There was, in fact, no
duty at all upon many of the things he consumed. There was no
duty, for example, upon shoes. The duty upon woolen goods gave a
smaller advantage to the manufacturer than the duty on wool gave
to the farmer. So with the duty on cotton goods. Automobiles were
cheaper in the United States than anywhere else on earth. So were
all agricultural implements. So were groceries. So were fertilizers.

But here I come to the brink of an abyss of statistics, and had better haul up. The enlightened reader is invited to investigate them
for himself; they will bring him, I believe, some surprises. They by
no means exhaust the case against the consecrated husbandman. I
have said that the only political idea he can grasp is one which
promises him a direct profit. It is, alas, not quite true: he can also
grasp one which has the sole effect of annoying and damaging his
enemy, the city man. The same mountebanks who get to Washington by promising to augment his gains and make good his losses devote whatever time is left over from that enterprise to saddling the
rest of us with oppressive and idiotic laws, all hatched on the farm.
There, where the cows low through the still night, and the jug of
Peruna stands behind the stove, and bathing begins, as at Biarritz,
with the vernal equinox—there is the reservoir of all the nonsensical
legislation which makes the United States a buffoon among the great
nations. It was among country Methodists, practitioners of a theology degraded almost to the level of voodooism, that Prohibition was
invented, and it was by country Methodists, nine-tenths of them ac-

tual followers of the plow, that it was [363/364] fastened upon the
rest of us, to the damage of our bank accounts, our dignity and our
viscera. What lay under it, and under all the other crazy enactments
of its category, was no more and no less than the yokel's congenital
and incurable hatred of the city man—his simian rage against everyone who, as he sees it, is having a better time than he is.

The same animus is visible in innumerable other moral statutes,
all ardently supported by the peasantry. For example, the Mann Act.
The aim of this amazing law, of course, is not to put down adultery;
it is simply to put down that variety of adultery which is most agree-
able. What got it upon the books was the constant gabble in the
rural newspapers about the byzantine debaucheries of urban anti-
nomians—rich stockbrokers who frequented Atlantic City from Friday to Monday, movie actors who traveled about the country with
beautiful wenches, and so on. Such aphrodisiacal tales, read beside
the kitchen-stove by hinds condemned to monogamous misery with
stupid, unclean and ill-natured wives, naturally aroused in them a
vast detestation of errant cockneys, and this detestation eventually
rolled up enough force to attract the attention of the quacks who
make laws at Washington. The result was the Mann Act. Since then
a number of the cow States have passed Mann Acts of their own,
usually forbidding the use of automobiles "for immoral purposes."
But there is nowhere a law forbidding the use of cow-stables, hay-
ricks and other such familiar rustic ateliers of sin. That is to say,
there is nowhere a law forbidding yokels to drag virgins into infamy
by the crude technic practised since Tertiary times on the farms;
there are only laws forbidding city youths to do it according to the
refined technic of the great Babylons.

Such are the sweet-smelling and altrustic agronomists whose sor-
rows are the *Leitmotiv* of our politics, whose welfare is alleged to be
the chief end of democratic statecraft, whose patriotism is the so-
called bulwark of this so-called Republic. [364]

WILLIAM ALEXANDER PERCY

Planters, Share-Croppers, and Such

FATHER was the only great person I ever knew and he would not have been great without Mother. They died two years after the flood, mercifully within a few weeks of each other. Without them my life seemed superfluous.

Holt, a hunting partner of Father's and an ex-slave, came up to the office to express his grief. I met him in the hall, but he motioned me to Father's desk, saying: "Set there where he sot. That's where you b'long." He took the chair across the desk from me, filling it and resting his strong hands on the heavy cane he always carried and needed. He was a magnificent old man with massive shoulders and a noble head. For some minutes he struggled silently, sitting there in what had been Father's office, then he let the tears gush unhindered from his eyes and the words from his heart: "The roof is gone from over my head and the floor from under my feet. I am out in the dark and the cold alone. I want to go where he is." He rose and hobbled out. Many of us felt that way.

From Father I inherited Trail Lake, a three-thousand-acre [270/271] cotton plantation, one of the best in the county and unencumbered. I was considered well-to-do for our part of the state. Father loved the land and had put into it the savings of a lifetime. Perhaps he loved it because he and his brothers and sisters had been born on it and had passed their childhood among country things. His grandfather had obtained title to the Percy Place about 1850. It was a patch of woods then and many slaves had to labor many months before it could properly be termed a cotton plantation. This grandfather, whom the family affectionately, but rather disrespectfully, referred to as Thomas G., had been the favorite son of old Don Carlos and had married a famous beauty from Huntsville named Maria Pope. If you had lived as long as I have with that oil

From William Alexander Percy, *Lanterns on the Levee: Recollections of a Planter's Son* (New York: Alfred A. Knopf, 1941), pp. 270–284.

painting of him in the library over the fireplace, you could easily deduce why Maria and Don Carlos loved him. It reticently and through a fume of chiaroscuro reveals a personable young chap in a black stock and a black waistcoat adorned with four stylish brass buttons. At first perhaps you won't notice his smile, but it's there, all right, at the corner of his mouth, very shadowy and knowing, a little hurt but not at all bitter. It's by that smile I really know him, and not by his descendants, who mostly are the kind you like to descend with, or by the tender trusting references to him in Don Carlos's will. Though I've always lived with the remnant of his brown English library (each leather volume numbered and marked with the book-plate bearing his name sans crest or escutcheon) and always loved his enormous mahogany dining-room table with its carved legs and brass claws, around which all of us have eaten meals together going on six generations now, it's not they but his smile that makes him a familiar and a confidant of mine—that and the fact he cut no very great figure in the world. He isn't a demanding ancestor. [271/272]

He seems to have felt that if he raised his sons to be gentlemen he would have done his full Christian duty by them and indeed by life. Training in a profession, though ornamental, was unnecessary for a gentleman, but of course you couldn't be one at all unless you owned land. Therefore, Thomas G. casually made doctors of his two older boys, Walker and LeRoy, and a lawyer of Fafar, after whom I was named, but having done that, without, of course, expecting them to practice medicine or law, he settled down gravely to the really serious business of getting them a plantation. He decided on a place in the Delta, paid for it, manned it with enough slaves to clear and cultivate it, and shipped his sons, all three of them, down to live on it.

When I was a youngster, I quite often spent the weekend on this plantation of theirs, which is still called the Percy Place. Already the slave quarters looked ramshackly, the woods had disappeared, the loamy creek land seemed thin, and the residence, from which the ells had fallen away, was ugly and plain, more full of room than anything else and split amidships by an enormous drafty hall, a very cave for coolness and emptiness.

I am sure in these days and times no wise father would dare bundle off three sons, two of them married, and expect them to live forever after under the same roof without kicking it off. Uncle Walker was married to Aunt Fannie, Fafar to Mur, and Uncle LeRoy (whom everybody loved and the youngsters called Uncle Lee) was the bachelor–scholar and gallivanter of the trio and so destined to endure gracefully occasional admonitions and rakings over the coals

from his young sisters-in-law. Yet all reports agree that the Percy
household was not only amiable but full of fun. Apparently they
were a cheery lot who liked life.

Then the war came, and everything changed. By the [272/273]
time of the surrender Uncle Walker had died, Uncle Lee had been
stricken with paralysis, and when Fafar, the youngest and the soldier
of the three, returned, it was to a diminished and penniless household of which he found himself the head and the bread-winner. The
women and children and sick were still clinging to the place, but
there wasn't a servant or a field-hand on it. All the slaves had left. I
suppose he and Mur must have done some pretty tragic planning together the night he got home. Mur brought out from hiding the last
of the plantation's horses, Fafar mounted this priceless, unlovely
steed—his name was Bill Jack—and jogged off to Greenville, which
then was a mere river-landing at the end of ten miles of impassable
road. Fafar was over thirty years old and a Colonel of a defeated
army. He hung out a shingle announcing to the bankrupt countryside that W. A. Percy had opened offices for the practice of law. In
time he became one of Mississippi's famous lawyers, but Father said
that right from the start he always managed to collect more clients
than fees.

Fafar was fifty-five years old when he died. Long before his death
people had been calling him "Old Colonel Percy" and "The Gray
Eagle." His life had been crowded with usefulness and honor, but it
ended when he was fifty-five. That is my age now. When I consider
all he did and all I haven't done, I feel the need of taking a good
long look at Thomas G., debonair and wistful, expecting nothing.

Of course the stage that Fafar trod after the war was no ordinary
stage, and the play no ordinary play. Those days you had to be a
hero or a villain or a weakling—you couldn't be just middling ordinary. The white people in the whole Delta comprised a mere handful, but there were hordes of Negroes. Poor wretches! For a thousand years and more they had been trained in tribal barbarism, for a
hundred and more in slavery. So equipped, they were presented
[273/274] overnight with freedom and the ballot and told to run
the river country. They did. They elected Negroes to every office.
We had a Negro sheriff, Negro justices of the peace, Negro clerks of
court. There were no white officials, not even carpetbaggers. It was
one glorious orgy of graft, lawlessness, and terrorism. The desperate
whites though negligible in number banded together to overthrow
this regime and chose Fafar as their leader. His life work became the
re-establishment of white supremacy. That work required courage,
tact, intelligence, patience; it also required vote-buying, the stuffing
of ballot-boxes, chicanery, intimidation. Heart-breaking business

and degrading, but in the end successful. At terrific cost white supremacy was re-established. Some of us still remember what we were told of those times, and what we were told inclines us to guard the ballot as something precious, something to be withheld unless the fitness of the recipient be patent. We are the ones I suppose who doubt despairingly the fitness of Negroes and (under our breath be it said) of women.

Father considered Fafar superior to any human being he had ever known: he insisted he had a finer mind, a greater gusto, a warmer love of people, and a more rigid standard of justice than of his sons. But for Fafar's efforts at running the plantation Father had only amused and tolerant scorn.

It appears that Fafar practiced law in order to be able to practice husbandry. He retained title to the Percy Place by paying its taxes with fees. But never, never, during all the years he managed it, did it yield one penny of profit. Father contended the reason for this deplorable result was Fafar's inability to say no to any Negro in wheedling mood. I suspect, however, the main reason was the low price of cotton and the South's economic collapse following Gettysburg. [274/275]

After the first fine frenzy of emancipation, although Negro politicians and carpetbaggers were riding high and making prosperity look like sin, the rank and file of ex-slaves, the simply country Negroes, found themselves faring exceedingly ill. They had freedom, but nothing else. It's a precious possession, but worthless commercially. The former slave-holders had land, but nothing else. It's as precious, nearly, as freedom, but without plow and plowmen equally worthless. On ex-slave and ex-master it dawned gradually that they were in great need of one another—and not only economically, but, curiously enough, emotionally. Holt killed a Yankee officer for insulting Colonel Howell Hines, his old master. Fafar had Negro friends without whose information and advice he and the other political rebels of the time would have suffered under this reign of scalawaggery even more grievously than they did. To each plantation drifted back puzzled, unhappy freedmen who had once worked it as slaves and who were discovering that though slaves couldn't go hungry, freedmen could and did. Ex-slaves returned to the Percy Place and asked for a chance to make a crop on it. Fafar had little to offer them except good land and leadership. He puzzled over what was just to do and what he could do. He concluded by offering his ex-slaves a partnership with him. The terms of it were simple.

In simple words, about like these, he explained it to them:

I have land which you need, and you have muscle which I need; let's put what we've got in the same pot and call it ours. I'll give you all the land you can work, a house to live in, a garden plot and room to raise chickens, hogs, and cows if you can come by them, and all the wood you want to cut for fuel. I'll direct and oversee you. I'll get you a doctor when you are sick. Until the crop comes in I'll try [275/276] to keep you from going hungry or naked in so far as I am able. I'll pay the taxes and I'll furnish the mules and plows and gear and whatever else is necessary to make a crop. This is what I promise to do. You will plant and cultivate and gather this crop as I direct. This is what you will promise to do. When the crop is picked, half of it will be mine and half of it yours. If I have supplied you with money or food or clothing or anything else during this year, I will charge it against your half of the crop. I shall handle the selling of the cotton and the cottonseed because I know more than you do about their value. But the corn you may sell or eat or use for feed as you like. If the price of cotton is good, we shall both make something. If it is bad, neither of us will make anything, but I shall probably lose the place and you will lose nothing because you have nothing to lose. It's a hard contract these hard times for both of us, but it's just and self-respecting and if we both do our part and have a little luck we can both prosper under it.

This was the contract under which Fafar operated the Percy Place during his lifetime, under which Mur operated it after his death, under which Father operated it from the time of her death to the time it was sold. It changed in no essential during all those years except that with better times the promise to keep the Negroes from going hungry and cold became a fixed obligation to lend them a stated amount of money each month from the first of March, when planting started, to the first of September, when cottonseed money began coming in. After the place had been worked for years under this arrangement—years during which nobody grew rich and nobody suffered for necessities—Father decided that it was getting run down, it was too old, it was worn out. Miserable, but feeling foresighted and awfully business-like, he sold the Percy Place. [276/277]

I rode through it last week and the crop was twice as big as either Fafar or Father had ever raised on it. Modern methods of farming, government-inspired diversification of crops, and the use of fertilizer have made it more productive than when Thomas G.'s sons planted their first cotton crop in its virgin soil with slave labor.

Let no one imagine that because Father sold the Percy Place he was landless. Far from it. Instead, he'd been watching longingly the new part of the county, the Bogue district, and little by little, bit by bit, over a period of ten years, he'd been buying a plantation there. It was his very own, his creation, and he loved it. He started with a batch of virgin timber and cleared that. Next he won in the cotton market and put the winnings into that section of Doctor Atterbury's, good land and mostly in cultivation. Then he added the desolate-looking deadening along Deep Slough. At last he bought the Cheek Place and the Ross Place. In all he finally acquired title to a single block of land of over three thousand acres—some cleared, some half-cleared, some in cultivation, part of it paid for, part mortgaged, most of it magnificent ridge-land, a few hundred acres swampy and sour. He named it Trail Lake after a singularly dilapidated-looking slough which meandered half-heartedly into the center of the place before petering out from sheer inertia. When I was going to Sewanee the whole property looked ragged and unkempt, full of fallen logs and charred stumps, standing and prone. It was at the end of the world, in a turkey and panther country. You could reach it only by a rocking impromptu trainlet called the Black Dog. The trip from Greenville and back required twenty-four hours.

Trail Lake was so far from anywhere, so inaccessible to "the law" and to the infrequent neighbors, that the Negroes ran off one manager after another and terrified the whole [277/278] countryside. Father almost lost the place because the Negroes wouldn't let any white man stay on it. At last, in desperation, he sent down a young manager from Arkansas, Billy Hardie, who shot a tenant the day of his arrival and single-handed dispersed a crap game his first Saturday night. Quiet ensued. It's a pleasant country, but even now not safe. If you haven't got a few pioneer virtues thrown in with the run-of-the-mill sort you'd better move on to a more cultured environment.

I have no love of the land and few, if any, pioneer virtues, but when Trail Lake became mine after Father's death, I must confess I was proud of it. I could reach it in three quarters of an hour. It was a model place: well drained, crossed by concrete roads, with good screened houses, a modern gin, artesian-well water, a high state of cultivation, a Negro school, a foolish number of churches, abundant crops, gardens and peach trees, quantities of hogs, chickens, and cows, and all the mules and tractors and equipment any place that size needed.

Father had operated it under the same contract that Fafar used on the Percy Place. The Negroes seemed to like it and I certainly did. I happen to believe that profit-sharing is the most moral system under which human beings can work together and I am convinced that if it were accepted in principle by capital and labor, our industrial troubles would largely cease. So on Trail Lake I continue to be partners with the sons of ex-slaves and to share fifty-fifty with them as my grandfather and Father had done.

In 1936 a young man with a passion for facts roved in from the

University of North Carolina and asked to be allowed to inspect
Trail Lake for the summer. He was Mr. Raymond McClinton, one
of Doctor Odum's boys, and the result of his sojourn was a thesis entitled "A Social-Economic Analysis of a Mississippi Delta Plantation." That's [278/279] coming pretty stout if you spend much of
your time trying to forget facts and are stone-deaf to statistics. But
some of his findings were of interest even to me, largely I suspect because they illustrated how Fafar's partnership-contract works in the
modern world. In 1936, the year Mr. McClinton chose for his study,
the crop was fair, the price average (about twelve cents), and the
taxes higher than usual. Now for some of his facts:

Trail Lake has a net acreage of 3,343.12 acres of which 1,833.66
are planted in cotton, 50.59 are given to pasture, 52.44 to gardens,
and the rest to corn and hay. The place is worked by 149 families of
Negroes (589 individuals) and in 1936 yielded 1,542 bales of cotton.
One hundred and twenty-four of the families work under Fafar's old
contract, and twenty-five, who own their stock and equipment,
under a similar contract which differs from the other only in giving
three-fourths instead of one-half of the yield to the tenant. The
plantation paid in taxes of all kinds $20,459.99, a bit better than
$6.00 per acre; in payrolls for plantation work $12,584.66—nearly
$4.00 an acre. These payrolls went to the Negroes on the place. The
124 families without stock of their own made a gross average income
of $491.90 and a net average income of $437.64. I have lost Mr.
McClinton's calculation of how many days of work a plantation
worker puts in per year, but my own calculation is a maximum of
150 days. There is nothing to do from ginning time, about October
the first, to planting time, about March the fifteenth, and nothing to
do on rainy days, of which we have many.

These figures, as I read them, show that during an average year
the 124 families working on Trail Lake for 150 days make each
$437.64 clear, besides having free water and fuel, free garden plot
and pasturage, a monthly credit for six months to cover food and
clothing, a credit [279/280] for doctor's bills and medicine, and a
house to live in. The Negroes who receive this cash and these benefits are simple unskilled laborers. I wonder what other unskilled
labor for so little receives so much. Plantations do not close down
during the year and there's no firing, because partners can't fire one
another. Our plantation system seems to me to offer as humane, just,
self-respecting, and cheerful a method of earning a living as human
beings are likely to devise. I watch the limber-jointed, oily-black,
well-fed, decently clothed peasants on Trail Lake and feel sorry for
the telephone girls, the clerks in chain stores, the office help, the unskilled laborers everywhere—not only for their poor and fixed wage

but for their slave routine, their joyless habits of work, and their insecurity.

Even with a place like Trail Lake, it's hard to make money farming. Although I kept myself helpfully obscure during the first years of my plantation-ownership, retaining the same excellent employees and following Father's practices, I began losing money almost at once, and in two years (they were depression years for everybody, I must confess) I had lost over a hundred thousand dollars and Trail Lake was mortgaged to the hilt. For the next four or five years I was in such a stew and lather getting that mortgage reduced and taxes paid, I lost track of goings-on in the outside world and missed the first tide of talk about sharecroppers. Those hundred and twenty-four families of mine with $437.64 in their jeans worked "on the shares" and called themselves "croppers," but I wasn't familiar with the term "share-croppers." As used by the press, it suggested to me no Delta group and I assumed vaguely that share-croppers must be of some perverse bucolic genus that probably originated in Georgia and throve in Oklahoma. But one day I read that the President of the United States had excoriated bitterly and sorrowfully "the infamous share-cropper [280/281] system." I asked a Washington friend of mine in what locality that system of farming prevailed. He knocked the breath out of me by answering: "On Trail Lake." I woke to the discovery that in pseudo-intellectual circles from Moscow to Santa Monica the Improvers-of-the-world had found something new in the South to shudder over. Twenty years ago it had been peonage. In the dark days when the collapse of the slave-trade had almost bankrupted good old New England, it had been slavery. Now it was the poor share-croppers—share-croppers over the whole South, but especially in the Delta. That very partnership of Fafar's which had seemed to me so just and practical now was being denounced as avaricious and slick—it was Mr. Roosevelt's "infamous system." We who had operated our plantations under it since carpet-bag days were taunted now with being little better than slave-drivers by the carpetbaggers' progeny and kin. Obviously we are given to depravity down here: the South just won't do. In spite of prayers and advice from the "holier-than-thou's" it's always hell-bent for some deviltry or other. At this moment there's another of those great moral daybreaks on, and its east is Washington. In the glow I realize that Fafar and Mur, Father and I suffered from moral astigmatism—for all I know, from complete moral blindness: we were infamous and didn't even suspect it. Well, well, well. That makes a Southerner feel pretty bad, I reckon.

Notwithstanding an adage to the contrary, truth, as I've observed it, is one of the least resilient of herbs. Crushed to earth, it stays crushed; once down, it keeps down, flatter than anything except an oat field after a wind-storm. The truth about share-croppers has been told and retold, but, being neither melodramatic nor evidential of Southern turpitude, it isn't believed. I am not a well-informed person, but I know the truth about share-cropping and in this [281/282] chapter I have told enough for earnest seekers to infer what it is; I have not done this, however, in the naïve hope that my words will do the slightest good or change the views of a single reader; my reason is other and quite unworthy: there's a low malicious pleasure in telling the truth where you know it won't be believed. Though rightly considered a bore and a pest in the best Trojan circles, Cassandra, no doubt, had her fun, but, at that, not nearly so much as the Knights of the Bleeding Heart who in politics and literature years from now will still be finding it fetching and inexpensive to do some of their most poignant public heart-bleeding over the poor downtrodden share-croppers of the deep South.

Share-cropping is one of the best systems ever devised to give security and a chance for profit to the simple and the unskilled. It has but one drawback—it must be administered by human beings to whom it offers an unusual opportunity to rob without detection or punishment. The failure is not in the system itself, but in not living up to the contractual obligations of the system—the failure is in human nature. The Negro is no more on an equality with the white man in plantation matters than in any other dealings between the two. The white planter may charge an exorbitant rate of interest, he may allow the share-cropper less than the market price received for his cotton, he may cheat him in a thousand different ways, and the Negro's redress is merely theoretical. If the white planter happens to be a crook, the share-cropper system on that plantation is bad for Negroes, as any other system would be. They are prey for the dishonest and temptation for the honest. If the Delta planters were mostly cheats, the results of the share-cropper system would be as grievous as reported. But, strange as it may seem to the sainted East, we have quite a sprinkling of decent folk down our way. [282/283]

Property is a form of power. Some people regard it as an opportunity for profit, some as a trust; in the former it breeds hubris, in the latter, noblesse oblige. The landed gentry of Fafar's time were of an ancient lineage and in a sober God-fearing tradition. Today many have thought to acquire membership in that older caste by acquiring land, naked land, without those ancestral hereditaments of virtue which change dirt into a way of life. On the plantation where there is stealing from the Negro you will generally find the owner to be a little fellow operating, as the saying goes, "on a shoe-string," or a nouveau riche, or a landlord on the make, tempted to take more than his share because of the mortgage that makes his title and his morals insecure. These, in their pathetic ambition to imitate what they do not understand, acquire power and use it for profit; for them the share-cropper system affords a golden opportunity rarely passed up.

Two courses of action would be effective against unworthy landlords: the Negroes could and should boycott such landlords, quietly and absolutely; the government could and should deny government benefits to the landlord who will not put the terms of his contract in writing, who will not carry out those terms and who will not permit the government to prove by its own inspection that they have been carried out. In place of these suggested remedies, I can only recommend changing human nature. All we need anywhere in any age is character: from that everything follows. Leveling down's the fashion now, but I remember the bright spires—they caught the light first and held it longest.

So much that was fine and strong went into the making of this Delta of ours! So much was conquered for us by men and women whose names we have forgotten! So much had to be overcome before ever this poor beautiful unfinished [283/284] present was turned over to us by the anonymous dead—malaria and yellow fever, swamp-water and rain-water and river-water, war and defeat, tropic heat and intemperate cold, poverty and ignorance, economic cruelty and sectional hatred, the pathos of a stronger race carrying on its shoulders a weaker race and from the burden losing its own strength! They must have been always in the front line fighting for us, those builders of the Delta; they could never have stopped long enough to learn of leisure and safety the graces of peace. But there are those who live in fear as in a native element, and they are beautiful with a fresh miraculous beauty. It is watching for unseen death that gives a bird's eyes their glancing brilliance. It is dodging eternal danger that makes his motions deft and exquisite. His half-wit testament to the delight of living, terror has taught him that, shaking the melody from his dubious innocent throat. Perhaps security is a good thing to seek and a bad thing to find. Perhaps it is never found, and all our best is in the search. [284]

JAMES AGEE
and
WALKER EVANS

———•·•———

Let Us Now Praise Famous Men

AT THE FORKS

ON A ROAD between the flying shadows of loose woods toward the middle of an afternoon, far enough thrust forward between towns that we had lost intuition of our balance between them, we came to a fork where the sunlight opened a little more widely, but not on cultivated land, and stopped a minute to decide.

Marion would lie some miles over beyond the road on our left; some other county seat, Centerville most likely, out beyond the road on our right; but on which road the woods might give way to any extension of farm country there was no deducing: for we were somewhere toward the middle of one of the wider of the gaps on the road map, and had seen nothing but woods, and infrequent woods farms, for a good while now.

Just a little behind us on our left and close on the road was a house, the first we had passed in several miles, and we decided to ask directions of the people on the porch, whom, in the car mirror, I could see still watching us. We backed slowly, stopping the car a little short of the house, and I got slowly out and walked back toward them, watching them quietly and carefully, and preparing my demeanors and my words for the two hundredth time.

There were three on the porch, watching me, and they must not have spoken twice in an hour while they watched beyond [32/33] the rarely traveled road the changes of daylight along the recessions of the woods, and while, in the short field that sank behind their

From James Agee and Walker Evans, *Let Us Now Praise Famous Men* (Boston: Houghton Mifflin Company, 1941), pp. 32–37.

house, their two crops died silently in the sun: a young man, a young woman, and an older man; and the two younger, their chins drawn inward and their heads tall against the grained wall of the house, watched me steadily and sternly as if from beneath the brows of helmets, in the candor of young warriors or of children.

They were of a kind not safely to be described in an account claiming to be unimaginative or trustworthy, for they had too much and too outlandish beauty not to be legendary. Since, however, they existed quite irrelevant to myth, it will be necessary to tell a little of them.

The young man's eyes had the opal lightings of dark oil and, though he was watching me in a way that relaxed me to cold weakness of ignobility, they fed too strongly inward to draw to a focus: whereas those of the young woman had each the splendor of a monstrance, and were brass. Her body also was brass or bitter gold, strong to stridency beneath the unbleached clayed cotton dress, and her arms and bare legs were sharp with metal down. The blenched hair drew her face tight to her skull as a tied mask; her features were baltic. The young man's face was deeply shaded with soft short beard, and luminous with death. He had the scornfully ornate nostrils and lips of an aegean exquisite. The fine wood body was ill strung, and sick even as he sat there to look at, and the bone hands roped with vein; they rose, then sank, and lay palms upward in his groins. There was in their eyes so quiet and ultimate a quality of hatred, and contempt, and anger, toward every creature in existence beyond themselves, and toward the damages they sustained, as shone scarcely short of a state of beatitude; nor did this at any time modify itself. [33/34]

These two sat as if formally, or as if sculptured, one in wood and one in metal, or as if enthroned, about three feet apart in straight chairs tilted to the wall, and constantly watched me, all the while communicating thoroughly with each other by no outward sign of word or glance or turning, but by emanation.

The other man might have been fifty by appearance, yet, through a particular kind of delicateness upon his hands, and hair, and skin —they were almost infantine—I was sure he was still young, hardly out of his twenties, though again the face was seamed and short as a fetus. This man, small-built and heavy jointed, and wandering in his motions like a little child, had the thorny beard of a cartoon bolshevik, but suggested rather a hopelessly deranged and weeping prophet, a D. H. Lawrence whom male nurses have just managed to subdue into a straitjacket. A broken felt hat struck through with grass hair was banged on flat above his furious and leaky eyes, and from beneath its rascally brim as if from ambush he pored at me walleyed while, clenching himself back against the wall, he sank along it trembling and slowly to a squat, and watched up at me.

None of them relieved me for an instant of their eyes; at the intersection of those three tones of force I was transfixed as between spearheads as I talked. As I asked my questions, and told my purposes, and what I was looking for, it seemed to me they relaxed a little toward me, and at length a good deal more, almost as if into trust and liking; yet even at its best this remained so suspended, so conditional, that in any save the most hopeful and rationalized sense it was non-existent. The qualities of their eyes did not in the least alter, nor anything visible or audible about them, and their speaking was as if I was almost certainly a spy sent to betray them through trust, whom they would show they had neither trust nor fear of. [34/35]

They were clients of Rehabilitation. They had been given a young sick steer to do their plowing with; the land was woods-clearing, but had been used as long as the house (whose wood was ragged and light as pith); no seed or fertilizer had been given them until the end of May. Nothing they had planted was up better than a few inches, and that was now withering faster than it grew. They now owed the Government on the seed and fertilizer, the land, the tools, the house, and probably before long on the steer as well, who was now so weak he could hardly stand. They had from the start given notice of the weakness and youth of the steer, of the nearly total sterility of the soil, and of the later and later withholding of the seed and fertilizer; and this had had a great deal to do with why the seed was given them so late, and they had been let know it in so many words.

The older man came up suddenly behind me, jamming my elbow with his concave chest and saying fiercely *Awnk, awnk,* while he glared at me with enraged and terrified eyes. Caught so abruptly off balance, my reflexes went silly and I turned toward him questioning 'politely' with my face, as if he wanted to say something, and could, which I had not quite heard. He did want urgently to say something, but all that came out was this blasting of *Awnk, awnk,* and a thick roil of saliva that hung like semen in his beard. I nodded, smiling at him, and he grinned gratefully with an expression of extreme wickedness and tugged hard at my sleeve, nodding violently in time to his voice and rooting out over and over this loud vociferation of a frog. The woman spoke to him sharply though not unkindly (the young man's eyes remained serene), as if he were a dog masturbating on a caller, and he withdrew against a post of the porch and sank along it to the floor with his knees up sharp and wide apart and the fingers of his left hand jammed as deep as they would go down his gnashing mouth, while he stayed his [35/36] bright eyes on me. She got up abruptly without speaking and went indoors and came back out with a piece of stony cornbread and gave it to him, and took her place again in her chair. He took the bread in both hands and struck his face into it like the blow of a hatchet, grappling with his jaws and slowly cradling his head like a piece of heavy machinery, while grinding, passionate noises ran in his throat, and we continued to talk, the young woman doing most of the talking, corroborative and protective of the young man, yet always respectful toward him.

The young man had the asthma so badly the fits of it nearly killed him. He could never tell when he was going to be any good for work, and he was no good for it even at the best, it was his wife did the work; and him—the third—they did not even nod nor shift their eyes toward him; he was just a mouth. These things were said in the voice not of complaint but of statement, quietly stiff with hatred for the world and for living: nor was there any touch of pride, shame, resentment, or any discord among them.

Some niggers a couple of miles down a back road let them have some corn and some peas. Without those niggers there was no saying what they'd be doing by now. Only the niggers hadn't had a bit too much for themselves in the first place and were running very short now; it had been what was left over from the year before, and not much new corn, nor much peas, was coming through the drought. It was——

The older man came honking up at my elbow, holding out a rolled farm magazine. In my effort to give him whatever form of attention could most gratify him I was stupid again; the idea there was something he wanted me to read; and looked at him half-questioning this, and not yet taking what he offered me. The woman, in a voice that somehow, though contemptuous [36/37] (it implied, You are more stupid than he is), yielded me for the first time her friendship and that of her husband, so that happiness burst open inside me like a flooding of sweet water, said, he wants to give it to you. I took it and thanked him very much, looking and smiling into his earnest eyes, and he stayed at my side like a child, watching me affectionately while I talked to them.

They had told me there was farm country down the road on the right a piece: the whole hoarded silence and quiet of a lonesome and archaic American valley it was to become, full of heavy sunflowers and mediocre cotton, where the women wore sunbonnets without shyness before us and all whom we spoke to were gracious and melancholy, and where we did not find what we sought. Now after a little while I thanked them here on the porch and told them good-bye. I had not the heart at all to say, Better luck to you, but then if I remember rightly I did say it, and, saying it or not, and unable to communicate to them at all what my feelings were, I walked back the little distance to the car with my shoulders and the back of my neck more scalded-feeling than if the sun were on them. As we started, I looked back and held up my hand. The older man was on the dirt on his hands and knees coughing like a gorilla and looking at the dirt between his hands. Neither of the other two raised a hand. The young man lowered his head slowly and seriously, and raised it. The young woman smiled, sternly beneath her virulent eyes, for the first time. As we swung into the right fork of the road, I looked back again. The young man, looking across once more into the woods, had reached his hand beneath the bib of his overalls and was clawing at his lower belly. The woman, her eyes watching us past her shoulder, was walking to the door. Just as I glanced back, and whether through seeing that I saw her I cannot be sure, she turned her head to the front, and disappeared into the house. [37]

5

The Machine in the Garden: Civilization, Progress, and Industry

AMERICA, since its discovery, has spoken symbolically to the imagination with a promise of liberation from social restraints and fulfillment of the corrupted ideals of Western man. Between the social restraints of the Old World and the liberating conquest of the wilderness, between the industrial civilization of the American East, modeled after the European, and the ever expanding frontier society, modeled after its own spirit, there has existed a tension which is observable in much of our literature. Unlike the hero of the nineteenth-century European novel, whose major struggle was to establish himself within a carefully ordered social structure, the hero of the American novel has continually sought to discover truth and self-knowledge by rejecting and escaping from the traditional social forms. By repudiating the disciplines of civilization, he acts out of a natural integrity that establishes him as morally superior to the conforming members of his oppressive society. This was the theme of Cooper's Leather-Stocking novels, whose Natty Bumppo was forced to stay one step ahead of encroaching civilization to maintain his peaceful, idyllic relationship with the natural environment and his fellow man. Following upon Natty's trail have been such travelers as Ishmael, Huck Finn, Nick Carraway, Ike McCaslin, Holden Caulfield, and Henderson the Rain King.

The dichotomies established by that tension, between the natural and the artificial, the virtuous and the corrupt, the independent and the conforming, the creative and the imitative, the spiritual and the material, carry naturally over into the tensions between agrarianism and industrialism—the harmonious, organic rural society as opposed

279

to the disintegrating, unnatural technological society. Politically, these dualities found expression in the contest between Hamilton's Federalists and Jefferson's Democratic-Republicans for the control of the nation's development, but American literature clearly carries the impact of the rivalry in the realm of the imagination.

If de Tocqueville read the American character accurately in 1840, there should never have been a contention, because it was his opinion that all democratic people were desirous of working and the form of labor they most preferred was the industrial or commercial. But he was emphasizing the profit motive, and the desire to make a fortune as quickly as possible, with but slight awareness of the kind of life full-scale industrial and manufacturing expansion would bring about. But to his credit, he did foresee the possible development of a wealthy capitalistic aristocracy which would be detrimental to democratic principles, and he perceived the great cost of industry in physical and intellectual health to the assembly line worker who "ultimately does his work with singular dexterity," but at the same time loses "the general faculty of applying his mind to the direction of his work."

Some historians have suggested that America's major internal conflict, the Civil War, was less a war over slavery and states' rights than simply a culmination and resolution of the long standing antagonism between the farm and the factory, between agrarianism based upon slave labor and industrialism based upon free labor. Henry Timrod's poem "Ethnogenesis," written as the first Confederate congress assembled on February 8, 1861, at Montgomery, Alabama, envisioned the coming battle essentially as a conflict between the virtuous agrarian and the satanic industrial systems, in which all the forces of nature and God ally themselves with the farmer. From this point of view, the developing success of the Hamiltonian doctrine with its exploding industrial expansion foretold the outcome of the War before it was fought. The defeat of the South, at any rate, marked the clear triumph of the capitalist over the independent farmer, the assembly line over the corn row, and established an economic course which this nation could never entirely alter. But this is not to say that the cause of the agrarians against industry was abandoned.

Writing shortly after the war, unreconstructed Tennessee humorist George Washington Harris, whose creation Sut Lovingood had long taken a stand against all social and philosophical hypocrisies, created an allegory about the unnatural character of technological and progressive experimentation and proposed a rather brutal solution to the problem: the castration of the machine age. At the turn of the century, Edwin Markham and Frank Norris turned their verse and prose to the cause of the independent farmer, oppressed and crushed by the larger, impersonal forces of capitalism. Treatment of the effect of the triumph of industrialism in the North and South are found in Robert Frost's poetry, and especially in the poems and stories produced by several of the earlier Southern Agrarians—John Crowe Ransom, Donald Davidson, Andrew Lytle, and Robert Penn Warren—who in 1930 had tried vainly to counteract its powerful, dehumanizing trends. The literary materials by these writers included in this unit offer a provocative variety of treatment of this theme.

The ultimate result of the struggle between the machine and the garden would be capitulation of the one to the other. If *Time's* report on the application of technological knowledge and tools to American husbandry is typical of contemporary agriculture, the verdict is clear. The machine has conquered the garden. But if the past history of the agrarian tradition is an indication of anything, the last agrarian, like the last puritan, has not been heard from yet.

JAMES FENIMORE COOPER

—•◆•—

The Pioneers

Men, boys, and girls
Desert th' unpeopled village; and wild crowds
Spread o'er the plain, by the sweet frenzy driven.
                                        Somerville.

FROM THIS TIME to the close of April the weather continued to be a
succession of great and rapid changes. One day, the soft airs of
spring seemed to be stealing along the valley, and in unison with an
invigorating sun, attempting covertly to rouse the dormant powers
of the vegetable world; while on the next, the surly blasts from the
north would sweep across the lake, and erase every impression left
by their gentle adversaries. The snow, however, finally disappeared,
and the green wheat-fields were seen in every direction, spotted with
the dark and charred stumps that had, the preceding season, supported some of the proudest trees of the forest. Ploughs were in motion, wherever those useful implements could be used, and the
smokes of the sugar-camps were no longer seen issuing from the
woods of maple. The lake had lost the beauty of a field of ice, but
still a dark and gloomy covering concealed its waters. For the absence of currents left them yet hidden under a porous crust, which,
saturated with the fluid, barely retained enough strength to preserve
the contiguity of its parts. Large flocks of wild geese were seen passing over the country, which hovered, for a time, around the hidden
sheet of water, apparently searching for a resting-place; and then, on
finding themselves excluded by the chill covering, would soar away
to the north, filling the air with discordant screams, as if venting
their complaints at the tardy operations of nature.

For a week, the dark covering of the Otsego was left to the undisturbed possession of two eagles, who alighted on the centre of its

From James Fenimore Cooper, *The Pioneers, or Sources of the Susquehanna, A
Descriptive Tale* (Boston and New York: Houghton, Mifflin and Company, 1876),
pp. 247–256. First published in 1823.

field, and sat eying their undisputed territory. [247/248] During the presence of these monarchs of the air, the flocks of migrating birds avoided crossing the plain of ice, by turning into the hills, apparently seeking the protection of the forests, while the white and bald heads of the tenants of the lake were turned upwards, with a look of contempt. But the time had come, when even these kings of birds were to be dispossessed. An opening had been gradually increasing at the lower extremity of the lake, and around the dark spot where the current of the river prevented the formation of ice, during even the coldest weather; and the fresh southerly winds, that now breathed freely upon the valley, made an impression on the waters. Mimic waves began to curl over the margin of the frozen field, which exhibited an outline of crystallizations that slowly receded towards the north. At each step the power of the winds and the waves increased, until, after a struggle of a few hours, the turbulent little billows succeeded in setting the whole field in motion, when it was driven beyond the reach of the eye, with a rapidity that was as magical as the change produced in the scene by this expulsion of the lingering remnant of winter. Just as the last sheet of agitated ice was disappearing in the distance, the eagles rose, and soared with a wide sweep above the clouds, while the waves tossed their little caps of snow into the air, as if rioting in their release from a thralldom of five months' duration.

The following morning, Elizabeth was awakened by the exhilarating sounds of the martins, who were quarreling and chattering around the little boxes suspended above her windows, and the cries of Richard, who was calling in tones animating as the signs of the season itself—

"Awake! awake! my fair lady! the gulls are hovering over the lake already, and the heavens are alive with pigeons. You may look an hour before you can find a hole through which to get a peep at the sun. Awake! awake! lazy ones! Benjamin is overhauling the ammunition, and we only wait for our breakfasts, and away for the mountains and pigeon shooting."

There was no resisting this animated appeal, and in a few minutes Miss Temple and her friends descended to the [248/249] parlor. The doors of the hall were thrown open, and the mild, balmy air of a clear spring morning was ventilating the apartment, where the vigilance of the ex-steward had been so long maintaining an artificial heat with such unremitted diligence. The gentlemen were impatiently waiting for their morning's repast, each equipped in the garb of a sportsman. Mr. Jones made many visits to the southern door, and would cry,—

"See, cousin Bess! see, 'Duke, the pigeon-roosts of the south have broken up! They are growing more thick every instant. Here is a flock that the eye cannot see the end of. There is food enough in it to keep the army of Xerxes for a month, and feathers enough to make beds for the whole country. Xerxes, Mr. Edwards, was a Grecian king, who—no, he was a Turk, or a Persian, who wanted to conquer Greece, just the same as these rascals will overrun our wheat-fields, when they come back in the fall. Away! away! Bess; I long to pepper them."

In this wish both Marmaduke and young Edwards seemed equally to participate, for the sight was exhilarating to a sportsman; and the ladies soon dismissed the party after a hasty breakfast.

If the heavens were alive with pigeons, the whole village seemed equally in motion, with men, women, and children. Every species of fire-arms, from the French ducking-gun with a barrel near six feet in length, to the common horseman's pistol, was to be seen in the hands of the men and boys; while bows and arrows, some made of the simple stick of a walnut sapling, and others in a rude imitation of the ancient cross-bows, were carried by many of the latter.

The houses and the signs of life apparent in the village, drove the alarmed birds from the direct line of their flight, toward the mountains, along the sides and near the bases of which they were glancing in dense masses, equally wonderful by the rapidity of their motion, and their incredible numbers.

We have already said, that across the inclined plane which fell from the steep ascent to the mountain to the [249/250] banks of the Susquehanna, ran the highway, on either side of which a clearing of many acres had been made at a very early day. Over those clearings, and up the eastern mountain, and along the dangerous path that was cut into its side, the different individuals posted themselves, and in a few moments the attack commenced.

Among the sportsmen was the tall, gaunt form of Leather-Stocking walking over the field, with his rifle hanging on his arm, his dogs at this heels; the latter now scenting the dead or wounded birds, that were beginning to tumble from the flocks, and then crouching under the legs of their master, as if they participated in his feelings at this wasteful and unsportsmanlike execution.

The reports of the fire-arms became rapid, whole volleys rising from the plain, as flocks of more than ordinary numbers darted over the opening, shadowing the field like a cloud; and then the light smoke of a single piece would issue from among the leafless bushes on the mountain, as death was hurled on the retreat of the af-frighted birds, who were rising from a volley, in a vain effort to es-cape. Arrows, and missiles of every kind, were seen in the midst of the flocks; and so numerous were the birds, and so low did they take their flight, that even long poles, in the hands of those on the sides of the mountain, were used to strike them to the earth.

During all this time, Mr. Jones, who disdained the humble and ordinary means of destruction used by his companions, was busily occupied, aided by Benjamin, in making arrangements for an assault of more than ordinarily fatal character. Among the relics of the old military excursions, that occasionally are discovered throughout the different districts of the western part of New York, there had been found in Templeton, at its settlement, a small swivel, which would carry a ball of a pound weight. It was thought to have been deserted by a war party of the whites, in one of their inroads into the Indian settlements, when, perhaps, convenience or their necessities induced them to leave such an incumbrance behind them in the woods. This miniature cannon had been released from the rust, and being mounted on little wheels, was now in a state for actual service. [250/251] For several years, it was the sole organ for extraordinary rejoicings used in those mountains. On the mornings of the Fourths of July, it would be heard ringing among the hills; and even Captain Hollister, who was the highest authority in that part of the country on all such occasions, affirmed that, considering its dimentions, it was no despicable gun for a salute. It was somewhat the worse for the service it had performed, it is true, there being but a trifling difference in size between the touch-hole and the muzzle. Still, the grand conceptions of Richard had suggested the importance of such an instrument in hurling death at his nimble enemies. The swivel was dragged by a horse into a part of the open space that the Sheriff thought most eligible for planting a battery of the kind, and Mr. Pump proceeded to load it. Several handfuls of duck-shot were placed on top of the powder, and the major-domo announced that his piece was ready for service.

The sight of such an implement collected all the idle spectators to the spot, who, being mostly boys, filled the air with cries of exultation and delight. The gun was pointed high, and Richard, holding a coal of fire in a pair of tongs, patiently took his seat on a stump, awaiting the appearance of a flock worthy of his notice.

So prodigious was the number of birds, that the scattering fire of the guns, with the hurling of missiles, and the cries of the boys, had no other effect than to break off small flocks from the immense masses that continued to dart along the valley, as if the whole of the feathered tribe were pouring through that one pass. None pretended to collect the game, which lay scattered over the fields in such profusion as to cover the very ground with the fluttering victims.

Leather-Stocking was a silent, but uneasy spectator of all these proceedings, but was able to keep his sentiments to himself until he saw the introduction of the swivel into the sports.

"This comes of settling a country!" he said; "here have I known the pigeons to fly for forty long years, and, till you made your clearings, there was nobody to skear or [251/252] to hurt them. I loved to see them in the woods, for they were company to a body; hurting nothing; being, as it was, as harmless as a garter-snake. But now it gives me sore thoughts when I hear the frighty things whizzing through the air, for I know it's only a motion to bring out all the brats in the village. Well! the Lord won't see the waste of his creatures for nothing, and right will be done to the pigeons, as well as others, by and by. There's Mr. Oliver, as bad as the rest of them, firing into the flocks, as if he was shooting down nothing but Mingo warriors."

Among the sportsmen was Billy Kirby, who, armed with an old musket, was loading, and without even looking into the air, was firing and shouting as his victims fell even on his own person. He heard the speech of Natty, and took upon himself to reply:—

"What! old Leather-Stocking," he cried, "grumbling at the loss of a few pigeons! If you had to sow your wheat twice, and three times, as I have done, you wouldn't be so massyfully feeling towards the divils. Hurrah, boys! scatter the feathers! This is better than shooting at a turkey's head and neck, old fellow."

"It's better for you, maybe, Billy Kirby," replied the indignant old hunter, "and all them that don't know how to put a ball down a rifle barrel, or how to bring it up again with a true aim; but it's wicked to be shooting into flocks in this wasty manner; and none do it, who know how to knock over a single bird. If a body has a craving for pigeon's flesh, why, it's made the same as all other creatures, for man's eating; but not to kill twenty and eat one. When I want such a thing I go into the woods till I find one to my liking, and then I shoot him off the branches, without touching the feather of another, though there might be a hundred on the same tree. You couldn't do such a thing, Billy Kirby—you couldn't do it, if you tried."

"What's that, old corn-stalk! you sapless stub!" cried the woodchopper. "You have grown wordy, since the affair of the turkey; but if you are for a single shot, here goes at that bird which comes on by himself."

The fire from the distant part of the field had driven a [252/253] single pigeon below the flock to which it belonged, and, frightened with the constant reports of the muskets, it was approaching the spot where the disputants stood, darting first to one side and then to the other, cutting the air with the swiftness of lightning, and making a noise with its wings, not unlike the rushing of a bullet. Unfortunately for the wood-chopper, notwithstanding his vaunt, he did not see this bird until it was too late to fire as it approached, and he pulled his trigger at the unlucky moment when it was darting immediately over his head. The bird continued its course with the usual velocity.

Natty lowered the rifle from his arm when the challenge was made, and waiting a moment, until the terrified victim had got in a line with his eye, and had dropped near the bank of the lake, he raised it again with uncommon rapidity, and fired. It might have been chance, or it might have been skill, that produced the result; it was probably a union of both; but the pigeon whirled over in the air, and fell into the lake, with a broken wing. At the sound of his rifle, both his dogs started from his feet, and in a few minutes the "slut" brought out the bird, still alive.

The wonderful exploit of Leather-Stocking was noised through the field with great rapidity, and the sportsmen gathered in, to learn the truth of the report.

"What!" said young Edwards, "have you really killed a pigeon on the wing, Natty, with a single ball?"

"Haven't I killed loons before now, lad, that dive at the flash?" returned the hunter. "It's much better to kill only such as you want, without wasting your powder and lead, than to be firing into God's creatures in this wicked manner. But I came out for a bird, and you know the reason why I like small game, Mr. Oliver, and now I have got one I will go home, for I don't relish to see these wasty ways that you are all practysing, as if the least thing wasn't made for use, and not to destroy."

"Thou sayest well, Leather-Stocking," cried Marmaduke, "and I begin to think it time to put an end to this work of destruction."

"Put an end, Judge, to your clearings. Ain't the woods [253/254] his work as well as the pigeons? Use, but don't waste. Wasn't the woods made for the beasts and birds to harbor in? and when man wanted their flesh, their skins, or their feathers, there's the place to seek them. But I'll go to the hut with my own game, for I wouldn't touch one of the harmless things that cover the ground here, looking up with their eyes on me, as if they only wanted tongues to say their thoughts."

With this sentiment in his mouth, Leather-Stocking threw his rifle over his arm, and followed by his dogs stepped across the clearing with great caution, taking care not to tread on one of the wounded birds in his path. He soon entered the bushes on the margin of the lake, and was hid from view.

Whatever impression the morality of Natty made on the Judge, it was utterly lost on Richard. He availed himself of the gathering of the sportsmen, to lay a plan for one "fell swoop" of destruction. The musket men were drawn up in battle array, in a line extending on each side of his artillery, with orders to await the signal of firing from himself.

"Stand by, my lads," said Benjamin, who acted as an aide-de-camp on this occasion, "stand by, my hearties, and when Squire Dickens heaves out the signal to begin firing, d'ye see, you may open upon them in a broadside. Take care and fire low, boys, and you'll be sure to hull the flock."

"Fire low!" shouted Kirby; "hear the old fool! If we fire low, we may hit the stumps, but not ruffle a pigeon."

"How should you know, you lubber?" cried Benjamin, with a very unbecoming heat for an officer on the eve of battle; "how should you know, you grampus? Haven't I sailed aboard of the Boadishey for five years? and wasn't it a standing order to fire low, and to hull your enemy? Keep silence at your guns, boys, and mind the order that is passed."

The loud laughs of the musket-men were silenced by the more authoritative voice of Richard, who called for attention and obedience to his signals.

Some millions of pigeons were supposed to have already [254/255] passed, that morning, over the valley of Templeton; but nothing like the flock that was now approaching had been seen before. It extended from mountain to mountain in one solid blue mass, and the eye looked in vain, over the southern hills, to find its termination. The front of this living column was distinctly marked by a line but very slightly indented, so regular and even was the flight. Even Marmaduke forgot the morality of Leather-Stocking as it approached, and, in common with the rest, brought his musket to a poise.

"Fire!" cried the Sheriff, clapping a coal to the priming of the cannon. As half of Benjamin's charge escaped through the touch-hole, the whole volley of the musketry preceded the report of the swivel. On receiving this united discharge of small-arms, the front of the flock darted upwards, while, at the same instant, myriads of those in the rear rushed with amazing rapidity into their places, so that when the column of white smoke gushed from the mouth of the little cannon, an accumulated mass of objects was gliding over its point of direction. The roar of the gun echoed along the mountains, and died away to the north, like distant thunder, while the whole flock of alarmed birds seemed, for a moment, thrown into one disorderly and agitated mass. The air was filled with their irregular flight, layer rising above layer, far above the tops of the highest pines, none daring to advance beyond the dangerous pass; when, suddenly, some of the leaders of the feathered tribe shot across the valley, taking their flight directly over the village, and hundreds of thousands in their rear followed the example, deserting the eastern side of the plain to their persecutors and the slain.

"Victory!" shouted Richard, "victory! we have driven the enemy from the field."

"Not so, Dickon," said Marmaduke: "the field is covered with them; and, like the Leather-Stocking, I see nothing but eyes, in every direction, as the innocent sufferers turn their heads in terror. Full one half of those that have fallen are yet alive; and I think it is time to end the sport, if sport it be." [255/256]

"Sport!" cried the Sheriff; "it is princely sport! There are some thousands of the blue-coated boys on the ground, so that every old woman in the village may have a pot-pie for the asking."

"Well, we have happily frightened the birds from this side of the valley," said Marmaduke, "and the carnage must of necessity end, for the present. Boys, I will give you sixpence a hundred for the pigeons' heads only: so go to work, and bring them into the village."

This expedient produced the desired effect, for every urchin on the ground went industriously to work to wring the necks of the wounded birds. Judge Temple retired towards his dwelling with that kind of feeling that many a man has experienced before him, who discovers, after the excitement of the moment has passed, that he has purchased pleasure at the price of misery to others. Horses were loaded with the dead; and, after this first burst of sporting, the shooting of pigeons became a business, with a few idlers, for the remainder of the season. Richard, however, boasted for many a year, of his shot with the "cricket;" and Benjamin gravely asserted, that he thought they killed nearly as many pigeons on that day, as there were Frenchmen destroyed on the memorable occasion of Rodney's victory. [256]

ALEXIS DE TOCQUEVILLE

Democracy in America

THAT ALMOST ALL THE AMERICANS FOLLOW INDUSTRIAL CALLINGS

AGRICULTURE is, perhaps, of all the useful arts that which improves most slowly amongst democratic nations. Frequently, indeed, it would seem to be stationary, because other arts are making rapid strides towards perfection. On the other hand, almost all the tastes and habits which the equality of condition engenders naturally lead men to commercial and industrial occupations.

Suppose an active, enlightened, and free man, enjoying a competency, but full of desires: he is too poor to live in idleness; he is rich enough to feel himself protected from the immediate fear of want, and he thinks how he can better his condition. This man has conceived a taste for physical gratifications, which thousands of his fellow-men indulge in around him; he has himself begun to enjoy these pleasures, and he is eager to increase his means of satisfying these tastes more completely. But life is slipping away, time is urgent —to what is he to turn? The cultivation of the ground promises an almost certain result to his exertions, but a slow one; men are not enriched by it without patience and toil. Agriculture is therefore only suited to those who have already large, superfluous wealth, or to those whose penury bids them only seek a bare subsistence. The choice of such a man as we have supposed is soon made; he sells his plot of ground, leaves his dwelling, and embarks in some hazardous but lucrative calling. Democratic communities abound in men of this kind; and in proportion as the equality of conditions becomes greater, their multitude increases. Thus democracy not only swells the number of workingmen, but it leads men to prefer one kind of

From Alexis de Tocqueville, *Democracy in America*, translated by Henry Reeve, Revised Edition (London and New York: Colonial Press, 1900), II, 163–167. First published in 1840.

labor to another; and whilst it diverts them from agriculture, it encourages their taste for commerce and manufactures.[a] [163/164]

This spirit may be observed even amongst the richest members of the community. In democratic countries, however opulent a man is supposed to be, he is almost always discontented with his fortune, because he finds that he is less rich than his father was, and he fears that his sons will be less rich than himself. Most rich men in democracies are therefore constantly haunted by the desire of obtaining wealth, and they naturally turn their attention to trade and manufactures, which appear to offer the readiest and most powerful means of success. In this respect they share the instincts of the poor, without feeling the same necessities; say rather, they feel the most imperious of all necessities, that of not sinking in the world.

In aristocracies the rich are at the same time those who govern. The attention which they unceasingly devote to important public affairs diverts them from the lesser cares which trade and manufactures demand. If the will of an individual happens, nevertheless, to turn his attention to business, the will of the body to which he belongs will immediately debar him from pursuing it; for however men may declaim against the rule of numbers, they cannot wholly escape their sway; and even amongst those aristocratic bodies which most obstinately refuse to acknowledge the rights of the majority of the nation, a private majority is formed which governs the rest.[b] [164/165]

[a] It has often been remarked that manufacturers and mercantile men are inordinately addicted to physical gratifications, and this has been attributed to commerce and manufacturers; but that is, I apprehend, to take the effect for the cause. The taste for physical gratifications is not imparted to men by commerce or manufacturers, but it is rather this taste which leads men to embark in commerce and manufacturers, as a means by which they hope to satisfy themselves more promptly and more completely. If commerce and manufacturers increase the desire of well-being, it is because every passion gathers strength in proportion as it is cultivated, and is increased by all the efforts made to satiate it. All the causes which make the love of worldly welfare predominate in the heart of man are favorable to the growth of commerce and manufacturers. Equality of conditions is one of those causes; it encourages trade, not directly by giving men a taste for business, but indirectly by strengthening and expanding in their minds a taste for prosperity.

[b] Some aristocracies, however, have devoted themselves eagerly to commerce, and have cultivated manufactures with success. The history of the world might furnish several conspicuous examples. But, generally speaking, it may be affirmed that the aristocratic principle is not favorable to the growth of trade and manufacturers. Moneyed aristocracies are the only exception to the rule. Amongst such aristocracies there are hardly any desires which do not require wealth to satisfy them; the love of riches becomes, so to speak, the high road of human passions, which is crossed or connected with all lesser tracks. The love of money and the

In democratic countries, where money does not lead those who possess it to political power, but often removes them from it, the rich do not know how to spend their leisure. They are driven into active life by the inquietude and the greatness of their desires, by the extent of their resources, and by the taste for what is extraordinary, which is almost always felt by those who rise, by whatsoever means, above the crowd. Trade is the only road open to them. In democracies nothing is more great or more brilliant than commerce: it attracts the attention of the public, and fills the imagination of the multitude; all energetic passions are directed towards it. Neither their own prejudices, nor those of anybody else, can prevent the rich from devoting themselves to it. The wealthy members of democracies never form a body which has manners and regulations of its own; the opinions peculiar to their class do not restrain them, and the common opinions of their country urge them on. Moreover, as all the large fortunes which are to be met with in a democratic community are of commercial growth, many generations must succeed each other before their possessors can have entirely laid aside their habits of business.

Circumscribed within the narrow space which politics leave them, rich men in democracies eagerly embark in commercial enterprise: there they can extend and employ their natural advantages; and indeed it is even by the boldness and the magnitude of their industrial speculations that we may measure the slight esteem in which productive industry would have been held by them, if they had been born amidst an aristocracy.

A similar observation is likewise applicable to all men living in

thirst for that distinction which attaches to power, are then so closely intermixed in the same souls, that it becomes difficult to discover whether men grow covetous from ambition, or whether they are ambitious from covetousness. This is the case in England, where men seek to get rich in order to arrive at distinction, and seek distinctions as a manifestation of their wealth. The mind is then seized by both ends, and hurried into trade and manufactures, which are the shortest roads that lead to opulence.

This, however, strikes me as an exceptional and transitory circumstance. When wealth is become the only symbol of aristocracy, it is very difficult for the wealthy to maintain sole possession of political power, to the exclusion of all other men. The aristocracy of birth and pure democracy are at the two extremes of the social and political state of nations: between them moneyed aristocracy finds its place. The latter approximates to the aristocracy of birth by conferring great privileges on a small number of persons; it so far belongs to the democratic element, that these privileges may be successively acquired by all. It frequently forms a natural transition between these two conditions of society, and it is difficult to say whether it closes the reign of aristocratic institutions, or whether it already opens the new era of democracy.

democracies, whether they be poor or rich. Those who live in the midst of democratic fluctuations have always before their eyes the phantom of chance; and they end by liking all undertakings in which chance plays a part. They are therefore all led to engage in commerce, not only for the sake of the profit it holds out to them, but for the love of the constant excitement occasioned by that pursuit. [165/166]

The United States of America have only been emancipated for half a century from the state of colonial dependence in which they stood to Great Britain; the number of large fortunes there is small, and capital is still scarce. Yet no people in the world has made such rapid progress in trade and manufactures as the Americans: they constitute at the present day the second maritime nation in the world; and although their manufacturers have to struggle with almost insurmountable natural impediments, they are not prevented from making great and daily advances. In the United States the greatest undertakings and speculations are executed without difficulty, because the whole population is engaged in productive industry, and because the poorest as well as the most opulent members of the commonwealth are ready to combine their efforts for these purposes. The consequence is, that a stranger is constantly amazed by the immense public works executed by a nation which contains, so to speak, no rich men. The Americans arrived but as yesterday on the territory which they inhabit, and they have already changed the whole order of nature for their own advantage. They have joined the Hudson to the Mississippi, and made the Atlantic Ocean communicate with the Gulf of Mexico, across a continent of more than five hundred leagues in extent which separates the two seas. The longest railroads which have been constructed up to the present time are in America. But what most astonishes me in the United States, is not so much the marvellous grandeur of some undertakings, as the innumerable multitude of small ones. Almost all the farmers of the United States combine some trade with agriculture; most of them make agriculture itself a trade. It seldom happens than an American farmer settles for good upon the land which he occupies; especially in the districts of the Far West he brings land into tillage in order to sell it again, and not to farm it: he builds a farmhouse on the speculation that, as the state of the country will soon be changed by the increase of population, a good price will be gotten for it. Every year a swarm of the inhabitants of the North arrive in the Southern States, and settle in the parts where the cotton plant and the sugar-cane grow. These men cultivate the soil in order to make it produce in a few years enough to enrich them; and they already look forward to the [166/167] time when they may return home to enjoy the competency thus acquired. Thus the Americans carry their business-like qualities into agriculture; and their trading passions are displayed in that as in their other pursuits.

The Americans make immense progress in productive industry, because they all devote themselves to it at once; and for this same reason they are exposed to very unexpected and formidable embarrassments. As they are all engaged in commerce, their commercial affairs are affected by such various and complex causes that it is impossible to foresee what difficulties may arise. As they are all more or less engaged in productive industry, at the least shock given to business all private fortunes are put in jeopardy at the same time, and the State is shaken. I believe that the return of these commercial panics is an endemic disease of the democratic nations of our age. It may be rendered less dangerous, but it cannot be cured; because it does not originate in accidental circumstances, but in the temperament of these nations. [167]

HENRY TIMROD

Ethnogenesis

WRITTEN DURING THE MEETING OF THE
FIRST SOUTHERN CONGRESS, AT MONTGOMERY,
FEBRUARY, 1861

I

HATH not the morning dawned with added light?
And shall not evening call another star
Out of the infinite regions of the night,
To mark this day in Heaven? At last, we are
A nation among nations; and the world
Shall soon behold in many a distant port
        Another flag unfurled!
Now, come what may, whose favor need we court?
And, under God, whose thunder need we fear?
        Thank Him who placed us here
Beneath so kind a sky—the very sun [150/151]
Takes part with us; and on our errands run
All breezes of the ocean; dew and rain
Do noiseless battle for us; and the Year,
And all the gentle daughters in her train,
March in our ranks, and in our service wield
        Long spears of golden grain!
A yellow blossom as her fairy shield,
June flings her azure banner to the wind,
    While in the order of their birth
Her sisters pass, and many an ample field
Grows white beneath their steps, till now, behold,
        Its endless sheets unfold
THE SNOW OF SOUTHERN SUMMERS! Let the earth

From *Poems of Henry Timrod,* Memorial Edition (Boston and New York:
Houghton, Mifflin and Company, 1899), pp. 150–154.

Rejoice! Beneath those fleeces soft and warm
    Our happy land shall sleep
    In a repose as deep
  As if we lay intrenched behind
Whole leagues of Russian ice and Arctic storm!

II

And what if, mad with wrongs themselves have wrought,
    In their own treachery caught,
    By their own fears made bold,
    And leagued with him of old,
Who long since in the limits of the North
Set up his evil throne, and warred with God—
What if, both mad and blinded in their rage,
Our foes should fling us down their mortal gage, [151/152]
And with hostile step profane our sod!
We shall not shrink, my brothers, but go forth
To meet them, marshaled by the Lord of Hosts,
And overshadowed by the might ghosts
Of Moultrie and of Eutaw—who shall foil
Auxiliary such as these? Nor these alone,
    But every stock and stone
    Shall help us; but the very soil,
And all the generous wealth it gives to toil,
And all for which we love our noble land,
Shall fight beside, and through us; sea and strand,
    The heart of woman, and her hand,
Tree, fruit, and flower, and every influence,
    Gentle, or grave, or grand;
    The winds in our defence
Shall seem to blow; to us the hills shall lend
    Their firmness and their calm;
And in our stiffened sinews we shall blend
    The strength of pine and palm!

III

Nor would we shun the battle-ground,
    Though weak as we are strong;
Call up the clashing elements around,
    And test the right and wrong!
On one side, creeds that dare to teach
What Christ and Paul refrained to preach;

Codes built upon a broken pledge,
And Charity that whets a poniard's edge; [152/153]
Fair schemes that leave the neighboring poor
To starve and shiver at the schemer's door,
While in the world's most liberal ranks enrolled,
He turns some vast philanthropy to gold;
Religion, taking every mortal form
But that a pure and Christian faith makes warm,
Where not to vile fanatic passion urged,
Or not in vague philosophies submerged,
Repulsive with all Pharisaic leaven,
And making laws to stay the laws of Heaven!
And on the other, scorn of sordid gain,
Unblemished honor, truth without a stain,
Faith, justice, reverence, charitable wealth,
And, for the poor and humble, laws which give,
Not the mean right to buy the right to live,
      But life, and home, and health!
To doubt the end were want of trust in God,
      Who, if he has decreed
   That we must pass a redder sea
Than that which range to Miriam's holy glee,
      Will surely raise at need
      A Moses with his rod!

IV

But let our fears—if fears we have—be still,
And turn us to the future! Could we climb
Some mighty Alp, and view the coming time,
    The rapturous sight would fill
      Our eyes with happy tears! [153/154]
Not only for the glories which the years
Shall bring us; not for lands from sea to sea,
And wealth, and power, and peace, though these shall be;
But for the distant peoples we shall bless,
And the hushed murmurs of a world's distress:
For, to give labor to the poor,
      The whole sad planet o'er,
And save from want and crime the humblest door,
Is one among the many ends for which
      God makes us great and rich!
The hour perchance is not yet wholly ripe
When all shall own it, but the type

Whereby we shall be known in every land
Is that vast gulf which lips our Southern strand,
And through the cold, untempered ocean pours
Its genial streams, that far off Arctic shores
May sometimes catch upon the softened breeze
Strange tropic warmth and hints of summer seas. [154]

GEORGE WASHINGTON HARRIS

Sut Lovingood's Allegory

THOSE OF US who have not yet reached that ferry, so dreaded by many, yet anxiously looked forward to by the footsore and weary ones, who have passed but few cool fountains, or hospitable shelters, along their bleak road, must well remember the good old days of camp meetings, battalion musters, tax gatherings, and shooting matches. Well! There was the house raising too, and the quiltings, and the corn shuckings, where the darkey's happy song was heard for the last time. And then, the moonlight dance in the yard—"Yas by geminey!" interrupted Sut, "an' the ridin home ahine the he fellers, on the same hoss, arter the dancin was done, an' the moon gone down. When, if hit hadent been for the well balanced gall, you couldn't a staid on yer critter, but would a bin foun' nex' morning, with yer hed in the branch, holdin a death holt to a willer root with yer teeth, whilst some feller rode like h—l arter the coroner, afore any body would venter to haul you out."—

I was just thinking boys, while Sut was speaking, whether we are the gainer by the discoveries—inventions—innovations, and prayers, of the last forty years. Whether the railway—telegraph—chloroform —moral reform, and other advancements, as they are termed, have really advanced us any, in the right direction or—

"Stop right thar, George, an' take my idear ove the thing, fresh from water. I know powerful well that I is a durn'd fool, an' all that but I can *see*, by golly! Don't the Bible tell about them seekin' out many strange inventions? Well! Thars the tex', now. An' if I wer a practiced hard shell, with ontax'd whisky in me deep enuff to swim a rat, I could make these woods quake, an' that ar mountain roar. But bein' as hit is, I mus' just talk, bein' content if ara one ove you boys will stay awake an' listen. Some ove you minds the boy that started to school one sleety mornin', an' slipp'd two steps backward for one forrid. He only got thar, you mine, by turnin' roun', an' gwine

From George Washington Harris, "Sut Lovingood's Allegory," Knoxville *Press and Messenger*, III (September 17, 1868), 1.

tother way. Well! That's the world's fix to-day, an' if heaven is the
hotel that they is aimin' to sleep in, if they don't turn an' go tother
way, I'm dod-drabitted if they don't 'lie out.'

"Nater, George, teaches the cow not to eat laurel or nightshade,
an' the dorg to hunt grass, when he has gorged too much 'turkey
with ister stuffin' (dorgs do eat sich things right often, you know).
So, as we grow old, nater makes some ove their instick grow an'
brighten in us, showin' one, now an' then, that we is on the wrong
road, an' might eat nightshade, for hit's plenty. That's what makes
you compar the days ove the fiddle, loom an' cradle with the pe-
aner, ball-room an' wetnurse, ove these days. In comparin' 'em, you
may take one person, a family, or a county, at a time, an' you'll find
that we haint gain'd a step on the right road, an' if the fog would
clear up we'd find heaven behine us, an' not strength enuff left to
reach hit alone, if we wer to turn back. No, boys, we aint as *good* as
we wer forty years ago. We am too dam artifichul, interprizin an'
sharp—we know too much. We ought to be sarved like Old Brakebill
sarved his black billy goat. We desarve hit, mos' all ove us.

"Old Brakebill was a Dutchman, a rale silver dollar Dutchman.
He wer fool enuff to think that both parties to a trade ought to hev
the best ove hit. That is, somehow in this way: If you had wheat, an'
to spare, an' wanted corn, an' I had corn, an' to spare, an' wanted
wheat, an' two bushels ove one was worth one bushel of t'other, all
the neighborhood over, then we ought to swap. On that sort ove
principle he'd trade, an' on no other. As to 'out smartin' ' anybody,
he know'd no more about hit than the rulin' politicians ove our day
know ove statesmanship, or the doctors ove mullygrubs in the brain.
He dident attrack much notice then, for he wer jist like most everybody else. But now, if he wer alive, he'd git his broad sturn kick'd
out ove church, an' be shot for a damfool, afore he could git out ove
the graveyard. 'Behine the age,' all that, you know.

"Well! Jist wish I wer behine the age mise'f, say some forty or fifty
years."

Well! Sut if you will not let me talk, suppose you tell us how
Brakebill served his black billy goat. And let us draw no comparisons between the lost past and the present, which we must endure.

"Oh'! I dont know much about hit. Only hearsay, from the old
folks, you know. Hit seems that he had, what would be call'd now a
days, a progressive billy goat—a regular, walkin insult to man, an'
beast; he strutted, with his hine laigs, and munched, like a fool gall
with hir fore ones. An' then his tail—hit said, 'you-be-dam,' all day
long, an' him as black as a coal cellar, at midnight at that. He would
a suited our day to a dot tho', an' our day would a suited him. He
could a hilt his own, even agin the 'busines men' (they am all the go

now, you know), an' durn my buttons, if he dident look an' act adzackley like 'em—beard, eyes, forred, dress, tail, and chewin, ways, an' voice. He did, by geminey!

"But, he wer altogether too dam smart for Brakebill, or Brake-bill's day, an' generashun beyant all sort of doubt. That ar meterfis-tickal, free will, billy goat wer forty years ahead ove *his* day. As they say in praise ove some cussed raskil, when he gets a million in a week, when at the gineril rate ove fortin makin, hit had orter took him sixty days. He had been showin many marks ove progress, an' higher law, for a good while, without attractin much notice anyway. Sich as buttin old misses Brakebill, bucket an' all, belly down, clean thru onder the cow, as she stoop'd to milk her. An' then buttin the cow herself out ove her slop tub, so that he could wet his own beard in her supper. That wer "higher law," warnt hit? Or he'd watch for the old man to go from the crib to the hog pen, with thirty big ears of corn, piled on his arm. When he'd make a de-monstrashun in the rear, that would send the old feller, spread eagle fashion, plowin gravel with his snout, while he impudently munch'd the hog's corn. That were financeerin, I s'pose. Or, he'd jump up an' but the under side ove the scaffol, whar the peaches wer spred to sun dry, an' then 'appropriate' all that he jar'd over the aidge. That mus' a ben what they now call 'strategy,' don't you recon?

"Old Misses Tardiff, a two hundred pound mother in the church, wer once out in the thicket alone, near the camp groun', durin the fall meetin, at secret prayer, an' hit wer away deep into a tolerable dark night. Benny (that wer the goat's name) were in the thicket too, an' seein her on her knees, bobbin her head up an' down, he tuck hit for a buttin challenge, or purtended that he did. So immejeretly he went for the 'bull curl' in her forred, turnin her numerous sum-mersets, down hill, into the branch, an' then runnin over her, with a 'B-Bu-Bub-Baa-a,' by golly. Geminey cricket! Don't you recon that ole 'oman tho't that the hill had blow'd up? Well, when she got able, an' her cloths sorter wrung dry—she went into camp, an' give in her 'sperience: That she had jist had a pussonel, breeches holt, wrastle, with the devil hissef, an' had come off conquerer, an' ment tharfore to wear the crown, but, that his smell ove brimstone an' hartshorn come mitey near chokin' her dead. Thar was ni onto eighty come up at the next call for mourners. But when they tried old man Brakebill, to git him up, he only smiled an' shook his head, sayin', 'Vait dill I shees if my Benny ishent in der dicket shum var.'

"Now, as I said afore, all this dident give the goat much ove a name, or attract much attenshun. He was look'd on as a raskil, that's a fact. But bein' a *beast,* he warn't dealt with like he would a been had he been a human, by them old time people. If he'd a lived now adays, I'l jist be durn'd if they hadent a made him President ove a college or the passun ove Plymouth Church, an' bilt him a harim or a corectory, which is hit? Them old fogy folks had a mitey poor idear ove progress, that's a fac'.

"But at last Mister Benny overdid the thing; he got to be a little too durn'd progressive for old Brakebill and his times. His sin foun' him out, an' he wer made to simmer down to a level surface with the loss ove all, that makes life wholesome to a goat. The fac' is, like mos' ove these yere human progress humbugs, he jis' played h—l with hissef.

"Old Brakebill got to noticin that thar was something wrong with his sheep. The ewes butted at the ram, spiteful like, butted one another an' behaved powerful bad ginerally. Arter a while, on 'zaminin he foun' that some ove the lambs had patches ove coarse har in their wool, an' were sproutin' beards. Nex' he found' his young pigs behavin' curious to be dutch hog's children. Rarin' up strait on thar hine laigs, clost fornint one another. Walkin' on top ove the fences —climbin' onto the shed roof ove the milk house, an' then buttin' one another off agin. An' every now an' then, one would hist his tail as straight up as a stack pole, an' put on a stiff strut. Venuses pups, too, seem'd to hev the very devil in'em. While one ove 'em lived on the goose grass in the yard, another one butted the house cat blind, to pussey's astonishment, wrath, an' hissin' disgust. Then another sprouted periwinkle shells above his ears, an' smelt like a bottle ove hartshorn, with a mouse in hit. An old, one-eyed goose laid aigs with har on, an' then give milk. A jinny's colt waked half hit's time on aind, an' on a par ove split huffs, chawin' a cud made ove an old shoe sole. The hempbrake even rared on *hit's* hine laigs, threatnin the cutin' box. Misses Brakebill left the plantation, an' the very devil was to pay generally. If you had a wanted to a bought the farm, you would a axed that dam goat the price ove hit, from his airs an' impudent ways, while the owner looked like a scared dorg, or a stepchild on the out aidge ove sufferance. Now, all this troubled the poor old Dutchman a power. He know'd that at the rate things were gwine on, his stock, very soon, wouldent be worth a tinker's durn. He had a hankerin' to believe in witches an' things, anyhow; so he tho't purty strong that some ove 'em must be arter his welfare. He toted a hoss shoe in his pocket, an' got rale serious. He often axed, 'how long it wer to camp meetin' time?' Jist like little children, sittin' round the fire ove a night, axin the knittin' mother, for the fiftieth time, 'how long will hit be till Christmas?' You must bar in mind that the poor feller dident know the fust durn'd thing about 'progress.' At last, by the livin' jingo! the *true* idear struck him, as hit mus *us* some time. So one mornin' arter drams, he come acrost a bran new, curious, little cuss, lookin' like a cross atwixt the devil an' a cookin' stove, standin' on hit's hine laigs, a suckin' the muley cow. Arter brainin' hit with a wagon standard, he jist sot down, an' whetted his knife, ontil it would shave the har off his arm. Now, boys, that's about all that anybody now livin' knows ove the matter. Only this much was noticed thararter: That Mister Benny, billy goat, instid ove chawin his cud, with a short, quick, sassey nip, nip, nip, arter that mornin', an' plum on, ontil he dried up an' died in a sink-hole, he chaw'd hit arter the fashion ove an old, lazy cow, when she is standin' onder the shade ove the willers, bellyfull, an' bellydeep in the creek. His tail never agin flaunted the sky, surjestin 'youbedam.' He wer the very last one that you'd a thought ove axin about the price ove the farm. An *he dident raise any more family.*

"For the sake ove this an' the nex generashun, I would like to know how Old Brakebill managed to straiten things out. If I only could find out, I'd tell Frank Blair, I would, by golly! He wouldent be afeard to surjest the idear, if he tho't hit a wholesome one. Would he?" [1]

EDWIN MARKHAM

The Man with the Hoe

WRITTEN AFTER SEEING MILLET'S WORLD-FAMOUS
PAINTING

God made man in His own image,
in the image of God made He him.
Genesis

BOWED by the weight of centuries he leans
Upon his hoe and gazes on the ground,
The emptiness of ages in his face,
And on his back the burden of the world.
Who made him dead to rapture and despair,
A thing that grieves not and that never hopes,
Stolid and stunned, a brother to the ox?
Who loosened and let down this brutal jaw?
Whose was the hand that slanted back this brow?
Whose breath blew out the light within this brain? [15/16]

Is this the Thing the Lord God made and gave
To have dominion over sea and land;
To trace the stars and search the heavens for power;
To feel the passion of Eternity?
Is this the Dream He dreamed who shaped the suns
And markt their ways upon the ancient deep?
Down all the caverns of Hell to their last gulf
There is no shape more terrible than this—
More tongued with cries against the world's blind greed—
More filled with signs and portents for the soul—
More packt with danger to the universe.

From Edwin Markham. *The Man with the Hoe and Other Poems* (Garden City N.Y.: Doubleday, Doran & Company, Inc., 1935), pp. 15–18. First published in 1899.

What gulfs between him and the seraphim!
Slave of the wheel of labor, what to him
Are Plato and the swing of Pleiades?
What the long reaches of the peaks of song,
The rift of dawn, the reddening of the rose? [16/17]
Through this dread shape the suffering ages look;
Time's tragedy is in that aching stoop;
Through this dread shape humanity betrayed,
Plundered, profaned and disinherited,
Cries protest to the Powers that made the world,
A protest that is also prophecy.

O masters, lords and rulers in all lands,
Is this the handiwork you give to God,
This monstrous thing distorted and soul-quencht?
How will you ever straighten up this shape;
Touch it again with immortality;
Give back the upward looking and the light;
Rebuild in it the music and the dream;
Make right the immemorial infamies,
Perfidious wrongs, immedicable woes?

O masters, lords and rulers in all lands,
How will the future reckon with this Man?
How answer his brute question in that hour
When whirlwinds of rebellion shake all shores [17/18]
How will it be with kingdoms and with kings—
With those who shaped him to the thing he is—
When this dumb Terror shall rise to judge the world,
After the silence of the centuries? [18]

FRANK NORRIS

A Deal in Wheat

I

THE BEAR—WHEAT AT SIXTY-TWO

As SAM LEWISTON backed the horse into the shafts of his buckboard and began hitching the tugs to the whiffletree, his wife came out from the kitchen door of the house and drew near, and stood for some time at the horse's head, her arms folded and her apron rolled around them. For a long moment neither spoke. They had talked over the situation so long and so comprehensively the night before that there seemed to be nothing more to say.

The time was late in the summer, the place a ranch in southwestern Kansas, and Lewiston and his wife were two of a vast population of farmers, wheat growers, who at that moment were passing through a crisis—a crisis that at any moment might culminate in tragedy. Wheat was down to sixty-six.

At length Emma Lewiston spoke.

"Well," she hazarded, looking vaguely out [3/4] across the ranch toward the horizon, leagues distant; "well, Sam, there's always that offer of brother Joe's. We can quit—and go to Chicago—if the worst comes."

"And give up!" exclaimed Lewiston, running the lines through the torets. "Leave the ranch! Give Up! After all these years!"

His wife made no reply for the moment. Lewiston climbed into the buckboard and gathered up the lines. "Well, here goes for the last try, Emmie," he said. "Good-by, girl. Maybe things will look better in town to-day."

"Maybe," she said gravely. She kissed her husband good-by and stood for some time looking after the buckboard traveling toward the town in a moving pillar of dust.

From Frank Norris, *A Deal in Wheat and Other Stories of the New and Old West* (New York: Doubleday, Page and Company, 1903), pp. 3–26.

"I don't know," she murmured at length; "I don't know just how we're going to make out."

When he reached town, Lewiston tied the horse to the iron railing in front of the Odd Fellows' Hall, the ground floor of which was occupied by the post-office, and went across the street and up the stairway of a building of brick and granite—quite the most pretentious structure of the town—and knocked at a door upon the first landing. The door was furnished with a pane of frosted glass, on which, in gold [4/5] letters, was inscribed, "Bridges & Co., Grain Dealers."

Bridges himself, a middle-aged man who wore a velvet skull-cap and who was smoking a Pittsburg stogie, met the farmer at the counter and the two exchanged perfunctory greetings.

"Well," said Lewiston, tentatively, after awhile.

"Well, Lewiston," said the other, "I can't take that wheat of yours at any better than sixty-two."

"Sixty-*two*."

"It's the Chicago price that does it, Lewiston. Truslow is bearing the stuff for all he's worth. It's Truslow and the bear clique that stick the knife into us. The price again this morning. We've just got a wire."

"Good heavens," murmured Lewiston, looking vaguely from side to side. "That—that ruins me. I *can't* carry my grain any longer—what with storage charges and—and—Bridges, I don't see just how I'm going to make out. Sixty-two cents a bushel! Why, man, what with this and with that it's cost me nearly a dollar a bushel to raise that wheat, and now Truslow——"

He turned away abruptly with a quick gesture of infinite discouragement.

He went down the stairs, and making his [5/6] way to where his buckboard was hitched, got in, and, with eyes vacant, the reins slipping and sliding in his limp, half-open hands, drove slowly back to the ranch. His wife had seen him coming, and met him as he drew up before the barn.

"Well?" she demanded.

"Emmie," he said as he got out of the buckboard, laying his arm across her shoulder, "Emmie, I guess we'll take up with Joe's offer. We'll go to Chicago. We're cleaned out!" [6/7]

II

THE BULL—WHEAT AT A DOLLAR-TEN

. . .——*and said Party of the Second Part further covenants and agrees to merchandise such wheat in foreign ports, it being under-*

*stood and agreed between the Party of the First Part and the Party
of the Second Part that the wheat hereinbefore mentioned is released and sold to the Party of the Second Part for export purposes
only, and not for consumption or distribution within the boundaries
of the United States of America or of Canada.*

"Now, Mr. Gates, if you will sign for Mr. Truslow I guess that'll
be all," remarked Hornung when he had finished reading.

Hornung affixed his signature to the two documents and passed
them over to Gates, who signed for his principal and client, Truslow
—or, as he had been called ever since he had gone into the fight
against Hornung's corner—the Great Bear. Hornung's secretary was
called in and witnessed the signatures, and Gates thrust the contract
into his Gladstone bag and stood up, smoothing his hat. [7/8]

"You will deliver the warehouse receipts for the grain," began
Gates.

"I'll send a messenger to Truslow's office before noon," interrupted Hornung. "You can pay by certified check through the Illinois Trust people."

When the other had taken himself off, Hornung sat for some moments gazing abstractedly toward his office windows, thinking over
the whole matter. He had just agreed to release to Truslow, at the
rate of one dollar and ten cents per bushel, one hundred thousand
out of the two million and odd bushels of wheat that he, Hornung,
controlled, or actually owned. And for the moment he was wondering if, after all, he had done wisely in not goring the Great Bear to
actual financial death. He had made him pay one hundred thousand
dollars. Truslow was good for this amount. Would it not have been
better to have put a prohibitive figure on the grain and forced the
Bear into bankruptcy? True, Hornung would then be without his
enemy's money, but Truslow would have been eliminated from the
situation, and that—so Hornung told himself—was always a consum-
mation most devoutly, strenuously and diligently to be striven for.
Truslow once dead was dead, but the Bear was never more dangerous than when deperate. [8/9]

"But so long as he can't get *wheat*," muttered Hornung at the end
of his reflections, "he can't hurt me. And he can't get it. That I
know."

For Hornung controlled the situation. So far back as the February
of that year an "unknown bull" had been making his presence felt
on the floor of the Board of Trade. By the middle of March the commercial reports of the daily press had begun to speak of "the powerful bull clique"; a few weeks later that legendary condition of affairs
implied and epitomized in the magic words "Dollar Wheat" had

been attained, and by the first of April, when the price had been boosted to one dollar and ten cents a bushel, Hornung had disclosed his hand, and in place of mere rumors, the definite and authoritative news that May wheat had been cornered in the Chicago pit went flashing around the world from Liverpool to Odessa and from Duluth to Buenos Ayres.

It was—so the veteran operators were persuaded—Truslow himself who had made Hornung's corner possible. The Great Bear had for once over-reached himself, and, believing himself all-powerful, had hammered the price just the fatal fraction too far down. Wheat had gone to sixty-two—for the time, and under the circumstances, an abnormal price. [9/10] When the reaction came it was tremendous. Hornung saw his chance, seized it, and in a few months had turned the tables, had cornered the product, and virtually driven the bear clique out of the pit.

On the same day that the delivery of the hundred thousand bushels was made to Truslow, Hornung met his broker at his lunch club.

"Well," said the latter, "I see you let go that line of stuff to Truslow."

Hornung nodded; but the broker added:

"Remember, I was against it from the very beginning. I know we've cleared up over a hundred thou'. I would have fifty times preferred to have lost twice that and *smashed Truslow dead*. Bet you what you like he makes us pay for it somehow."

"Huh!" grunted his principal. "How about insurance, and warehouse charges, and carrying expenses on that lot? Guess we'd have had to pay those, too, if we'd held on."

But the other put up his chin, unwilling to be persuaded. "I won't sleep easy," he declared, "till Truslow is busted." [10/11]

III

THE PIT

Just as Going mounted the steps on the edge of the pit the great gong struck, a roar of a hundred voices developed with the swiftness of successive explosions, the rush of a hundred men surging downward to the centre of the pit filled the air with the stamp and grind of feet, a hundred hands in eager strenuous gestures tossed upward from out of the brown of the crowd, the official reporter in his cage on the margin of the pit leaned far forward with straining ear to catch the opening bid, and another day of battle was begun.

Since the sale of the hundred thousand bushels of wheat to Trus-

low the "Hornung crowd" had steadily shouldered the price higher
until on this particular morning it stood at one dollar and a half.
That was Hornung's price. No one else had any grain to sell.

But not ten minutes after the opening, Going was surprised out of
all countenance to hear shouted from the other side of the pit these
words: [11/12]

"Sell May at one-fifty."

Going was for the moment touching elbows with Kimbark on one
side and with Merriam on the other, all three belonging to the
"Hornung crowd." Their answering challenge of *"Sold"* was as the
voice of one man. They did not pause to reflect upon the strangeness
of the circumstance. (That was for afterward.) Their response to the
offer was as unconscious as reflex action and almost as rapid, and before the pit was well aware of what had happened the transaction of
one thousand bushels was down upon Going's trading-card and fifteen hundred dollars had changed hands. But here was a marvel—
the whole available supply of wheat cornered, Hornung master of
the situation, invincible, unassailable; yet behold a man willing to
sell, a Bear bold enough to raise his head.

"That was Kennedy, wasn't it, who made that offer?" asked Kimbark, as Going noted down the trade—"Kennedy, that new man?"

"Yes; who do you suppose he's selling for; who's willing to go
short at this stage of the game?"

"Maybe he ain't short."

"Short! Great heavens, man; where'd he get the stuff?"

"Blamed if I know. We can account for [12/13] every handful of
May. Steady! Oh, there he goes again."

"Sell a thousand May at one-fifty," vociferated the bear-broker,
throwing out his hand, one finger raised to indicate the number of
"contracts" offered. This time it was evident that he was attacking
the Hornung crowd deliberately, for, ignoring the jam of traders
that swept toward him, he looked across the pit to where Going and
Kimbark were shouting *"Sold! Sold!"* and nodded his head.

A second time Going made memoranda of the trade, and either
the Hornung holdings were increased by two thousand bushels of
May wheat or the Hornung bank account swelled by at least three
thousand dollars of some unknown short's money.

Of late—so sure was the bull crowd of its position—no one had
even thought of glancing at the inspection sheet on the bulletin
board. But now one of Going's messengers hurried up to him with
the announcement that this sheet showed receipts at Chicago for that
morning of twenty-five thousand bushels, and not credited to Hornung. Some one had got hold of a line of wheat overlooked by the
"clique" and was dumping it upon them.

"Wire the Chief," said Going over his shoulder to Merriam. This one struggled out [13/14] of the crowd, and on a telegraph blank scribbled:

"Strong bear movement—New man—Kennedy—Selling in lots of five contracts—Chicago receipts twenty-five thousand."

The message was despatched, and in a few moments the answer came back, laconic, of military terseness:

"Support the market."

And Going obeyed, Merriam and Kimbark following, the new broker fairly throwing the wheat at them in thousand-bushel lots.

"Sell May at 'fifty; sell May; sell May." A moment's indecision, an instant's hesitation, the first faint suggestion of weakness, and the market would have broken under them. But for the better part of four hours they stood their ground, taking all that was offered, in constant communication with the Chief, and from time to time stimulated and steadied by his brief, unvarying command:

"Support the market."

At the close of the session they had bought in the twenty-five thousand bushels of May. Hornung's position was as stable as a rock, and the price closed even with the opening figure—one dollar and a half.

But the morning's work was the talk of all La Salle Street. Who was back of the raid? [14/15] What was the meaning of this unexpected selling? For weeks the pit trading had been merely nominal. Truslow, the Great Bear, from whom the most serious attack might have been expected, had gone to his country seat at Geneva Lake, in Wisconsin, declaring himself to be out of the market entirely. He went bass-fishing every day. [15]

IV

THE BELT LINE

On a certain day toward the middle of the month, at a time when the mysterious Bear had unloaded some eighty thousand bushels upon Hornung, a conference was held in the library of Hornung's home. His broker attended it, and also a clean-faced, bright-eyed individual whose name of Cyrus Ryder might have been found upon the pay-roll of a rather well-known detective agency. For upward of half an hour after the conference began the detective spoke, the other two listening attentively, gravely.

"Then, last of all," concluded Ryder, "I made out I was a hobo, and began stealing rides on the Belt Line Railroad. Know the road? It just circles Chicago. Truslow owns it. Yes? Well, then I began to catch on. I noticed that cars of certain number—thirty-one nought thirty-four, thirty-two one ninety—well, the numbers don't matter, but anyhow, these cars were always switched on to the sidings by Mr. Truslow's main elevator D soon [17/18] as they came in. The wheat was shunted in, and they were pulled out again. Well, I spotted one car and stole a ride on her. Say, look here, *that car went right around the city on the Belt, and came back to D again, and the same wheat in her all the time.* The grain was reinspected—it was raw, I tell you—and the warehouse receipts made out just as though the stuff had come in from Kansas or Iowa."

"The same wheat all the time!" interrupted Hornung.

"The same wheat—your wheat, that you sold to Truslow."

"Great snakes!" ejaculated Hornung's broker. "Truslow never took it abroad at all."

"Took it abroad! Say, he's just been running it around Chicago, like the supers in 'Shenandoah,' round an' round, so you'd think it was a new lot, an' selling it back to you again."

"No wonder we couldn't account for so much wheat."

"Bought it from us at one-ten, and made us buy it back—our own wheat—at one-fifty."

Hornung and his broker looked at each other in silence for a moment. Then all at once Hornung struck the arm of his chair with his fist and exploded in a roar of laughter. The [18/19] broker stared for one bewildered moment, then followed his example.

"Sold! Sold!" shouted Hornung almost gleefully. "Upon my soul it's as good as a Gilbert and Sullivan show. And we—— Oh, Lord! Billy, shake on it, and hats off to my distinguished friend, Truslow. He'll be President some day. Hey! What? Prosecute him? Not I."

"He's done us out of a neat hatful of dollars for all that," observed the broker, suddenly grave.

"Billy, it's worth the price."

"We've got to make it up somehow."

"Well, tell you what. We were going to boost the price to one seventy-five next week, and make that our settlement figure."

"Can't do it now. Can't afford it." "No. Here; we'll let out a big link; we'll put wheat at two dollars, and let it go at that."

"Two it is, then," said the broker. [19]

<h1 style="text-align:center">V</h1>

THE BREAD LINE

The street was very dark and absolutely deserted. It was a district on the "South Side," not far from the Chicago River, given up largely to wholesale stores, and after nightfall was empty to all life. The echoes slept but lightly hereabouts, and the slightest footfall, the faintest noise, woke them upon the instant and sent them clamouring up and down the length of the pavement between the iron shuttered fronts. The only light visible came from the side door of a certain "Vienna" bakery, where at one o'clock in the morning loaves of bread were given away to any who should ask. Every evening about nine o'clock the outcasts began to gather about the side door. The stragglers came in rapidly, and the line—the "bread line," as it was called—began to form. By midnight it was usually some hundred yards in length, stretching almost the entire length of the block.

Toward ten in the evening, his coat collar turned up against the fine drizzle that pervaded [21/22] the air, his hands in his pockets, his elbows gripping his sides, Sam Lewiston came up and silently took his place at the end of the line.

Unable to conduct his farm upon a paying basis at the time when Truslow, the "Great Bear," had sent the price of grain down to sixty-two cents a bushel, Lewiston had turned over his entire property to his creditors, and, leaving Kansas for good, had abandoned farming, and had left his wife at her sister's boarding-house in Topeka with the understanding that she was to join him in Chicago as soon as he had found a steady job. Then he had come to Chicago and had turned workman. His brother Joe conducted a small hat factory on Archer Avenue, and for a time he found there a meager employment. But difficulties had occurred, times were bad, the hat factory was involved in debts, the repealing of a certain import duty on manufactured felt overcrowded the home market with cheap Belgian and French products, and in the end his brother had assigned and gone to Milwaukee.

Thrown out of work, Lewiston drifted aimlessly about Chicago, from pillar to post, working a little, earning here a dollar, there a dime, but always sinking, sinking, till at last the ooze of the lowest bottom dragged at his feet and the rush of the great ebb went over him and [22/23] engulfed him and shut him out from the light, and a park bench became his home and the "bread line" his chief makeshift of subsistence.

He stood now in the enfolding drizzle, sodden, stupefied with fatigue. Before and behind stretched the line. There was no talking. There was no sound. The street was empty. It was so still that the passing of a cable-car in the adjoining thoroughfare grated like prolonged rolling explosions, beginning and ending at immeasurable distances. The drizzle descended incessantly. After a long time midnight struck.

There was something ominous and gravely impressive in this in-

terminable line of dark figures, close-pressed, soundless; a crowd, yet
absolutely still; a close-packed, silent file, waiting, waiting in the vast
deserted night-ridden street; waiting without a word, without a
movement, there under the night and under the slow-moving mists
of rain.

Few in the crowd were professional beggars. Most of them were
workmen, long since out of work, forced into idleness by long-con-
tinued "hard times," by ill luck, by sickness. To them the "bread
line" was a godsend. At least they could not starve. Between jobs
here in the end was something to hold them up—a small platform, as
it were, above the sweep [23/24] of black water, where for a moment they might pause and take breath before the plunge.

The period of waiting on this night of rain seemed endless to
those silent, hungry men; but at length there was a stir. The line
moved. The side door opened. Ah, at last! They were going to hand
out the bread.

But instead of the usual white-aproned undercook with his
crowded hampers there now appeared in the doorway a new man—a
young fellow who looked like a bookeeper's assistant. He bore in his
hand a placard, which he tacked to the outside of the door. Then he
disappeared within the bakery, locking the door after him.

A shudder of poignant despair, an unformed, inarticulate sense of
calamity, seemed to run from end to end of the line. What had happened? Those in the rear, unable to read the placard, surged forward, a sense of bitter disappointment clutching at their hearts.

The line broke up, disintegrated into a shapeless throng—a
throng that crowded forward and collected in front of the shut door
whereon the placard was affixed. Lewiston, with the others, pushed
forward. On the placard he read these words:

> "Owing to the fact that the price of grain has been increased to two
> dollars a bushel, there will be no [24/25] distribution of bread from this
> bakery until further notice."

Lewiston turned away, dumb, bewildered. Till morning he
walked the streets, going on without purpose, without direction. But
now at last his luck had turned. Overnight the wheel of his fortunes
had creaked and swung upon its axis, and before noon he had found
a job in the street-cleaning brigade. In the course of time he rose to
be first shift-boss, then deputy inspector, then inspector, promoted to
the dignity of driving in a red wagon with rubber tires and drawing
a salary instead of mere wages. The wife was sent for and a new start
made.

But Lewiston never forgot. Dimly he began to see the significance
of things. Caught once in the cogs and wheels of a great and terrible

engine, he had seen—none better—its workings. Of all the men who had vainly stood in the "bread line" on that rainy night in early summer, he, perhaps, had been the only one who had struggled up to the surface again. How many others had gone down in the great ebb? Grim question; he dared not think how many.

He had seen the two ends of a great wheat operation—a battle between Bear and Bull. The stories (subsequently published in the [25/26] city's press) of Truslow's countermove in selling Hornung his own wheat, supplied the unseen section. The farmer—he who raised the wheat—was ruined upon one hand; the working-man—he who consumed it—was ruined upon the other. But between the two, the great operators, who never saw the wheat they traded in, bought and sold the world's food, gambled in the nourishment of entire nations, practised their tricks, their chicanery and oblique shifty "deals," were reconciled in their differences, and went on through their appointed way, jovial, contented, enthroned, and unassailable. [26]

JOHN CROWE RANSOM

Antique Harvesters

(SCENE: *Of the Mississippi the bank sinister,*
and of the Ohio the bank sinister.)

TAWNY are the leaves turned but they still hold,
And it is harvest; what shall this land produce?
A meager hill of kernels, a runnel of juice;
Declension looks from our land, it is old.
Therefore let us assemble, dry, grey, spare,
And mild as yellow air.

"I hear the croak of a raven's funeral wing."
The young men would be joying in the song
Of passionate birds; their memories are not long.
What is it thus rehearsed in sable? "Nothing."
Trust not but the old endure, and shall be older
Than the scornful beholder.

We pluck the spindling ears and gather the corn.
One spot has special yield? "On this spot stood
Heroes and drenched it with their only blood."
And talk meets talk, as echoes from the horn
Of the hunter—echoes are the old men's arts,
Ample are the chambers of their hearts.

Here come the hunters, keepers of a rite;
The horn, the hounds, the lank mares coursing by
Straddled with archetypes of chivalry;
And the fox, lovely ritualist, in flight
Offering his unearthly ghost to quarry;
And the fields, themselves to harry. [50/51]

From John Crowe Ransom, *Selected Poems* (New York: Alfred A. Knopf, 1945),
pp. 50–51, 31–33. First published in 1924.

Resume, harvesters. The treasure is full bronze
Which you will garner for the Lady, and the moon
Could tinge it no yellower than does this noon;
But grey will quench it shortly—the field, men, stones.
Pluck fast, dreamers; prove as you amble slowly
Not less than men, not wholly.

Bare the arm, dainty youths, bend the knees
Under bronze burdens. And by an autumn tone
As by a grey, as by a green, you will have known
Your famous Lady's image; for so have these;
And if one say that easily will your hands
More prosper in other lands,

Angry as wasp-music be your cry then:
"Forsake the Proud Lady, of the heart of fire,
The look of snow, to the praise of a dwindled choir,
Song of degenerate specters that were men?
The sons of the fathers shall keep her, worthy of
What these have done in love."

True, it is said of our Lady, she ageth.
But see, if you peep shrewdly, she hath not stooped;
Take no thought of her servitors that have drooped,
For we are nothing; and if one talk of death—
Why, the ribs of the earth subsist frail as a breath
If but God wearieth. [51]

JOHN CROWE RANSOM

Captain Carpenter

CAPTAIN CARPENTER rose up in his prime
Put on his pistols and went riding out
But had got wellnigh nowhere at that time
Till he fell in with ladies in a rout.

It was a pretty lady and all her train
That played with him so sweetly but before
An hour she'd taken a sword with all her main
And twined him of his nose for evermore.

Captain Carpenter mounted up one day
And rode straightway into a stranger rogue
That looked unchristian but be that as may
The Captain did not wait upon prologue.

But drew upon him out of his great heart
The other swung against him with a club
And cracked his two legs at the shinny part
And let him roll and stick like any tub.

Captain Carpenter rode many a time
From male and female took he sundry harms
He met the wife of Satan crying "I'm
The she-wolf bids you shall bear no more arms."

Their strokes and counters whistled in the wind
I wish he had delivered half his blows
But where she should have made off like a hind
The bitch bit off his arms at the elbows. [31/32]

And Captain Carpenter parted with his ears
To a black devil that used him in this wise

318

O Jesus ere his threescore and ten years
Another had plucked out his sweet blue eyes.

Captain Carpenter got up on his roan
And sallied from the gate in hell's despite
I heard him asking in the grimmest tone
If any enemy yet there was to fight?

"To any adversary it is fame
If he risks to be wounded by my tongue
Or burnt in two beneath my red heart's flame
Such are the perils he is cast among.

"But if he can he has a pretty choice
From an anatomy with little to lose
Whether he cut my tongue and take my voice
Or whether it be my round red heart he choose."

It was the neatest knave that ever was seen
Stepping in perfume from his lady's bower
Who at this word put in his merry mien
And fell on Captain Carpenter like a tower.

I would not knock old fellows in the dust
But there lay Captain Carpenter on his back
His weapons were the old heart in his bust
And a blade shook between rotten teeth alack.

The rogue in scarlet and grey soon knew his mind
He wished to get his trophy and depart
With gentle apology and touch refined
He pierced him and produced the Captain's heart. [32/33]

God's mercy rest on Captain Carpenter now
I thought him Sirs an honest gentleman
Citizen husband soldier and scholar enow
Let jangling kites eat of him if they can.

But God's deep curses follow after those
That shore him of his goodly nose and ears
His legs and strong arms at the two elbows
And eyes that had not watered seventy years.

The curse of hell upon the sleek upstart
That got the Captain finally on his back
And took the red red vitals of his heart
And made the kites to whet their beaks clack clack. [33]

DONALD DAVIDSON

Prologue: the Long Street

Pacing the long street where is no summer
But only burning summer—looking for spring
That is not, spring that will not be here
But with its blunt remembrancer and friend,
Its blunt friend Death . . . Pacing the long street
That ends with winter that will never be
Winter as men would say it . . . Thinking of autumn—
What but a few blown leaves and the biting smoke
That feeds on all of these till autumn is not
Autumn? The seasons, even the seasons wither,
And all is mingled with a chaff of time
Till I must wonder, pacing the long street,
If anything in this vague inconceivable world
Can end, lie still, be set apart, be named.

Yet I would name and set apart from time
One sudden face, built from a clay and spittle
Ancient as time, stubborn as these square cliffs
Of brick and steel that here enclose my steps.
The grass cannot remember; trees cannot
Remember what once was here. But even so,
They too are here no longer. Where is the grass?
Only the blind stone roots of the dull street
And the steel thews of houses flourish here,
And the baked curve of asphalt, smooth, trodden,
Covers dead earth that once was quick with grass.
Snuffing the ground with acrid breath the motors [115/116]

From Donald Davidson, *Poems 1922–1961* (Minneapolis: University of Minnesota Press, 1966), pp. 115–116, 64. "Prologue: The Long Street" first published in 1927. "On a Replica of the Parthenon" first published in 1935.

Fret the long street. Steel answers steel. Dust whirls.
Skulls hurry past with pale flesh yet clinging
And a little hair. Fevered bones under clean
Linen. Aimless knuckles of bones
Within buttoned gloves waving to eyeless sockets:
"Good day, old friend! Good day, my girl! Good-bye!
So long, old man!"
                                    So long, forever so.
Forever, night after night, to say good-bye
Across the portals of an iron age
And close the ivory gate with hopeless stare
Down the long street and up and down again.
Again, old man? How shall we meet again . . .
Tonight, for lights bloom up uncertainly for us,
Or in this dead commingled smoke and dark take leave
Of dead men under a pall, nameless and choked? [116]

DONALD DAVIDSON

On a Replica of the Parthenon

WHY do they come? What do they seek
Who build but never read their Greek?
The classic stillness of a pool
Beleaguered in its certitude
By aimless motors that can make
Only incertainty more sure;
And where the willows crowd the pure
Expanse of clouds and blue that stood
Around the gables Athens wrought,
Shopgirls embrace a plaster thought,
And eye Poseidon's loins ungirt,
And never heed the brandished spear
Or feel the bright-eyed maiden's rage
Whose gaze the sparrows violate;
But the sky drips its spectral dirt,
And gods, like men, to soot revert.
Gone is the mild, the serene air.
The golden years are come too late.
Pursue not wisdom or virtue here,
But what blind motion, what dim last
Regret of men who slew their past
Raised up this bribe against their fate. [64]

ROBERT FROST

A Lone Striker

THE SWINGING mill bell changed its rate
To tolling like the count of fate,
And though at that the tardy ran,
One failed to make the closing gate.
There was a law of God or man
That on the one who came too late
The gate for half an hour be locked.
His time be lost, his pittance docked.
He stood rebuked and unemployed.
The straining mill began to shake.
The mill, though many, many eyed,
Had eyes inscrutably opaque;
So that he couldn't look inside
To see if some forlorn machine
Was standing idle for his sake.
(He couldn't hope its heart would break.)

And yet he thought he saw the scene:
The air was full of dust of wool.
A thousand yarns were under pull,
But pull so slow, with such a twist,
All day from spool to lesser spool,
It seldom overtaxed their strength;
They safely grew in slender length.
And if one broke by any chance,
The spinner saw it at a glance.
The spinner still was there to spin.

That's where the human still came in.
Her deft hand showed with finger rings

From *Complete Poems of Robert Frost* (New York: Henry Holt and Company, 1949), pp. 355–356. "A Lone Striker" first published in 1936.

Among the harp-like spread of strings.
She caught the pieces end to end [355/356]
And, with a touch that never missed,
Not so much tied as made them blend.
Man's ingenuity was good.
He saw it plainly where he stood,
Yet found it easy to resist.

He knew another place, a wood,
And in it, tall as trees, were cliffs;
And if he stood on one of these,
'Twould be among the tops of trees,
Their upper branches round him wreathing,
Their breathing mingled with his breathing.
If—if he stood! Enough of ifs!
He knew a path that wanted walking;
He knew a spring that wanted drinking;
A thought that wanted further thinking;
A love that wanted re-renewing.
Nor was this just a way of talking
To save him the expense of doing.
With him it boded action, deed.

The factory was very fine;
He wished it all the modern speed.
Yet, after all, 'twas not divine,
That is to say, 'twas not a church.
He never would assume that he'd
Be any institution's need.
But he said then and still would say
If there should ever come a day
When industry seemed like to die
Because he left it in the lurch,
Or even merely seemed to pine
For want of his approval, why,
Come get him—they knew where to search. [356]

ANDREW LYTLE

Jericho, Jericho, Jericho

SHE OPENED her eyes. She must have been asleep for hours or months. She could not reckon; she could only feel the steady silence of time. She had been Joshua and made it swing suspended in her room. Forever she had floated above the counterpane; between the tester and the counterpane she had floated until her hand, long and bony, its speckled dried skin drawing away from the bulging blue veins, had reached and drawn her body under the covers. And now she was resting, clear-headed and quiet, her thoughts clicking like a new-greased mower. All creation could not make her lift her thumb or cross it over her finger. She looked at the bed, the bed her mother had died in, the bed her children had been born in, her marriage bed, the bed the General [3/4] had drenched with his blood. Here it stood where it had stood for seventy years, square and firm on the floor, wide enough for three people to lie comfortable in, if they didn't sleep restless; but not wide enough for her nor long enough when her conscience scorched the cool wrinkles in the sheets. The two footposts, octagonal-shaped and mounted by carved pieces that looked like absurd flowers, stood up to comfort her when the world began to crumble. Her eyes followed down the posts and along the basket-quilt. She had made it before her marriage to the General, only he wasn't a general then. He was a slight, tall young man with a rolling mustache and perfume in his hair. A many a time she had seen her young love's locks dripping with scented oil, down upon his collar . . . She had cut the squares for the baskets in January, and for stuffing had used the letters of old lovers, fragments of passion cut to warm her of a winter's night. The General would have his fun. *Miss Kate, I didn't sleep well last night. I heard Sam Buchanan make love to you out of that farthest basket. If I hear him again, I mean to toss this piece of quilt in the fire.* Then he would chuckle in his round, soft voice; reach under the covers and pull her over to his

From Andrew Lytle, *A Novel, A Novella, and Four Stories* (New York: McDowell, Oblensky, Inc., 1958), pp. 3–18. First published in 1936.

side of the bed. On a cold and frosting night he would sleep with his nose against her neck. His nose was so quick to turn cold, he said, and her neck was so warm. Sometimes her hair, the loose unruly strands at the nape, would tickle his nostrils and he would wake up with a sneeze. This had been so long ago, and there had been so many years of trouble and worry. Her eyes, as apart from her as the mirror on the bureau, rested upon the half-tester, upon the enormous button that caught the rose-colored canopy and shot its folds out like the rays of the morning sun. She could not see but she could feel the heavy cluster of mahogany grapes that tumbled from the [4/5] center of the headboard—out of its vines curling down the sides it tumbled. How much longer would these never-picked grapes hang above her head? How much longer would she, rather, hang to the vine of this world, she who lay beneath as dry as any raisin. Then she remembered. She looked at the blinds. They were closed.

"You, Ants, where's my stick? I'm a great mind to break it over your trifling back."

"Awake? What a nice long nap you've had," said Doctor Ed.

"The boy? Where's my grandson? Has he come?"

"I'll say he's come. What do you mean taking to your bed like this? Do you realize, beautiful lady, that this is the first time I ever saw you in bed in my whole life? I believe you've taken to bed on purpose. I don't believe you want to see me."

"Go long, boy, with your foolishness."

That's all she could say, and she blushed as she said it—she blushing at the words of a snip of a boy, whom she had diapered a hundred times and had washed as he stood before the fire in the round tin tub, his little back swayed and his little belly sticking out in front, rosy from the scrubbing he had gotten. *Mammy, what for I've got a hole in my stummick; what for, Mammy?* Now he was sitting on the edge of the bed calling her beautiful lady, an old hag like her, beautiful lady. A good-looker the girls would call him, with his bold, careless face and his hands with their fine, long fingers. Soft, how soft they were, running over her rough, skinny bones. He looked a little like his grandpa, but somehow there was something missing . . .

"Well, boy, it took you a time to come home to see me die."

"Nonsense. Cousin Edwin, I wouldn't wait on a woman who had so little faith in my healing powers." [5/6]

"There an't nothing strange about dying. But I an't in such an all-fired hurry. I've got a heap to tell you about before I go."

The boy leaned over and touched her gently. "Not even death would dispute you here, on Long Gourd, Mammy."

He was trying to put her at her ease in his carefree way. It was so obvious a pretending, but she loved him for it. There was something

nice in its awkwardness, the charm of the young's blundering and of
their efforts to get along in the world. Their pretty arrogance, their
patronizing airs, their colossal unknowing of what was to come. It
was a quenching drink to a sin-thirsty old woman. Somehow his vitality had got crossed in her blood and made a dry heart leap, her
blood that was almost water. Soon now she would be all water, water
and dust, lying in the burying ground between the cedar—and fire.
She could smell her soul burning and see it. What a fire it would
make below, dripping with sin, like a rag soaked in kerosene. But
she had known what she was doing. And here was Long Gourd, all
its fields intact, ready to be handed on, in better shape than when
she took it over. Yes, she had known what she was doing. How long,
she wondered, would his spirit hold up under the trials of planting,
of cultivating, and of the gathering time, year in and year out—how
would he hold up before so many springs and so many autumns.
The thought of him giving orders, riding over the place, or rocking
on the piazza, and a great pain would pin her heart to her backbone.
She wanted him by her to train—there was so much for him to
know: how the creek field was cold and must be planted late, and
where the orchards would best hold their fruit, and where the frosts
crept soonest—that now could never be. She turned her head—who
was that woman, that strange woman standing by the bed as if she
owned it, as if . . . [6/7]

"This is Eva, Mammy."

"Eva?"

"We are going to be married."

"I wanted to come and see—to meet Dick's grandmother . . ."

I wanted to come see her die. That's what she meant. Why didn't
she finish and say it out. She had come to lick her chops and see
what she would enjoy. That's what she had come for, the lying little
slut. The richest acres in Long Gourd valley, so rich hit'd make yer
feet greasy to walk over'm, Saul Oberly at the first tollgate had told
the peddler once, and the peddler had told it to her, knowing it
would please and make her trade. *Before you die.* Well, why didn't
you finish it out? You might as well. You've given yourself away.

Her fierce thoughts dried up the water in her eyes, tired and resting far back in their sockets. They burned like a smothered fire
stirred up by the winds as they traveled over the woman who would
lie in her bed, eat with her silver, and caress her flesh and blood.
The woman's body was soft enough to melt and pour about him. She
could see that; and her firm round breasts, too firm and round for
any good to come from them. And her lips, full and red, her eyes
bright and cunning. The heavy hair crawled about her head to tangle the poor, foolish boy in its ropes. She might have known he

would do something foolish like this. He had a foolish mother. There warn't any way to avoid it. But look at her belly, small and no-count. There wasn't a muscle the size of a worm as she could see. And those hips—

And then she heard her voice: "What did you say her name was, son? Eva? Eva Callahan, I'm glad to meet you, Eva. Where'd your folks come from, Eva? I knew some Callahans who lived in the Goose-pad settlement. They couldn't be any of your kin, could they?" [7/8]

"Oh, no, indeed. My people . . ."

"Right clever people they were. And good farmers, too. Worked hard. Honest—that is, most of 'em. As honest as that run of people go. We always gave them a good name."

"My father and mother live in Birmingham. Have always lived there."

"Birmingham," she heard herself say with contempt. They could have lived there all their lives and still come from somewhere. I've got a mule older'n Birmingham. "What's your pa's name?"

"Her father is Mister E. L. Callahan, Mammy."

"First name not Elijah by an chance? Lige they called him."

"No. Elmore, Mammy."

"Old Mason Callahan had a son they called Lige. Somebody told me he moved to Elyton. So you think you're going to live with the boy here."

"We're to be married . . . that is, if Eva doesn't change her mind."

And she saw his arm slip possessively about the woman's waist. "Well, take care of him, young woman, or I'll come back and ha'nt you. I'll come back and claw your eyes out."

"I'll take very good care of him, Mrs. McCowan."

"I can see that." She could hear the threat in her voice, and Eva heard it.

"Young man," spoke up Doctor Edwin, "you should feel powerful set up, two such women pestering each other about you."

The boy kept an embarrassed silence.

"All of you get out now. I want to talk to him by himself. I've got a lot to say and precious little time to say it in. And he's mighty young and helpless and ignorant." [8/9]

"Why, Mammy, you forget I'm a man now. Twenty-six. All teeth cut. Long trousers."

"It takes a heap more than pants to make a man. Throw open them blinds, Ants."

"Yes'm."

"You don't have to close the door so all-fired soft. Close it naturally. And you can tip about all you want to—later. I won't be hurried to the burying ground. And keep your head away from that door. What I've got to say to your new master is private."

"Listen at you, mistiss."

"You listen to me. That's all. No, wait. I had something else on my mind—what is it? Yes. How many hens has Melissy set? You don't know. Find out. A few of the old hens ought to be setting. Tell her to be careful to turn the turkey eggs every day. No, you bring them and set them under my bed. I'll make sure. We got a mighty pore hatch last year. You may go now. I'm plumb worn out, boy, worn out thinking for these people. It's that that worries a body down. But you'll know all about it in good time. Stand out there and let me look at you good. You don't let me see enough of you, and I almost forget how you look. Not really, you understand. Just a little. It's your own fault. I've got so much to trouble me that you, when you're not here, naturally slip back in my mind. But that's all over now. You are here to stay, and I'm here to go. There will always be Long Gourd, and there must always be a McCowan on it. I had hoped to have you by me for several years, but you would have your fling in town. I thought it best to clear your blood of it, but as God is hard, I can't see what you find to do in town. And now you've gone and gotten you a woman. Well, they all have to do it. But do you reckon you've picked the right one—you must [9/10] forgive the frankness of an old lady who can see the bottom of her grave—I had in mind one of the Carlisle girls. The Carlisle place lies so handy to Long Gourd and would give me a landing on the river. Have you seen Anna Belle since she's grown to be a woman? I'm told there's not a better housekeeper in the valley."

"I'm sure Anna Belle is a fine girl. But Mammy, I love Eva."

"She'll wrinkle up on you, son; and the only wrinkles land gets can be smoothed out by the harrow. And she looks sort of puny to me, Son. She's powerful small in the waist and walks about like she had worms."

"Gee, Mammy, you're not jealous are you? That waist is in style."

"You want to look for the right kind of style in a woman. Old Mrs. Penter Matchem had two daughters with just such waists, but 'twarnt natural. She would tie their corset strings to the bed posts and whip'm out with a buggy whip. The poor girls never drew a hearty breath. Just to please that old woman's vanity. She got paid in kind. It did something to Eliza's bowels and she died before she was twenty. The other one never had any children. She used to whip'm out until they cried. I never liked that woman. She thought a whip could do anything."

"Well, anyway, Eva's small waist wasn't made by any corset strings. She doesn't wear any."

"How do you know, sir?"

"Well . . . I . . . What a question for a respectable woman to ask."

"I'm not a respectable woman. No woman can be respectable and run four thousand acres of land. Well, you'll have [10/11] it your own way. I suppose the safest place for a man to take his folly is to bed."

"Mammy!"

"You must be lenient with your Cousin George. He wanders about night times talking about the War. I put him off in the west wing where he won't keep people awake, but sometimes he gets in the yard and gives orders to his troops. 'I will sweep that hill, General'—and many's the time he's done it when the battle was doubtful —'I'll sweep it with my iron brooms'; then he shouts out his orders, and pretty soon the dogs commence to barking. But he's been a heap of company for me. You must see that your wife humors him. It won't be for long. He's mighty feeble."

"Eva's not my wife yet, Mammy."

"You won't be free much longer—the way she looks at you, like a hungry hound."

"I was just wondering," he said hurriedly. "I hate to talk about anything like this . . . ."

"Everybody has a time to die, and I'll have no maudlin nonsense about mine."

"I was wondering about Cousin George . . . If I could get somebody to keep him. You see, it will be difficult in the winters. Eva will want to spend the winters in town . . . ."

He paused, startled, before the great bulk of his grandmother rising from her pillows, and in the silence that frightened the air, his unfinished words hung suspended about them.

After a moment he asked if he should call the doctor.

It was some time before she could find words to speak.

"Get out of the room."

"Forgive me, Mammy. You must be tired."

"I'll send for you," sounded the dead voice in the still [11/12] room, "when I want to see you again. I'll send for you and—the woman."

She watched the door close quietly on his neat square back. Her head whirled and turned like a flying jennet. She lowered and steadied it on the pillows. Four thousand acres of the richest land in the valley he would sell and squander on that slut, and he didn't even know it and there was no way to warn him. This terrifying thought rushed through her mind, and she felt the bed shake with her pain, while before the footboard the specter of an old sin rose up to mock her. How she had struggled to get this land and keep it together—

through the War, the Reconstruction, and the pleasanter after days. For eighty-seven years she had suffered and slept and planned and rested and had pleasure in this valley, seventy of it, almost a turning century, on this place; and now that she must leave it . . .

The things she had done to keep it together. No. The one thing . . . From the dusty stacks the musty odor drifted through the room, met the tobacco smoke over the long table piled high with records, reports. Iva Louise stood at one end, her hat clinging perilously to the heavy auburn hair, the hard blue eyes and the voice:

"You promised Pa to look after me"—she had waited for the voice to break and scream—"and you have stolen my land!"

"Now, Miss Iva Louise," the lawyer dropped his empty eyes along the floor, "you don't mean . . ."

"Yes. I do mean it."

Her own voice had restored calm to the room: "I promised your pa his land would not be squandered."

"My husband won't squander my property. You just want it for yourself." [12/13]

She cut through the scream with the sharp edge of her scorn: "What about that weakling's farm in Madison? Who pays the taxes now?"

The girl had no answer to that. Desperate, she faced the lawyer: "Is there no way, sir, I can get my land from the clutches of this unnatural woman?"

The man coughed; the red rim of his eyes watered with embarrassment. "I'm afraid," he cleared his throat, "you say you can't raise the money . . . I'm afraid—"

That trapped look as the girl turned away. It had come back to her, now trapped in her bed. As a swoon spreads, she felt the desperate terror of weakness, more desperate where there has been strength. Did the girl see right? Had she stolen the land because she wanted it?

Suddenly, like the popping of a thread in a loom, the struggles of the flesh stopped, and the years backed up and covered her thoughts like the spring freshet she had seen so many times creep over the dark soil. Not in order, but as if they were stragglers trying to catch up, the events of her life passed before her sight that had never been so clear. Sweeping over the mounds of her body rising beneath the quilts came the old familiar odors—the damp, strong, penetrating smell of new-turned ground; the rank, clinging, resistless odor of green-picked feathers stuffed in a pillow by Guinea Nell, thirty-odd years ago; tobacco on the mantel, clean and sharp like smelling salts; her father's sweat, sweet like stale oil; the powerful ammonia of manure turned over in a stall; curing hay in the wind; the polecat's stink on the night air, almost pleasant, a sort of commingled scent of all the animals, man and beast; the dry smell of dust under a rug; the overstrong scent of too-sweet fruit trees blooming; the inhospitable wet ashes of a dead fire in a poor white's cabin; black [13/14] Rebecca in the kitchen; a wet hound steaming before a fire. There were other odors she could not identify, overwhelming her, making her weak, taking her body and drawing out of it a choking longing to hover over all that she must leave, the animals, the fences, the crops growing in the fields, the houses, the people in them . . .

It was early summer, and she was standing in the garden after dark—she had heard something after the small chickens. Mercy and Yellow Jane passed beyond the paling fence. Dark shadows—gay full voices. *Where you gwine, gal? I dunno. Jest a-gwine. Where you? To the frolic, do I live. Well, stay off'n yoe back tonight.* Then out of the rich, gushing laughter: *All right, you stay off'n yourn. I done caught de stumbles.* More laughter.

The face of Uncle Ike, head man in slavery days, rose up. A tall Senegalese, he was standing in the crib of the barn unmoved before the bush-whackers. *Nigger, whar is that gold hid? You better tell us, nigger. Down in the well; in the far-place. By God, you black son of a bitch, we'll roast ye alive if you air too contrary to tell. Now listen, ole nigger, Miss McCowan ain't nothen to you no more. You been set free. We'll give ye some of it, a whole sack. Come on, now*—out of the dribbling, leering mouth—*whar air it?* Ike's tall form loomed towards the shadows. In the lamp flame his forehead shone like the point, the core of night. He stood there with no word for answer. As she saw the few white beads of sweat on his forehead, she spoke.

She heard her voice reach through the dark—*I know your kind. In better days you'd slip around and set people's barns afire. You shirked the War to live off the old and weak. You don't spare me because I'm a woman. You'd shoot a woman quicker because she has the name of being frail. Well, I'm* [14/15] *not frail, and my Navy Six an't frail. Ike, take their guns.* Ike moved and one of them raised his pistol arm. He dropped it, and the acrid smoke stung her nostrils. *Now, Ike, get the rest of their weapons. Their knives, too. One of us might turn our backs.*

On top of the shot she heard the soft pat of her servants' feet. White eyeballs shining through the cracks in the barn. Then: *Caesar, Al, Zebedee, step in here and lend a hand to Ike.* By sun the people had gathered in the yard. Uneasy, silent, they watched her on the porch. She gave the word, and the whips cracked. The mules strained, trotted off, skittish and afraid, dragging the white naked bodies bouncing and cursing over the sod: *Turn us loose. We'll not bother ye no more, lady. You ain't no woman, you're a devil.* She turned and went into the house. It is strange how a woman gets hard when trouble comes a-gobbling after her people.

Worn from memory, she closed her eyes to stop the whirl, but clos-ing her eyes did no good. She released the lids and did not resist. Brother Jack stood before her, handsome and shy, but ruined from his cradle by a cleft palate, until he came to live only in the fire of spirits. And she understood, so clear was life, down to the smallest things. She had often heard tell of this clarity that took a body whose time was spending on the earth. Poor Brother Jack, the gen-tlest of men, but because of his mark, made the butt and wit of the valley. She saw him leave for school, where he was sent to separate him from his drinking companions, to a church school where the boys buried their liquor in the ground and sipped it up through straws. His letters: *Dear Ma, quit offering so much advice and send me more money. You send barely enough to keep me from stealing.* His buggy wheels scraping the gravel, driving up as the first roosters crowed. *Katharine,* [15/16] *Malcolm, I thought you might want to have a little conversation.* Conversation two hours before sun! And down she would come and let him in, and the General would get up, stir the fire, and they would sit down and smoke. Jack would drink and sing, *If the Little Brown Jug was mine, I'd be drunk all the time and I'd never be sob-er a-gin*—or, *Hog drovers, hog drovers, hog drovers we air, a-courting your darter so sweet and so fair.* They would sit and smoke and drink until she got up to ring the bell.

He stayed as long as the whiskey held out, growing more violent towards the end. She watered his bottles; begged whiskey to make camphor—*Gre't God, Sis Kate, do you sell camphor? I gave you a pint this morning.* Poor Brother Jack, killed in Breckinridge's charge at Murfreesboro, cut in two by a chain shot from an enemy gun. All night long she had sat up after the message came. His body scattered about a splintered black gum tree. She had seen that night, as if she had been on the field, the parties moving over the dark field hunting the wounded and dead. Clyde Bascom had fallen near Jack with a bad hurt. They were messmates. He had to tell somebody; and somehow she was the one he must talk to. The spectral lanterns, swinging towards the dirge of pain and the monotonous cries of *Water,* caught by the river dew on the before-morning air and held suspended over the fields in its acrid quilt. There death dripped to mildew the noisy throats . . . and all the while relief parties, moving, blots of night, sullenly moving in the viscous blackness.

Her eyes widened, and she looked across the foot posts into the room. There was some mistake, some cruel blunder; for there now, tipping about the carpet, hunting in her wardrobe, under the bed, blowing down the fire to its ashes until they glowed in their dryness, stalked the burial parties. They [16/17] stepped out of the ashes in twos and threes, hunting, hunting, and shaking their heads. Whom were they searching for? Jack had long been buried. They moved more rapidly; looked angry. They crowded the room until she gasped for breath. One, gaunt and haggard, jumped on the foot of her bed; rose to the ceiling; gesticulated, argued in animated silence. He leaned forward; pressed his hand upon her leg. She tried to tell him to take it off. Cold and crushing heavy, it pressed her down to the bowels of the earth. Her lips trembled, but no sound came forth. Now the hand moved up to her stomach; and the haggard eyes looked gravely at her, alert, as if they were waiting for something. Her head turned giddy. She called to Dick, to Ants, to Doctor Ed; but the words struck her teeth and fell back in her throat. She concentrated on lifting the words, and the burial parties sadly shook their heads. Always the cries struck her teeth and fell back down. She strained to hear the silence they made. At last from a great distance she thought she heard . . . *too late . . . too late.* How exquisite the sound, like a bell swinging without ringing. Suddenly it came to her. She was dying.

How slyly death slipped up on a body, like sleep moving over the vague boundary. How many times she had laid awake to trick the unconscious there. At last she would know . . . But she wasn't ready. She must first do something about Long Gourd. That slut must not eat it up. She would give it to the hands first. He must be brought to understand this. But the specters shook their heads. Well let them shake. She'd be damned if she would go until she was ready to go. She'd be damned all right, and she smiled at the meaning the word took on now. She gathered together all the particles of her will; the specters faded; and there about her were the anxious faces of kin and servants. Edwin had his hands under [17/18] the cover feeling her legs. She made to raise her own hand to the boy. It did not go up. Her eyes wanted to roll upward and look behind her forehead, but she pinched them down and looked at her grandson.

"You want to say something, Mammy?"—she saw his lips move.

She had a plenty to say, but her tongue had somehow got glued to her lips. Truly it was now too late. Her will left her. Life withdrawing gathered like a frosty dew on her skin. The last breath blew gently past her nose. The dusty nostrils tingled. She felt a great sneeze coming. There was a roaring; the wind blew through her head once, and a great cotton field bent before it, growing and spreading, the bolls swelling as big as cotton sacks and bursting white as thunder-heads. From a distance, out of the far end of the field, under a sky so blue that it was painful-bright, voices came singing, *Joshua fit the battle of Jericho, Jericho, Jericho—Joshua fit the battle of Jericho, and the walls came a-tumbling down.* [18]

ROBERT PENN WARREN

The Patented Gate and the Mean Hamburger

You HAVE seen him a thousand times. You have seen him standing on the street corner on Saturday afternoon, in the little county-seat towns. He wears blue jean pants, or overalls washed to a pale pastel blue like the color of sky after a shower in spring, but because it is Saturday he has on a wool coat, an old one, perhaps the coat left from the suit he got married in a long time back. His long wrist bones hang out from the sleeves of the coat, the tendons showing along the bone like the dry twist of grapevine still corded on the stove-length of a hickory sapling you would find in his wood box beside his cookstove among the split chunks of gum and red oak. The big hands, with the knotted, cracked joints and the square, horn-thick nails, hang loose off the wrist bone like clumsy, home-made tools hung on the wall of a shed after work. If it is summer, he wears a straw hat with a wide brim, the straw fraying loose around the edge. If it is winter, he wears a felt hat, black once, but now weathered with streaks of dark gray and dull purple in the sunlight. His face is long and bony, the jawbone long under the drawn-in cheeks. The flesh along the jawbone is nicked in a couple of places where the unaccustomed razor has been drawn over the leather-coarse skin. A tiny bit of blood crusts brown where the nick is. The color of the face is red, a dull red like the red clay mud or clay dust which clings to the bottom of his pants and to the cast-iron-looking brogans on his feet, or a red like the color of a piece of hewed cedar which has been left in the weather. The face does not look alive. It seems to be molded from the clay or hewed from the cedar. When the jaw moves, once, with its deliberate, massive motion on the quid of tobacco, [120/121] you are still not convinced. That motion is but the cunning triumph of a mechanism concealed within.

From Robert Penn Warren, *The Circus in the Attic and Other Stories* (New York: Harcourt, Brace and Company, 1948), pp. 120–133.

But you see the eyes. You see that the eyes are alive. They are pale blue or gray, set back under the deep brows and thorny eyebrows. They are not wide, but are squinched up like eyes accustomed to wind or sun or to measuring the stroke of the ax or to fixing the object over the rifle sights. When you pass, you see that the eyes are alive and are warily and dispassionately estimating you from the ambush of the thorny brows. Then you pass on, and he stands there in that stillness which is his gift.

With him may be standing two or three others like himself, but they are still, too. They do not talk. The young men, who will be like these men when they get to be fifty or sixty, are down at the beer parlor, carousing and laughing with a high, whickering laugh. But the men on the corner are long past all that. They are past many things. They have endured and will endure in their silence and wisdom. They will stand on the street corner and reject the world which passes under their level gaze as a rabble passes under the guns of a rocky citadel around whose base a slatternly town has assembled.

I had seen Jeff York a thousand times, or near, standing like that on the street corner in town, while the people flowed past him, under the distant and wary and dispassionate eyes in ambush. He would be waiting for his wife and three towheaded children who were walking around the town looking into store windows and at the people. After a while they would come back to him, and then, wordlessly, he would lead them to the store where they always did their trading. He would go first, marching with a steady bent-kneed stride, setting the cast-iron brogans down deliberately on the cement; then his wife, a small woman with covert, sidewise, curious glances for the world, would follow, and behind her the towheads bunched together in a dazed, glory-struck way. In the store, when their turn came, Jeff York would move to the counter, accept the clerk's greeting, and then bend down from his height to catch the whispered directions of his wife. He [121/122] would straighten up and say, "Gimme a sack of flahr, if'n you please." Then when the sack of flour had been brought, he would lean again to his wife for the next item. When the stuff had all been bought and paid for with the grease-thick, wadded dollar bills which he took from an old leather coin purse with a metal catch to it, he would heave it all together into his arms and march out, his wife and towheads behind him and his eyes fixed level over the heads of the crowd. He would march down the street and around to the hitching lot where the wagons were, and put his stuff into his wagon and cover it with an old quilt to wait till he got ready to drive out to his place.

For Jeff York had a place. That was what made him different

from the other men who looked like him and with whom he stood
on the street corner on Saturday afternoon. They were croppers, but
he, Jeff York, had a place. But he stood with them because his father
had stood with their fathers and his grandfathers with their grandfathers, or with men like their fathers and grandfathers, in other towns,
in settlements in the mountains, in towns beyond the mountains.
They were the great-great-great-grandsons of men who, half woods-
men and half farmers, had been shoved into the sand hills, into the
limestone hills, into the barrens, two hundred, two hundred and
fifty years before and had learned there the way to grabble a life out
of the sand and the stone. And when the soil had leached away into
the sand or burnt off the stone, they went on west, walking with the
bent-kneed stride over the mountains, their eyes squinching warily
in the gaunt faces, the rifle over the crooked arm, hunting a new
place.

But there was a curse on them. They only knew the life they
knew, and that life did not belong to the fat bottom lands, where
the cane was head-tall, and to the grassy meadows and the rich
swale. So they passed those places by and hunted for the place which
was like home and where they could pick up the old life, with the
same feel in the bones and the squirrel's bark sounding the same
after first light. They had walked a long way, to the sand hills of
Alabama, to [122/123] the red country of North Mississippi and
Louisiana, to the Barrens of Tennessee, to the Knobs of Kentucky
and the scrub country of West Kentucky, to the Ozarks. Some of
them had stopped in Cobb County, Tennessee, in the hilly eastern
part of the country, and had built their cabins and dug up the
ground for the corn patch. But the land had washed away there, too,
and in the end they had come down out of the high land into the
bottoms—for half of Cobb County is a rich, swelling country—where
the corn was good and the tobacco unfurled a leaf like a yard of
green velvet and the white houses stood among the cedars and tulip
trees and maples. But they were not to live in the white houses with
the limestone chimneys set strong at the end of each gable. No, they
were to live in the shacks on the back of the farms, or in cabins not
much different from the cabins they had once lived in two hundred
years before over the mountains or, later, in the hills of Cobb
County. But the shacks and the cabins now stood on somebody else's
ground, and the curse which they had brought with them over the
mountain trail, more precious than the bullet mold or grandma's
quilt, the curse which was the very feeling in the bones and the
habit in the hand, had come full circle.

Jeff York was one of those men, but he had broken the curse. It
had taken him more than thirty years to do it, from the time when

he was nothing but a big boy until he was fifty. It had taken him from sun to sun, year in and year out, and all the sweat in his body, and all the power of rejection he could muster, until the very act of rejection had become a kind of pleasure, a dark, secret, savage dissipation, like an obsessing vice. But those years had given him his place, sixty acres with a house and barn.

When he bought the place, it was not very good. The land was run-down from years of neglect and abuse. But Jeff York put brush in the gullies to stop the wash and planted clover on the run-down fields. He mended the fences, rod by rod. He patched the roof on the little house and propped up the porch, buying the lumber and shingles almost piece by piece [123/124] and one by one as he could spare the sweat-bright and grease-slick quarters and half-dollars out of his leather purse. Then he painted the house. He painted it white, for he knew that that was the color you painted a house sitting back from the road with its couple of maples, beyond the clover field.

Last, he put up the gate. It was a patented gate, the kind you can ride up to and open by pulling on a pull rope without getting off your horse or out of your buggy or wagon. It had a high pair of posts, well braced and with a high crossbar between, and the bars for the opening mechanism extending on each side. It was painted white, too. Jeff was even prouder of the gate then he was of the place. Lewis Simmons, who lived next to Jeff's place, swore he had seen Jeff come out after dark on a mule and ride in and out of that gate, back and forth, just for the pleasure of pulling on the rope and making the mechanism work. The gate was the seal Jeff York had put on all the years of sweat and rejection. He could sit on his porch on a Sunday afternoon in summer, before milking time, and look down the rise, down the winding dirt track, to the white gate beyond the clover, and know what he needed to know about all the years passed.

Meanwhile Jeff York had married and had had the three towheads. His wife was twenty years or so younger than he, a small dark woman, who walked with her head bowed a little and from that humble and unprovoking posture stole sidewise, secret glances at the world from eyes which were brown or black—you never could tell which because you never remembered having looked her straight in the eye—and which were surprisingly bright in that sidewise, secret flicker, like the eyes of a small, cunning bird which surprises you from the brush. When they came to town she moved along the street, with a child in her arms or later with the three trailing behind her, and stole her looks at the world. She wore a calico dress, dun-colored, which hung loose to conceal whatever shape her thin body had, and in winter over the dress a brown wool coat with a scrap of fur at the collar which looked like some tattered growth of fungus feeding on old wood. She [124/125] wore black high-heeled shoes, slippers of some kind, which she kept polished and which surprised you under that dress and coat. In the slippers she moved with a slightly limping, stealthy gait, almost sliding them along the pavement, as though she had not fully mastered the complicated trick required to use them properly. You knew that she wore them only when she came to town, that she carried them wrapped up in a piece of newspaper until their wagon had reached the first house on the outskirts of town, and that, on the way back, at the same point, she would take them off and wrap them up again and hold the bundle in her lap until she got home. If the weather happened to be bad, or if it was winter, she would have a pair of old brogans under the wagon seat.

It was not that Jeff York was a hard man and kept his wife in clothes that were as bad as those worn by the poorest of the women of the croppers. In fact, some of the cropper women, poor or not, black or white, managed to buy dresses with some color in them and proper hats, and went to the moving picture show on Saturday afternoon. But Jeff still owed a little money on his place, less than two hundred dollars, which he had had to borrow to rebuild his barn after it was struck by lightning. He had, in fact, never been entirely out of debt. He had lost a mule which had got out on the highway and been hit by a truck. That had set him back. One of his towheads had been sickly for a couple of winters. He had not been in deep, but he was not a man, with all those years of rejection behind him, to forget the meaning of those years. He was good enough to his family. Nobody ever said the contrary. But he was good to them in terms of all the years he had lived through. He did what he could afford. He bought the towheads a ten-cent bag of colored candy every Saturday afternoon for them to suck on during the ride home in the wagon, and the last thing before they left town, he always took the lot of them to the dogwagon to get hamburgers and orange pop.

The towheads were crazy about hamburgers. And so was his wife, for that matter. You could tell it, even if she didn't [125/126] say anything, for she would lift her bowed-forward head a little, and her face would brighten, and she would run her tongue out to wet her lips just as the plate with the hamburger would be set on the counter before her. But all those folks, like Jeff York and his family, like hamburgers, with pickle and onions and mustard and tomato catsup, the whole works. It is something different. They stay out in the country and eat hog-meat, when they can get it, and greens and corn bread and potatoes, and nothing but a pinch of salt to brighten it on the tongue, and when they get to town and get hold of beef and wheat bread and all the stuff to jack up the flavor, they have to swallow to keep the mouth from flooding before they even take the first bite.

So the last thing every Saturday, Jeff York would take his family over to Slick Hardin's *Dew Drop Inn Diner* and give them the treat. The diner was built like a railway coach, but it was set on a concrete foundation on a lot just off the main street of town. At each end the concrete was painted to show wheels. Slick Hardin kept the grass just in front of the place pretty well mowed and one or two summers he even had a couple of flower beds in the middle of that shirttail-size lawn. Slick had a good business. For a few years he had been a prelim fighter over in Nashville and had got his name in the papers a few times. So he was a kind of hero, with the air of romance about him. He had been born, however, right in town and, as soon as he had found out he wasn't ever going to be good enough to be a real fighter, he had come back home and started the dogwagon, the first one ever in town. He was a slick-skinned fellow, about thirty-five, prematurely bald, with his head slick all over. He had big eyes, pale blue and slick looking like agates. When he said something that he thought smart, he would roll his eyes around, slick in his head like marbles, to see who was laughing. Then he'd wink. He had done very well with his business, for despite the fact that he had picked up city ways and a lot of city talk, he still remembered enough to deal with the country people, and they were the ones who brought the dimes in. People who [126/127] lived right there in town, except for school kids in the afternoon and the young toughs from the pool room or men on the night shift down at the railroad, didn't often get around to the dogwagon.

Slick Hardin was perhaps trying to be smart when he said what he did to Mrs. York. Perhaps he had forgotten, just for that moment, that people like Jeff York and his wife didn't like to be kidded, at least not in that way. He said what he did, and then grinned and rolled his eyes around to see if some of the other people present were thinking it was funny.

Mrs. York was sitting on a stool in front of the counter, flanked on one side by Jeff York and on the other by the three towheads. She had just sat down to wait for the hamburger—there were several orders in ahead of the York order—and had been watching in her sidewise fashion every move of Slick Hardin's hands as he patted the pink meat onto the hot slab and wiped the split buns over the greasy iron to make them ready to receive it. She always watched him like that, and when the hamburger was set before her she would wet her lips with her tongue.

That day Slick set the hamburger down in front of Mrs. York, and said, "Anybody likes hamburger much as you, Mrs. York, ought to git him a hamburger stand."

Mrs. York flushed up, and didn't say anything, staring at her plate. Slick rolled his eyes to see how it was going over, and somebody down the counter snickered. Slick looked back at the Yorks, and if he had not been so encouraged by the snicker he might, when he saw Jeff York's face, have hesitated before going on with his kidding. People like Jeff York are touchous, and they are especially touchous about the women-folks, and you do not make jokes with or about their women-folks unless it is perfectly plain that the joke is a very special kind of friendly joke. The snicker down the counter had defined the joke as not entirely friendly. Jeff was looking at Slick, and something was growing slowly in that hewed-cedar face, and back in the gray eyes in the ambush of thorny brows.

But Slick did not notice. The snicker had encouraged him, [127/128] and so he said, "Yeah, if I liked them hamburgers much as you, I'd buy me a hamburger stand. Fact, I'm selling this one, You want to buy it?"

There was another snicker, louder, and Jeff York, whose hamburger had been about half way to his mouth for another bite, laid it down deliberately on his plate. But whatever might have happened at that moment did not happen. It did not happen because Mrs. York lifted her flushed face, looked straight at Slick Hardin, swallowed hard to get down a piece of the hamburger or to master her nerve, and said in a sharp, strained voice, "You sellen this place?"

There was complete silence. Nobody had expected her to say anything. The chances were she had never said a word in that diner in the couple of hundred times she had been in it. She had come in with Jeff York and, when a stool had come vacant, had sat down, and Jeff had said, "Gimme five hamburgers, if'n you please, and make 'em well done, and five bottles of orange pop." Then, after the eating was over, he had always laid down seventy-five cents on the counter—that is, after there were five hamburger-eaters in the family —and walked out, putting his brogans down slow, and his wife and kids following without a word. But now she spoke up and asked the question, in that strained, artificial voice, and everybody, including her husband, looked at her with surprise.

As soon as he could take it in, Slick Hardin replied, "Yeah, I'm selling it."

She swallowed hard again, but this time it could not have been hamburger, and demanded, "What you asken fer hit?"

Slick looked at her in the new silence, half shrugged, a little contemptuously, and said, "Fourteen hundred and fifty dollars."

She looked back at him, while the blood ebbed from her face. "Hit's a lot of money," she said in a flat tone, and returned her gaze to the hamburger on her plate.

"Lady," Slick said defensively, "I got that much money tied up here. Look at that there stove. It is a *Heat Master* and they cost. Them coffee urns, now. Money can't buy no better. And [128/129] this here lot, lady, the diner sets on. Anybody knows I got that much money tied up here. I got more. This lot cost me more'n . . ." He suddenly realized that she was not listening to him. And he must have realized, too, that she didn't have a dime in the world and couldn't buy his diner, and that he was making a fool of himself, defending his price. He stopped abruptly, shrugged his shoulders, and then swung his wide gaze down the counter to pick out somebody to wink to.

But before he got the wink off, Jeff York had said, "Mr. Hardin."

Slick looked at him and asked, "Yeah?"

"She didn't mean no harm," Jeff York said. "She didn't mean to be messen in yore business."

Slick shrugged. "Ain't no skin off my nose," he said. "Ain't no secret I'm selling out. My price ain't no secret neither."

Mrs. York bowed her head over her plate. She was chewing a mouthful of her hamburger with a slow, abstracted motion of her jaw, and you knew that it was flavorless on her tongue.

That was, of course, on a Saturday. On Thursday afternoon of the next week Slick was in the diner alone. It was the slack time, right in the middle of the afternoon. Slick, as he told it later, was wiping off the stove and wasn't noticing. He was sort of whistling to himself, he said. He had a way of whistling soft through his teeth. But he wasn't whistling loud, he said, not so loud he wouldn't have heard the door open or the steps if she hadn't come gum-shoeing in on him to stand there waiting in the middle of the floor until he turned round and was so surprised he nearly had heart failure. He had thought he was there alone, and there she was, watching every move he was making, like a cat watching a goldfish swim in a bowl.

"Howdy-do" he said, when he got his breath back.

"This place still fer sale?" asked him.

"Yeah, lady," he said.

"What you asken fer hit?"

"Lady, I done told you," Slick replied, "fourteen hundred and fifty dollars."

"Hit's a heap of money," she said. [129/130]

Slick started to tell her how much money he had tied up there, but before he had got going, she had turned and slipped out of the door.

"Yeah," Slick said later to the men who came into the diner, "me

like a fool starting to tell her how much money I got tied up here
when I knowed she didn't have a dime. That woman's crazy. She
must walked that five or six miles in here just to ask me something
she already knowed the answer to. And then turned right round and
walked out. But I am selling me this place. I'm tired of slinging hash
to them hicks. I got me some connections over in Nashville and I'm
gonna open me a place over there. A cigar stand and about three
pool tables and maybe some beer. I'll have me a sort of club in the
back. You know, membership cards to git in, where the boys will
play a little game. Just sociable. I got good connections over in
Nashville. I'm selling this place. But that woman, she ain't got a
dime. She ain't gonna buy it."

But she did.

On Saturday Jeff York led his family over to the diner. They ate
hamburgers without a word and marched out. After they had gone,
Slick said, "Looks like she ain't going to make the invest-mint.
Gonna buy a block of bank stock instead." Then he rolled his eyes,
located a brother down the counter, and winked.

It was almost the end of the next week before it happened. What
had been going on inside the white house out on Jeff York's place
nobody knew or was to know. Perhaps she just starved him out, just
not doing the cooking or burning everything. Perhaps she just quit
attending to the children properly and he had to come back tired
from work and take care of them. Perhaps she just lay in bed at
night and talked and talked to him, asking him to buy it, nagging
him all night long, while he would fall asleep and then wake up
with a start to hear her voice still going on. Or perhaps she just
turned her face away from him and wouldn't let him touch her. He
was a lot older than she, and she was probably the only woman he
had ever had. He had been too ridden by his [130/131] dream and
his passion for rejection during all the years before to lay even a
finger on a woman. So she had him there. Because he was a lot older
and because he had never had another woman. But perhaps she used
none of these methods. She was a small, dark, cunning woman, with a
widewise look from her lowered face, and she could have thought up
ways of her own, no doubt.

Whatever she thought up, it worked. On Friday morning Jeff
York went to the bank. He wanted to mortgage his place, he told
Todd Sullivan, the president. He wanted fourteen hundred and fifty
dollars, he said. Todd Sullivan would not let him have it. He already owed the bank one hundred and sixty dollars and the best he
could get on a mortgage was eleven hundred dollars. That was in
1935 and then farmland wasn't worth much and half the land in the
country was mortgaged anyway. Jeff York sat in the chair by Todd

Sullivan's desk and didn't say anything. Eleven hundred dollars would not do him any good. Take off the hundred and sixty he owed and it wouldn't be but a little over nine hundred dollars clear to him. He sat there quietly for a minute, apparently turning that fact over in his head. Then Todd Sullivan asked him, "How much you say you need?"

Jeff York told him.

"What you want it for?" Todd Sullivan asked.

He told him that.

"I tell you," Todd Sullivan said, "I don't want to stand in the way of a man bettering himself. Never did. That diner ought to be a good proposition, all right, and I don't want to stand in your way if you want to come to town and better yourself. It will be a step up from that farm for you, and I like a man has got ambition. The bank can't lend you the money, not on that piece of property. But I tell you what I'll do. I'll buy your place. I got me some walking horses I'm keeping out on my father's place. But I could use me a little place of my own. For my horses. I'll give you seventeen hundred for it. Cash."

Jeff York did not say anything to that. He looked slow at Todd Sullivan as though he did not understand. [131/132]

"Seventeen hundred," the banker repeated. "That's a good figure. For these times."

Jeff was not looking at him now. He was looking out the window, across the alleyway—Todd Sullivan's office was in the back of the bank. The banker, telling about it later when the doings of Jeff York had become for a moment a matter of interest, said "I thought he hadn't even heard me. He looked like he was half asleep or something. I coughed to sort of wake him up. You know the way you do. I didn't want to rush him. You can't rush those people, you know. But I couldn't sit there all day. I had offered him a fair price."

It was, as a matter of fact, a fair price for the times, when the bottom was out of everything in the section.

Jeff York took it. He took the seventeen hundred dollars and bought a dogwagon with it, and rented a little house on the edge of town and moved in with his wife and the towheads. The first day after they got settled, Jeff York and his wife went over to the diner to get instructions from Slick about running the place. He showed Mrs. York all about how to work the coffee machine and the stove, and how to make up the sandwiches, and how to clean the place up after herself. She fried up hamburgers for all of them, herself, her husband, and Slick Hardin, for practice, and they ate the hamburgers while a couple of hangers-on watched them. "Lady," Slick said, for he had money in his pocket and was heading out for Nashville on the seven o'clock train that night, and was feeling expansive, "lady, you sure fling a mean hamburger."

He wiped the last crumbs and mustard off his lips, got his valise from behind the door, and said, "Lady, git in there and pitch. I hope you make a million hamburgers." Then he stepped out into the bright fall sunshine and walked away whistling up the street, whistling through his teeth and rolling his eyes as though there were somebody to wink to. That was the last anybody in town ever saw of Slick Hardin.

The next day, Jeff York worked all day down at the diner. He was scrubbing up the place inside and cleaning up the trash which had accumulated behind it. He burned all the [132/133] trash. Then he gave the place a good coat of paint outside, white paint. That took him two days. Then he touched up the counter inside with varnish. He straightened up the sign out front, which had begun to sag a little. He had that place looking spick and span.

Then on the fifth day after they got settled—it was Sunday—he took a walk in the country. It was along toward sun when he started out, not late, as a matter of fact, for by October the days are shortening up. He walked out the Curtisville pike and out the cut-off leading to his farm. When he entered the cut-off, about a mile from his own place, it was still light enough for the Bowdoins, who had a filling station at the corner, to see him plain when he passed.

The next time anybody saw him was on Monday morning about six o'clock. A man taking milk into town saw him. He was hanging from the main cross bar of the white patented gate. He had jumped off the gate. But he had propped the thing open so there wouldn't be any chance of clambering back up on it if his neck didn't break when he jumped and he should happen to change his mind.

But that was an unnecessary precaution, as it developed. Dr. Stauffer said that his neck was broken very clean. "A man who can break a neck as clean as that could make a living at it," Dr. Stauffer said. And added, "If he's damned sure it ain't ever his own neck."

Mrs. York was much cut up by her husband's death. People were sympathetic and helpful, and out of a mixture of sympathy and curiosity she got a good starting trade at the diner. And the trade kept right on. She got so she didn't hang her head and look sidewise at you and the world. She would look straight at you. She got so she could walk in high heels without giving the impression that it was a trick she was learning. She wasn't a bad-looking woman, as a matter of fact, once she had caught on how to fix herself up a little. The railroad men and the pool hall gang liked to hang out there and kid with her. Also, they said, she flung a mean hamburger. [133]

TIME

-•-•-

The Pushbutton Cornucopia

AT 5:30 ONE FROSTY Indiana morning last week, Farmer Warren
North, 45, rolled out of bed to get at his chores. After a hearty
breakfast (orange juice, cereal, bacon and eggs), he left his twelve-
room white frame and fieldstone house, walked briskly to the barnyard. In the early morning mist the low-lying white barn, sur-
mounted by five giant blue-black silos, rode the frozen prairie like
an ocean liner. Like a rumble of surf came the hungry bellowing of
400 white-faced Herefords and the grunting of 500 Hampshire hogs,
waiting at row on row of troughs to be fed. In the barn, North
stepped up to an instrument panel as intricate as a ship's, began
pushing buttons and pulling switches. All around, the barn came to
vibrant life. From one silo dropped ground corn, from another si-
lage, from a third shelled corn.

By pushing other buttons, Farmer North shot in supplementary
vitamins, mineral and hormone nutrients. Then he cut in the big
noisemaker. In a channel in front of the silos a snakelike auger
began to turn. As it writhed, it propelled the feed up a steep incline
and sent it tumbling out through a conduit that passed directly over
330 feet of feed troughs. At regular intervals, trap doors automati-
cally distributed the individual animal's feed. When all the animals
on one side of a trough had been fed, the traps changed position,
shunted feed to the animals waiting on the other side.

Ten minutes later, Farmer North was through with a job that
would have taken five men half a day working with buckets and
pitchforks. He was ready to indulge his hobby. He returned to his
farmhouse and poured himself another cup of coffee. While it
cooled, he read a story on the "farm problem" in the *Wall Street
Journal*. Carrying his cup and a cigarette, he walked into his living
room, 40 feet long and beige-carpeted wall to wall. It was dominated
at the far end by a two-story pipe organ flanked by two electronic
organs and a grand piano. Farmer North sat down at the console,

From *Time*, LXXIII (March 9, 1959), pp. 74–78, 80.

and after running through a few warm-up chords and arpeggios, began to play Johann Sebastian Bach's chorale, *Jesu, Joy of Man's Desiring*.

Symbol & Example. Farmer North is a symbol—and a prime example—of the profound changes that have been wrought in U.S. agriculture by mechanization and automation, plus the new use of fertilizers. In the last 20 years, farming has changed more radically than in the previous two centuries. Once farmers used to dole out fertilizer thinking only of how much it cost them. Now they pour it on by the carload, confident of getting back bigger profits at harvest time. Farm use of fertilizer has risen in 20 years from 1,500,000 tons to 6,200,000 tons. To handle the huge increase in crops, farmers have had to mechanize almost every farm job. From 1938 to 1958, farmers more than trebled their ownership of tractors, to 4,700,000 (an average 1½ per commercial farm). Since 1945, they have increased their number of newer worksaving machinery by 1,200%—mostly with machines that had not even been [74/75] invented in 1938. Farmers have invested $17.5 billion in 1,040,000 combines, 745,000 cornpickers, 590,000 pickup hay balers, 255,000 field forage harvesters and other machinery. They spend $1.5 billion for gasoline and oil each year just to keep the equipment going.

Now farmers are taking the big step from mechanization to automation in the raising of animals and fowl; they are copying the assembly-line techniques of industry and bringing animals indoors. Once man felt he could not provide an environment for animals as good as nature's. Now he knows he can do a whole lot better. Behind him, giving him confidence, are ever-new discoveries in antibiotics, hormones, climate control, nutrition and plant and animal genetics.

Failure & Scandal. The result of all this is that farm productivity is soaring at a rate that once nobody believed possible. From 1938 through 1957, overall farm labor productivity rose at an annual average rate of 4.7% (*v.* 2.2% for the rest of the economy). Even more significant, productivity is increasing at an accelerating rate. Last year, it jumped 8%, as much as the increase for the decade 1920-30. This technological fact, ignored by the politicians, is what has made the farm-support program such a failure and scandal. Last year, with farmers paid $620 million to put land in the soil bank, the planted acreage was reduced to the smallest since 1919. But the yield was 11% greater than in the previous record year of 1957. This year, in many crops, the U.S. is headed for even bigger surpluses. The 1959 wheat harvest was forecast last week at 1.2 billion bu. This will add 200 million bu. to the record 1.3 billion bu. wheat carryover expected this July 1. With productivity shooting up like the kudzu vine, even veteran farm lobbyists are beginning to wonder if any kind of a subsidized farm program can be anything but a failure and scandal.

In the Box. For Farmer North, the revolution in farming came at precisely the right time. Twenty years ago Warren North could not afford a pair of new work shoes; he did his chores in an overshoe and a boot. Today, by taking full advantage of all the scientific advances, plus an amount of hard work that would have broken a weaker man, North is comfortably a millionaire. But he remembers every struggling step of the way up. Born in 1913 on the farm he now owns, near Brookston (pop. 1,100), in northwest Indiana, North started in field work at the age of seven, the year after his mother died. His father bolted a box to a harrow, and North, riding in the box, drove the team. His father followed, driving another team pulling a corn planter.

At nine, North was experienced enough to work in the fields alone. Life around Brookston was grim for all farmers in those days after the collapse of prices following the World War I boom, and it was harsh at the North farm. Dale North, the father, was not satisfied unless everybody got up at 3:30 to milk, eat and harness up, so they could get into the fields by 5:30. The cheerless life in Widower North's house still troubles Warren North: "We never even had a Christmas tree." By 1930 the father saw the way clear to let Warren's twin sister Wanda go off to teachers college. Warren himself was ready to go away in three months, study the organ for a term, then enter engineering school the following fall.

All this changed when Dale North had a heart attack. Before he died, he told Warren: "Get an education. Don't be a farmer. I wish I hadn't been." The death left Warren North alone at 17 with an $8,500 mortgage on the 180 acres, $1,500 in funeral and other personal debts. He could go away, let the farm go in a forced sale to satisfy the debt. Or he could stay and try to salvage something. He decided to stay: "I was young and strong," he says now with a slow smile. "And I already had done the spring plowing."

Ten-Cent Dates. Of the next four years, Warren North remembers little except being bone-weary at all times. His father had got up at 3:30. He got up at 1:30 to milk and set the cans out on the road for the creamery that paid him 2¢ a quart. He had to cut his luxuries to 10¢ a week for old Buffalo roll-your-own tobacco. On his rare dates, he limited the evening to a dime "for two Cokes." Such ruthless self-denial paid off financially. Warren not only kept Wanda in school but paid off the $1,500 of his father's personal debts to close the estate so he and Wanda could legally inherit the 180 acres.

The years left scars. Withdrawn to begin with, Warren became more so. He married three times. He and his third wife separated six years ago. He found consolation in music, the farm and religion; a Baptist, he has long been organist for the Federated Church. The more unlucky he was in love the more his daring touch with farming coined gold. He was one of the first in Indiana to use fertilizer on wheat, pioneered with hybrid corn in 1937. His yield rose from 50 bu. to 65 bu. and ultimately 100 bu. per acre. He made up his own mind. When the experts said Russian hard wheat would not grow in his area, he planted Russian hard wheat. His yield went from 30 bu. to 42 bu. per acre.

Bigger & Bigger. He developed a passion for the latest in machinery. He bought his first tractor in 1933 for $550. Gradually he went in for bigger and more expensive models. By 1950 he was paying $3,000 for a tractor. Later he paid $4,800 apiece for three more. In 1952 he bought a $5,500 combine, decided he had made a good deal when the price rose to $8,000. He early realized that to make costly equipment pay he had to have more land to operate it more of the time. He bought Wanda's 90 acres, partly to save the land from going to another buyer, inherited 25 acres from his grandmother. The rest he picked up at steadily rising market prices from other farmer's. Year by year he mortgaged and paid off, [75/76] mortgaged and paid off. Gradually his property line stretched out to enclose 300 acres, then, 500, then two years ago 1,000 acres of the finest land in northern Indiana—worth $500 an acre. When his land got ahead of his equipment, he switched from four-blade to six-blade plows to cut plowing time by one third.

By 1957 Warren North had all the land he wanted. The question was how he could best use it. He was selling grain and feeding hogs and some cattle. He decided that raising grain did not pay enough and that he had to go in for mass production of livestock, use all his grain for his own animals. Through the years North had kept a tight rein on his wage outlay. He employed only two year-round hired hands, plus two part-time men in summer. But the going wage in his area had gone up from $100 to $180 a month plus a house, utilities, etc. "I figured even if I could get more men they would not be any account."

The Drive to Automate. For the same reason that inspired many an industrialist faced with similar cost-price squeeze, North decided to automate his livestock feeding, bought glass-lined steel Harvestore silos, developed by the A. O. Smith Corp. of Milwaukee, Wis., for $55,000. Hermetically sealed to prevent decay, the silos permitted him to store corn and silage as soon as cut, thereby giving it all the feed value of green produce. Since the corn did not have to be dried to bone hardness as in ordinary storage, it would also be easily digestible. (Around Warren North, in a more primitive cycle, many farmers still followed the traditional and inefficient practice of feeding dried corn to cattle, running in hogs to pick out undigested kernels from the manure, then letting chickens clean up.)

North spent another $75,000 on equipment to go with the silos. The result is that he can swiftly raise his livestock feeding output without more capital. By turning his animals over three times a year, he is already running at the rate of 1,200 head of cattle 1,500 hogs a year. Depending on the market outlook, he can increase this to 1,800 cattle and 4,000 hogs with no additional labor.

Last year *Prairie Farmer*, the leading midwestern farm magazine (circ. 415,000), was so impressed by North that it held its annual farm progress show on his farm. Two hundred tents were set up. In two days 215,000 visitors tramped over the place to see how he does it. Said Jim Thomson, managing editor of *Prarie Farmer:* "North is one of America's great farmers...."

Corn the Key. If any single event can be said to have touched off the farm revolution, it was the development of hybrid corn. It opened the eyes of farmers and scientists alike to the vast increase that could be made in food production. Following Mendelian genetic principles, Professor George Harrison Shull of the Carnegie Institution of Washington developed the first hybrid corn in 1908. This was more than mere crossing: by generations of inbreeding he got pure strains which when mated yielded an almost explosive yield increase given the name of "hybrid vigor." But Shull's work was commercially valueless; the seed was too expensive. Not till 1935, after further discoveries by U.S. Department of Agriculture Researcher Donald Jones and commercial seedsmen, such as Henry A. Wallace, one time (1933-40) U.S. Secretary of Agriculture, could commercial seed companies put hybrid corn on the market.

Last year U.S. farmers seeded 90% of their corn acreage with hybrid corn, got a total yield of 3.4 billion bu.—750 million bu. higher than they could have produced with regular corn. The wonders of hybrid corn are still surprising the scientists. For example, last year Illinois Farmer James Holderman decided to try a new type of hybrid corn, even though the experts warned him it was not suitable for his land. He doubled the amount of fertilizer, planted the rows closer together, and his yield jumped to 175 bu. an acre, compared to an average 70 bu. The corn was so thick that his mechanical picker just barely got through it. Now corn experts are studying Holderman's experiment to see exactly what happened—and if it should be recommended to everyone.

At the University of Illinois, Associate Professor Earl R. Leng has developed a dwarf corn that he hopes will some day end farmers'

worries from wind-storm damage. The short stalk is also ideal for automated pickers. By crossing his dwarf corn with teosinte, a Mexican
grass, he has also developed a stalk with 20 small ears all along the
stalk. If he can increase the size of the ears, the corn of 1965 may
well resemble a hat tree. . . . [76/77]

The Machine Mother. What is happening in corn and other crops
can be matched in animals and fowl. One of the pioneer researchers
was Dr. E. Parmalee Prentice, a son-in-law of John D. Rockefeller.
In the 1920s, at his farm in Massachusetts, many strains were combined to produce the superior White Leghorn, now the basic egg-lay-
ing hen in the U.S. Today some 30 hatcheries specialize in producing laying pullets, have helped to push U.S. yearly egg production
per hen up from 134 in 1940 to 200 in 1958.

The demand for the more prolific egg layer has required more
and more automation. Near Atlanta, Ga., Layer Breeder Roy Durr
produced 500,000 chickens last year trying to keep up with orders for
layers. He puts the eggs in special incubators that vastly improve on
the maternal solicitude of real hens. A hen often forgets to turn her
eggs (causing the membrane lining to adhere to the shell and killing
the fetus), or in hot dry weather leaves the nest and lets them dry
out. Durr's mechanical mother turns each egg every hour, and when
a thermometer warns that the relative humidity is too low, shoots in
a fine spray of water. Durr staggers the eggs in each incubator, because from the 16th day until the 21st, when the chick breaks
through the shell, a hatching chicken gives off heat, thereby thriftily
helps incubate the eggs put in later. This way Durr has to turn on
the electricity only about 75% of the time.

The laying pullets are sold to other farmers who do nothing but
produce eggs for the table in a completely automatic fashion. The
hens are kept in individual cages. They stick their heads out to feed
from a continuously filled feed trough, turn around to a drinking
fountain, drop their eggs on the inclined wire floor. The eggs roll
outside through an automatic counter onto a conveyor belt that
takes them to a human sorter who puts them in boxes. Another conveyor belt takes away the droppings. One man can easily take care of
7,000 birds with an output of 4,000 eggs a day. Outside each cage is
the laying record. When this drops, the hen goes to the stewing pot.
. . . [77/78]

Showers for Pigs. The indoor life cycle of the chickens forecasts
the future for all farm animals. Purdue University has a $700,000
climate-control program in which, among other things, pigs take regular shower baths. Says Animal Science Professor Frederick N. Andrews: "Pigs do not wallow in mud because they like to be dirty.
They wallow in mud because they have no sweat glands to keep

them cool." With daily or even hourly shower baths, meticulous regulation of the temperature, humidity and even the air movement around them for each day of their lives, Purdue's hogs grow on less feed, gain 1¾ lbs. per day, compared to 1½ lbs. for hogs forced to put up with natural weather.

Purdue has also brought sheep indoors. Not only do the sheep seem to be happier but Purdue can regulate the amount of light they get. Normally, sheep breed only once a year, when the autumn days begin to shorten. By changing the lighting indoors, Purdue can make sheep think it is autumn any time of the year, get two or more lamb crops, schedule spring lamb around the calendar.

Cradle to Grave. U.S. manufacturers are turning out fully automated cages designed with the idea of giving each animal precision comfort. Ranger Equipment Co. is on the market with the Porkliner, claims that with $112,000 worth of its equipment one man can raise 7,000 hogs a year with only half-day help. The Porkliner is a hog's country club. The little pigs begin with private rooms, to avoid being stepped on by the sow. A hydraulic lift is used to stack the cages six rows high. Manure falls through the cage bottoms and is mechanically removed to be used as fertilizer. In their whole lives, until they are made into ham, sausages and bacon, the hogs never know weight-killing struggle.

Such confinement and automation of animals is possible and profitable because of a raft of new chemical discoveries. In 1948 Purdue's Dr. Andrews discovered how to put tiny pellets of stilbestrol, a synthetic female sex hormone, under the skins of cattle and sheep to make them gain weight 15% faster. Today 80% of the nation's beef cattle get stilbestrol. This helps farmers produce an estimated billion pounds more meat than they could have got for the same amount of feed without stilbestrol. . . .

Fewer Farms. Where all this is leading to is obvious to farm experts. The number of farmers will steadily drop as more mechanization and automation increases the investment needed to farm. Economists of the Department of Agriculture estimate that the 3,100,000 commercial farms of 1954 may well be 2,000,000 by 1975. But they see rising prices for land and even used equipment making it easy for farmers to sell out at good prices. Those who stay in will have bigger markets. In 1940 each U.S. farmer fed himself and ten others. He now feeds 20 others. In 1975 experts expect it will be about 42. Increasing agricultural efficiency will make the job easier and more profitable.

Whether the U.S. can much longer afford the huge surpluses being piled up by this efficiency is doubted by most farm experts. Even if the support scandal continues, there is something for U.S.

taxpayers to be cheerful about. Rising efficiency keeps down the cost of food. The mountainous grain surplus currently is causing a build-up in cattle-breeding—pointing to an eventual price break.

For the world, the enormous success of Farmer North and thousands like him may be even more significant. The new methods have proved just as successful abroad as in the U.S. For example, in England, Farmer Anthony Fisher tried his hand at dairying. After his herd died of [78/80] foot-and-mouth disease he was about ready to quit. Hearing about the U.S. system of raising broilers, he wrote to Ralston Purina Co. to get free brochures on how to do it. He started out with 200 birds. Now his output has grown to 1,000,000 a year. The broiler king of England, he has one packing plant, plans another to process his chickens and those of his imitators. The broiler is fast becoming as cheap and popular in England as in the U.S.

Thus the new methods of mechanization and automation developed by the U.S. farmer can show the world how to solve the food shortages brought on by the explosion in population. In the next decade, the most important U.S. export may well be the lessons that Farmer North and others learned down on the farm. [80]

Epilogue

THE PART the agrarian tradition played in the life and work of William Faulkner, this century's and one of America's greatest novelists, is singular evidence of its consequence in the history of American ideas. Thomas Jefferson had a habit throughout his busy career as one of America's greatest statesmen of insisting that his true vocation was farming, that the natural life was the rural life and not the frenzied existence in metropolitan Washington. Faulkner was then clearly imitating the Jeffersonian pattern when he insisted, as he always did throughout his life, that farming was his primary occupation and writing was only a hobby. In a meeting with citizens of Nagano during his visit to Japan in 1955, Faulkner proudly asserted, "I'm a countryman. My life is farmland and horses and the raising of grain and feed. I took up writing simply because I liked it . . ., but just to be a writer is not my life; my life is a farmer, so in that sense, I'm not a writer because that doesn't come first." It is needless to point out that Jefferson and Faulkner were both being disingenuous, as they were fully aware that their achievements were in the political and literary arenas, respectively, and neither was likely to be remembered for his agricultural pursuits.

Of more importance is the part agrarian themes play in the life's work Faulkner devoted to his fictional saga of Yoknapatawpha County. The American Adam's second fall from grace in the new Garden of Eden, because of his attempts to establish property rights in God's soil and his fellow man, is a reiterated theme in his fiction. The passing away of the wilderness in the face of industrialism and commercialism is the theme of his great story "The Bear." In the Snopes trilogy, *The Hamlet, The Town,* and *The Mansion,* Faulkner projected on a broad canvas the conflict between agrarianism and materialism, the principles of the one embodied in the defeated Sartoris family, and the valueless animalism of the other embodied in the successful Snopes breed. Like Captain Carpenter of John Crowe Ransom's poem, the ritualistic, chivalric gestures of the Sartoris clan are but empty, self-defeating postures in an increasingly Snopes-ordered world. While the independent, small-farm families do not play a large part in Faulkner's fiction, they do appear occasionally—such as the McCallums and the McCaslins—and he treats

them in the favorable light so often enjoyed by the American yeomen. He considers in much of his work the transformation of the
agrarian into the modern urban industrial society; and Popeye, of
Sanctuary, described as a mechanical robot with a face of stamped
tin, and who grows hysterical at the sight of fields and trees, stands
as the ultimate symbol of the machine and its effect on society.

That Faulkner accepted many of the agrarian principles as a part
of his moral vision is explicit in a speech he made to his fellow Mis-
sissippians in 1952 and reprinted here. It is upon the survival of
these principles that he based his optimistic hope expressed in his
Nobel Prize acceptance address of 1949 that man will not merely
endure, he will prevail.

WILLIAM FAULKNER

The Rights of Man

WHEN THE INVITATION to be here today first reached me, it came from Mr. Billy Wynn. It contained one of the nicest compliments anyone ever received. Mr. Wynn said, "We not only want to honor this particular fellow-Mississippian, we want him to honor us."

You can't beat that. To reverse a metaphor, that is a sword with not only two edges, but with both edges on the same side; the receiver is accoladed twice with one stroke: He is honored again in honoring them who proffered the original honor. Which is exactly the sort of gesture which we Southerners like to believe that only another Southerner could have thought of, invented. And, sure enough, it happens so often as to convince us that we were right.

He also gave me the Council's permission to speak on any subject I liked. That subject won't be writing or farming either. In my fan mail during the past year, there was a correspondence with another Mississippi gentleman, who takes a very dim view of my writing ability and my ideas both. He is a Deltan, he may be here today, and can ratify this. In one of his last letters, having reviewed again his opinion of a Mississippian who could debase and defile his native state and people as I have done, he said he not only didn't believe I could write, he didn't even believe I knew anything about farming, either. I answered that it wasn't me who made the claims about my degree as a writer, and so I would agree with him on that one; and after fifteen years of trying to cope not only with the Lord but with the federal government too to make something grow at a profit out of the ground, I was willing to agree with him on both of them.

So I shan't talk about either writing or farming. I have another subject. And, having thought about it, maybe I don't know very much about this one either, for the reason that none of us seem to

From William Faulkner, *An Address Delivered at the Seventeenth Annual Meeting of Delta Council*, May 15, 1952, Delta State Teachers College Campus, Cleveland, Mississippi. Page numbers have been supplied by the editor for this pamphlet. Reprinted with the kind permission of the Delta Council.

know much about it any more, that all of us may have forgotten one of the primary things on which this country was founded. [3/4]

Years ago, our fathers founded this country, this nation, on the premise of the rights of man. As they expressed it, "the inalienable right of man to life, liberty, and the pursuit of happiness." In those days, they knew what those words meant, not only the ones who expressed them, but the ones who heard and believed and accepted and subscribed to them. Because until that time, men did not always have those rights. At least, until that time, no nation had ever been founded on the idea that those rights were possible, let alone inalienable. So not only the ones who said the words, but the ones who merely heard them, knew what they meant. Which was this: "Life and liberty in which to pursue happiness. Life free and secure from oppression and tyranny, in which all men would have the liberty to pursue happiness." And both of them knew what they meant by "pursue." They did not mean just to chase happiness, but to work for it. And they both knew what they meant by "happiness" too: not just pleasure, idleness, but peace, dignity, independence and self-respect; that man's inalienable right was, the peace and freedom in which, by his own efforts and sweat, he could gain dignity and independence, owing nothing to any man.

So we knew what the words meant then, because we didn't have these things. And, since we didn't have them, we knew their worth. We knew that they were worth suffering and enduring and, if necessary, even dying to gain and preserve. We were willing to accept even the risk of death for them, since even if we lost them ourselves in relinquishing life to preserve them, we would still be able to bequeath them intact and inalienable to our children.

Which is exactly what we did, in those old days. We left our homes, the land and graves of our fathers and all familiar things. We voluntarily gave up, turned our backs on, a security which we already had and which we could have continued to have, as long as we were willing to pay the price for it, which price was our freedom and liberty of thought and independence of action and the right of responsibility. That is, by remaining in the old world, we could have been not only secure, but even free of the need to be responsible. Instead, we chose the freedom, the liberty, the independence and the inalienable right to responsibility; almost without charts, in frail wooden ships with nothing but sails and our desire and will to be free to move them, we crossed an ocean which did not even match the charts we did have; we conquered a wilderness in order to establish a place, not to be secure in because we [4/5] did not want that, we had just repudiated that, just crossed three thousand miles of dark and unknown sea to get away from that; but a place to be free in, to be independent in, to be responsible in.

And we did it. Even while we were still battling the wilderness with one hand, with the other we fended and beat off the power which would have followed us even into the wilderness we had conquered, to compel and hold us to the old way. But we did it. We founded a land, and founded in it not just our right to be free and independent and responsible, but the inalienable duty of man to be free and independent and responsible.

That's what I am talking about: responsibility. Not just the right, but the duty of man to be responsible, the necessity of man to be responsible if he wishes to remain free; not just responsible to and for his fellow man, but to himself; the duty of a man, the individual, each individual, every individual, to be responsible for the consequences of his own acts, to pay his own score, owing nothing to any man.

We knew it once, had it once. Because why? Because we wanted it above all else, we fought for it, endured, suffered, died when necessary, but gained it, established it, to endure for us and then to be bequeathed to our children.

Only, something happened to us. The children inherited. A new generation came along, a new era, a new age, a new century. The times were easier; the life and future of our nation as a nation no longer hung in balance; another generation, and we no longer had enemies, not because we were strong in our youth and vigor, but because the old tired rest of earth recognized that here was a nation founded on the principle of individual man's responsibility as individual man.

But we still remembered responsibility, even though, with easier times, we didn't need to keep the responsibility quite so active, or at least not so constantly so. Besides, it was not only our heritage, it was too recent yet for us to forget it, the graves were still green of them who had bequeathed it to us, and even of them who had died in order that it might be bequeathed. So we still remembered it, even if a good deal of the remembering was just lip-service.

Then more generations; we covered at last the whole face of the western earth; the whole sky of the western hemisphere was one loud American affirmation, one vast Yes; we were the whole [5/6] world's golden envy; never had the amazed sun itself seen such a land of opportunity, in which all a man needed were two legs to move to a new place on, and two hands to grasp and hold with, in order to amass to himself enough material substance to last him the rest of his days and, who knew? even something over for his and his

wife's children. And still he paid lip-service to the old words "freedom" and "liberty" and "independence"; the sky still rang and ulu-
lated with the thunderous affirmation, the golden Yes. Because the
words in the old premise were still true yet, for the reason that he
still believed they were true. Because he did not realize yet that
when he said "security", he meant security for himself, for the rest of
his days, with perhaps a little over for his children: not for the children and the childrens' children of all men who believed in liberty
and freedom and independence, as the old fathers in the old strong,
dangerous times had meant it.

Because somewhere, at some moment, something had happened to
him, to us, to all the descendants of the old, tough, durable, uncompromising men, so that now, in 1952, when we talk of security, we
don't even mean for the rest of our own lives, let alone that of our
and our wife's children, but only for so long as we ourselves can
hold our individual place on a public relief roll or at a bureaucratic
or political or any other organization's gravy-trough. Because somewhere, at some point, we had lost or forgot or voluntarily rid ourselves of that one other thing, lacking which, freedom and liberty
and independence cannot even exist.

That thing is the responsibility, not only the desire and the will to
be responsible, but the remembrance from the old fathers of the
need to be responsible. Either we lost it, forgot it, or we deliberately
discarded it. Either we decided that freedom was not worth the responsibility of being free, or we forgot that, to be free, a man must
assume and maintain and defend his right to be responsible for his
freedom. Maybe we were even robbed of responsibility, since for
years now the very air itself—radio, newspapers, pamphlets, tracts,
the voices of politicians—has been loud with talk about the rights of
man,—not the duties and obligations and responsibilities of man,
but only the "rights" of man; so loud and so constant that apparently we have come to accept the sounds at their own evaluation,
and to believe too that man has nothing else but rights:—not the
right to independence and freedom in which to work and endure in
his own sweat in order to earn for himself what the old ancestors
meant by happiness and [6/7] the pursuit of it, but only the chance
to swap his freedom and independence for the privilege of being free
of the responsibilities of independence; the right not to earn, but to
be given, until at last, by simple compound usage, we have made respectable and even elevated to a national system, that which the old
tough fathers would have scorned and condemned: charity.

In any case, we no longer have responsibility. And if we were
robbed of it by such as this which now seems to have taken over responsibility, it was because we were vulnerable to that kind of rav-

ishment; if we simply lost or forgot responsibility, then we too are to be scorned. But if we deliberately discarded it, then we have condemned ourselves, because I believe that in time, maybe not too long a time, we will discover that, as was said about one of Napoleon's acts, what we have committed is worse than a crime: it was a mistake.

Two hundred years ago, the Irish statesman, John Curran, said, "God hath vouchsafed man liberty only on condition of eternal vigilance; which condition if he break it, servitude is the consequence of his crime and the punishment of his guilt." That was only two hundred years ago, because our own old New England and Virginia and Carolina fathers knew that three hundred years ago, which was why they came here and founded this country. And I decline to believe that we, their descendants, have really forgotten it. I prefer to believe rather that it is because the enemy of our freedom now has changed his shirt, his coat, his face. He no longer threatens us from across an international boundary, let alone across an ocean. He faces us now from beneath the eagle-perched domes of our capitols and from behind the alphabetical splatters on the doors of welfare and other bureaus of economic or industrial regimentation, dressed not in martial brass but in the habiliments of what the enemy himself has taught us to call peace and progress, a civilization and plenty where we never before had it as good, let alone better; his artillery is a debased and respectless currency which has emasculated the initiative for independence by robbing initiative of the only mutual scale it knew to measure independence by.

The economists and sociologists say that the reason for this condition is, too many people. I don't know about that, myself, since in my opinion I am even a worse sociologist and economist than my Delta fan considers me a writer or a farmer. But even if I were a sociologist or economist, I would decline to believe this. Because to believe this, that man's crime against his freedom is that there are too many of him, is to believe that man's [7/8] sufferance on the face of the earth is threatened, not by his environment, but by himself: that he cannot hope to cope with his environment and its evils, because he cannot even cope with his own mass. Which is exactly what those who misuse and betray the mass of him for their own aggrandisement and power and tenure of office, believe: that man is incapable of responsibility and freedom, of fidelity and endurance and courage, that he not only cannot choose good from evil, he cannot even distinguish it, let alone practice the choice. And to believe that, you have already written off the hope of man, as they who have reft him of his inalienable right to be responsible, have done, and you might as well quit now and let man stew on in peace in his own recordless and oblivious juice, to his deserved and ungrieved doom.

I, for one, decline to believe this. I decline to believe that the only true heirs of Boone and Franklin and George and Booker T. Washington and Lincoln and Jefferson and Adams and John Henry and Paul Bunyan and Johnny Appleseed and Lee and Crockett and Hale and Helen Keller, are the ones denying and protesting in the newspaper headlines over mink coats and oil tankers and federal indictments for corruption in public office. I believe that the true heirs of the old tough durable fathers are still capable of responsibility and self-respect, if only they can remember them again. What we need is not fewer people, but more room between them, where those who would stand on their own feet, could, and those who won't, might have to. Then the welfare, the relief, the compensation, instead of being nationally sponsored cash prizes for idleness and ineptitude, could go where the old independent uncompromising fathers themselves would have intended it and blessed it: to those who still cannot, until the day when even the last of them except the sick and the old, would also be among them who not only can, but will. [8]

Questions for Study, Discussion, and Writing

I. AN AMERICAN ARCADIA: THEORETICAL PERSPECTIVES

Eliot: *Essays Upon Field-Husbandry*. What has prompted Eliot to pick up the pen in the service of agriculture? How does he reconcile his profession of the ministry with his interest in farming? Why has writing about the subject fallen into general neglect? How does he distinguish between nominal or artificial and natural or real wealth? What is the relationship of husbandry to the social unit?

Jefferson: *Notes on the State of Virginia, "Query XIX."* How does the importance of manufacturing in Europe compare with its importance in America? At what point in his essay does Jefferson shift out of the objective, logical style of the recorder of fact and into the emotional, metaphoric style of the poet? Select examples of his use of imagery of degeneration and disease (such as "mobs," "sores on the body," "canker") and define the intent of his rhetorical effects.

Taylor: *The Pleasures of Agriculture*. What are the psychological and physical effects of agricultural labor? What virtues does it foster? How does agriculture relate to religion and patriotism? Why should the scientist and politician know more about it?

Emerson: *Farming*. How does the occupation of husbandry relate to all other occupations? Make a list of the advantages and virtues Emerson finds in farming. Why is the farmer a true abolitionist? How does his work relate to the operation of the universe? What is Emerson's reply to the Malthusian theory that population increases at a faster rate than its means of subsistence? Compare the significance of nature in the philosophy of transcendentalism and in the life of the farmer. Compare Emerson with Jefferson in both theme and style.

Greeley: *The Farmer's Calling*. How does Greeley disagree with Jefferson and Emerson on the significance and virtues of agriculture? Then why would he encourage anyone to go into the vocation? How has Greeley applied the ethics of capitalism and the American dream of success to the idyllic life of the farmer? How does his essay reflect an early use of the techniques of modern advertising and public relations propaganda?

Sidney Lanier: *Corn.* What purpose is served by the lengthy introductory descriptions of nature? Look up a definition of the pathetic fallacy and determine how Lanier has used it as his basic method of conveying his theme. How would you state the poem's theme in a complete sentence? Why is corn appropriate as his controlling symbol? What is Lanier's opinion of trade and commerce? What is the point of the allegoric narrative in the next to the last unit? How appropriate is the identification of the hill with King Lear from Shakespeare's play in the concluding lines? Would you define Lanier's agrarianism as intellectual or emotional?

Cauley: *The Merits of Agrarianism.* In what ways is the farmer truly more independent and self-sufficient than other citizens? What is Cauley's proposal for the best method of satisfying our material wants? Is it a realistic one? Have all the material benefits brought by progress, according to Cauley, made man happier or wiser? What are some of the therapeutic and healthy effects of farming? How many of the virtues encouraged by the agrarian community does Cauley convincingly illustrate?

Brownell: *The Community and Rural Life.* How does Brownell define rural life? What makes it the seat of true community? What are the dangers in losing man's alliance with nature?

Bromfield: *Out of the Earth,* from "Out of the Sea." What kind of training and knowledge does Bromfield consider necessary for the good farmer? Why? What does comparative embryology and biochemistry contribute to his argument? Is his opinion of the farmer's view of immortality reflective of traditional or liberal theology?

"Epilogus: A Philosophical Excursion." Does Bromfield's list of virtues instilled by husbandry differ any from those of earlier celebrations of the agrarian life? Is he any more or less romantic than they are? How has farm life improved or changed in the twentieth century? What modern sociological and economic theories are challenged by Bromfield in the statement, "More than any other member of our society—indeed, perhaps alone in our society—the farmer has learned how to use machinery to serve him rather than his serving machinery"? Does his use of specific descriptive detail contribute anything to his thesis?

II. THE GOOD LIFE: AS IT IS LIVED

Crèvecoeur: *On the Situation, Feelings, and Pleasures of an American Farmer.* What are the reasons Crèvecoeur is especially glad to be an American farmer rather than one of some other nationality? What are the specific ties that seem to bind him to the soil? Determine what are some of the lessons taught him by nature and how they relate to agrarian ideals. Crèvecoeur's appeal rests upon a convincing use of descriptive detail based apparently upon experience. Although he did become an American farmer, he was a Frenchman by birth and a scion of the *petite noblesse*—not the son of an American farmer as he pretended to be. Does his use of such fictionalized details in any way affect the validity of his arguments?

William Cooper: *Letter to William Sampson, Esq.* What is Cooper's attitude toward the value of untamed and uncultivated land? What were the sources of difficulties in settling the Otsego territory? By what providential means was survival possible? Does Cooper seem to suggest that the virtues and pleasures of farming lie elsewhere than in the labor and soil?

Lanier: *The Waving of the Corn.* From whose point of view is this poem written and how might this affect its persuasiveness? Can we clearly identify the specific virtues Lanier is celebrating? State the theme of the poem. Is it sufficiently supported?

Whitman: *The Common Earth, the Soil.* Should this brief piece be classified as an essay, a poem, or as a prose poem? (Look up definitions of each in a handbook of literary terms.) What does it lack for easy identification as either prose or poetry? Is it less or more effective than Lanier's poem?

Garland: *The Return of a Private.* Does the beginning description of the returning Civil War veterans and their reception provide any commentary on civilian reaction to the war? What does the story suggest about the economic security of the farmer following the war? As the story develops, what do we learn about the character of the returned farmers? Formulate the qualities of Edward Smith's character and the commentary they make on the larger American society. Identify the virtues of rural life as Garland has illustrated them. This subject matter is easily susceptible to sentimental treatment. Has Garland successfully avoided it? What techniques does he use in attempting to do so? Does his use of descriptive detail and point of view contribute anything to his effect?

Norris: *The Octopus.* Would the pleasures of cultivation described by Norris be classified as aesthetic or physical? Analyze his use of sexual and copulatory imagery as an effective literary technique. Compare his use of personification or the pathetic fallacy with Lanier's use of it in "Corn." Is either more effective? Why?

Frost: *Mowing.* What is distinctive about Frost's attempt to capture the pleasures of an agricultural task in comparison with those of the nineteenth-century poets, as in the selections in this volume by Lanier, Timrod, and Whitman? Note Frost's use of alliteration (especially words beginning with "s" and "w"). How does this technique effectively add sound to sense in the poem? What does the scythe seem to be whispering to the laborer? Is it the scythe, nature, the laborer, or the poet who says, "The fact is the sweetest dream that labor knows"? Does it make any difference? What exactly does this sentence mean?

Lytle: *The Hind Tit.* Lytle begins with a highly concrete, detailed description of the physical exterior and the activities of farm life. How does this support his thesis? Are there any wasted activities or products in the day's work? How is this way of life superior to the new way brought about by industrialism? How are charms and signs as useful as scientific data in predicting natural phenomena? Compare Lytle with Huey Long (in section 3) on the potency and virtues of potlikker. How are even the games and amusements of country folk reflective of their patterns of life? What is Lytle's purpose in dropping dialect words occasionally into his prose, sometimes within quotation marks (such as "chillurn" for children, "sallet" for salad, "jine" for join, "gals" for girls, "ballets" for ballads, "figgers" for figures, and "h'isted" for hoisted)?

Roberts: *On the Mountainside.* What first brings Newt a sense of dissatisfaction with his way of life and extent of experience? How does Miss Roberts use the dancing at the party in the beginning to indicate the moods of the people? How are Newt's emotions played upon by the sights, smells, and sounds of his rural life? What is the message of the stranger Newt encounters at the house near Bee Gum Mountain? Does he heed it? What is achieved by the limited omniscient point of view? How does it enable the writer subtly or implicitly to suggest the values and virtues Newt is abandoning by his move to the settlement?

III. THE YEOMAN AND THE AMERICAN POLITICAL CHARACTER

Jefferson: *Letters.* In his letter to Jean Baptiste Say in 1804, what differences does Jefferson note between Europe and America concerning the ratio between population and agricultural produce, and the ratio of manufacturers to farmers? Writing to a Mr. Lithson in 1805, Jefferson indicates certain revisions he would like to make in his *Notes on the State of Virginia,* especially Query XIX. Why does he wish to make them and do they reflect any basic changes in his agrarian principles?

Franklin: *The Internal State of America.* What is the point of Franklin's historical parable about the farmer? How important is agriculture in the national economy? What is his general attitude towards merchants and shopkeepers? What seems to be Franklin's gauge for success, wealth, and prosperity in America?

Hamilton: *Report on Manufactures.* What are his basic findings on the importance of manufacturing in the national economy? Why are some unfriendly to the encouragement of manufacturing? What are their arguments? Basically, what parts does he feel agriculture and industry should play in the national economy? How objective and fair has Hamilton been in his presentation of the agrarian point of view? Are his concessions merely rhetorical?

Taylor: *Arator,* "No. 3, The Political State of Agriculture." How does government support of commerce and manufacturing damage the welfare of agriculture? What does Taylor mean by his fear of "rendering governments too strong for nations"? Why should agriculture and manufacturing be permitted to compete on the open market, without government support of either?

"No. 60, The Rights of Agriculture." Summarize Taylor's estimate of the rights of agriculture in America. What is Taylor's purpose in drawing an analogy between the actions of the federal government and the act of excommunication by the Catholic pope? Is the use of the parody of the excommunication speech a persuasive rhetorical strategy?

Cooper: *The American Democrat,* "On Property." How does Cooper support his thesis that property is at the base of civilization and is indispensable to social improvement? Why do communist experiments fail? Is the desire for property a natural instinct? How does instruction in respect for property rights improve civic morality? Are property rights ever detrimental to the common good? What are the dangers of wealth? Can property be considered a fair test for the extension of political rights to the owner?

"On Commerce." What is the character of a nation whose government is strongly influenced by commerce? Whose interest does it protect? What are the rights and responsibilities of commerce? Is Cooper in greater accord with Hamilton, or Jefferson and Taylor, regarding government support of manufacturing?

Fitzhugh: *Cannibals All!,* "Slavery—Its Effect on the Free." How does Fitzhugh refute the theory that slavery has a harmful effect on those whites who own none. What does it suggest about agricultural labor? How are slaves better off than menial free whites in the North? Why is the North more dependent on slavery than the South?

"Deficiency of Food in Free Society." What is Fitzhugh's opinion of agricultural labor? Why is it the proper pursuit of slaves? How is slavery comparable to socialism? How does the agricultural condition of New England make talk of disunion folly?

Whitman: *Democratic Vistas.* What to Whitman is the importance of property ownership, political partisanship, female suffrage, and the rural settlements in the West to the future of American democracy? What are the qualities of the ideal community he envisages and what part does agriculture play in it?

George: *Of Property in Land in the United States.* Why did the discovery of gold in California revive an older concept of property? What is wrong with the modern concept of private property in land? Why wasn't it rejected, along with the concepts of aristocracy and monarchy, when the country was first founded? How does it endanger the rights to life and liberty? Why haven't the American people realized the injustices of private property in land? What will be the effect of the exhaustion of open land fit for agriculture?

Garland: *Under the Lion's Paw.* What are the qualities and characteristics of the Midwestern farmer exemplified in the Council and Haskins families? What exactly is the "lion's paw" of the title? How does Jim Butler and his dealings with Mr. Haskins illustrate the injustices of private property in land about which Henry George wrote? How are women and children treated under this agricultural serfdom? Does Garland succeed in this story in combining stark realism with an implicit moral point? At what places in the story does he revert to explicit moral preachment?

Carnegie: *Triumphant Democracy.* What basic agrarian principles are repeated by Carnegie? What is the measuring rod by which he determines the success or prosperity of an agricultural nation? What advancements have been made in agriculture? Who is responsible for them? What appears to be the tendency toward the size of farms? What is his reply to the criticisms of the national economy by Henry George?

Dunning: *The Farmers' Alliance,* "Introductory History." What has been the effect of the moneyed aristocracy in American society? Does labor always receive its just reward? What conditions have caused farmers to create organizations for the protection of their interests? Why must individual enterprise be replaced by group effort?

National People's Party Platform. Who are responsible for the series of grave injustices and corruptions listed in the preamble? Who is the "grand and general chief" mentioned in the fifth paragraph of the preamble? How does the platform attempt to combine the forces of industrial labor with those of farming? What disposition should be made of the land? Have any of their resolutions been fulfilled? Would any of them now be considered radical?

Twelve Southerners: *A Statement of Principles.* What exactly are the Southern Agrarians proposing for the South and the nation as a solution to their economic ills? What is the "American industrial ideal" which they oppose? How have science and technology affected

American society? What are the evils of industrialism? What is its impact on religion, art, and the social amenities? Do the Agrarians wish to abandon industrialism entirely? What is their concept of an ideal agrarian society? Have any of their warnings about the problems industrialism would create in modern society proved to be true?

Davidson: *"I'll Take My Stand": A History.* What had the Southern Agrarians hoped would be the reaction to their book, *I'll Take My Stand?* Were their expectations fulfilled? How does their original intent compare with the way it was popularly understood? What was the significance of their common Southern backgrounds in their collaboration? What especially did they find distressing in contemporary life? To whom did they look in the past as spiritual leaders? Why did the title chosen for the book create misunderstanding? Why did they refrain from proposing a specific economic or political program? What does Davidson mean when he says that they favored a true federalism and opposed Leviathanism? Why did they disagree with Roosevelt's New Deal?

Long: *Every Man a King,* "Cotton Reduction Plan—Potlikker Episode." Why aren't federal farm relief programs working? What are the economic and nutritional virtues of potlikker? Is his potlikker plan merely an example of Long's famed homely sense of humor?

Anderson: *Blue Smoke.* How is the tobacco market important to the rural town and the farmers? What does Anderson find admirable in the way Virginians identify themselves? Why has there been a shift in the attitude of these farmers toward government men? Is the auction or sale of tobacco crops a fair, equitable system? What are some of the fictional techniques Anderson used in this sketch that make it more effective than an essay would be?

Roosevelt: *President's Message to Congress: Farm Tenancy.* What American dream have modern conditions corrupted? How does the report of the Special Committee on Farm Tenancy indicate that Henry George's prophecies were fulfilled? What practical action does Roosevelt recommend?

IV. THE WEEDS IN THE GARDEN: DISSENT AND DISILLUSIONMENT

Byrd: *History of the Dividing Line.* How productive are the soil and the farmers in the area of North Carolina surveyed by Byrd? In the society he observes, who are the more responsible and productive members? What is to account for the general aversion to labor and poverty witnessed by Byrd?

Hawthorne: *The Blithedale Romance*. What effect does the natural environment have on the inhabitants of the Blithedale community? What sort of people were attracted to the experimental socialistic community? How do the neighboring farmers react to their experiment? Are the narrator-poet's preconceptions of the spiritual and physical pleasures in agricultural labor fulfilled? What, according to Zenobia, is the result of trying to combine the physical and intellectual lives? Does Hollingsworth agree?

Alcott: *Transcendental Wild Oats*. What were the purposes and principles behind the founding of Fruitlands? What part was to be played by agriculture? How do Timon Lion, Abel Lamb, and Lamb's wife Hope differ in temperament? How capable are the new farmers as husbandmen? How do the reactions of outsiders compare with those depicted in Hawthorne's episode from *The Blithedale Romance?* Compare Miss Alcott's story with those of realists like Garland, Mrs. Freeman, or Miss Roberts, in characterization, use of descriptive detail, dialogue, and general style. Note the significance of characters' names in the story. Is Miss Alcott closer to nineteenth-century writers like Hawthorne or the twentieth-century realists? Support your conclusions with specific examples. Select lines and passages illustrating Miss Alcott's gentle irony and good humor toward these events in her early life. How does her view of this experience compare with Hawthorne's view of a similar kind in his novel?

Thoreau: *The Bean-Field*. In this chapter from *Walden,* Thoreau describes his attempt to live the role of the American husbandmen in his idyllic garden of Eden. By taking careful note of his use of such comic and satiric devices as irony, exaggeration, the mock heroic, and parody, indicate how Thoreau finds the virtues of the agrarian existence to be mythical. Is the outcome of his experiment in growing beans economically successful? Does it support the traditional theory that the farmer is totally independent? In the next to the last paragraph, what does Thoreau indicate has corrupted American farming? How do his comments compare with those of Henry George in section 3 on the issue of private property? Of what genuine significance in the total scheme of things is the farmer, according to the final paragraph?

Lanier: *Thar's More in the Man Than Thar Is in the Land*. What does Lanier achieve by the use of a first-person narrator and native dialect in this poem? What sort of person is Jones? Why is Brown able to succeed where Jones failed? What is Lanier's main point?

Veblen: *The Independent Farmer*. How has the idealized concept of the independent yeoman disadvantaged him in the modern national economy and the system of absentee ownership? What has been the significance of farming in the development of America, economically and politically? How does Veblen characterize the motivations of the farm population? What specifically does he charge them with? What can we deduce is Veblen's general opinion of the agrarian "good life" and the American farmer?

Mencken: *The Husbandman*. How many of the criticisms of the American farmer voiced by Mencken are also voiced by Thorstein Veblen? What have been the farmer's contributions to American political theory? What would the application of an industrial organization to farming achieve? Does he feel that the farmer has been unfairly treated by capitalism, industry, and government regulation? How was the farmer responsible for Prohibition and the Mann Act? Compare the vituperative, ironic, emotional overstatement of Mencken's essay with the calm, rational logic of Veblen's. Who is more convincing?

Percy: *Planters, Share-Croppers, and Such*. What is Percy's attitude toward his father and ancestors? What does their history indicate about the nture of Southern antebellum plantation life and the problems of adjustment to Reconstruction? How, according to Percy, did profit-sharing or sharecropping come about? What are the weaknesses of the system? What can be done to strengthen it? Does Percy consider himself an agrarian? Would he consider James Agee and Walker Percy among his "Knights of the Bleeding Heart"?

Agee [and Evans]: *Let Us Now Praise Famous Men*, "At the Forks." Note Agee's highly figurative language in his descriptions. What does he achieve thereby? How has government rehabilitation affected the lives of this rural family? How is the action of the senile old man, who gives a rolled farm magazine to Agee, symbolic of the plight of these farmers? Define the feelings and attitude of Agee toward these people.

V. THE MACHINE IN THE GARDEN:
CIVILIZATION, PROGRESS, AND INDUSTRY

Cooper: *The Pioneers*. Why does Cooper paint such a carefully detailed portrait of the beauties of an orderly, balanced nature before beginning his narrative? How does it contrast with the frenzied activity of the following pages? Why does Leatherstocking consider the carnage of the pigeons wasteful and unsportsmanlike? What finally causes him to break his silence over the proceedings? What is to be held responsible for the occurrence, according to Natty Bumppo? What point is Natty's feat meant to illustrate?

De Tocqueville: *Democracy in America*. Why, according to de

Tocqueville, are labor and the earning of a living held in such high regard in America? What part does the profit motive play in the pursuit of labor? Why do the democratic conditions of equality engender commerce and industry, but not agriculture? What is his assessment of America's commercial promise in 1840? How has land speculation affected the farmer? How is it that manufacturing may demean and lower the class of workmen while raising the class of industrialists to a new aristocracy? How does it differ from the European aristocracy? What danger does this possibility hold for the future of America?

Timrod: *Ethnogenesis*. What event is celebrated in the opening lines of the poem? How do the forces of nature and the products of the soil react to this event? How are Northern industrialism and Southern agrarianism characterized? On whose side is God to be found? What are to be the responsibilities of the Confederacy? What is the meaning of the title? With the work of which other poet in this volume is Timrod's closest in style and technique?

Harris: *Sut Lovingood's Allegory*. What is the point of Sut's little parable (in paragraph 3) about the boy going to school on a sleety morning? How does it relate to the earlier comments? How does Sut feel about technological and material progress? What is wrong with his contemporary men? Why would Old Brakebill, if still alive, be considered "behind the time"? What characteristics of the times were possessed by Brakebill's billy goat? What finally drives Brakebill to curtail the goat's unusual activities? What drastic measure does he take and what, therefore, is Harris suggesting as a solution to the perversions of the machine age? Look up the definition of *allegory* in a literary handbook and determine how well Harris' story complies with the description. Analyze and discuss Harris' use of a rich metaphoric and figurative language.

Markham: *The Man with the Hoe*. What are the forces and conditions responsible for the pathetic state in which Markham views the yeoman in 1899? What prophetic warning is issued by the poet? Find a reproduction of Millet's painting and judge how well Markham has interpreted it.

Norris: *A Deal in Wheat*. Norris provides the reader with the causes and results of a deal in wheat from both the farmer's point of view and the professional speculator's. What illegal trick does Truslow pull on Horning? Why doesn't he prosecute him? What is its impact on the farmers and the working men, such as Sam Lewiston? What are the tragic ironies about industrial society that Norris is underlining? What does Norris achieve artistically by beginning and ending with the story of Sam Lewiston?

Ransom: *Antique Harvesters*. What are some of the activities closely associated with the antebellum agrarian South depicted in this poem? Is the poet describing actual activity or an artistic portrayal of life, perhaps a painting or tapestry? What does the stylized tone of the poem suggest about this question? Why does Ransom make heavy use of the language of chivalry? The hunters, as "keepers of a rite," are symbolic of what in the Old South? The "Proud Lady" of the last four stanzas probably represents the Southland and its attendant qualities and virtues. What is the religious source of this metaphor? Are her worshippers willing to forsake her? What is the poet's injunction to moderns in the last stanza?

Captain Carpenter. If one reads this poem as an allegory of the agrarian attempting to maintain a grasp on the traditional virtues of courage, courtesy, dignity, and ceremony in the modern world, what could be concluded about the meaning of the poem? Why is Captain Carpenter so easily defeated? What is the poet's attitude toward his Quixotic hero? Does he ridicule or approve of him? Why has the author imitated the medieval ballad form, used such formal diction, and treated the violence with such ironic detachment? Why does the final combatant choose Captain Carpenter's heart over his tongue as a trophy?

Davidson: *Prologue: The Long Street.* What is "the long street" intended to represent as a metaphor? What appears to be the dilemma of the narrator? What is the one thing of which he can be certain? What is responsible for his corrupted and sterile environment?

On a Replica of the Parthenon. This poem is about a full-sized reproduction of the Parthenon built in Centennial Park in Nashville, Tennessee, to commemorate its centennial in 1898; thus its self-description as the "Athens of the South." While it is the location of numerous colleges and universities, Nashville has been in this century a center for Southern industrialism, and more recently, the "Country Music Capital of the World." What are some of the ironies in this situation that Davidson is underlining? Do those who come to view the Greek temple recognize its significance? In what sense is it a "bribe" raised up against man's fate?

Frost: *A Lone Striker.* What is responsible for the laborer's forced exclusion from the factory? Would his absence be noted within the factory and its operation? Why does he desert to the woods? Is his act a retreat, or an affirmation of something? How can we tell? How would Frost's theme be stated in prose?

Lytle: *Jericho, Jericho, Jericho.* What does the reader gradually learn about the situation and condition of the narrator as the story opens and progresses? What distinctive qualities of her character and personality emerge, and what do these reveal about her agrarian world of the past? Why is she called "a sin-thirsty old woman"? How has she come by Long Gourd and what has motivated her to possess and enlarge it? What is the source of antipathy between her and Dick's fiancé, Eva? What device has Lytle used in order to compress a life's history into a brief compass? Note his effective use of symbolic detail. What do the following signify: the cluster of mahogany grapes on her bed headboard, the odors that are remembered as her life passes before her eyes, the cotton field that she envisions in the final paragraph, and the lines from the spiritual at the conclusion? Is Lytle's description of death from the point of view of a dying person convincing?

Warren: *The Patented Gate and the Mean Hamburger.* What function does the composite portrait of a rural type serve in the beginning? How does Jeff York differ from the other sharecroppers? How did he achieve independence? What symbolic function does the patented gate serve for Jeff York. What is the symbolic significance of the hamburger stand? Are they appropriate symbols? What causes Jeff to commit the act he does at the end? What are the Jeffersonian agrarian assumptions behind this story?

Time: *The Pushbutton Cornucopia.* How is Warren North a typical example of the modern American husbandman? How have science and technology affected his life and the agrarian existence? What has he learned from mechanization and automation? How does his early life reflect the virtues of the typical agrarian husbandman? How does it later contradict parts of the agrarian mystique? What has brought about the technological revolution in farming? What areas of agriculture has it reached? What impact will this have on the number of independent farmers? Does *Time* feel that all this harbors well for the future of American agriculture? What would an agrarian say?

EPILOGUE

Faulkner: *The Rights of Man.* What are the attitudes of Faulkner toward his work as a writer and as a farmer? What does he feel are the basic virtues upon which America was founded? What do they have in common with agrarian principles? What is the virtue upon which all the others rest? How did times change after the nation's foundation? What does modern man need to relearn? Who are America's real enemies? Does Faulkner have hope for the future?

Suggestions for Further Reading

THE SECONDARY MATERIALS and critical studies on the agrarian theme in American literature are very few. The best single study is Leo Marx's *The Machine in the Garden: Technology and the Pastoral Ideal in America* (1964), which offers a perceptive survey of the conflict in American thought and literature between the pastoral and technological images and ideals. From the historical perspective, Henry Bamford Parkes' *The American Experience* (1947) is a brilliant analysis of the significance of agrarian ideals in the nation's political development. More specialized studies are *Farming and Democracy* by A. Whitney Griswold (1948), a thorough treatment and criticism of the idea that farming as a family enterprise is the backbone of democracy; and *The Age of Reform: From Bryan to F. D. R.* by Richard Hofstadter (1955), which emphasizes the place of agrarian theories in the reform movements of the period 1890 to 1940.

Other books that contain material that directly or indirectly relate to agrarianism are Frederick Jackson Turner's *The Frontier in American History* (1920), a landmark statement in historiography of the impact on the American character of the frontier movement, though now seriously questioned by modern historians; *Virgin Land: The American West as Symbol and Myth* by Henry Nash Smith (1954), a provocative study of several myths and symbols of the westward movement, including that of the virtuous yeoman-farmer; R. W. B. Lewis' *The American Adam: Innocence, Tragedy and Tradition in the Nineteenth Century* (1955), which assesses the intellectual influence of the concept of the American as a new Adam in a second Garden of Eden; and Howard Mumford Jones' *O Strange New World* (1964), a survey of the development of American culture, with fascinating material on the ideas and images generated in the minds of Europeans about the New World. Roy W. Meyer's *The Middle Western Farm Novel in the Twentieth Century* (1956) is a summary analysis of the social commentary implicit in 140 novels dealing with agrarian life in the Middle West. An excellent account of the agricultural revolution in eighteenth-century England and its influence on literary thought is Kenneth MacLean's *Agrarian Age: A Background for Wordsworth* (1950).

The best introduction to the Populist movement is John D. Hicks' *The Populist Revolt* (1931), and an interesting collection of primary documents is George B. Tindall's edition of *A Populist Reader: Selections from the Works of American Populist Leaders* (1966). The Southern Agrarians of 1930 have been the subject of two books, John L. Stewart's *The Burden of Time: The Fugitives and Agrarians* (1965) and Alexander Karanikas' *Tillers of a Myth: Southern Agrarians as Social and Literary Critics* (1966), both of which are provocative but not entirely dependable. What may prove to be the best study is being prepared by Virginia Rock, based upon her 1961 University of Minnesota dissertation, "The Making and Meaning of *I'll Take My Stand:* A Study in Utopian-Conservatism, 1925–1939." A new edition of *I'll Take My Stand,* the Agrarian symposium, was published in 1962 with an introduction by Louis D. Rubin, Jr., and biographical sketches by Virginia Rock.

American literature offers an abundance of varied and interesting novels, poems, and stories that deal in imaginative ways with the theories and realities of agrarianism. A complete list of authors and specific titles would be extensive and inconvenient. But the student interested in pursuing the subject in the works of a particular novelist or poet would find it rewarding to examine in the nineteenth century the works of John Esten Cooke, Mary E. Wilkins Freeman, Hamlin Garland, Joel Chandler Harris, Richard Malcolm Johnston, John Pendleton Kennedy, Mary Noailles Murfree, Thomas Nelson Page, William Gilmore Simms, Henry Timrod, and Mark Twain. In the twentieth century, the writers whose fiction and poetry are highly reflective of agrarian problems and principles include Sherwood Anderson, Louis Bromfield, Erskine Caldwell, Truman Capote, Willa Cather, Donald Davidson, William Faulkner, Robert Frost, Ellen Glasgow, Caroline Gordon, Andrew Lytle, Frank Norris, Flannery O'Connor, John Crowe Ransom, Conrad Richter, Elizabeth Madox Roberts, Carl Sandburg, John Steinbeck, Jesse Stuart, Allen Tate, Robert Penn Warren, Eudora Welty, and Stark Young. Many of these authors are represented by selections in this volume. If one had to pick the three most important novels dealing in this century with the transition from an agrarian to an industrial society, they would be *The Octopus* by Frank Norris (1901), *Winesburg, Ohio* by Sherwood Anderson (1919), and *The Grapes of Wrath* by John Steinbeck (1939).

An invaluable specialized bibliography which appeared while this book was in galley proof is Virginis Rock's "Agrarianism: Agrarian Themes and Ideas in Southern Writing," *Mississippi Quarterly*, XXI (Spring, 1968), 145-156. A student of the subject may profitably consult this bibliography for readings beyond the brief list provided here.

Notes on the Authors

JAMES AGEE (1909–1955): The brief but bright career of James Agee was spent producing a body of fiction, poetry, and film criticism that was as perceptive as it was sensitively written. His fiction was based on his experiences in Knoxville, Tennessee, where he was born and raised, and it reflects his deep love of the land. When *Fortune* magazine sent him to Alabama in 1936 to do a story on the sharecropper families, it developed into a book-length manuscript published as *Let Us Now Praise Famous Men* (1941), with photographs by Walker Evans.

LOUISA MAY ALCOTT (1832–1888): One of the most widely read juvenile authors in America, Louisa May Alcott largely drew from the life and activities of the Alcott family for her fiction. Strong-willed, independent, and practical, she proved a mainstay to her visionary, idealistic father, Bronson Alcott, who had a checkered career as a peddler, philosopher, and educator. The good-natured way in which she viewed his often futile plans and notions is reflected in "Transcendental Wild Oats," based on his unsuccessful establishment of a cooperative community.

SHERWOOD ANDERSON (1876–1941): When Sherwood Anderson abandoned his position as president of a paint manufacturing business, he had gathered wide experience for use in his fiction as a soldier, laborer, farmer, and advertising copy writer. His life and his work showed the profound impact of the tensions between agrarian rural communities and cosmopolitan industrial cities. While much of his fiction now appears outmoded and imperfect, a few short stories and *Winesburg, Ohio* assure him of a place among America's best writers.

LOUIS BROMFIELD (1896–1956): Although his reputation has fallen into neglect in recent years, during his lifetime the novels of Louis Bromfield were best sellers and brought him plaudits as a writer of skill and perception. During the last part of his career, he established a farm in Ohio called Malabar, which became a showplace for the demonstration of the success of his agricultural theories. His several books about this aspect of his career have been regarded as agrarian documents equal in importance to Jefferson's *Notes on the State of Virginia*.

BAKER BROWNELL (1887–1965): Having studied at Harvard under such philosophers as Royce and Santayana, Baker Brownell did not devote his career to serious philosophical inquiry and teaching until he had spent twenty-five years as a journalist, editor, and poet. Once he became engaged in teaching philosophy and sociology, he produced a large number of books and devoted much of his research to a study of the rural community in hopes of rehabilitating this source of democratic stability.

WILLIAM BYRD (1674–1744): One of colonial Southern society's true gentlemen, William Byrd of Westover was a well-known planter, lawyer and public official in his age. He also dabbled in science, wrote several books, and kept private diaries that have proved to be some of the richest most fascinating social documents to come out of his time. They reveal Byrd as an eminently vulnerable man but also a man of great wit and warm humor.

ANDREW CARNEGIE (1835–1919): A man whose life exemplified the "rags to riches" story was Andrew Carnegie, who worked his way up from bobbin boy in a cotton mill to become one of America's largest steel industralists. When he retired in 1901, he devoted the rest of his life to administering his fortune for the public welfare, through establishing libraries and educational facilities, a consequence of his belief that wealth entails an ethical responsibility that it be profitably employed for the common good.

TROY J. CAULEY (b. 1902): A native of Texas, Troy J. Cauley had taught economics at several Southern and Midwestern universities before he wrote his study of the economics of agrarianism, published in 1935. After working for the federal government for twelve years as an economist and soil conservationist, he returned to teaching in 1947, and has published further important studies in economics and regionalism.

JAMES FENIMORE COOPER (1789–1851): The novels of James Fenimore Cooper form a vast panorama of the settling of the frontier and the attendant conflicts between the natural and the civilized man. His serious criticisms of American life, less obvious in his novels than in his essays, often brought him sharp censure by American newspapers. While his skill was not of the first order, his memorable characters, like Natty Bumppo, and his narrative technique assure him of a continuing readership.

WILLIAM COOPER (1754–1809): Usually called "Judge Cooper" by those who knew him, William Cooper, father of James Fenimore Cooper, was responsible for the founding of Cooperstown, New York, where he occupied a huge unexplored estate that once contained 750,000 acres. He published in 1810 *A Guide to the Wilderness*, describing his experience as a frontier settler. He reportedly served as a model for Judge Temple in his son's novel *The Pioneers*.

MICHEL-GUILLAUME JEAN DE CRÈVECOEUR (1731–1813): Although by birth and temperament a European, Crèvecoeur saw more sharply into the American character and foresaw more prophetically into the American future than any other member of his generation. His great love for the country first led him to settle as a farmer in New York state in 1754, and after a return to Europe because of a conflict of sympathies during the Revolution, he returned to America as French consul in 1783.

DONALD DAVIDSON (1893–1968): No single member of the original Southern Agrarians continued to develop and uphold the agrarian principles as faithfully or as ardently as Donald Davidson. His creative work as a skilled essayist, acute social and literary critic, well-informed historian, and sensitive poet assure him of an important place in contemporary letters, although his firm convictions have often brought disfavor among literary critics. Some of the brightest young writers in the modern South began their careers under his guidance as a teacher of creative writing at Vanderbilt University, where he taught from 1920 until his retirement in 1964.

NELSON A. DUNNING: An associate editor of the weekly *National Economist*, organ of the Southern Alliance for Farmers, Nelson A. Dunning published in 1891 a compendium of Populist doctrine, *The Farmers' Alliance History and Agricultural Digest*. His introductory history to the volume is a well-written expression of Populist philosophy and economic thought.

JARED ELIOT (1685–1763): While he spent the major part of his life at Killingworth, Connecticut, as New England's most respected and widely known minister and physician, Jared Eliot also made contributions to the advancement of metallurgy and scientific agriculture. This latter interest led to the writing of *Essays Upon Field-Husbandry*, the first colonial work on the subject and one that brought him much recognition in his time.

RALPH WALDO EMERSON (1803–1882): Deserting the Christian ministry when it proved too narrow a vocation for the full exercise of his intellectual and spiritual ambitions, Ralph Waldo Emerson became the foremost American exponent of Transcendentalism. While his prose style was not always crystal clear, and some have considered him a philosophical virgin, his writing has had a profound influence on American life and thought perhaps unequaled by any other philosopher.

WILLIAM FAULKNER (1897–1962): While William Faulkner was in no sense a systematic social or cultural historian, the total body of his fiction furnishes fascinating data for understanding the mind of the modern South—its complexities, contradictions, and inner divisions. The reader should not, however, fail to remember that he was primarily an artist and all that he wrote contains the impress of his distinctive point of view and imagination.

GEORGE FITZHUGH (1806–1881): After he had traveled through the Northern states in 1854 and 1856, where he probably encountered Harriet Beecher Stowe, the Virginia-born lawyer George Fitzhugh became confirmed in his proslavery views and launched his eloquent and passionate defense of the slave system with two books, *Sociology for the South* (1854) and *Cannibals All!* (1857). His main arguments were based on the evils of the Northern industrial and captalistic society, and the virtues he saw in the patriarchal system possible in the Southern slave economy.

BENJAMIN FRANKLIN (1706–1790): In every sense—philosophically, socially, and culturally—Benjamin Franklin was an epitome of his age and time. His work as a statesman, scientist, and writer clearly mark him not simply as a reflector but as an intellectual pioneer in eighteenth-century rationalism. Without him, the character of American culture today might have been drastically different, and the folk would have been without one of their favorite symbolic heroes of the spirit of American progress.

ROBERT FROST (1874–1963): An excellent example of the regional artist who uses the experience of his local environment as subject matter for making transcendent statements about man is Robert

Frost. Wherever Frost looked in his beloved New England, at what ever finite aspect of nature, he found a spiritual truth, and his material was inexhaustible. He was one of the few modern poets capable of spanning the ever broadening gap between poet and reader, his poems being easily appreciated on the literal level, yet capable of yielding intricate technical and thematic complexities upon careful analysis.

HAMLIN GARLAND (1860–1940): Compelled to express in his fiction a demand for social justice by the depiction of the actualities of Midwestern farm life as he knew it, Hamlin Garland became an early American realist. While the reading public often found his grim regional stories not to their liking, he persisted in his studies of economic and social problems in works of fiction and autobiography. His writing is clearly of another era, yet it still retains a certain power and force that keeps a few of his best books in print.

HENRY GEORGE (1839–1897): An early itinerant life as a sailor and printer brought Henry George to a realization of the great disparity in America between prosperity and poverty, between wealth and want. First as a journalist, then the author of books, and later as a politician, this shocking contrast became the theme of his work, and his "single tax" theory of appropriating only unearned increment on land was his proposal for righting the balance of national prosperity. His economic thought has been perpetrated by numerous editions of his famed *Progress and Poverty* (1879) and the Henry George School of social science in New York City.

HORACE GREELEY (1811–1872): Undoubtedly one of the great reformers of his and all time, Horace Greeley spent a provocative and vigorous life writing, lecturing, and politicking in behalf of his causes. Both the laboring classes of the city and the yeomen of the country elicited his support, but his radicalism often alienated important and influential people. He was not a talented writer, but as an acute editor he brought to his newspaper, the New York *Tribune,* some of the period's best journalists and correspondents.

ALEXANDER HAMILTON (1755–1804): In the earliest political pamphlets written by Alexander Hamilton as a student at Columbia University, he demonstrated a keen and mature grasp of the principles of constitutional government. His labors in behalf of an industrial economy, a strong federal authority, and the national treasury have left a profound impress on the foundations of political and economic life in America.

GEORGE WASHINGTON HARRIS (1814–1869): Although he spent his life engaged in a number of professional activities, such as metal-worker, steamboat pilot, farmer, surveyor, postmaster, railroad superintendent, and would-be politician, George Washington Harris succeeded in none of them and is now remembered only for the humorous sketches and stories he wrote in his leisure. His hell-raising, often vulgar-mouthed creation, Sut Lovingood, was based on Tennesseeans much like him in reality, and was used to embarrass and criticize genteel literature, social conventions, religious hypocrites, reformers, filiopietists, and Yankee politics.

NATHANIEL HAWTHORNE (1804–1864): As an early perceptive writer of fiction about the nature of sin and the great inner struggles of the American conscience and soul, Nathaniel Hawthorne is in a class by himself. While he rejected the outer forms of the Puritan faith, he found that its estimate of human nature as depraved and in need of salvation was accurate, and his great romances, written in his uniquely symbolic and allegoric mode, demonstrate the moral difficulties which perpetually confront humanity.

THOMAS JEFFERSON (1743–1826): Like his contemporary Benjamin Franklin, Thomas Jefferson had a marvelously eclectic mind which led him to achievements, minor and major, in politics, diplomacy, law, science, architecture, and agriculture. Through his masterful leadership, Jefferson instilled in American democracy its great concern for equality, the lot of the common man, the sanctity of private property and the necessity of public education. The spirit of his personality and intellect abides in American political and social thought.

SIDNEY LANIER (1842–1881): As a poet, critic, and musician, Sidney Lanier was one of the most accomplished and well-known Southern writers to emerge after the Civil War. A follower of Poe's poetic theories, which emphasize the importance of sound and rhythm over sense, his harmonious, lilting verses are not likely to appeal to the modern reader. While his work reflects little attempt at a consistent philosophic pattern, he did celebrate the agrarian life as healthier and more virtuous than cosmopolitan industrial existence.

HUEY LONG (1893–1935): One of the most unashamedly cynical and opportunistic politicians to appear in America was Huey Long, who rose from a rustic origin as son of a Louisiana farmer to become head of that state's most vicious political machine. Nothing stood in the way of the "Kingfish's" programs of building good highways and good schools, be it bribe, blackmail, or fraud. The question of whether he would have proved to be a fascist dictator was left forever unsolved when Dr. Carl A. Weiss, Jr., gunned him down in the state capitol.

ANDREW LYTLE (b. 1902): The traditions of the Southern agrarian way of life, with its strong family ties and matriarchial social system, has formed the subject matter of the novels and stories of Andrew Lytle, one of the twelve contributors to the 1930 agrarian manifesto, *I'll Take My Stand.* His work as a teacher of creative writing, a literary critic, and since 1961, editor of the *Sewanee Review,* are significant contributions to modern Southern literature.

EDWIN MARKHAM (1852–1940): His boyhood experiences in Oregon as a shepherd and farmhand influenced the lifelong sympathy of Edwin Markham for the lot of the exploited poor. The success which his poem "The Man with the Hoe" brought him in 1899 enabled him to give up teaching for writing poetry and lecturing on social problems, but his work, though popular in its time, has proved to have little staying power either in relevance or technical achievement. He is said to have served as a model for the sensitive poet Presley in Norris' novel *The Octopus.*

H. L. MENCKEN (1880–1956): The American way of life has had few critics as vituperative, vicious, and raucous as Baltimore journalist H. L. Mencken. His definition of democracy was "the worship of jackals by jackasses." Yet if his significant contributions to American literature, linguistics, and humor count for anything, few native sons have contributed as much to this country's heritage.

FRANK NORRIS (1870–1902): After spending the early part of his career as a foreign correspondent, Frank Norris spent his few remaining years writing a small body of fiction which established his reputation as America's first great naturalist. He had projected a panoramic trilogy on the production and marketing of wheat, for which he completed only two volumes—*The Octopus* (1901) and *The Pit* (1903)—which reflected some inconsistency both in economic attitude and stylistic development. He was Zola's nearest but imperfect American disciple.

WILLIAM ALEXANDER PERCY (1885–1942): The poetry and prose of Mississippian William Alexander Percy reflect his agrarian disposition, his love of nature and rejection of industrial materialism. But he is less known for his four volumes of traditional verse than for his finely written autobiography *Lanterns on the Levee* (1941), which captures the attitudes of a cultivated and compassionate soul trapped in a modern world little to his liking.

JOHN CROWE RANSOM (b. 1888): An unusual feat was performed by John Crowe Ransom, who in less than a decade wrote a significant body of highly refined poetry, which brought him wide and well-deserved acclaim, and then turned to create for himself a reputation as one of this century's most creative and influential literary critics. Along with Donald Davidson and Allen Tate, Ransom was a prime mover in the group of Southern Agrarians who declared war on industrial society in 1930. The tensions of his concerns over the loss of faith and ritual in our traditionless modern culture create in his poetry a delicately balanced wit and wry irony.

ELIZABETH MADOX ROBERTS (1886–1941): Although Kentucky-born Elizabeth Madox Roberts began her career as a poet, she attracted attention as a highly sensitive interpreter in fiction of the psychological stresses which occur in Southern rural and mountain life. The lyricism of her style and the mysticism of her philosophy lift her stories from the realm of local color to the level of symbolic drama of universal relevance.

FRANKLIN D. ROOSEVELT (1882–1945): One of the most gifted, best loved, and at the same time feared American Presidents was Franklin D. Roosevelt, who put into action at a time of national despair a New Deal that put the common man back on his feet, but also same time threatened to begin an era of government beauracracy and authoritarian control of private business and economic life. He had a remarkable facility for communicating with the citizens of all classes, and he was a virtuoso of political power. His administration established trends in the national development that remain with us today.

JOHN TAYLOR (1753–1824): Recognized by V. L. Parrington as "the most original economist of his generation," John Taylor of Caroline County, Virginia, published in 1814 his massive but perceptive *An Inquiry into the Principles and Policies of the Government of the United States,* wherein he attacked Hamilton's "system of paper and patronage" and took a firm stand for private property, states' rights, and federal nonintervention. But he considered himself first of all a farmer, and his agricultural essays, published in *Arator,* are among the most important agrarian theoretical documents of the nineteenth century.

HENRY DAVID THOREAU (1817–1862): If Emerson was the great expositor of Transcendental theory, Henry David Thoreau was its greatest practitioner. Always taking the unconventional approach to anything, Thoreau acted upon the courage of his convictions, abandoned them if they proved wanting, and always assumed responsibility for the consequences. The depth of his insight, the warmth of his emotions, and the humor of his intellect distinguish his prose works as unlike anything else in American letters.

HENRY TIMROD (1828–1867): A lamentable career of poverty and misfortune was the lot of Henry Timrod, Columbia, South Carolina, poet and war correspondent. A classicist by training and inclination, his poetry reflects this interest, and his spirited treatment of Civil War subject matter earned for him the title of "Poet Laureate of the Confederacy."

ALEXIS DE TOCQUEVILLE (1805–1859): Sent by the French Government in 1831 to observe the American penal system, Alexis de Tocqueville also began to gather data for his masterful analysis of *Democracy in America,* published in 1835 and 1840 in two volumes simultaneously in French and an English translation by Henry Reeve. Considered by some the greatest work ever written about one country by a member of another, the book continues to hold interest for all generations as a political treatise of great insight and prophetic judgment.

THORSTEIN VEBLEN (1857–1929): One of America's most original economists, social philosophers, and eccentrics was Thorstein Veblen. A son of hardy Norwegian immigrants and a product of the Midwestern agricultural frontier society, he distinguished himself in intellectual circles by his acute analyses of social, cultural, and economic institutions. Once he achieved fame with his book *The Theory of the Leisure Class* (1899), his personal irregularities and impetuous actions increased and earned for him an occasionally scandalous reputation.

ROBERT PENN WARREN (b. 1905): Among the twelve Southerners who contributed to the agrarian symposium *I'll Take My Stand,* Robert Penn Warren has proven to be the most remarkably versatile, having experienced great success as a novelist, poet, critic, and teacher. Next to Faulkner's novels, Warren's reveal more about the complexities of Southern life and thought than those of any other writer, *All the King's Men* (1946) being his masterpiece. His textbook *Understanding Poetry* (1938), written with Cleanth Brooks, brought about a revolution in the teaching of poetry in American classrooms.

WALT WHITMAN (1819–1892): The voice of poet-prophet Walt Whitman symbolically absorbed and embodied the total spirit of America and her people more fully than the voice of any other philosopher or artist. He spent a lifetime revising and perfecting his volume *Leaves of Grass* (1855–1892), which constitutes the single most profound, complex, and influential poetic document in American literature.